KOREA –
A RELIGIOUS HISTORY

A revision of the original work of 1989, which established itself as the authoritative work in the field, this book is an historical survey of all the religious traditions of Korea in relation to the socio-cultural trends of seven different periods of Korean history. Beginning in the middle of the first millennium BC, the work has been revised to bring the story to the end of the twentieth century. The book includes a discussion of the history of the study of religion in Korea, and a chronological description of Korean folk religion including shamanism, Buddhism, Confucianism, Roman Catholicism and Protestantism, Islam, and Korean New Religions. There are also some final observations about the unique characteristics of religious beliefs and practices in Korea.

James Huntley Grayson is Reader in Modern Korean Studies in the School of East Asian Studies at the University of Sheffield, and Dean of the Faculty of Social Sciences. His research interests are in traditional Korean religion, Korean Christianity and Korean oral folklore. His most recent work, *Myths and Legends from Korea*, was published by Curzon Press in 2001.

Great Buddha of the Sŏkkur-am Grotto, Kyŏngju, c. 750. Reproduced by courtesy
of the National Museum of Korea, Kyŏngju Branch.

KOREA –
A RELIGIOUS HISTORY

Revised edition

James Huntley Grayson

RoutledgeCurzon
Taylor & Francis Group

First edition published in 1989
This revised edition published 2002
by RoutledgeCurzon
11 New Fetter Lane, London EC4P 4EE

Simultaneously published in the USA and Canada
by RoutledgeCurzon
29 West 35th Street, New York, NY 10001

RoutledgeCurzon is an imprint of the Taylor & Francis Group

© 2002 James Huntley Grayson

Typeset in Times by LaserScript Ltd, Mitcham, Surrey

Printed and bound in Great Britain by
Antony Rowe Ltd, Chippenham, Wiltshire

British Library Cataloguing in Publication Data
A catalogue record of this book is available from the British Library

Library of Congress Cataloging in Publication Data
A catalog record for this book has been requested

ISBN 0–7007–1605–X

For Ruth, Andrew and Christopher
with love

CONTENTS

CONTENTS

CONTENTS

LIST OF FIGURES

LIST OF ILLUSTRATIONS

Frontispiece. Great Buddha of the Sŏkkur-am Grotto, Kyŏngju, c. 750.

The following illustrations appear between pages 48–49.

1 *Wang och'ŏnch'uk-guk chŏn* (Record of a Journey to the Five Kingdoms of India). Manuscript. Written by Hyech'o c. 750.

2 Tae'ung-jŏn (Main Hall) of T'ongdo-sa temple, South Kyŏngsang Province, 1644.

3 Pagoda at T'ongdo-sa containing a relic of the Buddha brought to Silla by the monk Chajang, c. mid-seventh century.

4 Tae'ung-jŏn, Pongwŏn-sa, Sŏul. Head Temple of the Taego Buddhist Order. Late eighteenth century.

5 Vairocana Buddha in the Samch'ŏnbul-jŏn (Three Thousand Buddha Hall) of Pongwŏn-sa. Mid-1990s.

6 Taesŏng-jŏn, principal shrine of the Mun-myo or central Confucian shrine for Korea. Sŏul. Erected 1398; rebuilt 1601.

7 Group of Confucian scholars in traditional scholars' clothing in front of the Mŏngnyun-dang, lecture hall of the Sŏngggyun-gwan or Confucian academy in Sŏul. Building erected in 1398; rebuilt 1606.

8 Chŏng-jŏn (part view), principal shrine of the Chong-myo, the royal ancestral shrine in Sŏul. Erected in 1396 and extended on various occasions.

9 Tong-myo, a shrine in Chinese style dedicated to Kuan Yü, the Chinese God of War. Erected in 1602 at the command of the Ming emperor Shên-tsung (r. 1572–1620).

10 Cathedral Church of the Immaculate Conception of St Mary (popularly Myŏng-dong Cathedral), Roman Catholic cathedral of Sŏul. Erected in 1892–8 as a martyrium over the site of the home of the first Korean martyr, Kim Pŏmu.

11 Ch'ŏltu-san martyrs' church and museum. Dedicated in 1967, the church and museum is on a hill overlooking a site on which numerous Korean Catholics were executed.

PREFACE TO THE REVISED EDITION

When I wrote the first edition of this book in the late 1980s, I remarked that there was a need for a connected history of the development and condition of religion in Korea. Since that time the situation has changed little as the only other English, indeed Western-language, history to be published is a translation of a Korean-language text. I have taken the opportunity afforded by the re-publication of this work by the Curzon Press to amend the text, adding in material where I thought the original text was insufficiently clear or where further information was required. I have also taken advantage of recent scholarship to make changes in the text where there was a need to do so, and I have expanded the bibliography to include more recent scholarly works. I have also taken the narrative down to the end of the twentieth century. Otherwise, the text remains essentially as in the first edition.

I am especially pleased that this book is appearing in a paperback edition as it will now be able to fulfil the original intention of the author, to write a general history of religion in Korea which could be used as a standard source for students doing course subjects in East Asian religions and history in general or specifically in Korean religions, culture or history. It is not intended to be an exhaustive, monographic study of a particular aspect of Korean religions, but only to provide the general reader with an overall view of the history of the subject.

With regard to the Romanisation of Korean words, names and place names, I have continued to follow the universal scholarly practice of using the so-called McCune-Reischauer system because it provides the closest approximation in Roman letters to the sounds of Korean terms, and because it is necessary to maintain consistency in the representation of terms to avoid confusion for introductory students and the general reader. Likewise, I have continued to use the Wade-Giles system for Romanising Chinese terms rather than the *pinyin* system as the former system still has greater currency amongst scholars of East Asian religions. However, I have provided a conversion table from Wade-Giles into the *pinyin* system for the most important terms.

Finally, but not least importantly, I want to thank all the many people who helped me in making the revisions for this work including librarians who have helped me to find difficult-to-obtain materials and friends and colleagues who have made many useful suggestions and comments. I am solely responsible, however, for any errors of fact or interpretation. This edition is dedicated to my family as a reminder of the happy years we spent in Korea and in rediscovering it on later occasions.

J.H.G.
2001

PREFACE TO THE FIRST EDITION

For some years, the need for a connected history of religion in Korea has been obvious. Good books on the general subject of the history of religion or about the history of specific religious traditions have been written about China, Japan, and other Asian nations. However, in the past sixty years, only two books on the history of religion in Korea have appeared in Western languages, one in English and more recently one in German. For various reasons, each of these books has some shortcomings, and it was felt that a fresh attempt was necessary to describe the religions of Korea. It has been the author's intention that this book should not only be a history of religions in Korea, but that it should show the development of each tradition in relation to the others and that this development should be related to the general flow of Korean history. The author sincerely hopes that the reader will find this attempt to present the complex and significant history of religions in Korea to be both successful and interesting.

Any work which attempts to cover such a wide-ranging subject must draw on material from a variety of sources. Because this book is a cultural history as much as a religious history, there is technical vocabulary which is drawn from many different languages. Buddhist words use the standard Sanskrit or Pali transcription unless transcription according to Chinese, Korean, or Japanese pronunciation is deemed important. All Chinese vocabulary items, including many familiar place names, are transcribed according to the Wade-Giles system of Romanization. The author has decided to do this as many of the common terms used by historians of religion have been and still are in this transcription. Japanese words follow the Hepburn system. Korean words are transcribed according to the McCune-Reischauer system. As there is some variation in the application of this system of transcription, the author wishes to point out that it is his practice to use the hyphen to connect class words to titles, thus Pŏmŏ-sa, Han-gang, and Sŏrak-san. I have also used the hyphen to tie bound morphemes to their principal words, thus Han'gug-ŭi. I have not, however, as I had often done previously, placed the hyphen between the two characters of the personal name of a historic figure, thus Kim Chŏnghyŏn, rather than Kim Chŏng-hyŏn. All place names, including Sŏul (Seoul), and familiar names of people have been Romanized according to the McCune-Reischauer system. Names of people known by another transcription have that transcription used in parentheses at the first occurrence of the person's name.

During the years in which this book was being written, the author has benefited from the advice and suggestions of many friends and colleagues, both Korean and Western. They are too many to mention here by name, but I wish to indicate here my indebtedness to them all. No one but myself, however, is responsible for any errors of fact or interpretation. One person must be singled out for her unfailing support, my wife Dr Ruth Hildebrandt Grayson. She has given me support and assistance throughout, and without it, in a very real sense, this book would not have been written. Therefore it is only fitting that this book should be dedicated to her.

J.H.G.
1989

1

INTRODUCTION

1. The Subject and Purpose of this Book

In her justly famous travelogue *Korea and Her Neighbours*, Mrs Isabella Bird
Bishop wrote that when she set out on her journey to Korea in 1894 some of her
friends ventured guesses as to the location of this exotic nation. Mrs Bishop
commented that 'It was curious that not one of these educated, and, in some
cases, intelligent people came within 2,000 miles of its actual latitude and
longitude!' In the intervening hundred years, the academic world has fared little
better in its understanding of this nation on the tip of North-east Asia. Korea's
important role in the cultural and religious history of East Asia is either ignored
or passed over with comments to the effect that it was a bridge for the
transmission of Chinese civilization to Japan. This latter remark would leave the
untutored reader with the feeling that Korea had little to contribute to the general
process of cultural development and merely acted as some sort of passive
conduit. Statements of this type are wrong historically and in terms of the
importance of Korean religions in the modern world.

Korean Buddhism and Confucianism have played significant parts in the
development of Korean culture and have made unique contributions to the growth
of each of these religious traditions generally. Although much is made of
Japanese *Zen* Buddhism in courses which deal with the history of world
religions, Korean *Sŏn* Buddhism not only was established earlier than the
Japanese form of meditative Buddhism, but it has been the predominant form of
Korean monastic Buddhism since the tenth century.

In modern times, it is no exaggeration to say that the most dynamic form of
orthodox or traditional Buddhism in East Asia is to be found in Korea. Monastic
Buddhism in Japan would appear to be nearly dead, while monastic Buddhism in
Korea thrives. One indication of this vitality may be seen in the way in which
Korean Buddhist orders have been actively promoting the propagation of
Buddhism in the West. Although Confucianism is a Chinese philosophico-
religious system, it is only in Korea that an entire society became thoroughly
Confucianised. Christianity, a late-comer on the Korean religious scene, has
made dramatic progress there. The national census conducted in 1995 indicated

that more than one quarter of the national population self-identified themselves as a Protestant or Roman Catholic Christian. Thus, Korea is the only nation in Asia where Christianity has established itself during the past two hundred years as a significant component of the national culture.

This book has been written with the intention of redressing the neglect of Korean religions and their history. As any writer would, the author has brought to this work his own points of view and interpretations of history. Firstly, the author is a Christian minister. This means that his interpretation at certain points will be different from that of, for instance, a Buddhist scholar, or an agnostic.

Secondly, the author does not believe that there is such a 'thing' as Korean religion, but only Korean religions, or better, Korean religious traditions. Granted that there are certain cultural influences which give religion in Korea a different character from religion in China or Japan, none the less, the author does not think that taken as a whole there is a phenomenon which can be labelled as Korean religion. In this book, the various religious traditions will be dealt with separately.

Thirdly, this is a book of history. The author intends to deal with religion in Korea not as an abstract phenomenon, but as a component of Korean culture which has grown and developed through time. Therefore Korean history has been divided into eight large time periods. The condition of the various religious traditions in each period has been treated separately, and this religious history has been set against the contemporary political and cultural history. In this way, the author hopes to show not only how a particular religious tradition was related to the culture of a particular period, but also how the various traditions related to each other at a certain time.

Fourthly, in each period of Korean history, the writer has tried to indicate that one of the traditions was the predominant force, influencing the other traditions both structurally and doctrinally. In each of the four parts of the book, I have indicated this priority by arranging the order in which I discussed the various traditions according to the influence which I perceived them to have exercised. Because Confucianism was the dominant expressed mode of religion and philosophy during the Chosŏn Dynasty, the discussion of Confucianism precedes the discussion of Buddhism or Catholicism. As it is my opinion that currently Protestant Christianity is the most dynamic, if not yet *the* dominant, form of religion in Korea, the discussion of this tradition precedes the discussion of Catholicism, Confucianism, and Buddhism. Likewise, the other traditions are ranked in order amongst themselves.

Fifthly, it is the author's strongly held opinion that Korean traditional religion, commonly and mistakenly called shamanism, has greatly influenced all forms of religion in all periods of Korean history, including Christianity in modern times.

2. A Short History of the Study of Our Subject

(a) The Period of Early Contact

Although Europeans have known about the existence of Korea since the late medieval period through such accounts as the travelogue of Marco Polo (1254–1324), knowledge of her manners and customs did not become known until sometime in the late seventeenth century. Perhaps the earliest description of Korean religious life occurs in the account given by the shipwrecked Dutch seaman Hendrik Hamel (1630–92), *An Account of the Shipwreck of a Dutch Vessel on the Coast of the Isle of Quelpaert, Together with the Description of the Kingdom of Corea* (1668). Among the matters which Hamel discusses are religious practices, but unfortunately his description is too brief and the material which he does include is not clearly described. It is also difficult to compare what Hamel says with what we know of religion in that period from Korean sources. It is, none the less, a valuable account in so far as it is a record based on the author's own direct observations.

A far better description of certain aspects of Korean religious practices is contained in Père Jean-Baptiste du Halde's (1674–1743) massive four-volume work, *Description géographique, historique, chronologique et physique de l'Empire de la Chine et la Tartarie Chinoise* (1735), drawn from the letters of French Jesuit missionaries in China to society headquarters in France. This work, also translated and published in English in 1736, greatly influenced the picture which the European intelligentsia had of China. It contains an entire chapter devoted to Korea—the first time that an extensive description of that country was made available to the Western reader. The legend of the founder of Koguryŏ, Ko Chumong (see Appendix A. 4), is introduced to the reader of this work. The structure and content of this legend drew the attention of scholars who were beginning to take an interest in the religious traditions of the non-European world, and the story subsequently appeared in collections of world mythology and folklore.

In 1747, Thomas Astley wrote a compilation of various travel accounts entitled *Voyages and Travels* in which there is a chapter called 'A Description of Korea, Eastern Tartary, and Tibet'. The material in this chapter is drawn entirely from Père du Halde's work and Hamel's account. More influential than this work was a book specifically devoted to religion which included an account of the legend of Ko Chumong, founder-monarch of Koguryŏ. The Abbé Antoine Banier's (1673–1741) *La Mythologie et les fables expliquées par l'histoire* (1738) drew on the Jesuit accounts of Korea and in turn became an important source for later students. It was translated into English in 1739 by A. Millar and was used by subsequent scholars of religion and mythology in Britain. In 1816, George Stanley Faber (1773–1854) wrote *The Origin of Pagan Idolatry Ascertained from Historical Testimony and Circumstantial Evidence*, in which he recounted for his readers the legend of Ko Chumong. Even though stories

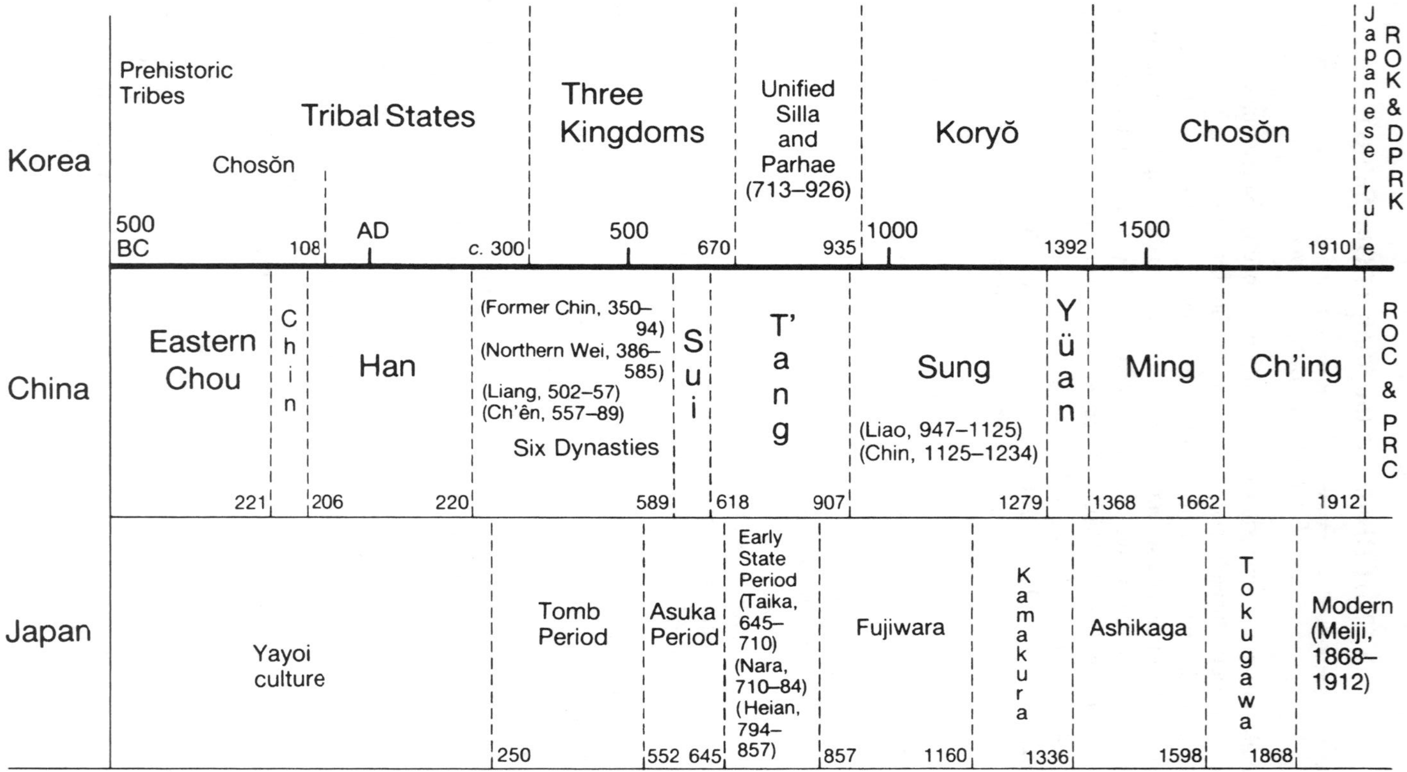
Korea
Prehistoric Tribes
Chosŏn
Tribal States
Three Kingdoms
Unified Silla and Parhae (713–926)
Koryŏ
Chosŏn
Japanese rule
ROK & DPRK
500 BC
108
AD
c. 300
500
670
935
1000
1392
1500
1910
China
Eastern Chou
Chin
Han
(Former Chin, 350–94)
(Northern Wei, 386–585)
(Liang, 502–57)
(Ch'ên, 557–89)
Six Dynasties
Sui
T'ang
Sung
(Liao, 947–1125)
(Chin, 1125–1234)
Yüan
Ming
Ch'ing
ROC & PRC
221
206
220
589
618
907
1279
1368
1662
1912
Japan
Yayoi culture
Tomb Period
Asuka Period
Early State Period (Taika, 645–710) (Nara, 710–84) (Heian, 794–857)
Fujiwara
Kamakura
Ashikaga
Tokugawa
Modern (Meiji, 1868–1912)
250
552
645
857
1160
1336
1598
1868

Figure 1 Comparative Schematic Diagram of East Asian History such as this were well known in the early nineteenth century amongst students of folklore and mythology, by the end of the century virtually all knowledge of Korea and its religions had disappeared from Western books.

One exception to this trend was the two-volume work by Père Charles Dallet (1829–78), *Histoire de l'Église de Corée* (1874) which was based upon letters and other materials written by French missionaries in Korea and sent to the headquarters of the Paris Missionary Society. The first volume of this history of the Roman Catholic Church in Korea is preceded by an introduction of 192 pages which provides the first exhaustive account of the culture, society, mores, politics, and religion of the Korean people to appear in any Western language. Chapter 11 of the Introduction is devoted to the religious life of Korea. In thirteen terse pages it provides the first coherent description of Korean Confucianism, Buddhism, and folk religion. This book became a major source of information for decades, and is still a useful source for historical research. Significantly, it was the first book after Hamel's account to be based upon the direct observations of people who were working and living in Korea.

(b) The Period of Western Imperial Expansion

With the advent of Western imperial expansion throughout the globe, Europeans in the late nineteenth century more than at any other time took an interest in the culture, customs, mores, and religious beliefs of 'exotic' peoples. Often one of the major sources of information for scholarly research came from the writings of foreign missionaries, and in many instances missionaries were the first scholars to study non-European peoples. This was certainly the case for Korea. During the period from the late nineteenth to the middle of the twentieth century, the first scholars of the Korean religious scene came from the ranks of the foreign missionaries.

From the time of their arrival in Korea in the middle of the 1880s, Protestant missionaries studied the religious practices of the Koreans for several reasons, including the evangelistic need to know the beliefs and thought of the people amongst whom they worked, and the theological interest in contrasting indigenous beliefs and practices with the Christian religion. Important early missionary scholars included Homer B. Hulbert (1863–1949), George Heber Jones (1867–1919), James Scarth Gale (1863–1937), Bishop Mark Napier Trollope (1862–1930), and Charles Allan Clark (1878–1961).

Hulbert, a member of the northern Methodist mission, USA, was one of the most original thinkers amongst the first generation of missionaries to Korea. During his editorship of the *Korea Review*, he published in 1903 a series of articles entitled 'The Korean Mudang and P'ansu' which was the first thorough description of the rituals and practices of Korean shamanism. It is still an important source for research into the primal religion of Korea. In 1906, Hulbert wrote a book entitled *The Passing of Korea* which decries the destruction of an independent Korean state by the Japanese and in which he gives a survey of

Korean history and describes the culture and customs of old Korea. Hulbert devotes chapters to 'Folklore', 'Religion and Superstition', and geomancy. The chapter on folklore in particular is a seminal analysis of the subject and is based upon an earlier article entitled 'Korean Folktales' which had appeared in the *Transactions of the Korea Branch of the Royal Asiatic Society* for 1902. In 1925, years after his expulsion from Korea by the Japanese, Hulbert compiled a popular collection of Korean folk-tales called *Omjee the Wizard: Korean Folk Stories*.

Like Hulbert, George Heber Jones, who was also a northern Methodist, was one of the first missionaries to express an interest in Korean indigenous religious practices. His classic work is 'The Spirit Worship of the Koreans', which also appeared in the *Transactions* for 1902. Unlike Hulbert's series of articles which had appeared in the *Korea Review*, Jones's article does not attempt to describe in detail shamanistic practices, but rather attempts to create an analytical framework to organize the entire pantheon of Korean spirits and the various religious beliefs of the Koreans. Jones also contributed to knowledge about the history of Korean Confucianism. In 1903 he wrote an article for the *Transactions* on the life and work of the most significant Confucian scholar of the Silla period, Ch'oe Ch'iwŏn (857–?). This was probably the first piece of detailed research on Ch'oe by a Western scholar.

The article by Jones on spirit-worship formed the basis of later work done by such missionary scholars as C. A. Clark of the northern Presbyterian mission. The latter published in 1932 a book based on a series of lectures first given at Princeton Theological Seminary entitled *Religions of Old Korea*. This was the first comprehensive treatment of the history of Korean religious beliefs and practices. Apart from descriptions of Buddhism and Confucianism, Clark also discusses Roman Catholic and Protestant Christianity, Korean shamanism, and the syncretic religion, *Ch'ŏndo-gyo*.

Bishop Trollope of the Church of England mission likewise contributed several articles to the *Transactions*, including an essay of 1917 entitled 'Introduction to the Study of Buddhism in Corea'. This article considered the origin of Buddhism in Korea, certain key figures in Buddhist history, and some doctrinal contributions of Korean Buddhism. The bishop concluded with four suggestions for future research which are still relevant today – the writing of a detailed and connected history of Korean Buddhism, the study of the history of the Buddhist scriptures used in Korea to determine which are the historically primary works, the detailed historical study of the individual monasteries of Korea, and the study of the history of the architectural layouts of Korean temples.

James Scarth Gale, as a member of the translation committee for the Bible, was a particularly gifted linguist and literary figure amongst the members of the early missionary community. Like Hulbert and Jones, Gale was interested in the myths and folk-beliefs of the Koreans and wrote about them in various scholarly journals. Gale also applied his linguistic skills to the translation of materials relating to Korean religions, perhaps the first Westerner to do so. He translated into English two traditional collections of Korean folk-tales by the scholars Yi Yuk (15th cent.) and Im Pang (1640–1724). These stories were published in 1913 as *Korean Folk Tales: Imps, Ghosts and Fairies*. Gale also translated the seventeenth-century novel *Ku'un-mong* by Kim Manjung (1637–92) as *The Cloud Dream of the Nine: A Korean Novel* (1922). Although the translation of this novel was not a piece of academic research as such, Gale's ability to convey the rich Buddhist imagery of the original text provides some insight into the popular Buddhist thinking of that period.

Finally, mention must be made of the seminal work in Korean studies done by the French scholar and diplomat Maurice Courant (1865–1935). He not only compiled the first significant bibliography of Korean materials, he also wrote an important early introduction to Korean religion, 'Sommaire et historique des cultes coreéns', *T'oung Pao* (Leiden and Paris, 1900).

At the same time that the early missionaries were examining the religious life of Korea, other early foreign residents and visitors were taking an interest in the folk art of the Korean people, which primarily used motifs having religious themes. Two early collectors are important, Major John Baptiste Bernadou (1858–1908), United States Naval Attaché in Sŏul in the early 1880s, and the French traveller Charles Varat (1842?–1893). Major Bernadou's collection of folk materials and his extensive descriptive notes now form the core of the collection of Korean folk materials at the Smithsonian Institution in Washington. This collection is important to any student of Korean religion, as it contains valuable materials which may be seen nowhere else. Varat visited Korea in 1888 and 1889 and amassed a collection of photographs of Korean folk paintings which was not only a major resource for scholarly researchers, but also evoked considerable interest amongst French painters at the turn of the nineteenth century.

During the first third of the twentieth century, Korean Buddhism aroused some interest among scholars in the English- and German-speaking worlds. Heinrich Friedrich Hackmann (1864–1935) translated his own German-language work into English in 1910, entitling it *Buddhism as a Religion: Its Historical Development and its Present Condition*. This work gives a none too flattering picture of the state of Korean Buddhism at that time. This picture is confirmed by Frederick Starr (1858–1933), an American anthropologist who had visited Korea, in his *Korean Buddhism* (1918), a valuable record of the condition of Buddhism in the second decade of this century. The philosopher James Bissett Pratt (1875–1944), after making an extensive study of world Buddhism, published *The Pilgrimage of Buddhism and a Buddhist Pilgrimage* (1928) in which he comments, as had previous observers, on the general ignorance of many of the Korean clergy. Apart from such general studies as these, there were also individual studies of various aspects of Korean Buddhism. Examples would be Bertha Gottsche's examination of the Sŏkkur-am grotto in an article of 1918–19, or the research of Walter Fuchs (1935) on Hyech'o's record of his journey to India in the early eighth century.

Concurrent with the development of Western interest in Korean religion, we may note the development of Western-style Korean scholarship of religion. The foremost indigenous scholar of Korean religions in the first half of this century was the Buddhist Yi Nŭnghwa (1869–1945). His works, largely descriptive rather than analytical, include *Chosŏn pulgyo t'ongsa* (A Complete History of Korean Buddhism, 1918), *Chosŏn kidokkyo-gŭp oegyo-sa* (A History of Korean Foreign Relations and Christianity, 1925), *Chosŏn musok-ko* (Records of Korean Shamanism, 1927), and *Han'guk togyo-sa* (A History of Korean Taoism, 1959). These books bring together many different sources for the history of religion in Korea and are principal resources for anyone researching any aspect of Korean religions. Modern researchers, such as Yu Tongsik, have used the materials in them extensively.

(c) The Period of an Independent Korea

Research into Korean religions waned, naturally, during the years of the Second World War, the Korean War, and throughout the dreadful years following in the wake of the cessation of hostilities on the peninsula. Since the late 1960s and throughout the 1970s to the present, however, the scope and quality of research by both Korean and Western scholars has increased greatly. In the present era, research is dominated largely by academic interests, rather than as in the past by the particular religious interests of the writers. There would seem to be three main lines of interest which are being pursued, namely, anthropological studies, textual studies, and historical studies.

Anthropological studies attempt to examine religious practices and beliefs within the context of a particular social setting, such as a village or a sub-community within an urban society. Social, economic, political, and psychological influences are examined, and detailed descriptions of particular rituals or practices are presented to the reader. This development in research is typical of both Korean and Western researchers. One thinks here of the important contributions made by Kim T'aegon (1937–1996), Ch'oe Kilsŏng (1940–), Laurel Kendall (1947–), Dawnhee and Roger Janelli, and others. With the single exception of the work of Homer Hulbert, previous Western scholarship on Korean religions did not describe specific practices, but dealt primarily with such abstract concepts as types and essences. With the advent of research using an anthropological methodology, there are for the first time thorough descriptions of discrete religious practices. These descriptions are set against and compared with those of other social institutions, to illustrate the interconnected relationship of religion with all aspects of society. This type of research has been applied primarily to folk religious practices, but it has considerable potential for describing the beliefs of Buddhists, Christians, and believers in the new religions as well.

Concurrent with the interest in anthropological studies, which by their nature are concerned with contemporary thought, beliefs, and practices, an interest in an examination of Korean religious texts has developed which has contributed to an understanding of the historical development of the various religious traditions of Korea. Lewis Lancaster and his associates are particularly to be singled out here for their contributions to the description and analysis of manuscripts and texts relating to Korean Buddhism. Lancaster's *The Korean Buddhist Canon: A Descriptive Catalogue* (1979) is a primary source for anyone doing research in this area. Robert E. Buswell, jun.'s study of Chinul (1983) is especially significant for its textual analysis, for its biographical description of one of the seminal figures of Korean Buddhism, and for its presentation of some of the unique features of Korean Buddhist belief and practice.

Textual studies have not been limited to Buddhism. Important contributions have been made in the area of Confucian thought. Some of the fruits of this research may be found in *The Rise of Neo-Confucianism in Korea* (1985), edited by Wm. Theodore de Bary and JaHyun Kim Haboush. Nor has textual research been limited to the great religions alone; it has also encompassed research in materials relating to folk religion. To cite only one example, the Dutch scholar B. C. A. Walraven (1947–) has made a considerable study of ancient and modern texts relating to shamanistic practices especially in his work *Songs of the Shaman* (1994). Textual analysis of materials relating to Buddhism, Confucianism, and the folk traditions has provided us with specific knowledge about the philosophical and religious concepts of concrete individuals, thus allowing us to arrive at more certain and specific conclusions about the religious beliefs and practices of a particular era.

General historical studies have also recently appeared which have outlined the course of development of a particular religion in a specific period or which have dealt with the development of a religious tradition or traditions over an extended period of time. The first book since Clark's *Religions of Old Korea* (1932) to survey the entire history of Korean religious experience was *Die Religionen Koreas* (1977) by the Dutch scholar Frits Vos (1918-2000). This work has a comprehensive bibliography which may still be consulted profitably by any researcher.

Although there has been academic interest in Buddhist and Confucian history for some decades, it is only in recent years that there has been an attempt to write a connected history of Christianity in Korea. The early years of Korean Protestantism have been well documented by George Paik (1895–1984) in his *The History of Protestant Missions in Korea: 1832–1910* (1929). However, until very recently, virtually nothing had been written in either English or Korean about the years following the Japanese annexation of Korea. Donald N. Clark's *Christianity in Modern Korea* (1986) and the author's *Early Buddhism and Christianity in Korea* (1985) attempt to redress this imbalance.

Korean Protestant scholars such as Min Kyŏngbae (1934–) and Yi Manyŏl (1938–) have written biographies of early Protestant figures, as well as connected histories of the several Protestant missions and Korean denominations, which have greatly contributed to our knowledge of recent Christian history. On the

Roman Catholic side there has been even greater progress through the work of Father Ch'oe Sŏgu and his associates at the *Han'guk kyohoe-sa yŏn'gu-so* 'Korean Church History Research Institute'. They have done much as regards the discovery, preservation, and analysis of early Catholic documents and the creation of local Catholic histories. Perhaps the major academic achievement of the institute to date is the *Han'guk kat'ollik taesajŏn* (Dictionary of Korean Catholicism, 1985).

Continuing anthropological, textual, and historical research will add to our knowledge and appreciation of the religious experience of the Korean people, contribute to a better understanding of Korea's place in the progress of world culture, and facilitate the growth of greater inter-religious understanding. It is the hope of the author that this general survey of Korean religion and history will in some measure contribute to these three scholastic goals.

Part I

EARLY KOREA

2

KOREA PRIOR TO CHINESE CIVILIZATION

The Palaeolithic Period to the Fourth Century

1. The Culture of the Earliest Period

(a) Prehistoric Times

The question of who the Koreans are is an archaeological and historical puzzle which cannot yet be fully and properly resolved. Recent archaeological work indicates that Palaeo-Asiatic peoples inhabited the Korean peninsula more than two hundred millennia before the present, which is within the period of Neanderthal man. As with all peoples with a primitive technology, the culture and economy of these early races was strongly affected by the climate and geography of the area where they lived. Discoveries of palaeolithic sites indicate that the early settlers of the Korean peninsula were fishermen residing near the mouths of the great rivers, or hunters in those areas distant from river valleys. Apart from such basic information, little is known at present about the culture of the most distant past, and certainly nothing of what language these people spoke or what ideas they thought or what gods they worshipped. The archaeological evidence does tell us, however, that the material culture of these prehistoric groups was comparable to the culture of similar Palaeo-Asiatic societies in Eastern Siberia and Manchuria. This is an important point because it reminds us that, whatever the origins of the Korean people are, the Koreans are not of Chinese stock nor is their primal culture derived from China. They are North-east Asiatics.

As elsewhere in the world, the archaeological record shows a progressive development of culture from a palaeolithic culture through an early agricultural society to a society with a metallurgic technology. This shift in cultural status seems to have been related to a flow of culture from Manchuria into Korea. Whether or not the advent of agriculture in the peninsula was accompanied by the arrival of another racial group displacing the earlier inhabitants, it is plain that the shift to metallurgy, to a technology of bronze, was accompanied by the arrival of a new racial group, presumably of Tungusic stock, which merged with the ancient inhabitants.

Agriculture first appeared around the third millennium BC in the northern part of the peninsula, and somewhat later in the south. Bronze technology, of the

Scytho-Siberian tradition, appeared in northern Korea some time after 1000 BC. Bronze Age culture did not emerge in southern Korea until 600 BC. In our discussions of the development of Korean culture, it is important to remember this time-lag between the north and the south, especially the south-east, as it will be typical of all new cultural innovations until the modern period. It also seems reasonable to date the emergence of the immediate ancestors of the present Korean people to around 600 BC. The present Korean race is an amalgamation of the pre-Bronze Age inhabitants of the peninsula who were related to the most ancient tribes of North-east Asia, and certain Tungusic peoples who brought Bronze Age civilization with them. The merger of these two racial and cultural groups was probably completed around 600 BC with the development of bronze technology in the south.

The emergence of Bronze Age technology also brought with it certain changes in social structure. Typical archaeological remains of this period are dolmens, menhirs, and elaborate tombs of stone slabs which indicate that certain members of the society of that time could utilize the labour of other members to construct these monuments. The emergence of a stratified society with at least a ruling and a subservient class is clearly indicated. The occurrence of copper and bronze ornaments amongst the burial items in the grander tombs is further evidence of this important change in society.

There is only indirect evidence of the religious beliefs of this time. The burial of the dead with ceremony and the inclusion of beautiful ornaments with the corpse probably indicate some concept of an afterlife. The use of horse, tiger, and bird motifs on bronze objects would seem to reflect shamanistic religious beliefs similar to beliefs current in modern Siberia. These few facts fit well with what we know of the origins of the Koreans, but it is not until the Iron Age that there is specific archaeological and written evidence for the Koreans' religion.

(b) Proto-historic Times

Korean history may be said to begin with the Iron Age, because it was during this period that distinct tribal groupings began to form which became the direct ancestors of the first Korean states. The advent of Iron Age technology and culture brought with it increased social change which took place in direct relation to the proximity of the tribal area to the centre of Chinese civilization. Thus Ancient Chosŏn attained true state structure earlier than any other society, because of its geographic closeness to China.

It is important to remember in this discussion that Koreans have claimed as their land and their ancestors, territories and peoples well beyond the area of the Korean peninsula. In addition to the Korean peninsula, a large section of southern Manchuria, including the Liaotung Peninsula and all the land west to the Liao River, north to the Sungari River, and east to the Sea of Japan, is said to have been the primal territory of the Korean people. In this vast territory grew up the following ethnic groups (see Fig. 2): the people of the state of

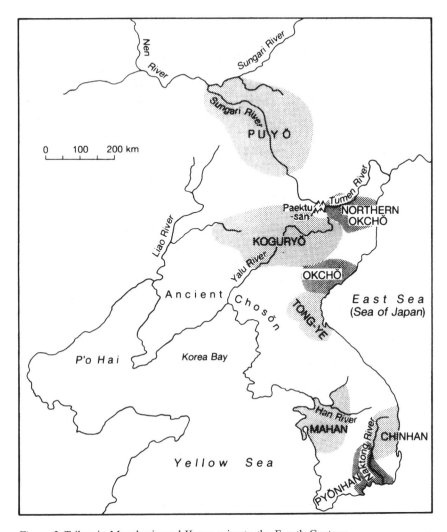

Figure 2 Tribes in Manchuria and Korea prior to the Fourth Century

Ancient Chosŏn, occupying the north-western portion of the Korean peninsula, the Liaotung Peninsula, and lands to the east of the Liao River; the Puyŏ tribal group occupying the vast territories along the fertile plains of the valley of the Sungari River; the Koguryŏ tribal group, possibly a break-off from the Puyŏ, occupying the mountain valleys to the north of the middle reaches of the Yalu River; the Okchŏ and Tong-ye tribal groups, possibly branches of the Koguryŏ, occupying the areas around the modern cities of Hamhŭng and Wŏnsan respectively; and the Mahan, Pyŏnhan, and Chinhan tribal groups occupying the area of the west coast of Korea south of the Han River, the course of the

15

Naktong River, and the south-eastern part of the peninsula east of the Naktong River respectively.

The Iron Age reached the area of Ancient Chosŏn first, with the result that a state emerged in this region during the fourth century before Christ, the same era as the Period of Warring States in China (403–221 BC). This ancient state was very much affected by the political and cultural currents of the time, and undoubtedly the rise of an independent non-Chinese state in this area must be attributed to the contemporary state of disunion in China. When union was established there under the Chin (249–207 BC) and Han (206 BC to AD 220) dynasties, Ancient Chosŏn suffered. Suppression of revolts in the north-eastern region of the Han Empire led to the flight of numerous refugees into Ancient Chosŏn, some of whom were employed by the state to defend its vulnerable northern border. One of these refugees, Wiman, led a revolt in 190 BC, usurping the throne and establishing a state called Wiman Chosŏn. Wiman and his descendants, however, were only able to enjoy the fruits of their exploits for eighty years. In 109 BC, the Emperor Wu-ti (r. 141–87 BC) of the Han Dynasty conquered Ancient Chosŏn in an attempt to protect his sensitive north-east border. The incorporation of the most ancient Korean state into the Han Empire led to the creation of the Lolang (Nangnang in Korean) commanderies, which were to play an important part in the diffusion of Chinese civilization into the Korean tribal areas.

The introduction of iron technology greatly aided the military strength of Ancient Chosŏn. Iron swords and arrowheads quickly replaced ones made of bronze during the Period of Warring States in China, and clearly enabled this group to maintain and secure its position against the various neighbouring Chinese states. Iron also led to certain improvements in living conditions. Iron tools could more easily fashion wood, which led to homes made of wood replacing the mud homes of the past. The *ondol* or Korean hypocaust system of underfloor heating traces its origins to this period, a significant advance in home heating. During this era the use of the dolmen declined and finally ceased, to be replaced by interment of the remains in large burial mounds or in large, round coffin jars. The cultural influence of this state extended beyond the Korean cultural sphere to Japan, where we may see its effect on the Yayoi (*c.* 300 BC to AD 300) culture.

Puyŏ, the furthest north of the Korean tribal groups, had a mixed pastoral/agricultural economy, the only one of the tribal groups to practise the herding of animals. This group emerged onto the historical scene much later than Ancient Chosŏn, and did not attain prominence until the first century AD. As it was surrounded by various 'barbarian' tribes such as the Hsienpei on the north, and by Koguryŏ and China on the south and west, Puyŏ sought politically to balance its relations between these various groups. This policy of alliance worked well for some time, but after the disastrous defeat by the Hsienpei in 346, Puyŏ went into an irreversible decline until the tribal leaders were forced to place themselves under the authority of Koguryŏ in 494. Although the supreme tribal leader referred to himself as *wang* (king) when corresponding with the Chinese emperor as a sign of subservience, Puyŏ never attained the status of a kingdom but only of a tribal league. Its social structure was composed of the basic clan units which merged to form the various tribes of the league. The patriarchs of the various clans and the chieftains of the several tribes had authority over matters of local or immediate concern. Graver matters of concern to the whole league, such as war, were debated at a general council of the tribal league. A pastoral and agricultural, clan-based society, the Puyŏ practised the enslavement of non-clan members, such as prisoners of war or criminals. They also possessed a primitive legal code which would appear to be a formalization of traditional practices. The culture of the Puyŏ, by the time of their extinction as an independent entity, had attained the level of a sophisticated tribal society relatively uninfluenced by the development of Chinese civilization.

Koguryŏ, on the other hand, lying astride the main route of cultural and technological diffusion into the peninsula and being in close proximity to the territory of Lolang, was more sinified than Puyŏ. The legendary founder of Koguryŏ, Ko Chumong, was said to have been one of the chieftains of a Puyŏ tribe who was forced to flee south. Koguryŏ, like Puyŏ, found itself in a geo-politically delicate situation and responded by developing a warrior tradition. Clashes with the Chinese colonies in Korea are recorded as early as 128 BC. Significantly, Koguryŏ conquered the Chinese colony of Hsüan-t'u (*Hyŏnt'o* in Korean) in 75 BC, the first of many future conquests. By the beginning of the second century after Christ, Koguryŏ had begun to transform itself into a true kingdom and had begun the series of spectacular conquests which were to lead to its supremacy in North-east Asia. Throughout the second and third centuries, Koguryŏ pursued a policy of southward expansion threatening both the Liaotung Peninsula and the colonies in north-western Korea. Finally, taking advantage of the weakness of the Chinese state, Koguryŏ conquered the Chinese commanderies in 313, ending four centuries of Chinese dominance in the area, and firmly establishing itself as *the* power in North-east Asia.

Like Puyŏ, Koguryŏ was a tribal league; it was composed of five tribes, the head of one of which would be selected as the supreme leader of the league. Before the emergence of Koguryŏ as a kingdom, the great chief was chosen most often from the Sono tribe. However, by the period in which Koguryŏ began to transform itself into a kingdom, the Kyeru tribal chieftains had begun to predominate. Beneath the great chief were various ranked chiefs and petty chieftains. The regularity and order of the terms for these various positions is one indication that by the second century a government bureaucracy had begun to take shape. As the kingship became hereditary, the premiership tended to remain elective amongst the various tribal chiefs and chieftains. This highly stratified society was a warrior society. As in Puyŏ, slavery was practised utilizing prisoners of war and criminals to perform tasks beneath the dignity of the ordinary man. Rank was indicated by the apparel worn, and at death the status of the deceased was indicated by the type of tomb and burial items. Although similar to the Puyŏ in many ways, the Koguryŏ made more rapid progress in the transition to a true kingdom, began earlier to adapt sinitic culture, and more thoroughly developed the traditions of a warrior class.

The Tong-ye and Okchŏ tribal groups in north-eastern Korea were more primitive than the tribes discussed previously. They had many customs in common with Koguryŏ, yet never rose above the level of a tribal society. The several clans remained comparatively independent, and the overall tribal structure was weak. A tribal league as in Puyŏ and Koguryŏ never developed. Clan land was jealously guarded and most decisions regarding justice were made by the clan patriarchs. Because of their proximity to the sea, the Okchŏ and Tong-ye had a mixed economy of fishing and agriculture. A certain amount of trading of a primitive nature did exist, mostly in fish, salt, seaweed, and sealskins, but a rudimentary system of money exchange did not develop. Although it is unclear when the Tong-ye and Okchŏ disappeared as independent entities, they seem to have been absorbed by Koguryŏ by the middle of the first century.

South of the Han River, we find the Sam-Han or three Han tribes. The entire southern area of the peninsula was late in receiving metallurgic culture, so late in fact that there are not distinct bronze and iron ages. Metallurgy appeared by the third century BC. One early tribal state was Chin-guk, which apparently was founded by the last king of Ancient Chosŏn, who fled to an area south of modern Sŏul after the usurpation of the kingship by Wiman in 190 BC. The Sam-Han tribal groups of Mahan, Pyŏnhan, and Chinhan came into existence around the time of the advent of metallurgic culture and persisted until the third century AD, or possibly later. The first of the tribal leagues to develop into a kingdom was Mahan, which became the nucleus around which the Kingdom of Paekche began to form. This development seems to have taken place under the aegis of chieftains from tribes from the north, for Paekche preserved the tradition that Onjo, a Puyŏ tribal chieftain, had fled from Koguryŏ and established himself as head of a new tribal league. The Pyŏnhan formed themselves into tribes no later than the second century AD, and by the third century had created a tribal league called the Kaya Federation. Excavations in the area of the federation demonstrate that Kaya enjoyed considerable trade, as is confirmed by ancient records which show that the Kaya states exported iron ore to China, the Tong-ye, and Japan. The Chinhan tribes began to form a tribal league based on the tribe of Saro near modern Kyŏngju. However, remoteness from the centre of cultural activity and the impediment to communication by the great Sobaek Mountains meant that this league emerged later than, and did not achieve the status of a kingdom until some time after, its neighbours. The Kingdom of Silla did not emerge until the fifth century, well after similar developments elsewhere. As with the northern tribal groups, society was stratified, but it was seemingly less structured and more primitive than elsewhere. Clothing type was used to indicate social status. Slavery was practised, the slaves often being Chinese who had been apprehended while cutting trees in the tribal forests. Mineral ores were mined and smelted, and metal objects were made locally. Housing was very primitive, with only one room being used by all members of commoners' families, which shocked visiting Chinese.

2. Korean Primal Religion

By the opening of the fourth century AD, the peoples within the Korean cultural sphere, comprising the areas of eastern and southern Manchuria plus the Korean peninsula, had attained the height of their development as a comparatively independent cultural entity. The culture which was characteristic of the various tribal groups and incipient states of that time, we term Korean Primal Culture. This culture, regardless of superficial embellishments which were derived from Chinese civilization, was entirely Korean and owed its origins to developments in Siberia and Central Asia. The religious traditions of the several tribes were more uniquely Korean than were the governmental and political systems. We term this religious tradition Korean Primal Religion. From the fourth through to the end of the fifth century, and in the case of Silla to the end of the sixth century, the Korean people experienced more cultural and social change than at any time before the end of the nineteenth century. From this period onwards, the Korean people became a part of the Chinese cultural sphere and came to accept the sinified form of Buddhism as their own. In order to understand later religious developments, it is important to identify the primal religion of Korea. The nature of this religion will explain in part why and how Confucianism, Buddhism, and Christianity have been accepted in Korea, and why Taoism and Shintō have experienced little success there.

The primal religion of Korea in the fourth century reflects both its descent from ancient Siberian shamanism and the adjustment which this precursor religion made to the settled conditions of an agricultural society. The shamanistic influence may be seen in the indigenous belief in a supreme, heavenly spirit called *Hanŭllim* in Korean or *Ch'ŏnsin* in Sino-Korean, and in the body of heavenly spirits which carry out his will. Shamanistic also is the belief in the ability of certain unusual persons to communicate with the realm of spirits, in particular with *Hanŭllim*, the Lord of Heaven. The antiquity of the belief in a supreme being is indicated by the mention of this great god in the foundation myths of the Korean tribal states, and the occurrence of the name of the Mountain God, a modern guise of the Ruler of Heaven, on a stele dated to AD 85 in the area of the state of Ancient Chosŏn. The stele, containing a petition for a bountiful harvest, tells us that by the first century agriculture played an important part in the principal rituals of the state and people. All of the major rituals of the various groups were addressed in the first instance to the Lord of Heaven and were concerned with aspects of the agricultural cycle.

The Puyŏ, largely a pastoral people, had a great festival called *Yŏnggo-je* which was celebrated in the first month of the lunar calendar. This was not a harvest festival, but a great rite conducted at the end of the grazing season. The *Yŏnggo-je* is comparable to similar rites of other pastoral peoples which took place when the animals for breeding were separated from those selected for slaughter. Such rites have a function which is analogous to harvest rites amongst agricultural peoples. The Puyŏ also had a service of divination in which cracks in the hoof of a sacrificed ox were scrutinized to prognosticate the future. The Koguryŏ had a harvest rite called the *Tongmaeng-je*, celebrated during the tenth month. They also honoured a spirit called *Susin*, symbolic of male reproductive power, an obvious corollary to agricultural fertility rites. The more primitive Tong-ye also had a harvest festival in the tenth lunar month, which they called *Much'ŏn-je*. Further south, we note that the Han tribes had two principal festivals, one for the planting of grain in the spring (fifth lunar month) and one for the harvest in the autumn (tenth lunar month). These were called *Suritnal* and *Sangdal* respectively. These rites were held at altars erected on the tops of mountains or, in the case of the more southern tribes, in sacred groves called *sodo*. The officiants at these rites were men called *Ch'ŏn-gun* or Prince of Heaven who were either the sovereigns of their tribe or members of the ruling family. They were the great shamans who interceded with Heaven on behalf of their people and who were seen by their people as being *sinin* or divine men.

The great festivals were times of much festivity, with dancing and drinking. These sacred festivals, however, could be used for other purposes. The Puyŏ brought criminals to justice at this time and freed prisoners as an act of benevolence. The *sodo*, typical of southern Korea, was a sacred grove, marked off by a bell and a drum suspended on a pole to symbolize the presence of divine beings. Apart from the function which these groves played as the location of the great rites, they also offered protection to the refugee. A criminal or other person fleeing an enemy could claim asylum within the holy precincts of the *sodo*, as was the case with churches in medieval Europe. Often myths of the founding ancestors of a state or clan are associated with a particular clan *sodo*.

It is interesting to observe that the names of these various tribal rites betray their shamanistic ancestry. The drum is an important instrument used by the shaman to create the ecstatic state necessary for the journey to Heaven. The name of the Puyŏ festival the *Yŏnggo-je* contains the term *ko* for drum, indicative of its importance to that rite. Likewise, the name of the Tong-ye festival the *Much'ŏn-je* means 'dancing before Heaven', a reference to the state of ecstasy prior to the shaman's journey. The title of the Sam-Han festival *Suritnal* contains the word *suri* or eagle. Ornithological motifs are common symbols in the legends of Siberian shamanism, as they represent the flight of the soul of the shaman to the realm of the spirits.

Besides these great rites, each of the clans and tribes held ceremonies in honour of their ancestors and maintained separate shrines to perpetuate their memory. When the tribal league emerged, with a single family in which the rulership became hereditary, the rites concerning the founding ancestor of the royal line took on increased importance and became national rites. Legends developed around these figures and these stories took on the character of national foundation myths. All of the stories reflect a belief in a Supreme Being,

20

who was the creator of the universe, of culture and society, and to whom the royal family was related. The earliest of these stories is the Myth of Tan'gun of Ancient Chosŏn, but Puyŏ, Koguryŏ, Kaya, and Silla all had their own versions. For the interest of the reader, translations of these myths have been included in Appendix A. The purpose of these stories was two-fold, to demonstrate that the kings ruled by divine right, and that they could intercede with *Hanŭllim* for their people because they were his royal descendants.

The shamanistic role of the Korean sovereigns is well illustrated by the royal regalia excavated from the great tumuli in the capital of Silla, Kyŏngju. Although the regalia date from the sixth century and later, they preserve the religious sentiment of an earlier era. The royal regalia consist of three items of ceremonial dress, the crown, the belt, and shoes, all three of which are important elements of the dress of modern Siberian shamans. The crowns of pure gold sheets consist of a gold circlet surmounted by golden uprights in the form of trees and deer antlers. From these dangle comma-shaped pieces of jade called *kogok*. Some crowns have an inner crown with wings of beaten gold, and one crown is surmounted by a double arch of gold topped by a golden phoenix. From the circlet of the crown dangle golden chains with various golden objects and *kogok* suspended from them. The gold belts similarly have many objects, including *kogok*, suspended from them. Tree, deer, and bird motifs are typical designs which modern Siberian shamans use to adorn their clothing. They also place bear or tiger claws on their clothing in the belief that they may obtain the power of those beasts. The *kogok* may reasonably be interpreted as an animal claw.

A belief in the afterlife amongst the non-royal members of society may be deduced from the ceremony with which persons were buried, and especially the types of items buried with them. In particular, the Pyŏnhan buried bird-wings with the deceased. Birds are symbolic of the belief in the upward ascent of the soul, especially the soul of the shaman.

An examination of the myths and legends from the tribal states reveals that there were three principal religious concerns in the tribal period. These were the offering of prayers for the prosperity of the land, the curing of disease, and the propitiation of and the sending-off of the soul of the deceased to the next world. These functions were performed then as now by the shaman and have remained as diagnostic characteristics of Korean religious experience throughout the ages.

3

THE THREE KINGDOMS
The Advent of Chinese Civilization

1. The Historical Background

The next four hundred years of Korean history, from the opening of the fourth century to the latter quarter of the seventh century, were dominated by the contest between the various Korean powers for supremacy on the peninsula. This contest culminated in the great wars of the 660s which firmly established Silla's suzerainty over most of the Korean peninsula. Throughout this long period, China was divided into various petty states fighting over the remains of the Han Empire, which had collapsed in the first part of the third century. Political disunion in China, and particularly the dominance of the states of northern China by 'barbarian' tribes, contributed substantially to the development of the Korean states and to the spread of Chinese culture into the peninsula.

Two Korean powers emerged, Paekche and Koguryŏ, which for more than 200 years engaged in constant warfare. As Puyŏ in the far north had entered into a state of decline, and the tribal states in the south-east did not develop into true kingdoms until much later, the field of battle was divided initially between these two states. Although Koguryŏ entered the fourth century as the dominant power, she was defeated in several wars with Paekche, the last of which in 371 resulted in the sacking of P'yŏngyang and the death of her king. At this point Koguryŏ entered into an alliance with the barbarian empire of Former Chin (351–94) in northern China, whilst Paekche allied itself with Eastern Chin (317–420) in southern China and developed trading relations with Japan.

The reverses of the fourth century were overcome in the fifth century when Koguryŏ re-established its power and expanded its territory under the aegis of King Changsu (r. 413–91). Realizing the danger which a revitalized Koguryŏ posed to his kingdom, the King of Paekche established diplomatic relations with the Empire of Northern Wei (386–534) in north China and with the emergent state of Silla in the south-eastern part of the peninsula. In spite of these precautions, Koguryŏ's power continued to grow and in 475, a hundred years after Koguryŏ's humiliating defeat at the hands of Paekche, troops sacked the capital of Paekche south of the Han River and killed her king. Paekche lost her importance as a power on the peninsula and never recovered her former strength.

Her territory was diminished and her capital moved to a more secure place in the southern part of the peninsula.

At the opening of the sixth century, it seemed virtually certain that Koguryŏ would soon dominate the entire peninsula as well as eastern and southern Manchuria. Paekche, Kaya, and the incipient state of Silla were all stuffed into the southernmost part of the peninsula, seemingly ripe for absorption into the Kingdom of Koguryŏ. This did not happen. Paekche secured her position by entering into an alliance with the Liang Empire (502–57) in southern China and by strengthening her ties with Silla and Japan. Although politically weakened, Paekche attained the height of her cultural development at this time; a sophistication she used in the diplomatic manoeuvres of this century. For a short period Paekche and Silla were allied in an attempt to drive Koguryŏ out of the Han River Valley in central Korea. This alliance was abruptly broken when in mid-century Silla seized the valley for herself. A counter-attack by Paekche was disastrously defeated, resulting in the death of King Sŏng (r. 523–54), who had been responsible for the brilliance of Paekche's culture. This defeat sealed the fate of Paekche as an important contender in the peninsular power-struggle and established Silla as the opponent of the expansion of Koguryŏ. At the same time that Silla seized the Han River Valley, she also absorbed the Kaya Federation and the tribal state of Talgubŏl on the east bank of the Naktong River.

By the opening of the seventh century, Koguryŏ still remained the dominant power, but Silla possessed large portions of the north-eastern part of the peninsula in addition to the Han River Valley and the whole south-eastern part of the peninsula. Paekche was left with only a small portion of the south-western part of the peninsula. Until the final third of the sixth century, China remained in a state of disunion. Full union was restored only with the emergence of the Sui Empire (581–618), which attempted to eliminate the threat of Koguryŏ on its north-eastern frontier. Several unsuccessful attempts were made to conquer Koguryŏ, the last one in 612 being so disastrous that it contributed directly to the fall of the state in 618 and the establishment of the T'ang Empire (618–907). To counterbalance the power of Koguryŏ, Silla allied itself with the new T'ang Dynasty, and Koguryŏ and Paekche entered into an alliance with each other. The struggle for a unified government on the peninsula thus entered the realm of international politics. Until mid-century, Koguryŏ was able to fend off all attacks on itself. At that time, T'ang and Silla agreed to a joint pincer attack, first on Paekche and then on Koguryŏ. This plan was successfully implemented. Paekche collapsed in 660 and Koguryŏ by the end of the decade. Originally T'ang had intended to absorb these conquered states into the empire, but Silla was ultimately successful in driving out the Chinese from the former area of Paekche and southern Koguryŏ. Her northernmost boundary was established in the vicinity of P'yŏngyang. Subsequently, former Koguryŏ military leaders re-established a separate kingdom in the northern part of the former realm of Koguryŏ, an event which began the era of northern and southern states, Unified Silla (660–936) and Parhae (699–926).

During these centuries, culture and society were affected by influences from China, and the Korean states began more and more to take on the appearance of miniature Chinese realms. The Korean states, though fiercely independent, were now securely within the Chinese sphere of culture. Titles for the rulers of the states and their subordinates assumed Chinese styles, and the form of government was made to conform in appearance with what was known of the Chinese government. Often, however, these forms were merely means to mask the actual aristocratic nature of society. It is in this period that knowledge of the Chinese written language and the Confucian Classics became an important element in the education of the upper classes of all three societies. Buddhism was also transmitted to the peninsula at this time, and introduced not only new philosophical concepts but also more sophisticated forms of art. The influence of the Empire of Northern Wei was particularly important in the growth of a sophisticated art tradition.

One of the peculiar characteristics of the society of Silla was the Bone Rank System, or *kolp'um-je*. The aristocracy was divided into three broad classes: *sŏnggol*, or holy bone class, from which the sacred kings of Silla derived; the *chin'gol*, true bone class or the upper aristocracy; and the *tup'um*, or head classes, which included all other members of the aristocracy. The *tup'um* consisted of six further subdivisions, the upper two classes (the fifth and sixth head classes) being members of the regional aristocracy.

Koguryŏ still retained many qualities of the clan-based society of a previous age. Positions in government seem to have been reserved for members of the aristocracy according to their rank. For example, the *taedaero* or prime minister was elected once every three years from the senior tribal leaders and could not succeed himself. Limitation of the prime minister to a single term of office was a new feature of the constitution of the government of Koguryŏ. Paekche's system was somewhat different. As tribal union had been imposed from without by a branch of the royal house of Puyŏ, leadership tended to be hereditary in that group of people. More quickly than either Koguryŏ or Silla, Paekche adopted the Chinese system of bureaucracy and the use of colours in the official costume to distinguish the various bureaucratic levels. Koguryŏ and Paekche, significantly, adopted very early on the use of the Chinese word *wang* for king, whilst Silla used the pure Korean term *maripkan* or great khan until well into the sixth century. This development is some measure of the rapidity of the spread of Chinese political concepts in the former two states.

2. The Advent of Buddhism

(a) The Period of Contact and Accommodation

Although it is said that Buddhism formally entered Korea in the latter part of the fourth century, there is good reason, at least in the case of Koguryŏ, to think that there was some Buddhist presence before the middle of the century (see Fig. 3).

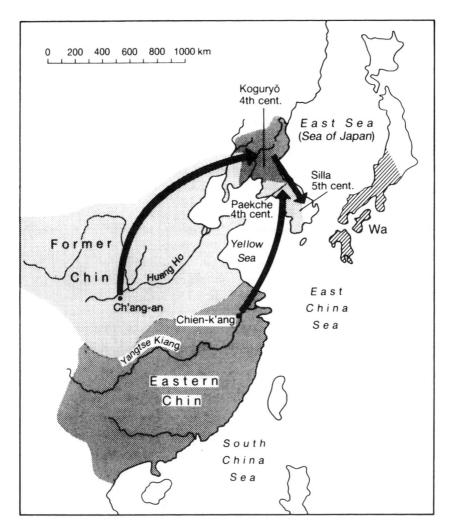

Figure 3 Diffusion of Buddhism into Korea

Murals from tombs of that period show clear Buddhist influence, such as the inclusion of the lotus motif in the decoration of the walls. The *Liang Kao-sêng ch'uan* (Lives of Eminent Monks, written in the Liang Dynasty, *c.* 519) mentions the fact that the fourth-century Chinese monk Chih Tun (314–66) carried on a correspondence with a monk from Koguryŏ. This would imply the presence of some sort of monastic community prior to 372, the date of the formal recognition of Buddhism in Koguryŏ. The dates for the official acceptance of Buddhism, 372 in the case of Koguryŏ and 384 in the case of Paekche, are significant indicators of the political and cultural relations which existed between the states of North-east Asia. In 372, the Emperor Fu-ch'ien (r. 357–85) of Former Chin sent the monk Sundo (4th cent.) and his entourage to King Sosurim (r. 371–83) with the suggestion that Buddhism would protect the state against its enemies. After the collapse of the state of Former Yen (349–70), Former Chin and Koguryŏ became allied against the various northern tribes threatening their borders. In this era, political ties were often cemented through the establishment of cultural links, such as the sending of the Buddhist monk Sundo. Buddhism became acceptable to the élite of Koguryŏ because it came with the prestige of a Chinese state supporting it.

Mālānanda, an Indian monk sojourning in the state of Eastern Chin (317–420) in southern China, met an official from Paekche and returned home with the latter in the year 384. Upon his arrival in the capital of Paekche, the *Haedong kosŭng-jŏn* (Lives of Eminent Korean Monks, *c.* 1215) tells us that Mālānanda was met at the outskirts of the city by the king, who personally escorted the monk to his palace where he listened respectfully to the monk's sermon. As in the case of Koguryŏ, the ready acceptance of the Buddhist monk by the King of Paekche was due to the associations which Buddhism appeared to have with Chinese culture. The political and cultural prestige of China enabled Buddhism to gain a ready hearing in the élite circles of the early Korean states. Buddhism entered the area of Silla, however, much later than Koguryŏ and Paekche. As its development in Silla was dependent on events taking place in those latter two states, the advent of Buddhism in Silla will be discussed in a later section.

There were two other Buddhist monks who arrived in Koguryŏ before the beginning of the fifth century, Ado and T'an-shih. Ado, who arrived in 383, was said to have been the offspring of a Koguryŏ woman and an official from Northern Wei, called Agulma. Ado's mother must have been a practising Buddhist, for it is related by the *Samguk yusa* (Memorabilia of the Three Kingdoms, *c.* 1285) that she sent Ado to a monastery at the age of 5 to become a monk. At the age of 16, Ado went to Northern Wei in search of his father. After meeting him, he then settled down to study for three years under a monk called Hsüan-chang. When Ado returned to his native country in 383, King Sosurim ordered a temple to be constructed for his use, as had been done for the monk Sundo.

The Chinese monk T'an-shih was a native of Kuanchung, now modern Shensi Province. He came to Koguryŏ in 395, during the reign of King Kwanggaet'o (r. 391–413), and stayed for ten years. Although the *Samguk yusa* and other ancient records make few references to this monk, he was apparently held in high esteem. There were also several rather mysterious events associated with him. He was called the 'White Footed Master' because his feet were supposed to be whiter than his face and would not be sullied even by a muddy stream.

Not only did the government of Koguryŏ willingly accept foreign missionaries, but even at this early date it promoted the growth of Buddhist institutions throughout the country. King Sosurim's successor, King Kogugyang

(r. 384–91), made strenuous efforts to spread Buddhism beyond the court circle to the general mass of the people. His successor, King Kwanggaet'o, attempted to turn Koguryŏ into a thoroughly Buddhist state. Around the area of P'yŏngyang, the southern capital, he ordered the construction of nine temples to aid in the dissemination of Buddhist knowledge. Many monks began to make the journey from Koguryŏ to China to study Buddhism more thoroughly, the most notable of whom was Sŭngnang (Sêng-lang in Chinese, 5th cent.). A student of an otherwise unknown Koguryŏ monk called Pŏpto, Sŭngnang is said to have studied for a while with the great Kumārajīva (344–413). Known as a proponent of the Hua-yen and San-lun doctrines, Sŭngnang was instrumental in the formation of the San-lun School in Northern Wei.

The *Haedong kosŭng-jŏn* mentions that in the year following Mālānanda's arrival in Paekche, the king built a temple for his use, and that ten monks were ordained upon its completion. Following these brief mentions, the historical records are silent as to further developments in either Koguryŏ or Paekche. None the less, it is plain that Buddhism was readily accepted by the élite in both societies, that in both cases royal patronage was extended, and that efforts were made by the king and the court within the first few decades after contact to spread the new doctrine amongst the general populace. Further, efforts were made to ensure that the standards of Buddhist knowledge were maintained, as exemplified by the sending of Sŭngnang to China to study.

(b) The Fifth Century

The fifth century is a surprising blank in the historical record of the two states of Paekche and Koguryŏ. None of the standard historical sources make any direct reference to the development of Buddhism, which had made such a dramatic start in the fourth century. There are some clues, however, to the continued development of Buddhism in Koguryŏ and Paekche. As a result of the jockeying for power between these two states, Paekche developed diplomatic ties with the state of Northern Wei (see Fig. 4). This state was ruled by the 'barbarian' T'o-pa people who had been greatly influenced by Buddhist missionaries from Central Asia, such as Fo-t'u-teng (?–349), who had brought with them a syncretic Buddhism rich in magic and shamanism. They had also brought with them the superb traditions of Buddhist art which had evolved in Central Asia. The unique form of Buddhist art which grew up in the T'o-pa empire came to be known as the Northern Wei style and was transmitted to Paekche during this period. Some of the greatest artistic treasures of Korea are the result of the diffusion of this style of art. Paekche in her turn transmitted the Northern Wei style to Japan, where it had a great influence on the formative period of Japanese Buddhist art.

Another clue to the continued growth of Buddhism in Koguryŏ and Paekche is the transmission of Buddhism to the area of the state of Silla. The *Haedong kosŭng-jŏn* gives us several clues concerning the first appearance of Buddhism in the region which was to become Silla. This ancient book refers to two

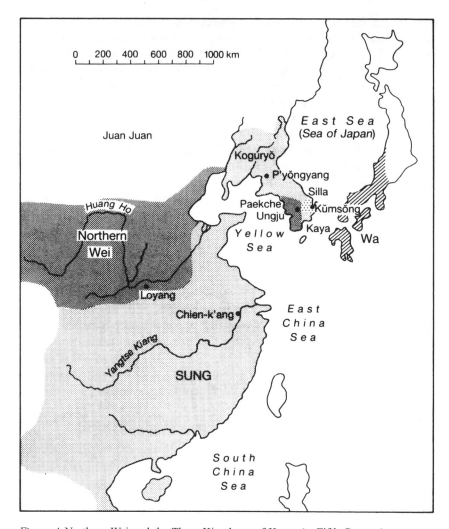

Figure 4 Northern Wei and the Three Kingdoms of Korea (*c.* Fifth Century)

Buddhist missionaries, Hŭkhoja (Black Barbarian) and Ado who arrived from Koguryŏ, but they apparently were not the first propagators of Buddhism to appear in the Silla area, for the account of the monk Hŭkhoja tells us that while he was residing in the home of a secret believer Morye, he learned of the martyrdom of two earlier missionaries, Chŏngbang and Myŏlgubi. These two martyrs must have arrived in the Silla region no later than the first part of the reign of King Nulchi, the first quarter of the fifth century. The story of Hŭkhoja indicates that the reception of Buddhism in Silla was radically different from its reception in Koguryŏ or Paekche. In the Silla area the initial reaction would seem to have been one of fear at the importation of foreign or novel ideas and beliefs. The first missionaries became martyrs for their cause, and the believers had to go underground.

The story of Hŭkhoja continues by saying that when King Nulchi's daughter fell ill, Hŭkhoja's presence was revealed to the king and the monk was summoned to the palace to effect a cure of the royal illness. Hŭkhoja was able to do this by burning incense before the diseased princess and by making a vow to one of the Bodhisattvas. The miraculous cure of the princess brought favour to the monk and to his religion. Whatever serious opposition there had been to Buddhism must have been contained by royal patronage, and from that time onwards the foreign religion appears to have been practised as a cult of the royal court. Shortly after this, the *Haedong kosŭng-jŏn* records that the monk vanished.

During the reign of King Soji (r. 479–500), the *Haedong kosŭng-jŏn* mentions the appearance of yet another monk from Koguryŏ, Ado. Ado arrived in Silla accompanied by three other monks. Like his predecessor Hŭkhoja, Ado and his entourage established themselves in the home of Morye. Shortly after his arrival there, Ado died, but it is said that his companions remained, daily reciting the sutras and teaching the *vinaya* or monastic rules. Several persons were said to have been converted through their efforts.

Because the ancient records claim that Ado and Hŭkhoja were thought to be similar in appearance, many scholars feel that they were one and the same person. This may well have been the case. Hŭkhoja's name literally means 'Black Barbarian', which would indicate that although he came to the Silla area from Koguryŏ, he was by origin either Indian or Serindian. Whether Ado and Hŭkhoja are one or two persons, their physical appearance would indicate that even at this early date the Korean states had direct contact with the Buddhist kingdoms of Central Asia and beyond.

One further clue to the advance of Buddhism in Silla may be found in the regnal styles of the kings who succeeded King Nulchi prior to King Pŏphŭng (r. 514–39), under whose aegis Buddhism was formally adopted as the state religion. An examination of the regnal names of the kings in the *Samguk sagi* (History of the Three Kingdoms, c. 1145) and in the *Samguk yusa* indicate that all of them may be given a Buddhist interpretation, which is not possible for the regnal names prior to Nulchi.

The question of whether Buddhism existed in the area of the Kaya Federation prior to its absorption into the rising Kingdom of Silla is a hotly debated issue. There are no temples in this area which can claim confidently an origin as early as the fifth century. However, there are two clues to the presence of Buddhism in Kaya during this period. First, in the area of the modern city of Koryŏng, the ancient state of Tae Kaya, there is a chambered tomb with murals, totally dissimilar to other tombs in this area. The murals of this tomb obviously demand comparison with those in Koguryŏ. The Kaya tomb mural includes colourful lotus flowers, a Buddhist motif. Second, the foundation myth of the state of Pon

Kaya, modern Kimhae, says that its first king, Suro (traditional regnal dates, 42–199), married a mysterious princess who is said to have come by boat from the ancient Indian city of Ayodhya along with a magnificent entourage. Furthermore, the foundation legend of the Changyu-sa temple near Kimhae claims that the temple had been founded by the princess's brother the monk Changyu who had accompanied her to Tae Kaya. Whether or not the story of the Indian origin of the princess is correct, it is clear that through this marriage with a foreign princess King Suro effected some significant cultural changes, one of which may have been the introduction of Buddhism.

(c) The Sixth Century

The sixth century was a century of ferment in Buddhist Korea. It was during this period that Buddhism in Koguryŏ and Paekche achieved its first period of maturity. It was also during this period that Buddhism in Silla, following official acceptance by King Pŏphŭng, showed the first fruits of what was to be a flourishing religion. There are four events which are characteristic of this period: the sending of scholars to China, the pilgrimage of monks to India, the development of Korean Buddhist traditions congruent with the traditions of Korean primal religion, and the initiation of Buddhist evangelism in Japan. Each event demonstrated the vigour of Korean Buddhism throughout this century.

During this period, Koguryŏ produced four monks worthy of note: Ŭiyŏn, Chihwang, Sŭngsil, and Sŭngin. Ŭiyŏn was an important Buddhist thinker of the mid-sixth century who was not only a Buddhist adept but was reputed to have a profound knowledge of both Confucian philosophy and *Hsüan-hsüeh* or Dark Learning. Dark Learning was a form of philosophical speculation in the Taoist schools which became prominent at the end of the Three Kingdoms Period (220–65) in China. As Han Confucianism had lost its appeal to the literati during the last days of the empire, the literati had turned more and more to speculative metaphysics. One resolution of the problem of universal metaphysics was the development of *Hsüan-hsüeh*, which in turn prepared the way for the acceptance of Buddhism by the literati. The fact that Ŭiyŏn was aware of Confucian thought and Taoist metaphysics as well as Buddhist philosophy would indicate that he was fully conversant with the philosophical and religious trends of China.

The *Haedong kosŭng-jŏn* records the story that the prime minister of Koguryŏ, who was a widely read man, was unclear about certain points of Buddhist doctrine. The prime minister sent Ŭiyŏn to Northern Chi (550–77) to present his queries to the monk Fa-shang. The *Haedong kosŭng-jŏn* concludes this story with the pious remark that Ŭiyŏn returned to Koguryŏ stimulated, and so renewed his efforts for the propagation of Buddhism. The remark that he 'skilfully' persuaded and led the 'straying masses' would indicate that although he himself was a member of the intellectual élite, he was vitally concerned with the dissemination of Buddhism to the common man. This story also tells us that the intellectual culture of Koguryŏ was in no way inferior to that of China, and that regular cultural and intellectual interchange between China and Koguryŏ existed. Also, the prime minister of Koguryŏ was sufficiently cognizant of intellectual trends in China to know which scholars could be relied upon to give correct answers to his many questions. Finally, the story illustrates the concern of the intelligentsia for the dissemination of Buddhism amongst the masses.

Chihwang was a Koguryŏ monk who went to study in China during the early years of the Sui Dynasty, where it is said that he was tutored by monks of the Hīnayāna tradition. Although the Mahāyāna traditions must have been dominant in Koguryŏ, Chihwang's experience shows that Hīnayāna also played a role in the growth of Buddhist thought there. Shortly before the departure of Chihwang for China, the monks Sŭngsil and Sŭngin made the journey to China to study in the state of Ch'ên (557–89). Although they had been given permission to travel freely within Ch'ên, the monks found themselves trapped in the turbulence which surrounded the demise of this state and the rise of the Sui Empire. Finding their way home blocked, the two Koguryŏ monks set out for the nation of Nan-chiao (modern Szechuan Province), and it is said that they were responsible for the spread of Buddhism into that region. This missionary effort was sparked by the same evangelical concern which led to the evangelization of Japan.

In addition to the monks mentioned above, there is also a record of the monk P'ayak who went to study the T'ien-t'ai doctrines under the monk Chih-i (538–97), the first Korean monk known to have gone to China for this purpose. P'ayak's journey is one further indication of the degree to which Koguryŏ monks were aware of the current intellectual trends of China.

During the same period in which these Koguryŏ monks set out to study in the Middle Kingdom, other Koguryŏ monks were actively pursuing a programme of evangelism in Japan. Although the efforts of these Koguryŏ monks was crucial to the development of Buddhism in Japan, the honour of initiating Buddhist missions in that country belongs to Paekche and not Koguryŏ. King P'yŏngwŏn (r. 559–90) of Koguryŏ dispatched the monk Hyep'yŏn (Keiben in Japanese) in 560 to the court of the Japanese king, Bidatsu (r. 539–571). This monk was responsible for the conversion of the eminent nun, Zenshin, who in turn was the spiritual mentor of Zenzō and Keizen. However, no monk who crossed over to Japan proved to be more influential than Hyeja (Keiji in Japanese), tutor of the crown prince Shōtoku Taishi (573–621) who was responsible for the significant political reforms of the seventh century and for the adoption of Buddhism in Japan. Hyeja went over to Japan in the year 595 and apparently died there. The movement of Buddhist missionary monks to Japan which these two monks symbolized gathered momentum during the seventh century.

For Paekche, the sixth century was the golden age of Buddhist culture. Like Koguryŏ, Paekche sent monks to study in China and played a major role in the evangelization of Japan. Paekche was also the first Korean state to send a monk to study in India. Buddhism not only flourished in Paekche during this century, but the ancient records make it clear that it was in a positive state of ferment. Possibly the first person from Paekche to study abroad was Palchŏng, about whom little is known other than that he arrived in Liang in southern China sometime during the T'ien-chien period (502–20) of the Emperor Wu-ti (r. 502–49). One account of him indicates that he had a great interest in the *Avatamsaka-sūtra* (*Hua-yen Ching* in Chinese) and in the Lotus Sutra. The former sutra, which teaches that all beings possess the Buddha nature, became the principal scripture of the Hua-yen School. The Lotus Sutra teaches the principle of universal salvation and the compassion of the Bodhisattva Avalokiteśvara. Palchŏng was the first Korean monk who is known to have studied the doctrines of these sutras, which became the foundation of important schools of Korean Buddhism.

The Paekche monk Hyŏn'gwang went to the state of Ch'ên to study the T'ien-t'ai doctrines under Hui-ssu, the second patriarch of the sect. The *Sung Kao-sêng Ch'uan* (Lives of Eminent Monks, written in the Sung Dynasty, c. 988) tells us that after thorough indoctrination by the patriarch, Hyŏn'gwang returned to Paekche where he helped to establish the T'ien-t'ai School.

The most eminent of these peripatetic Paekche monks was Kyŏmik, who made the arduous trek to India. Kyŏmik left Paekche in 526 during the early years of the reign of King Sŏng (r. 523–54), who was largely responsible for the development of Paekche's sophisticated Buddhist culture. Kyŏmik's travels to India are symbolic of the efforts which King Sŏng was making to raise the level of his nation's civilization. At first Kyŏmik went to China, but after a brief sojourn there, he pressed on to India. It is possible that he may have got the idea to travel to India from reading Fa-hsien's (died c. 418/423) record of his journey there a hundred years earlier. Kyŏmik spent five years studying at the Mahāvinaya Vihāra, or Temple of the Grand Discipline, in Sankisa. This city is mentioned both by Fa-hsien and by Hsüan-tsang (602–64) in their travel records. After completing his studies in Sankisa, Kyŏmik returned home, bringing with him copies of the *Abhidharma-pitaka* in Sanskrit. The king placed Kyŏmik in charge of the Hŭngnyung-sa temple and commanded that he should undertake the translation of the sutras into Chinese at the head of a committee of twenty-eight learned monks.

King Sŏng, like the prime minister of Koguryŏ, sent an emissary to China to enquire about abstruse questions of Buddhist doctrine. The emissary was sent to the state of Liang in 551, shortly before its collapse, and returned home with a copy of the *Nirvāna-sūtra*. This is the first time that this sutra is known to have been disseminated to Korea. It teaches the universal salvation of mankind, and the eternal life of the soul in a state of perpetual bliss, and became the foundation scripture of an important school of Korean Buddhism in a later age. Some time after the visit of the Paekche emissary, the Emperor of Liang sent artists and temple artisans to Paekche, one further indication of the continuous flow of cultural and artistic influences into this tiny state.

Possibly the most important cultural accomplishment of King Sŏng's reign was the initiation of Buddhist missionary work in Japan. The importance of this effort and its impact on later Japanese Buddhism and culture cannot be overstated. Too often discussions of the introduction of Buddhism to Japan leave one with the impression that the Korean states were only passive conveyers of the Buddhist tradition to the island nation. In fact, Korean Buddhist missionaries were directly involved in the development of Buddhism in Japan for over 150 years. Of the three states, the influence of Paekche was paramount. It was Paekche which initiated Buddhist missions in Japan. It was Paekche which over several generations transmitted the sophisticated art and architecture of the Chinese world, notably the Northern Wei style. It was Paekche which was largely responsible for the early training of Japanese monks and nuns. Paekche, in this century of cultural ferment, was the principal transmitter and active agent in the early development of Japanese Buddhist civilization.

On three occasions, in 538, 545, and 552, King Sŏng sent Buddhist statues and scriptures to the Japanese king with the request that he give the new doctrines careful consideration. In 552, it is recorded that King Sŏng sent a bronze statue and a carved stone statue of Maitreya along with various scriptures. In his letter to the King of Japan, King Sŏng recommended Buddhism to his counterpart on the basis that it was a doctrine far superior to Confucianism, and that it had found great favour in India, China, and Paekche. Subsequently, the new doctrine found adherents amongst certain members of the aristocracy, whilst others found themselves strongly opposed to anything which was contrary to the indigenous traditions. The Soga clan in particular took up the cause of Buddhism and extended its patronage to the Koguryŏ monk Hyep'yŏn, who had come over in 560. Before the arrival of this important monk, however, King Sŏng in the final year of his reign in 554 had sent two scholarly monks, Tamhye and Tosim, and sixteen preaching monks to Japan to spread Buddhism there.

The programme of sending missionaries to Japan was continued by King Sŏng's successor, King Widŏk (r. 554–98), who sent nine more monk-evangelists to Japan during the first year of his reign. In 577, King Widŏk sent a number of sutras, teachers of the Buddhist Law, masters of Ch'an Buddhism (*Zen* in Japanese), nuns, and exorcists, as well as numerous artisans to assist in the construction of the Taiben-ō Temple. Shortly after this, a further group of artisans, workers in stone, wood, and tile, were sent over. Again, in the year 587 King Widŏk sent more temple artisans to Japan. These are the first artisans whose names are recorded for posterity, which is some indication of the esteem in which they were held. They were T'ae Yangmal, T'ae Mun, and Ko Koja. While sending artisans and teachers to Japan, King Widŏk continued to make gifts of Paekche *objets d'art*, such as the stone statue of Maitreya given in 584. By the 580s, the flow of Koreans into Japan to propagate Buddhism was matched by the return flow of Japanese going to Paekche to study. The Soga clan, for example, sent Zenshin and several of her disciples to Paekche for further study, in spite of the fact that her own teacher was a Koguryŏ monk. Possibly one reason why Paekche was held in such high regard was the tradition of scholarship which had been established under Kyŏmik in the earlier part of the century.

Silla, as in most cultural affairs, lagged behind her more sophisticated neighbours Koguryŏ and Paekche in the development and spread of Buddhism. The sixth century, however, was of great importance to her in her attempt to achieve parity with the intellectual and political standards of her neighbours. The most significant event of the sixth century in Silla was the official adoption of Buddhism as the state religion. Although Buddhism seems to have been practised as a cult of the immediate court circle throughout the fifth century, since the latter part of King Nulchi's reign, King Pŏphŭng was actually the first king of Silla who was an avowed Buddhist.

The *Haedong kosŭng-jŏn* records the story that King Pŏphŭng wished to declare Buddhism as the official religion of the land, but was afraid to do so because of strong opposition from the conservative quarter of the aristocracy. In his court entourage there was a young Buddhist believer, Pak Yŏmch'ok, otherwise known as Ich'adon. The king and this courtier both felt that a dramatic event was needed to break the impasse. Ich'adon offered to sacrifice his life in the cause of Buddhism. The two men worked out a plan whereby Ich'adon would appear to have usurped royal authority by ordering the construction of a temple without royal assent. This was done and the enraged aristocracy brought the matter to the attention of the king, who ordered the courtier's execution. Before his death, Ich'adon predicted two miracles which would prove the veracity of Buddhism – that his blood would flow as white as milk, and that his decapitated head would fly to the top of a nearby hill. Legend says that the occurrence of these events so overawed the aristocracy that they readily accepted the adoption of Buddhism in Silla.

King Pŏphŭng ordered the construction of a great temple, the Taewang hŭngnyun-sa, in 534. Upon its completion in 539, he abdicated in favour of his nephew, who succeeded as King Chinhŭng (r. 540–76). Pŏphŭng changed his name to Pŏpkong, and retired to spend the remainder of his life as a monk in the great temple which he had built. Similarly, Pŏphŭng's queen retired from secular life, spending her final years as a nun at the Yŏnghŭng-sa. The martyrdom of Ich'adon was commemorated every year on the fifth day of the eighth lunar month, the alleged day of his execution.

These facts tell us many things about the vitality of early Silla Buddhism. First, in spite of decades of royal patronage, there was tremendous opposition to the new cult, which had to be overcome by the dramatic martyrdom of Ich'adon. Second, the adoption of Buddhism signalled the beginning of the sinification of Silla's culture. Pŏphŭng was the first monarch to use the Chinese word *wang* for king in his regnal style rather than the Korean word *maripkan*. Also, Pŏphŭng's regnal name is the first such name to incorporate an avowedly Buddhist concept – the Advancement of the Dharma. The name of the temple to which the king retired might be translated as the Temple of the Great King Who Turns the Wheel of the Dharma. This must be a reference to Pŏphŭng himself. In Sanskrit, such a great king is called a *cakravartī-rāja* (*wangsŏn* in Korean). Unquestionably, the descendants of the divine kings of

Silla used Buddhist concepts to lend credence to traditional concepts of kingship.

Chinhŭng came to the throne as a minor; nevertheless, throughout his long reign one senses a great vigour in everything which was undertaken. At this time, Silla began to develop more contacts with the Chinese world. Envoys came and went; monks travelled to China for study and returned. In 549, the Liang emperor sent an envoy to King Chinhŭng with a gift of several Buddhist relics. He arrived in the company of Kaktŏk, who is the first Silla monk known to have gone to a Chinese state to study. Then, in 565 a representative of the Lord of Ch'ên arrived in Silla with a gift of several hundred rolls of sutras and other Buddhist works. He was accompanied by Myŏnggwan, a Silla monk who had studied in Ch'ên.

The construction of Buddhist places of worship was furthered in this period. One of the most famous temples constructed in Chinhŭng's reign was the Hwangnyong-sa, or Temple of the Yellow Dragon. In 558 the king had ordered the erection of a new palace, but the construction was halted when it was discovered that a yellow dragon lived in a pond on that spot. Construction was resumed, but the palace became a great temple. This is one early indication of the amalgamation of Buddhism with native practices. Buildings which in an earlier period might have been dedicated to the spirits of the land or sky were now built for the same reasons but in a Buddhist guise.

In King Chinhŭng's reign, we discern the first distinctive Korean Buddhist rites. The first instance would be the commemorative rite for the martyrdom of Ich'adon, similar to the rites of propitiation offered up by the shamans to soothe the souls of the dead. The *P'algwan-hoe*, a Buddhist memorial-rite for the spirits of soldiers who had fallen in battle, was performed for the first time for a week during the tenth lunar month of 572. This would have been a significant national undertaking. There is a traditional story that the founder of the Pŏpchu-sa temple, Ŭisin, returned to Silla from India bringing with him numerous sutras. Whether this story is historically correct or not, it is one indication of the sophistication of Buddhist culture during Chinhŭng's reign. As his uncle had done, King Chinhŭng abdicated in favour of his successor and retired to a monastery, taking the Buddhist name of Pŏbŭn. He was buried in a tumulus near his uncle, King Pŏphŭng.

Under the reign of King Chinp'yŏng (r. 579–631), Silla became involved in the Buddhist missionary movement in Japan. One of the first actions of this king's reign was the gift of a Buddhist statue to the King of Japan. In the first half of his reign three important monks were sent to study in China, Chimyŏng who set out in 586, Wŏn'gwang who went in 589, and Tamyuk who left in 596. Of these three monks, Wŏn'gwang was unquestionably the greatest. He spent ten years in China, first studying in Chin-ling in Ch'ên. Later, he spent considerable time travelling throughout the new Sui Empire. Wŏn'gwang emphasized the study of two sutras, the *Nirvāna-sūtra*, and the *Prajña-sūtra*, which stresses the illusory nature of the universe. Wŏn'gwang returned to Silla in 599 at the request of King Chinp'yŏng. As the impact of Wŏn'gwang's work properly belongs to the seventh century, we will treat his accomplishments in the next section.

(d) The Seventh Century

By the seventh century the strength of Buddhism in Koguryŏ had begun to wane, while enthusiasm for the religion seemed to gain even more momentum in Silla. The history of Buddhism in Korea in the seventh century is largely a record of developments within Paekche and Silla. Both Silla and Paekche continued to take an interest in the Buddhist missionary movement in Japan, while at the same time Silla gave expression to its piety by the number of scholarly pilgrims it sent to India, the homeland of the Buddha.

Koguryŏ continued to play an important role in the evangelization of Japan. In 602, the monks Sŭngnyung (Sōryū in Japanese) and Unch'ong (Unshū in Japanese) crossed over, followed eight years later in 610 by the artist-monks Tamjing (Donchō in Japanese) and Pŏpchŏng (Hotei in Japanese). Tamjing in particular is credited with the creation of the beautiful murals in the famed Kintō hall of the Hōryū-ji temple in Nara. One of the greatest Koguryŏ monks to make the journey to Japan was Hyegwan (Keikan in Japanese), who had studied the San-lun doctrines in China under Chi-tsang. After the establishment of the T'ang Empire, he left China to go as a missionary to Japan, arriving there in 625 towards the end of the reign of the Empress Suiko (r. 592–628). He was joined in 628 by a Koguryŏ monk, Todŭng (Doto in Japanese, 7th cent.), who had also been in China studying the San-lun doctrines. These two monks, along with the Paekche monk Kwallŭk, helped to establish the Sanron School in Japan. This school traces its origins to Nāgārjuna in India and to the Serindian, Kumārajīva. Nāgārjuna taught that the phenomenal world is unreal and that the recognition of this fact leads to *prajña* or wisdom. To obtain knowledge of this absolute truth, the student must first pass through a lower level of worldly knowledge. This is the same school with which the Koguryŏ monk Sŭngnang had been associated.

Hyegwan was granted the highest clerical title in Japan, *sōjō*, by the Empress Suiko. The prompt advent of rain after the completion of ceremonies which Hyegwan had been asked to perform had the twofold result of the elevation of the Koguryŏ monk and the creation of imperial patronage for the Sanron School. Koguryŏ monks continued to enter Japan until the fall of the kingdom. The last of them known to have entered Japan was Tohyŏn (Tōgen in Japanese, 7th cent.), who resided in the Daian-ji temple and is credited with the authorship of an historical work the *Nihon segi* which is no longer extant. It is said that when Tohyŏn observed a mouse clinging to the tail of a horse, he had a sudden premonition of the demise of Koguryŏ.

Podŏk, the most eminent Buddhist monk of late Koguryŏ times, had a great interest in Taoism as well. During his sojourn in China, Podŏk spent considerable effort in the collection of Taoist writings. Ever since the late sixth century, Taoist influence on the élite of Koguryŏ had begun to surpass that of

Buddhism. Podŏk's collection of Taoist materials must have been part of some scheme to combat this influence through a thorough knowledge of the philosophy and metaphysics of Taoism. He was a proponent of the doctrines of the *Nirvāna-sūtra*, which taught the imperishable character of the Buddha Nature to be found within each person. This was surely a counterfoil to Taoist concepts of immortality. Feeling frustrated in his attempts to stem the tide of Taoist influence, Podŏk exclaimed that the people of Koguryŏ believed only in Taoism and rejected Buddhism. So saying, he decamped for Paekche.

Buddhist culture in Paekche continued to flourish, one symbol of which was the prosecution of Buddhist missions in Japan. In 602, Kwallŭk (Kanroku in Japanese, 6th–7th cent.) crossed over to Japan bringing with him a number of sutras, historical books, and works on astronomy, geography, and the occult arts. Along with Hyegwan, he was instrumental in the creation of the Sanron School. Kwallŭk established himself at the Genkō-ji temple and, like Hyegwan, was granted the title of *sōjō* in 624. In the *Nihon shoki* (Chronicles of Japan, c. 720) there is an interesting story which demonstrates the personal influence of this Paekche monk. Kwallŭk is said to have intervened at one point to save the lives of several Japanese monks who had been accused of various offences. He memorialized the throne and asked for clemency on the grounds that Buddhism had not been in Japan long enough to provide a background for the spiritual growth of the offending monks. The fact that Kwallŭk was successful in his petition and that he was shortly afterwards elevated to the status of *sōjō* indicates the immense personal prestige which he possessed.

Internally, Paekche Buddhism flourished until the demise of the state. The short-reigned King Pŏp (r. 599–600) in the year of his ascension promulgated a law which forbade the taking of any life, including the killing of a bird. This was an obvious, if idealistic, attempt to make the laws of Paekche conform with Buddhist doctrine. King Pŏp also began construction of the great national temple, the Wanghŭng-sa, which was completed in 635 during the reign of his successor, King Mu (r. 600–41). This temple is referred to in ancient records as a *tae karam*, a term derived from the Sanskrit word *sanghārāma* (monastery), and meaning a grand temple. King Mu also ordered the construction of another grand temple, the Mirŭk-sa, the Temple of Maitreya. Recent excavations of the temple site indicate that it was the largest temple ever built in Korea. In China, the cult of the saviour Maitreya reached the height of its popularity in the sixth and early seventh centuries. The erection of this great temple to Maitreya shows that Paekche continued to keep abreast of the trends of spirituality in the continental empire.

Peaceful relations existed between Paekche and Silla throughout the reign of King Mu. The marriage of the king to the daughter of King Chinp'yŏng of Silla was followed by the sending out of artists and temple artisans to Silla to assist in the construction of temples there. At one point, King Mu sent a hundred artisans to Silla, symbolic of the great flow of culture which was taking place between the two states.

In the *Nihon shoki*, there is a curious account of a Paekche ship which was blown off course on a return journey from China in the year 609. The passengers were twelve monks and seventy-eight laymen who had been on a pilgrimage to various sites in the southern part of the Sui Empire. The leaders of the group informed the Japanese authorities that they had been sponsored by the King of Paekche. After negotiations with the authorities, some of the passengers elected to stay on in Japan. This story tells us that not only did the King of Paekche actively pursue cultural contacts as a matter of state policy, but that there must have been a significant community of persons of Paekche descent already in Japan, enough to make those cast up on its shores feel at home. The last Buddhist cleric from Paekche known to have gone to Japan was the nun Pŏmmyŏng (Hōmyō in Japanese), who arrived in 655 shortly before the demise of her homeland.

As in Silla, the names of the kings of Paekche contain concepts traceable to Buddhist influence such as Sŏng ('holy'), Widŏk ('strong virtue'), Hye ('mercy'), Pŏp ('law' = *dharma*), Ŭija (r. 641–60, 'righteous mercy') and are a further confirmation of the development of Buddhist culture in this small state.

The history of Silla during the first third of the seventh century was dominated by the character of King Chinp'yŏng, one of the longest-lived monarchs of Silla. Although he began his reign in the final quarter of the sixth century, the most significant events in Buddhist history took place during the latter part of his reign. There are three significant events of seventh-century Silla Buddhism which have their origin in this remarkable period: the reorganization of the Hwarang Troop, the pilgrimage of many Silla monks to India, and the development of an indigenous, sophisticated form of Silla Buddhism.

Wŏn'gwang, who had returned to Silla at the request of King Chinp'yŏng, quickly assumed the role of the leading monk of his day. He was considered to be not only a spiritual leader, but also a cultural and civic leader. He was used by the king on diplomatic missions, such as a mission to the Emperor Yang-ti (r. 605–16) of Sui in 608. Wŏn'gwang was also responsible for the creation of new Buddhist rituals. In 613, he presided over the second *Paekchwa-hoe*, at which he expounded on various scriptures.

Wŏn'gwang's greatest contribution, however, was in the reorganization of the Hwarang Troop. Although this group traces its origins to the sixth century or earlier, the troop as we know it was the work of Wŏn'gwang. The *Haedong kosŭng-jŏn* contains the story of two young men who approached Wŏn'gwang to learn simple principles by which a Buddhist layman could live. The precepts which Wŏn'gwang expounded became known as the *sesok ogye* (Five Principles for Secular Life) or the *Hwarang-do* (Law of the Hwarang). The five principles which Wŏn'gwang taught may be stated succinctly as (1) loyalty to the sovereign, (2) filial piety, (3) loyalty to one's friends, (4) to fight in battle without retreating, and (5) to kill only when necessary. These precepts show an obvious blending of Buddhist, Confucian, and native concepts. The emphasis on the code of the warrior, in particular, contradicts the Buddhist precept of reverence for life, and is a clear sign of the state of Buddhist syncretism with indigenous ideas and attitudes.

The troop of young aristocrats whom Wŏn'gwang gathered around him and to whom he taught these five precepts was called the Hwarang. Patriotism became an important element in the instruction of these youth, and it should be no surprise to learn that two of their number became leaders in the fight for Silla's dominance in the peninsula and for the unification of the three kingdoms. Kim Yusin (595–673), a member of the former royal house of Pon Kaya, and Prince Ch'unch'u (604–61), first king of *chin'gol* rank, were the most outstanding of several warriors who helped make Silla the dominant military power of the seventh century. It is significant to note that the Hwarang Troop represented not only a blend of Buddhist and Korean thought, but also the general social change which was taking place in Silla at that time. The old élite was passing away, and members of a conquered nation (Pon Kaya) or of the non-divine aristocracy (*chin'gol*) assumed the leadership of the nation. It was the Hwarang Troop which trained this new élite class, and it was the precepts of the Hwarang by which they came to live.

The *Samguk yusa* contains a story that the members of the Hwarang Troop were especially devoted to the cult of Maitreya and that they took names based on Buddhist legendary and historical figures. At this time, the cult of Maitreya was widely practised in Silla and Paekche, the result of cultural influence from Northern Wei. With the establishment of the T'o-pa dynasty in northern China, there had been the hope that Maitreya would descend from the Tushita Heaven, ushering in an era of peace and prosperity. Amongst the aristocracy of seventh-century Silla there was a similar hope that Maitreya would bring about peace and the unification of the kingdoms under Silla's rule.

The second major event of importance during King Chinp'yŏng's reign was the pilgrimages to India undertaken by monks from Silla (see Fig. 5). Although the first monk to travel to India was from Paekche, and although there are records of other monks from Korea having made the trip, Silla holds the record for the number of monks who underwent the arduous overland journey. It is an interesting fact that in I-ching's (635–713) *Ta T'ang hsi-yü ch'iu-fa kao-sêng ch'uan* (Biographies of Eminent Monks of T'ang Who Sought the Dharma in the Western Regions), fully one-sixth of the biographies are about monks from Silla. This is an astounding figure considering the disparity in the size of the population of T'ang and Silla, and considering how recently Silla had become a civilized state. I-ching records the name of only one monk from Koguryŏ, and there are no mentions of Japanese monks who completed the journey.

Chollyun (Āryavarman in Sanskrit) came to Ch'ang-an to study during the reign of the Emperor Kao-tsung (r. 650–83). After an unspecified period of study in China, Chollyun decided to go on to India. He studied at the Nālandā University, a major Buddhist centre in central India, and died there at the age of 70. He is said to have specialized in the study of the *vinaya* texts. Hyeŏp also made the journey to India, first residing in the Mahābodhi Temple in Bodhgaya,

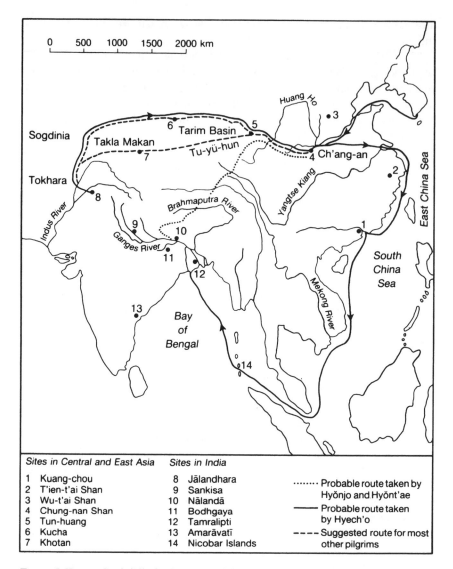

0   500   1000   1500   2000 km

Figure 5 Korean Study/Pilgrim Routes and Sites in India and China

the site of the Buddha's enlightenment, before he went on to Nālandā. He is said to have died there at the same time as Chollyun. Hyŏnt'ae (Sarvajña-deva in Sanskrit) made the pilgrimage not via Central Asia and Gandhāra as had the others, but over the more arduous diplomatic route via Nepal. He also studied in the Mahābodhi Temple, and then set off for home. In T'u-yü-hun, an area between modern western China and eastern Tibet, Hyŏnt'ae met a monk who urged him to go back to India for further study – which he did. Following his second period of study in India, Hyŏnt'ae returned to T'ang. While in India, he is said to have visited Sankisa, where Kyŏmik had resided.

The most important of these peripatetic monks was Hyŏnjo. He went to India with two of his disciples, Hyŏn'gak and Hyeryun. They travelled via Central Asia, entering the Indian subcontinent at Jālandara, where they stayed for four years. They then travelled to Bodhgaya, where they studied at the Mahābodhi Temple for three years, finally pushing on to Nālandā, where they resided for another three years. Hyŏnjo returned to the T'ang capital, but had hardly settled in before the Emperor Kao-tsung sent him back to India on a diplomatic mission. Following the completion of this duty, Hyŏnjo went back to Nālandā for further study and then pressed on to the great Buddhist centre at Amarāvatī in south India, where he died. Hyŏnjo was accompanied to Amarāvatī by his disciple Hyeryun. After his master's death, Hyeryun stayed at the Cincā Vihāra and later at the Gandhārachanda, a school for monks from Central Asia. Hyeryun's Indian name was Prajñavarman.

Hyŏn'gak, another of Hyŏnjo's disciples, remained at Nālandā, where he died at the age of forty. Kubon, yet another Silla monk, was at Nālandā at the same time as Hyŏn'gak and also died there at an early age. In another work of I-ching, the *Nan-hai chi-kuei nei-fa ch'uan* (A Record of the Buddhist Kingdoms in the Southern Archipelago), there is a mention of two other Silla monks who attempted to reach India by sea but died *en route* near northern Sumatra. Unfortunately neither their names nor a record of their lives has been preserved.

From the very end of the reign of King Chinp'yŏng, through the reigns of the two great queens of Silla, Queens Sŏndŏk (r. 632–47) and Chindŏk (r. 647–54), and through the reigns of their successors, King Muryŏl (Prince Ch'unch'u, r. 654–61) and King Munmu (r. 661–8), Silla Buddhism was dominated by the three greatest figures of its entire history, Chajang (590–658), Wŏnhyo (617–86), and Ŭisang (625–702). The middle third of the seventh century was unquestionably the golden age of Silla Buddhism. It is worthy of note that this was both a time of general cultural ferment and the period during which the rulers of Silla were laying plans for their political supremacy on the peninsula. Each of these three monks made a unique and lasting contribution to Buddhism in Silla.

Chajang was a member of the royal house of Silla of *chin'gol* rank. His father, a fervent Buddhist, had vowed that if he were granted a son, the boy would be dedicated to the Buddha. The *Samguk yusa* says, however, that Chajang, growing up in such a pious environment, came to his own decision and vowed to lead a monastic life. A small hut was built near the family home where the young Chajang began to develop his powers of meditation. Because of his reputation, King Chinp'yŏng wished to honour Chajang with an official appointment. Chajang's rejection of these overtures enraged the king, who then threatened Chajang with death. Chajang's cool response was that it was better to live by the *dharma* for one day rather than to live a hundred years by avoiding it. The king relented and Chajang was given permission to lead a monastic life.

In 636, Chajang took ten disciples with him on a journey to T'ang. He visited the famed Wu-t'ai Shan mountain where he is said to have had a vision of the Bodhisattva Mañjuśrī, who taught the monk a cryptic phrase in Sanskrit. The following morning, as Chajang was puzzling over the phrase, a strange monk came up to him and instructed him in the sacred mystery behind the words. This monk also gave Chajang some relics. Suddenly, Chajang realized that he had again met Mañjuśrī.

Although the emperor granted Chajang permission to stay in one of the greatest temples in the T'ang capital, Chajang preferred to stay in a small hut near Chung-nan Shan mountain. During the three years he was resident there, many Chinese monks sought to study under him. When Chajang was called back to Silla in 643 at the request of Queen Chindŏk, the Emperor T'ai-tsung (r. 626–49) gave a magnificent banquet in his honour and presented him with many sutras and ritual implements to take back to Silla.

Queen Chindŏk assigned the Punhwang-sa as Chajang's residence from where it was expected that he would make short trips to the royal palace or the Hwangnyong-sa to expound on the scriptures and on aspects of Buddhist doctrine. He was also honoured with the title of *taegukt'ong* or supreme cleric, through which office it was anticipated he would effect a reformation of Silla Buddhism. However, upon his return to Silla, Chajang set out for a range of mountains on the eastern seaboard near modern Kangnŭng in search of an experience of Mañjuśrī. He failed in this attempt due to the extreme mistiness of the weather. Returning to a nearby temple, he did have a sudden experience of this Bodhisattva. As a consequence, Chajang named this range of mountains Odae-san (Wu-t'ai Shan in Chinese). Chajang believed that these mountains were the abode of Mañjuśrī and that this was proof that in a former era Silla had been a Buddhist nation.

Chajang was the first person to name a range of Korean mountains after a Buddhist concept. Many of the names of important mountains in Korea have a Buddhist derivation, such as Kŭmgang-san (Diamond Mountains = Vajra Mountains), Sŏrak-san (Snowy Mountains = Himālaya Mountains), Kaya-san (Bodhgayā Mountains), Chiri-san (Wisdom Mountains). The fashion for naming mountains in this way began in this period and must be related to the ancient cult of the mountain god, San-sin.

The experience of Mañjuśrī was a turning-point in the life of Chajang. Following this dramatic event, he devoted the rest of his life to the dissemination of Buddhism from the aristocratic circle to which he belonged to the general mass of the people. Using his influence as *taegukt'ong*, Chajang reorganized Buddhism in Silla by issuing four general commands for clerical discipline:

1   intensified study of the sutras;
2   attendance at twice-yearly seminars on doctrines followed by mandatory examinations on the content of the lectures;

3   the establishment of the T'ongdo-sa temple as the only place within the kingdom where clergy could be ordained;

4   the creation of a government department to oversee the maintenance of temples, images, and other Buddhist property.

Chajang's actions not only effected a general reformation in the standards of the Silla clergy and novitiates, but they were also instrumental in the creation of the *Yul-chong* or Disciplinary Sect. This sect emphasized the role of monastic discipline in the attainment of enlightenment. As in the Buddhist community, so also in general society Chajang urged the adoption of higher standards of civilization. To this end, he urged the adoption of the T'ang style of dress and the use of the T'ang calendar as more appropriate to a sophisticated society. Chajang died at the Suda-sa temple near Kangnŭng which he had built. He is presumed to have passed away in Queen Chindŏk's reign as there is no mention of him in the reign of King Muryŏl.

Discussions of Chajang's contributions to Korean Buddhism and culture often overlook his interest in esoteric Buddhism, especially in the cult of Mañjuśrī. This Bodhisattva is a prime figure in esoteric Buddhism with its occult rituals and use of magic. Esoteric Buddhism is a far cry from the disciplinary Buddhism of the *Yul-chong* with which Chajang is normally associated. His interest in the subject is one further indication of the amalgamation of Buddhism and Silla's primal religion which was taking place at this time. It is also significant to remember that Chajang was a member of the royal house which claimed divine descent. His ecstatic experiences of Mañjuśrī in T'ang and in Silla would not seem strange to members of a family whose antecedents had based their prestige and power on the ability to communicate with the spiritual world.

Wŏnhyo, said by many to be the greatest of all Silla monks, was born into a provincial family by the name of Sŏl in 617. As a novice he studied the Lotus Sutra under Yangji at the Pan'go-sa. He later studied the *Nirvāṇa-sūtra* with the Koguryŏ monk Podŏk when the latter was resident in Silla. Upon completing these studies, Wŏnhyo felt that he could learn no more within the narrow confines of Silla and set off with his friend Ŭisang to study in China. On their way, it is said that Wŏnhyo had a curious experience. One night during a rainstorm the two friends took shelter in a cave and went to sleep. In the middle of the night, being thirsty, Wŏnhyo got up and drank some water from a vessel which he found in the cave. In the morning, the two monks arose to discover that they had slept in a grave which had been opened by robbers. To his horror, Wŏnhyo realized that he had drunk out of the skull of the deceased. He immediately felt a sense of revulsion and nausea overtaking him – when suddenly, he gained enlightenment. Wŏnhyo said afterwards that from this incident he learned the relativity of everything. Things are what we imagine them to be. Reality is based upon our perceptions. Having grasped this great insight, he decided not to go to T'ang, for in his new state of knowledge he felt that there was nothing which he could learn from the Chinese. Wŏnhyo returned home, but his unenlightened friend Ŭisang continued his journey to China.

Wŏnhyo was unquestionably the most unique, even eccentric, figure of Silla Buddhism. He refused to become a member of any of the new doctrinal sects which were then beginning to develop in Silla. Based on his experience in the tomb, he felt that the study of particular sutras or other materials by themselves would not lead to enlightenment. Likewise, he felt that the meditation practices of the monasteries and monastic discipline by themselves were insufficient to lead the uninitiated to enlightenment. He was strongly convinced of the idea that Buddhism should be a unified organization rather than a group of loosely affiliated schools. Wŏnhyo's ecumenical sentiments were the first serious attempt to unify the various sects. His movement was known as *Ilsŭng pulgyo* (Buddhism of the Single Vehicle) or as *T'ong pulgyo* (Unified Buddhism).

More important, however, than Wŏnhyo's efforts to reorganize and unify Buddhism was his attempt to spread Buddhism amongst the masses. His method was eccentric, extraordinary, and highly effective. For the better part of his life, he wandered around the realm of Silla as a vagabond hermit carrying with him a six-stringed zither, the *kŏmun-go*. He would play this instrument for the amusement of farmers who might be gathered at some local shrine for a ritual. He frequented wine-shops and played for the amusement of the local folk; he practised meditation in the mountains, and sang Buddhist songs as he passed through the countryside and the mountain passes. In fact, it is said that some of the songs which Wŏnhyo composed became so widely used that even non-Buddhists sang them frequently. In order to propagate Buddhism, Wŏnhyo attempted to live a life which was not cloistered, but close to the common man. Strongly eschewing doctrinal and monastic Buddhism, Wŏnhyo preached to the common people the hope of *Chŏngt'o pulgyo* (Pure Land Buddhism) and the cult of the saviour Buddha Amitābha. The popularity of this cult in later centuries, the hope which it offered the ordinary man of being reborn in the Western Paradise in the presence of the loving Buddha Amitābha, had its origin in the popular evangelistic movement which Wŏnhyo initiated.

Wŏnhyo was not simply a renegade from orthodox Buddhism, nor only a popularizer of its teachings for the masses. He was a major scholar who was said to have composed during his lifetime at least five important treatises. Works which have been attributed to him are the *Pŏphwa-gyŏng chong'yo* (Thematic Essentials of the Lotus Sutra), the *Tae yŏlban-gyŏng chong'yo* (Thematic Essentials of the *Nirvāna Sūtra*), the *Kŭmgang sammae kyŏngnon* (Essay on the Diamond Sutra), the *Taesŭng kisil-lon so* (Commentary on the *Mahāyāna Śraddhotpāda Śāstra*), and the *Yusim allak-to*. The first three of these works are commentaries on the universalistic doctrines of salvation (the ubiquity of the Buddha nature, for example) taught in three of the most important Buddhist scriptures used thoroughout East Asia. The Lotus and *Nirvāna* sutras in particular were the scriptures which Wŏnhyo had first studied and in which, evidently, he maintained a lifelong interest. The fourth work is a commentary on

44

an important treatise known in English as the *Awakening of Faith* and frequently attributed to Aśvaghoṣa (2c.?). The concepts in this treatise were considered by Wŏnhyo to be an excellent means to draw together the various doctrines of Mahāyāna Buddhism. The final work is a guide for the layman who is seeking the path to Buddhist salvation, but it is now thought that it may not actually be the work of Wŏnhyo. These writings show that Wŏnhyo was deeply concerned to find a means to draw the various elements of Mahāyāna Buddhism together into a coherent, universalistic teaching.

Wŏnhyo violated every standard for an ordinary monk and yet was revered as a saint. Late in life, he sensed sexual urges which he had never known before. Hearing of the beauty of one of the royal princesses, he desired to know her. He went round the Silla capital Kyŏngju singing a bawdy song, would anyone give him an axe without a handle? The song's lyrics implied that the Princess Yosŏk-kung was already having an affair with Wŏnhyo. Once this state of affairs was made public, it was easy for Wŏnhyo to have his liason with the princess. The issue of this union was a boy, Sŏl Ch'ong (7th cent.), who grew up to become one of the great Confucian scholars and literary figures of Silla. Wŏnhyo died at the age of sixty-nine in the year 686.

Ŭisang was the third of the three great monks who were active during the golden age of Silla Buddhism. Born in the year 625, Ŭisang decided to enter the monastic life in 644 at the age of nineteen. He resided for a while in the Hwangbok-sa and became friendly with the monk Wŏnhyo, who was eight years his senior. They resolved to travel together to China to study Buddhist doctrines there. Because of his peculiar experience *en route*, Wŏnhyo returned to Silla, but Ŭisang pressed on. Due to the unsettled political conditions in Koguryŏ at that time, Ŭisang was prevented from going on to T'ang.

Ŭisang never gave up his desire to go to China. In 650, he was able to attach himself to the entourage of the embassy of the Emperor Kao-tsung, which was returning home to Ch'ang-an. Ŭisang settled down in Ch'ang-an at the Chih-hsiang Temple on Chung-nan Shan, the place in the T'ang capital where Chajang had earlier sojourned. Ŭisang studied the *Hua-yen Ching* under Chih-yen (602–88), who was the second patriarch of the Hua-yen School. At the same time that Ŭisang was studying at the Chih-hsiang Temple, Master Chih-yen had a young Serindian boy with him, Fa-tsang (643–712), with whom Ŭisang struck up a lifelong friendship. Fa-tsang later became the third patriarch of the Hua-yen School. Even after twenty years had passed since they were parted, Fa-tsang remembered his friend from Silla and wrote a letter to him praising his profound knowledge of the *Hua-yen Ching* and his efforts to propagate Buddhism in his homeland. Fa-tsang is considered by many to have been the real founder of the school, as it was he who systematized the doctrines which the school taught. Ŭisang's relationship with both Fa-tsang and Wŏnhyo placed him in a unique intermediary position between these two important thinkers.

In 670, following the turbulent decade which led to Silla's supremacy in the Korean peninsula, Ŭisang heard a rumour that the Emperor Kao-tsung was making plans to attack Silla. The Silla monk abruptly ended his twenty-year stay in T'ang and hurried home to report this story to King Munmu. After fulfilling this duty, Ŭisang then retired to the Sŏrak Mountains on the east coast, residing for six years in the Kwanŭm Cave (Cave of Avalokiteśvara). He then emerged from this self-imposed retirement and began the vigorous dissemination of the doctrines of the Hua-yen (Hwaŏm in Korean) School.

The Hua-yen School was the most abstruse and philosophical of the Buddhist schools which were transmitted early on to Silla. The school's principal doctrine was a theory of causation by the universal principle, the *dharmadhātu*, which taught that all the *dharmas* in the universe emerged together. Thus the school taught that the universe was self-created, that principle and phenomena are mutually part of each other, and that all phenomena are likewise identified with each other. Ŭisang helped found numerous temples, many of which are still among the best known in Korea. In 676, he received permission to construct the Pusŏk-sa near Yŏngju, which was to be the centre of the Hwaŏm School. This temple was followed by the Pimara-sa in Wŏnju, the Haein-sa on Kaya-san, the Pŏmŏ-sa on Kŭmjŏng-san, and the Hwaŏm-sa on Chiri-san. Although an important school in the intellectual history of Korea, the Hwaŏm School did not become a popular sect. However, the school does represent the first flowering of the sophisticated, philosophical aspect of Silla Buddhism which developed during the later Silla era. Ŭisang died in 702 at the age of seventy-seven.

In any discussion of the important monks of Silla in the seventh century, one cannot overlook the work of Wŏnch'ŭk (613–96), even though he spent most of his life in T'ang. He was born in 613, a member of the royal house of Silla. At a very young age he was set aside for the monastic life, and in 627, at the age of fourteen, he was sent to T'ang to study. There is a story that as a child Wŏnch'ŭk could recall verbatim anything which was said within his hearing. This faculty enabled him to learn to speak other languages well. He is said to have had a flawless Chinese pronunciation and an unusually good understanding of written Sanskrit. Wŏnch'ŭk was trained at the Yüan-fa Temple in Ch'ang-an, where he studied the *Abhidharma-śāstra* and the *Abhidharma-kośa-śāstra*, Hīnayāna writings teaching the eternal nature of the *dharmas* in the universe. Wŏnch'ŭk then became a student of Hsüan-tsang (602–64), the great traveller and Buddhist philosopher. The Silla monk was reckoned second in importance after K'uei-chi (632–82) as Hsüan-tsang's principal disciple.

There was considerable rivalry between K'uei-chi and Wŏnch'ŭk. For one thing, Wŏnch'ŭk was not above misusing his talents. He was said to have overheard Hsüan-tsang teaching a new doctrine, contained in the master's *Wei-shih Lun* (Ideation Only Philosophy), to K'uei-chi. When the discourse was over, Wŏnch'ŭk hastened over to the Hsi-ming Temple and preached the discourse as if it were his own teaching. This incident not only resulted in Hsüan-tsang writing a new treatise, the *Yu-chia Lun* (Philosophy of Yoga), for his premier disciple, but it was the beginning of a long period of cool rivalry between the two disciples.

Whatever one may think of Wŏnch'ŭk's ethics, he was one of the most important translators in seventh century T'ang China. He was one of five monks who helped in the translation of the large numbers of sutras brought to T'ang by the Indian monk Śivahara in 676 and he was also responsible for translations of the *Ta-ch'êng Hsien-shih Ching* and the *P'u-yü Ching*. Even in the final year of his life, he remained active in the work of translation. When the Khotanese monk Śilananda arrived in Ch'ang-an in 695, Wŏnch'ŭk assisted him in translating the *Avatamsaka-sūtra* [Garland Sutra]. He died in 696 at the age of 83.

Concurrent with the development of a more orthodox monastic and doctrinal Buddhism was the growth of esoteric Buddhism. We know from records of curative ceremonies held in Silla that there had been practitioners of a magical form of Buddhism in previous centuries. However, it is in the seventh century that we first hear of schools of esoteric Buddhism. The foremost esoteric monk of the seventh century was Myŏngnang, who was the son of Lady Namgan, the sister of Chajang. Myŏngnang was not only born into a family of privilege, but also into one with a strong interest in Buddhism. It is also important to recall his uncle Chajang's interest in the occult figure Mañjuśrī. Obviously, Myŏngnang's interest in the esoteric and occult was not a solitary one, even amongst the élite.

Myŏngnang went to T'ang in 632, before Chajang went there, and while in T'ang he learned the secrets and rituals of the esoteric school. When he returned to Silla, he seems to have become an adviser to the sovereign. The *Samguk yusa* records the story that when T'ang was threatening to invade Silla in the year 668, King Munmu asked Myŏngnang to protect the nation against invasion by use of his great powers. At first Myŏngnang wanted to build a temple to the Four Heavenly Kings, the guardians of the four quarters of the universe. Realizing that he would have to act more quickly, the occult monk gathered twelve esoteric monks together and performed a secret rite using a cosmic *mandala* diagram. The story says that as a result the T'ang navy was sunk *en route* to Silla. These same events were repeated the next year. In 679, the Sach'ŏnwang-sa (Temple of the Four Heavenly Kings) was constructed as a cosmic diagram of immense magical power. In fulfilment of a vow made to the Dragon King on his return to Silla, Myŏngnang dedicated his home as a temple devoted to the worship of this spirit. The Dragon King, of course, plays an important role in Korean primal religion as the ruler of the sea. Myŏngnang gathered disciples of occult Buddhism around him and founded the *Sinin-jong* (Spirit Seal School), a branch of the Chên-yen (True Word) School in China.

Myŏngnang was not the only monk who investigated the occult practices of Buddhism. Hyet'ong, who established the Chinŏn Sect (Chên-yen School in Chinese), studied the secrets of this school for many years whilst resident in T'ang under the tutelage of Wu-wei San-tsang. During his stay in T'ang, Hyet'ong developed such a reputation as an occult adept that he was summoned by the Emperor Kao-tsung to cure his daughter. This patronage greatly enhanced the Silla monk's prestige. Upon his return to Silla, King Hyoso (r. 692–701) asked him to cure his daughter's illness, which he did. The *Samguk yusa* contains a curious story in which it is related that Hyet'ong fell foul of King Hyoso at one point, and was ordered to be taken into custody and executed. When the soldiers came to take Hyet'ong from his temple, the monk climbed up onto the roof, holding a bottle and brush. In full view of the assembled soldiers, he painted a red line around the bottle's neck. Instantly, there appeared a red line around the necks of the soldiers. Hyet'ong then threatened to break the neck of the bottle, causing the soldiers to retreat in a panic.

Milbon was another esoteric of the seventh century. He was called upon to use his occult powers to cure both Queen Sŏndŏk and her prime minister. Myŏnghyo (8th cent.) spent a number of years in China, after which he returned to Silla, spreading the doctrines taught by the *Mahāvairocana-sūtra*, a principal scripture of the Chên-yen Sect. Myŏnghyo in particular seems to have been influenced by Vajrabodhi (671–741), an Indian resident in T'ang who was also the teacher of Hyech'o, a pilgrim to India. The appeal of these esoteric sects was due in no small measure to their similarity to Korean primal religion. The emphasis on the curing of disease, the use of magic, and the appeal to spirits to protect the nation were concepts which were rooted as much in Korean shamanism as in Buddhism. The ready acceptance of these practices and their advocates was the consequence of esoteric Buddhism being viewed as a superior form of shamanism.

3. The Advent of Confucianism

Certain modern scholars, such as Yi Ŭrho,[1] claim that before the diffusion of Chinese civilization into Korea there was a primitive form of folk philosophy, characteristic of the tribal states, which had certain essential similarities to Classical Confucianism. The evidence for this folk philosophy, termed *Han sasang* (Concept of Unity), comes from an analysis of the ancient foundation myths of Korea, particularly the Myth of Tan'gun (see Appendix A.1). According to Yi, three principal relations are stressed in this myth: (1) the relationship between the Lord of Heaven, *Hwanin*, and his son, *Hwanung*; (2) the relation between Hwanung and his subordinates; and (3) the relation between Hwanung and the Bear Woman. These are the three fundamental Confucian relationships between father and son, lord and subject, and husband and wife. Although Yi does not mention it, there is also the relation between Heaven and earth, symbolized by Hwanung and the Bear-woman. Yi stresses the fact that this most ancient of all Korean legends contains three of the five fundamental social relationships of Confucianism (ruler/ruled, parent/child, husband/wife, elder/young siblings, friend/friend), indicating that even before the advent of Confucian philosophy, Koreans accepted these relationships as essential to their understanding of the social world.

---

1 Yi Ŭrho, *Han'guk kaesin yuhak-sa siron* (Sŏul, Pagyŏng-sa, 1980), pp. 11–29.

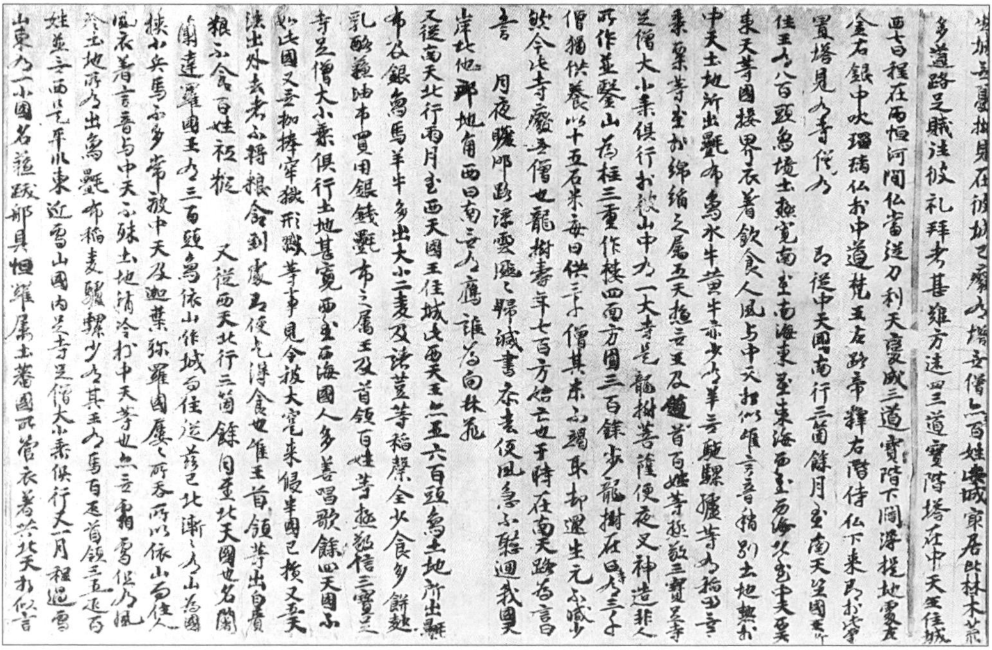

Plate 1 *Wang och'ŏnch'uk-guk chŏn* (Record of a Journey to the Five Kingdoms of India). Manuscript. Written by Hyech'o c. 750.

Plate 2 Tae'ung-jŏn (Main Hall) of T'ongdo-sa temple, South Kyŏngsang Province, 1644.

Plate 3 Pagoda at T'ongdo-sa containing a relic of the Buddha brought to Silla by the monk Chajang, c. mid-seventh century.

Plate 4 Tae'ung-jŏn, Pongwŏn-sa, Sŏul. Head Temple of the Taego Buddhist Order. Late eighteenth century.

Plate 5 Vairocana Buddha in the
Samch'ŏnbul-jŏn (Three Thousand
Buddha Hall) of Pongwŏn-sa.
Mid-1990s.

Plate 6 Taesŏng-jŏn, principal shrine of the Mun-myo or central Confucian shrine for Korea. Sŏul. Erected 1398; rebuilt 1601.

Plate 7 Group of Confucian scholars in traditional scholars' clothing in front of the Mŏngnyun-dang, lecture hall of the Sŏngggyun-gwan or Confucian academy in Sŏul. Building erected in 1398; rebuilt 1606.

Plate 8 Chŏng-jŏn (part view), principal shrine of the Chong-myo, the royal ancestral shrine in Sŏul. Erected in 1396 and extended on various occasions.

Plate 9 Tong-myo, a shrine in Chinese style dedicated to Kuan Yü, the Chinese God of War. Erected in 1602 at the command of the Ming emperor Shên-tsung (r. 1572–1620).

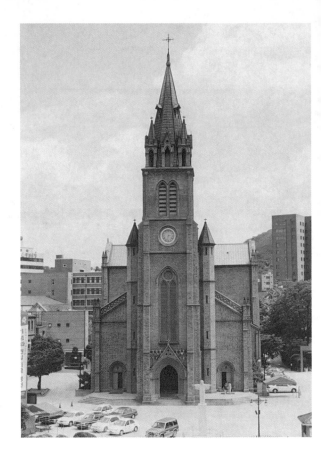

Plate 10 Cathedral Church of the Immaculate Conception of St Mary (popularly Myŏng-dong Cathedral), Roman Catholic cathedral of Sŏul. Erected in 1892–8 as a martyrium over the site of the home of the first Korean martyr, Kim Pŏmu.

Plate 11 Ch'ŏltu-san martyrs' church and museum. Dedicated in 1967, the church and museum is on a hill overlooking a site on which numerous Korean Catholics were executed.

Plate 12 Original quadrangle, Yonsei University, Sŏul. Main building erected c. 1920.

Plate 13 Ch'ŏndo-gyo Central Church, Sŏul. Building completed in 1923.

Plate 14 Chonggyo Methodist Church in central Sŏul. A typical example of a contemporary large Korean Protestant Church. Erected 2001.

The nature of these social relationships is based on the concept of the harmony between different social statuses. In no place does the Myth of Tan'gun indicate strife, conflict, or discord. Thus, harmony implies an underlying unity despite differences, a concept which Yi compares to the Confucian concept *jên* (benevolence). *Han sasang* or *Yi-yi il* (Two but One) is the heart of the *Yin-Yang* (*Ŭmyang* in Korean) philosophy and is unquestionably one of the primal concepts of East Asia. It is Yi's contention that it was just such concepts of Korean folk philosophy which prepared the people for the acceptance of the formal system of Confucian philosophy.

In the fourth century, as the Korean states Koguryŏ and Paekche adopted sinitic culture, they also began to absorb Confucianism. The adoption of Confucian learning and the Confucian system of education was an important means by which the cultural and political standards of the Korean states were elevated. However, two points need to be made here. The adoption of Confucianism in one form or another did not mean that these states therefore became Confucian societies, but only that they received certain Confucian influences which were of a cultural nature. Second, when we speak of Confucian influence, we may speak broadly of three ways in which Confucianism affected Korean culture: cultural influence, political influence, and social influence. By cultural influence, we shall mean that influence which Confucianism exercised over arts, letters, education, and philosophy. The influence of Confucianism in the ancient states of Korea initially meant the adoption of a writing system (Chinese), the study of the Confucian canonical works and the acceptance of their philosophical concepts, the establishment of a formalised system of education. This was the first level of influence which was exercised over the ancient Korean kingdoms. By political influence, we shall mean that influence which Confucianism exercised in the reformation of and creation of systems of government. Political influence builds on the existing cultural influences of Confucianism and adopts the developed political philosophy which leads to the creation of a regularised state bureaucracy and a formalised governmental structure with diversified political functions and checks on the functioning of government. Finally, by social influence, we shall mean that influence which Confucianism had on the fundamental restructuring of society, encompassing changes in mores and values, especially as these are represented by changes in social relationships. This was the last level of Confucian influence on Korea and it is important to note that until the Chosŏn Dynasty, Confucian influence on the Korean nation was largely in the area of political and cultural affairs, hardly touching the social sphere.

In the same year in which King Sosurim of Koguryŏ welcomed the foreign monk Sundo to his palace, and two years after Koguryŏ's disastrous defeat at the hands of Paekche, the king established a national college for the education of the sons of the aristocracy, the T'aehak. The establishment of this college in 372 was followed shortly by the founding of various private academies called *kyŏngdang*. Although the purpose of these schools was to educate the youth of

Koguryŏ in the Confucian classics, Chinese literature, and the martial arts, their rules of limitation undermined one of the essential aspects of Confucianism. By opening their doors only to the scions of the aristocracy, these academies not only denied access to education to the ordinary man, but also denied him the opportunity to participate in the government of the nation. Until the end of the Chosŏn Dynasty, this limitation of Confucian education to the aristocracy was a fatal flaw in Korean Confucianism.

Confucian influence in Paekche, as in Koguryŏ, was of a cultural not a political nature. Records indicate that by the late fourth century, at the same time that Buddhism was being received, Confucian thought and letters were also being accepted. Under the reigns of Kings Kŭnch'ogo (r. 346–75) and Kŭn'gusu (r. 375–84), Confucianism was transmitted to Japan through the agency of two scholars, A Chikki and Wang In. A Chikki became the tutor of the Japanese crown prince, and subsequently requested that Wang In should also be brought to Japan. The latter, accompanied by a Paekche prince, brought with him ten copies of the Analects of Confucius and one copy of the *Chien-cha Wên* (The Thousand-character Classic), a basic text for teaching Chinese characters. In spite of the existence of such internationally recognized scholars, it does not seem that there were Confucian academies in Paekche as in Koguryŏ.

From the fourth century onwards, an important cultural influence of Confucianism was in the development of literary scholarship and the keeping and writing of historical records. Dictionaries also began to appear at this time. The Koguryŏ court kept records of the history of each reign called *yugi*, and the victories of King Kwanggaet'o were recorded on a great stele near the Koguryŏ capital Kungnae-sŏng in 414. The Koguryŏ dynastic records were compiled into a hundred-*chüan* work called the *Kuksa* (National History), and then in the year 600 were condensed into a connected five-volume work, the *Sinjip* (New Compilation) by a scholar of the National Academy, Yi Munjin. The Paekche scholar Ko Hŭng (4th cent.) wrote the first connected history of Paekche called the *Sŏgi* (Documentary Records) in 375. This was followed in later times by the *Paekche-gi* (Records of Paekche) and the *Paekche pon'gi* (Original Records of Paekche) and the *Paekche sinch'an* (New Records of Paekche). Unfortunately, these records have since disappeared. In the mid-sixth century, in 545, the Silla scholar Kŏch'ilbu (6th cent.) wrote the first history of his native state, the *Kuksa* (National History), no longer extant.

In the Three Kingdoms Period, Confucianism seems to have had mostly an indirect influence on Silla. Kŏch'ilbu, perhaps the first scholar known to have worked within the Confucian framework, does not seem to have created a school of Confucian scholars around himself. Even though there was no formal school of Confucianism, there was a distinct Confucian cultural influence on Silla. We have noted at the end of the sixth century and the beginning of the seventh century how the Buddhist monk Wŏn'gwang reorganized the education of the aristocratic youth through the Hwarang Troop and the Law of the Hwarang. Only one of the laws derives from Buddhism, and at that it is a perversion of the

Buddhist reverence for life. The first three laws – loyalty to king, parents, and friends – are taken from Confucian thought. It is a sure sign of the prestige of Confucian learning when the most prominent Buddhist leader of the day based his philosophy on fundamental Confucian concepts. The mixture of part Buddhist and part common-sense rules with Confucian thought also shows the degree to which the intermixture of the various Chinese traditions had taken place. Clearly, in Koguryŏ, Paekche, or Silla, one cannot speak of the growth of a Confucian tradition prior to the mid-seventh century. There was influence on thought and letters, but there was not yet the development of a defined school of Confucian philosophy. There was cultural influence and political influence to a limited extent, but there was virtually no social influence.

4. Taoism: The Lack of a Tradition

The Chinese say that their religion has three pillars, Confucianism, Buddhism, and Taoism. However, Taoism has never existed as an organized religious body or as a separate school of philosophy in Korea. Charles Allen Clark, one of the early Protestant missionaries to Korea, remarks in *Religions of Old Korea* (1932) that it seemed strange as he crossed from Manchuria into Korea to see a magnificent Taoist temple perched high on a cliff overlooking the Yalu River on the Chinese side. It was as if Taoism had got so far and no further. Why was this so?

Taoism is both a religious and a philosophical system. The philosophical system has had an important but indirect influence on Korean thought. As the tradition of Ch'an (*Sŏn* in Korean) Buddhism developed in China, it was greatly influenced by the speculative philosophy of Taoism. This influence may be found in the history of Korean Sŏn Buddhism, but it has not been an especially important aspect of it. Taoist thought, particularly the concept of the *T'ai-chi* and the *Yin-Yang*, helped to shape the thought of Chu Hsi (1130–1200), the Sung Dynasty Confucian scholar whose system of philosophy came to dominate Korean Confucian thinking during the Chosŏn Dynasty. What knowledge Koreans have about Taoist concepts has been largely mediated through the metaphysics of Chu Hsi's form of Neo-Confucianism. Suitably, the *Yin-Yang* symbol and four of the eight trigrams compose the design elements of the flag of the Republic of Korea. Individual Korean scholars over the centuries have been aware of Taoism; many have read the important works of Taoist philosophy. Yet no one ever formed a school of Taoism in Korea. Philosophy in Korea has meant Confucianism, especially Chu Hsi's version of Neo-Confucian philosophy.

Religious Taoism, as organized by Chang Tao-ling (34–156) and others, systematized Chinese folk religion into a body of rituals and belief with a hierarchical structure of priests and patriarchs. It should come as no more of a surprise that this systematized folk religion did not gain acceptance during the Three Kingdoms period than that Shintō had no appeal to twentieth-century Korea. Koreans have been aware of philosophical Taoism for some time and have been familiar with the *Tao-tê Ching* and the *Chuang-tzu* for centuries. Through their numerous contacts over the centuries, Koreans have known of the religious practice of Taoism in China, yet not even the great prestige of Chinese culture could make them adopt this formalized folk religion as their own. Over the centuries, Korean folk religion has blended with Buddhism or been rejected by Confucianism. Whatever the attitude towards this folk religion was, it was Korea's own. Korea did not need to import someone else's folk-beliefs.

Only during one period of Korean history did organized Taoism make any headway. During the last phase of the Koguryŏ kingdom, the élite members of society began to take more interest in Taoist speculative thought and Taoist concepts of immortality than in Buddhism. In 624, the Emperor Kao-tsu (r. 618–26) of T'ang sent a Taoist priest with some Taoist scriptures and a statue to King Yŏngnyu (r. 617–42) of Koguryŏ as a gesture of goodwill. This priest lectured the court on the precepts of the *Tao-tê Ching*, which resulted in a number of élite converts to the Chinese religion. In the following year, the king sent a number of persons to China to study Taoism. Among the élite converts to Taoism was the Koguryŏ strongman Yŏn Kaesomun (?–666), who actively encouraged the religious cult of Taoism. In 642, Yŏn had King Pojang (r. 642–68) make a request to the Emperor T'ai-tsung to send a learned priest to expound on Taoist thought. The priest Shu-ta arrived in the same year bringing with him a copy of the *Tao-tê Ching* and accompanied by seven other Taoist priests. The king made over several Buddhist temples for their use. It was actions such as these which made the eminent Buddhist monk Podŏk despair. Feeling that Koguryŏ had gone over entirely to Taoism, he left his homeland in 650.

There are other clues to the cultural influence which religious Taoism exercised on early Korea. Examination of tiles from the tomb of King Muryŏng (r. 501–23) of Paekche show images of the Taoist Land of the Immortals. The same kinds of scenes may also be found on tiles from the Unified Silla period. The names of members of the Silla Hwarang Troop, such as Kuksŏn (national immortal) and Sŏnnang (immortal man), also reveal Taoist influence. In the eighth century there seems to have been a renewed interest in divination and occult practices which some scholars want to link with Taoism. Fascination with the Taoist Immortals continued through to the end of the Chosŏn Dynasty. However, this fascination never led to the creation of a full-fledged religious cult. Consequently, we may speak of Taoist philosophical or even religious influence from a very early period, but we may not speak of a Taoist religious tradition in Korea.

4

SILLA AND PARHAE
Two Powers in North-east Asia

1. The First North–South Division

With the collapse of Koguryŏ in 670, the entire geo-political structure of North-east Asia was dramatically altered. It had originally been the intention of T'ang to bring most of Manchuria and the Korean peninsula under its direct control. To that end, following the defeat of Paekche, T'ang established an administrative body in the Paekche area. Silla, however, was able to thwart T'ang's designs. Although she was unable to expel T'ang from the entire peninsula, T'ang recognized Silla's *de facto* control of the peninsula south of the Taedong River. Theoretically, this ought to have left T'ang in control of virtually all of the former territory of the Kingdom of Koguryŏ and vast areas to the west of the Liao River. However, eleven of the walled cities of Koguryŏ never submitted to T'ang's authority, and held out against the imposition of T'ang imperial rule. This condition of instability on its north-eastern border caused T'ang to set up military commanderies there to prevent incursions of former Koguryŏ warriors and their tribal allies.

Until Silla was able to firmly resist T'ang's plan to incorporate the peninsula into the empire, it had been the intention of the Chinese to use the last king of Koguryŏ, Pojang, as their instrument in governing the peninsula. Pojang was to have been given the titles of Governor-General of Liaotung and King of Chosŏn. This plan came to nought, but his son Tongmu was made Governor-General of Andong, an area extending from the Liao River to the Taedong River including the Liaotung Peninsula, but largely confined in the Korean peninsula to the west coast. By the creation of military commanderies in north-east China and the establishment of a viceroyalty in southern Manchuria, the Chinese hoped both to contain the expansion of Manchurian tribal peoples, including the remnants of the Koguryŏ, and to prevent the northern expansion of Silla (see Fig. 6).

In 696, Li Chin-ch'ung, the Khitanese commander who had been selected by T'ang to defend the Jehol area of the north-east, rose in rebellion against the imperial government, setting the whole area of north-east T'ang into political confusion. Among his subordinates was a Koguryŏ general, Tae Choyŏng (?–719), who fled from Jehol to the area of modern Tunhua in Chilin Province.

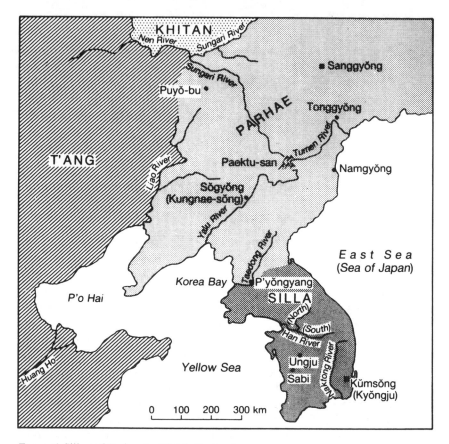

Figure 6 Silla and Parhae (*c.* Eighth Century)

There he formed a new alliance with several of the tribal peoples who had composed the Kingdom of Koguryŏ. The Moho, Sushen, and Yemaek tribes recognized Tae Choyŏng as their king and he took the regnal name of King Ko (r. 699–719) of Ching-guk. In 713, King Ko changed the name of the kingdom to Parhae (in Chinese, P'o-hai). Contrary to what most schoolchildren in Korea are taught, Silla did not unify the Korean peninsula into a single nation. From the end of the seventh century, there existed two Korean states, Parhae and Silla. Parhae was the direct political descendant of Koguryŏ, and may be thought of as its cultural and social successor as well. Parhae was keen to indicate its descent from Koguryŏ as is evidenced by letters sent to the Japanese emperor with whom the new state maintained friendly relations. King Mu (r. 719–37), King Ko's successor, stressed the point that the new state was built upon the territory of Koguryŏ and kept to the customs of Puyŏ. King Mun (r. 737–93), the third king, referred to himself as *Koguryŏ kugwang* (King of Koguryŏ). This was all part of a diplomatic war to enlist the support of the former allies of Paekche and Koguryŏ. Unquestionably, the new state was threatened by the pressure being applied on the west from T'ang and on the south from Silla.

T'ang was concerned by the presence of a rejuvenated, powerful state on its sensitive north-east border and connived at destroying the delicate tribal relationships which existed within Parhae. T'ang encouraged a branch of the Moho people living near the confluence of the Sungari and Amur Rivers to rebel against the King of Parhae in 732. Parhae retaliated by sending its navy to attack the Shantung Peninsula. T'ang and Silla then entered into an alliance to destroy Parhae. Hoping to repeat the successful pincer movement which had destroyed Koguryŏ in the previous century, attacks were launched from T'ang and Silla against Parhae. The war ended without the destruction of Parhae, and a treaty of peace was entered into between Parhae and T'ang. Silla, however, was excluded from this arrangement, and the two Korean states entered into a chilly relationship which lasted until the demise of both states in the early tenth century.

Unfortunately, very little is known of the culture and society of Parhae. The only sources of information are brief references in a few ancient books and scant archaeological evidence. Parhae was very much in the orbit of the cosmopolitan culture of T'ang. The capital city, Sanggyŏng (Upper Capital), was patterned after the city plan of Ch'ang-an, the T'ang capital. The structure of the government bureaucracy and the names of the various ministries show a strong Confucian influence on the style of government. Buddhism was also an extremely strong cultural force, as is indicated by the number of monks and temples thought to have existed in the state. The eighth-century Japanese monk Ennin in his diary mentions two incidents which occurred in his travels, a story about a Parhae monk and an encounter with a Parhae prince who was a devout Buddhist, which give some indication of the continuity of Buddhism in the former territory of Koguryŏ. Excavations at Sanggyŏng also indicate the strong influence which Buddhism exercised on the arts and architecture of Parhae. After 732, cultural relations began to flourish between Parhae and its former enemy, T'ang. Students from the national Confucian college of Parhae were sent to T'ang to study Confucianism, and as we have seen Buddhist monks also travelled to China to study Buddhist doctrine and practice. By the early ninth century, Parhae had reached such a degree of prosperity that it was referred to by the Chinese as *hai-tung shêng-kuo* (Prosperous State to the East of the Sea).

In the early part of the tenth century, the Khitan tribes rose up against Chinese authority in North-east Asia and created their own state which came to be known as Liao (907–1125). Their incursions into the surrounding states led to the collapse of all three states of North-east Asia, T'ang, Parhae, and Silla. Parhae, which had been a union of Koguryŏ and other tribal groups, came apart forever under the pressure of the Khitan invasion of 926. The union of the various tribal peoples had proved unstable in the end, each group going its own way. The ruling élite, who claimed descent from the aristocracy of Koguryŏ, fled to the area of the new state of Koryŏ on the Korean peninsula, thus showing their affinity to the peninsular peoples. A branch of the Moho attempted to establish a state, Chŏngan-guk, in the area of the first capital of Koguryŏ, Kungnae-sŏng, on the Yalu River. This proved to be ephemeral and the state was destroyed by the Khitan.

After having successfully repulsed T'ang attempts to incorporate Silla into the empire in the 670s, Silla entered into a period of cultural and political florescence. During the next hundred years, Silla was to attain the summit of its cultural and political development, which was never to be surpassed nor ever again to be attained. The zenith of Silla's economic prosperity and cultural achievements were reached during the reign of King Kyŏngdŏk (r. 742–65). During the hundred-year period following unification, the finest works of stone sculpture, bronze casting, and temple architecture were created. The greatest of all these cultural achievements was unquestionably the magnificent Sŏkkur-am grotto on the outskirts of Kyŏngju. From the reign of Kyŏngdŏk's successor King Hyegong (r. 765–80) onwards, Silla society entered into a long period of social decline typified by unceasing political strife. Wanne J. Joe has aptly said that the final period of Silla's history was a record of the gradual loosening of the glue which had held together the various components of the social structure.[1] Until the middle of the eighth century, the kings of Silla had been able to enhance royal authority and the power of the central government according to Confucian principles. However, this process tended to increase the contradictions already present in Silla society, which had originally been organized along clan lines under aristocratic leadership. The centralized Confucian bureaucratic system was alien to this social system and created tensions at all levels of society. During the reign of Hyegong, a group of conservative aristocrats joined cause with a group of ninety-six clan chiefs who revolted against the central government. Social advances which had been made during the reign of King Kyŏngdŏk were rescinded during Hyegong's reign in an attempt to appease these groups. This was unsuccessful, and dissension and rebellions continued to plague the land until the king himself was murdered in 780. At this point, two branches of the royal family emerged vying for power. King Sŏndŏk (r. 780–5), who was considered to be a more malleable man than the previous king, was brought to the throne. Sŏndŏk was from a branch of the ruling Kyŏngju Kim clan which claimed descent from King Naemul (r. 356–402), whereas all previous kings from the middle of the seventh century were descendants of King Muryŏl. From this time until the demise of Silla in the tenth century, most of the kings were drawn from the former branch of the royal clan.

From this period, Silla society began rapidly to divide into various warring factions and communities. On the aristocratic level, there were the Muryŏl and Naemul branches of the royal clan, each with its own political policy. The

1 Wanne J. Joe, *Traditional Korea: A Cultural History* (Sŏul, Chungang UP, 1972), p. 148.

Muryŏl line was associated with a more liberal, bureaucratic Confucian policy. Set against their faction was the Naemul line and its associates among the grand aristocrats, who pursued a conservative policy designed to enforce the Bone Rank system. With the Naemul clan and its associates holding the levers of government, the lesser aristocrats became alienated from the government. This malaise was paralleled amongst the Confucian-trained scholars who held in contempt the autocratic and non-Confucian pattern of late Silla government. These two factions of the petty nobility formed an important anti-government bloc which created an increasing state of social instability. Members of the Muryŏl line finally rose up in revolt against the authoritarianism of the king. Kim Hŏnch'ang, the pretender to the throne from this branch of the royal clan, was sent down from the capital as a result of various intrigues at the court. As an effort at appeasement he was created governor of Ungch'ŏn Province. However, he used his position as a base for increasing his own power, and in 822 he rebelled against the central authority. He attempted to create an independent kingdom, Changan, but was killed in the ensuing conflict. His son, however, continued the rebellion. This rebellion was the first of many which were to characterize the political situation in ninth-century Silla. These revolts were directly responsible for the collapse of the central government and the creation of small states which gradually carved up the territory of the kingdom.

At the same time that members of the aristocratic classes were vying with each other for power, the power of the merchant class was steadily increasing. As the central government was less and less able to control trade, in particular international trade, individual merchants conducted trade with foreign governments on their own authority. Korean ship-building and navigation became increasingly sophisticated as a consequence of this increase in commerce. Silla merchants and merchants from other nations were able to establish extraterritorial rights for themselves in various ports in the T'ang empire. The Japanese, as Ennin's diary well documents, availed themselves of both the Korean shipping fleet and the extraterritorial rights of the Sillans. The economic power of these Silla merchants in turn gave them considerable political power at home. The most notable of them was Chang Pogo (?–846), who rose to power as a merchant and as a guardian of the shipping lanes from piracy. The power which he wielded through his army and navy led him to take an increasing interest in the affairs of the royal court. In 839, he placed his own candidate on the throne, King Sinmu (r. 839), but later overreached himself and was killed in the resulting conflict.

The weakness of the central authority throughout the area of the Silla kingdom meant that locally powerful groups were not only able to dominate affairs in their areas but were actually able to act independently of the government. There were three such groups which all enlarged the area of their personal estates, and refused to remit taxes to the central government as a way of withdrawing their support from it. The first group was composed of those grand aristocrats who had been left out of or who had been banished from the ruling court circle and who increased their family landholdings as a way of consolidating regional power. The second group consisted of those local headmen and petty aristocrats who used the chaotic social conditions of the ninth century to increase their own landholdings. The third group was composed of those Buddhist monasteries which had acquired considerable wealth in money, land, and slaves. Originally, land and slaves had been donated to the temples as a pious act by members of the laity. By the ninth century, however, these holdings were being aggressively expanded. The three groups either bought out poor farmers or seized land by sheer force. Tax revenues and the local administrative apparatus were withdrawn from the control of the central government. Increasingly, these landed estates took on the appearance of the feudal *demesnes* of medieval Europe. The squeeze which these great estates placed on the ordinary man became so intolerable that many farmers began to turn to banditry as a means of survival. By the close of the ninth century, farmers' revolts had become quite common.

The crumbling authority of the central government, beset by challenges from dissident aristocrats, scholars, landholders, merchants, and peasants, received a disastrous blow when certain powerful figures in the provinces began to form alternative central governments. Two leaders in particular were important. In the area of the old Paekche state, a local powerbroker, Kyŏn Hwŏn (867–935), arose and established the state of Later Paekche in 892. This king was very successful in international relations and was able to establish diplomatic ties with the states of Wu and Wu-yüeh in southern China, and to enter into cordial contact with Later T'ang (888-937) in northern China. Another rebel leader, Kungye (?–918), who controlled large sections of northern Silla, felt strong enough by the year 901 to declare the establishment of the state of Later Koguryŏ. He was an illegitimate son of King Hŏnan (r. 857–61) and had pretensions to the throne of Silla. However, his attempt to maintain amongst his followers the Bone Rank system and other marks of Silla aristocracy led to a revolt against his rule. He was succeeded by a lieutenant, Wang Kŏn (877–943). Thus by the end of the ninth century and the beginning of the tenth century, the central government of Silla in Kyŏngju controlled barely more than the area immediately surrounding the capital city. The peninsula itself was consumed in a war of dynastic succession between Later Koguryŏ and Later Paekche. In 927, Later Paekche sacked the Silla capital, murdered the king and his courtiers who were revelling at the P'osŏk Pavilion, and carried away slaves and booty. Kyŏn Hwŏn then placed a king of his own choice on the throne of Silla, King Kyŏngsun (r. 927–35). Later Koguryŏ was able skilfully to counteract the diplomatic and military advantages of Later Paekche by instilling dissension within the court circle of Later Paekche which eventually led to the collapse of the state. With the eventual capitulation of the royal court in Kyŏngju in 935, a new central government was established over all the area formerly administered by Silla. This state took the name of Koryŏ and ushered in a new period of dynastic history. At the same time as Silla collapsed, the entire T'ang world-order came apart. A new dynasty arose in China, and Manchuria passed forever from Korean control. In establishing his new kingdom, the first king of Koryŏ showed great wisdom by taking as members of his own royal family the former king of Silla and the crown prince of Parhae, thus symbolically uniting the various strains of the Korean race.

2. The Growth of Doctrinal Buddhism

(a) The O-gyo: The Orthodox Sects

As Silla's culture became more sophisticated, Buddhist thought and practice also became more complex and sophisticated. The most notable trend in Korean Buddhism during the hundred years following the unification of the Korean states was the emergence of genuine schools of Buddhist thought (see Fig. 7). The roots of this trend may be found in the work of Chajang, Wŏnhyo, and especially Ŭisang, but the development of genuine schools of Buddhist doctrine took place in the generation after these great figures. These sects were called the *O-gyo* or Five Schools. Interestingly, four of these five schools were present in China, but those schools which were most prominent in T'ang were not necessarily the most prominent in Silla.

The Five Buddhist Schools of Silla were the *Yul-chong* (*Lü-tsung* in Chinese), the *Hwaŏm-jong* (Hua-yen Sect in Chinese), the *Pŏpsang-jong* (Fa-hsiang Sect in Chinese), the *Yŏlban-jong* (*Nieh-p'an tsung* in Chinese) or Nirvana Sect, and the *Haedong-jong*, an indigenous sect. In addition to these five sects, there was also the T'ien-t'ai School, known as the *Ch'ŏnt'ae-jong* in Korean, and two major schools of esoteric Buddhism, the *Sinin-jong*, and the *Chinŏn-jong* (Chên-yen sect in Chinese). The latter two schools, however, have traditionally been excluded from the list of the principal schools of Buddhism in Silla, as they have been considered to be beyond the pale of orthodoxy.

The *Lü-tsung* or Disciplinary School was founded by the T'ang monk Tao-hsüan (596–667), who emphasized the teaching of the *Ssu-fen-lü* (Vinaya in Four Parts). For Tao-hsüan, acceptance of Buddhism meant not only assent to a certain set of doctrines but also adherence to a strict set of rules for the monastic life, called *vinaya*. The *Ssu-fen-lü* is a corpus of monastic regulations containing 250 sets of rules governing the lives of monks and a separate set of 348 regulations for nuns. The regulations listed in the *Ssu-fen-lü* are of two types, positive instructions for the proper conduct of ceremonies and the practice of the religious life, and negative rules or prohibitions against the commission of specified sins, such as lying, stealing, killing, and committing adultery. Part of the Hīnayāna tradition, this scripture had been widely accepted in East Asia by the Mahāyāna schools. Although not popular in T'ang, the *Lü-tsung* did attract the attention of the Silla monk Chajang. Chimyŏng had attempted to introduce the *Yul-chong* to Silla before Chajang, but had failed to gain acceptance for the sect. Greatly concerned with raising the standards of the Buddhist clergy, Chajang encouraged the growth of this sect which emphasized

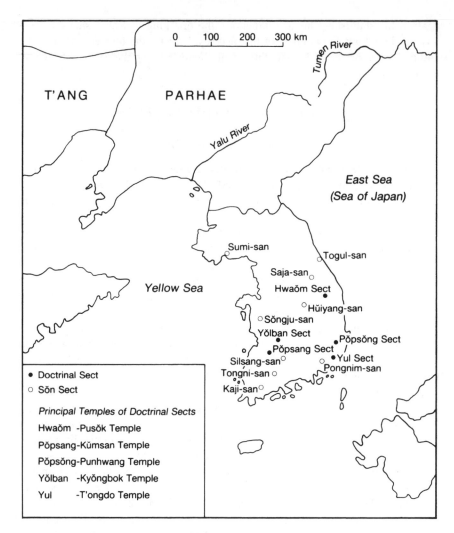

Figure 7 Location of Doctrinal and Sŏn Sect Head Temples in Unified Silla

monastic discipline. He also attempted to formalize the education of the clergy and to centralize the ordination of monks and insisted on attendance at yearly lectures and examinations on the contents of the talks. Chajang created a central national temple at T'ongdo-sa and stipulated that all persons seeking ordination must receive it on the ordination platform at this temple, the pagoda of which enshrines a relic of the Buddha.

The second sect of the *O-gyo* was the Hwaŏm Sect. The Hua-yen School owes its origins to the monk Fa-shun (557–640) who emphasized the study of the *Avatamsaka-sūtra* (Garland Sutra). The school is indigenous to China and has no precedent in India. Fa-shun was the teacher of both Fa-tsang, who became the third patriarch of the school, and Ŭisang. As discussed before, the core doctrine of this school is the concept of *dharmadhātu*, or universal principle, called *li* in Chinese. Principle and the phenomenon of the universe are interchangeable as are all of the individual phenomenon in it. Thus everything in the universe is a manifestation of the supreme mind, which is the Buddha. Because of its authoritarian or centralist tendency, this school was popular with the rulers of East Asian monarchies because it helped to strengthen the central national government. When Ŭisang returned to Silla, he began to disseminate this abstruse doctrine and established ten major monasteries for the propagation of the concepts of the school, the first of which was the Pusŏk-sa. Ancient records preserve a list of the names of the many disciples of Ŭisang, indicating the great success which he had in winning converts to his point of view. To instruct his disciples, Ŭisang used commentaries on the *Avatamsaka-sūtra* which had been brought back from T'ang in 692 by Sŭngjŏn. This sect remained influential amongst the metropolitan élite in Kyŏngju until the end of the Silla kingdom and is known to have existed in one form or another until the fifteenth century.

The third school, the *Haedong-jong*, is related to the development of the Hwaŏm School. The founder of this school was Ŭisang's friend Wŏnhyo, who differed from Ŭisang in the importance which he attached to the *Avatamsaka-sūtra*. Ŭisang insisted on the exclusive use of this sutra as the path for salvation, while Wŏnhyo felt that it was the greatest of sutras. For Wŏnhyo, salvation could come through the study of the other sutras properly understood. The choice of name for this sect indicates an element of nationalism, as *haedong* (east of the sea) is a poetic reference to Silla. This school is also called the *Pŏpsŏng-jong* (School of the Dharma Nature, Fa-hsing School in Chinese), a reference to a minor school of this name in China which was associated with the San-lun School. The principal temple was the Punhwang-sa in Kyŏngju.

The fourth school of the *O-gyo* was the *Pŏpsang-jong* (Fa-hsiang School in Chinese, Dharma Characteristics School). In China, the school was also known as the Wei-shih School or Ideational Only School. This school had its origins in India and was brought back to T'ang by the traveller Hsüan-tsang. At Nālandā, Hsüan-tsang had studied under Śilabhadra, who stood in the fourth generation from the founders of the school, Asanga and Vasubandhu. Initiated in China by Hsüan-tsang, this sect was widely propagated by Hsüan-tsang's premier disciple, K'uei-chi. The sect flourished for the next 200 years until it entered into a state of intellectual decline under the criticism of the Hua-yen School, and it disappeared altogether after the suppression of Buddhism in 845 under the nationalist emperor Wu-tsung (r. 840–6).

Like the Hua-yen School, the Fa-hsiang School emphasizes a doctrine of the mind. In its view, all phenomena in the universe are the creation of our consciousness, and thus ultimately illusory. Unlike the Hua-yen School, this sect did not believe that all sentient beings had the Buddha nature. The Fa-hsiang School taught that 'mind' possesses eight consciousnesses, one each for the five senses, one consciousness which creates individual conceptions from the perceptions received from the senses, the mind itself which exercises reason and will, and finally the *ālaya-vijñāna* or the storehouse of consciousness. The latter consciousness possesses the effects of *karma* from the distant past. In this great storehouse all ideas whether pure or impure exist intermingled, side by side. Through the interaction of the other consciousnesses, these ideas come into the world manifesting themselves in individual phenomena. The pure ideas which come from the perfect enlightenment of the Buddha lead the impure ideas to a higher state of truth where subject and object are not distinguished. The school argued that since not everyone possessed pure seeds in their storehouse, not everyone could attain Buddhahood. The concept of the storehouse has certain obvious parallels to Platonism, although the outcome of the Fa-hsiang School's ideational thinking is rather different.

The *Pŏpsang-jong*, the Korean form of the Fa-hsiang School, derives from Wŏnch'ŭk, another disciple of Hsüan-tsang. Although he never returned to Silla, many of his students from Silla did, and they helped to establish this school there. Three monks in particular were instrumental in bringing this school to their native land, Sŭngjang, Tojŭng, and Kyŏnghŭng. The latter is credited with the founding of the first temple of the *Pŏpsang-jong*, the Samnyang-sa in Kyŏngju.

The fifth of the five sects founded in the Silla period was the *Yŏlban-jong* or Nirvana School. This school developed in China as a result of the esteem in which the Chinese monk Tao-sheng (?360–434) held the *Nirvāna-sūtra* (in full the *Mahāparinirvāna-sūtra*). He taught that he even those whose principal interest was the gratification of their own desires possessed the Buddha-nature. In China, the Nirvana Sect existed as a separate entity until it was absorbed into the T'ien-t'ai School in the sixth century. However, the intellectual and spiritual influence of this school continued well into the seventh century. The Koguryŏ monk Podŏk studied the doctrines of the Nirvana Sect whilst he was in T'ang. Leaving Koguryŏ in disgust over the rise of Taoism, Podŏk settled in Paekche. His disciples created temples from which the doctrines of the sect were propagated. As it was through their efforts that the Nirvana Sect was brought to Silla, Podŏk is counted as the founding patriarch of the school there. Podŏk's influence extended beyond this school itself. His teachings about the *Nirvāna-sūtra* shaped the thinking of such great monks as Wŏnhyo, Ŭisang, and Kyŏnghŭng. As a sect, however, the Nirvāna Sect does not seem to have been numerically strong, in spite of the influence of its teaching.

The *Nirvāna-sūtra* teaches that all beings possess the Buddha nature and as a result everyone may attain to the state of *nirvāna*, a teaching which may not seem to be different from what is understood about the teaching of Primitive Buddhism. However, this sutra goes on to claim that the Buddha possesses an eternal self which lives in a state of bliss in *nirvāna*. *Nirvāna* itself is not an abstract experience or expression but is personal, eternal, and full of joy. All beings possess the nature of the Buddha and consequently they can enter into this personal, eternal state of happiness. The sutra also refers to the beings of this world as the children of Buddha, because they have participated in the Buddha nature since the beginning of the world. Obviously, there are many points of comparison here with core Christian theology which emphasises the universal potential of salvation, humanity as being the children of God, the eternality of God, and the blissfulness of Heaven.

(b) The Ch'ŏnt'ae-jong

The *Ch'ŏnt'ae-jong* (T'ien-t'ai School in Chinese), another doctrinal sect which developed in Silla, is not normally enumerated amongst the *O-gyo* which flourished after the unification of the Three Kingdoms. In China, the school owes its origin to Chih-i (538–97), who attempted to make sense of the contradictory mass of Buddhist scriptures. Because of the diversity of the sutras, and the contradictions between the teachings of the various sutras, many persons questioned how the corpus of scriptures could be accepted as the teaching of one man. Chih-i attempted to show how the teachings of the sutras could be arranged according to a historical chronology and also how they could be organized according to the type of doctrine. In the early stages of his teaching the Buddha taught only basic concepts, while later on he taught more complex ideas. This constituted the chronological aspect of Chih-i's system. Chih-i also thought that for more advanced thinkers, the Buddha taught some abstruse matters even at the earliest stage of his work. This concept led to a doctrinal or conceptual organization of the Buddhist corpus. This philosophical system was not merely a bibliophile's attempt to intellectually arrange matters, but was a major effort to systematize and synthesize all Buddhist teachings.

The T'ien-t'ai School in China, while emphasizing the teaching of each sutra, also stressed the importance of three sutras as having greater importance than the others. These were the Lotus Sutra, the *Nirvāna-sūtra*, and the *Mahāprajñāpāramitā-sūtra*. It is believed that Chih-i obtained some of the ideas for the systematic arrangement of the sutras from his teacher Hui-szu (515–77).

During the same period when Chih-i was studying with his master Hui-szu, the Paekche monk Hyŏn'gwang was also studying under the same teacher. When Hyŏn'gwang returned to Paekche, he taught principles similar to those of Chih-i, which in turn led to the development in Paekche of a movement parallel to the T'ien-t'ai School. However, this movement did not emerge as an organized school of Buddhism until the reign of King Hyegong (r. 765–79) of Silla. During his reign, a great interest in the T'ien-t'ai School was aroused by the teachings of the ninth patriarch of the Chinese sect, Chan-jan (711–82). For Chan-jan everything was a manifestation of Absolute Mind. The ninth patriarch is credited with the remark that even a grain of dust contains the Buddha Nature. Interest was so stimulated in his concept of universal salvation that numerous monks crossed from Silla to T'ang, who in turn became responsible for the formal foundation of this school in Silla after their return. However, after a period of popularity, the *Ch'ŏnt'ae-jong* fell from favour and was not a powerful force in subsequent generations.

(c) Esoteric Buddhism

Concurrent with the development of the doctrinal schools of Buddhism was the growth of esoteric Buddhism. We have already referred to such esoteric masters as Myŏngnang and Hyet'ong and have mentioned the rise of the mysterious *Sinin-jong* and *Chinŏn-jong* schools. These trends continued throughout the hundred years or so following the wars for unification. Two monks are of particular importance here, Chinp'yo and Hyech'o.

Chinp'yo is supposed to have left his family at the age of 12 in order to enter a monastery. He took up residence at the Kŭmsan-sa where he studied Ch'an practices under the master Sŭngje. Chinp'yo's teacher had made a journey to Wu-t'ai Shan where he had had an ecstatic experience of the Bodhisattva Mañjuśrī, and where he had received a set of five commandments from this mysterious figure. As a young man Chinp'yo desired to have the same type of experience. He retreated to a hermitage deep in the mountains where he underwent a series of strenuous, ascetic exercises which culminated in an experience of the Bodhisattva Ksitigarbha, guardian of the souls of the dead. Moving to another location, Chinp'yo again had an ecstatic experience, this time of Maitreya, and received from Maitreya three objects: a set of commandments called the *manbun'gye*, a copy of a book of divination called the *Chan-ch'a Ching*, and 189 divination sticks. Two of the divination sticks were supposed to be the fingers of Maitreya himself.

Returning to Kŭmsan-sa from his mountain retreat, Chinp'yo erected a statue of Maitreya and gathered around himself a community of monks who ordered their lives according to the commandments which he had received from Maitreya. Chinp'yo also instituted a yearly service of divination. The school which grew up around Chinp'yo has been called the *Yoga-jong* or Yoga School.

Like Chajang in a previous century, Chinp'yo's authority had been validated by an ecstatic experience, and like his teacher Sŭngje and Chajang, Chinp'yo had received a set of commandments from the Bodhisattva. When a shaman in modern times is called by the spirits to be their intermediary with this world, the shaman encounters the spirit in a dream or in a state of ecstasy. While the shaman is in this trance, the spirit will teach an esoteric formula for the shaman to use in curing disease, or will make a gift of some object. This type of experience is precisely the kind of experience which these esoteric monks had of a Buddhist divinity. The *Samguk yusa* also says that the disciples of Chinp'yo used *mandalas* or sacred diagrams in the course of performing esoteric rites. The use of these sacred diagrams and magical formulas is parallel to the rites and practices of Korean primal religion. The growth of esoteric Buddhism in Silla is an example of a religious syncretism where the primal religious tradition adopts the form of a foreign religion because of its outward similarity to concepts and practices of the primal religion. In so doing, such a syncretic religion may ignore or be unaware of the content of the foreign religion.

Hyech'o (704–87) is usually regarded as the greatest of the monks of the eighth century. Although not the last in the line of famous travellers to India, Hyech'o is remembered for the record of his travels, the *Wang och'ŏnch'uk-kuk-chŏn* (Record of a Journey to the Five Kingdoms of India, 8th cent.). Hyech'o left Silla at the age of 19 to study with the famous Indian monk Vajrabodhi and his disciple Amogha (704–74), who were resident in Kuang-chou in south China. Vajrabodhi was so impressed by the aptitude of the Silla monk that he urged him to make the sea-journey to India to study Buddhism at its source.

Hyech'o's record tells us that he went out by sea from Kuang-chou, passed by the Nicobar Islands, and entered India at Tāmralipti, near modern Calcutta. He travelled widely in India and returned to T'ang via the land-route, arriving in Kucha in 727. In India, he went to the Magadha region in the valley of the River Ganges, where he visited Kuśinagara, Vārānasī (Benares) and its famous Deer Park, Bodhgayā, and Rājagrha. He also visited the Chalukya kingdom in south India, the Valabhī kingdom in west India, and Jālandhara in north India. Hyech'o's record also includes information on Persia and the Byzantine Empire, about which he heard during the course of his travels, and on several of the Central Asian states through which he passed on his way to China. His account demonstrates the extent to which Islam had penetrated into the southern part of Central Asia by the middle of the eighth century. When he returned to China, he took up residence at a temple in Ch'ang-an and assisted his master Vajrabodhi in the translation of an esoteric sutra dedicated to Mañjuśrī. After his master's death, Hyech'o continued to work with Amogha until that monk's death in 774.

Normally, Korean histories mention Hyech'o's importance as an observer of contemporary India, but ignore his role in the development and transmission of the esoteric tradition of Buddhism. Although he never returned to Silla, Hyech'o must have had unquestioned influence on the Buddhism of his time not only as a Buddhist pilgrim, but as a disciple of the leading teacher of the esoteric school in China. Vajrabodhi was the chief propagandist for the Tantric school, and his biography shows that he indulged in the use of the *mandala*, predicted rain, and cured disease. Vajrabodhi also propagated the use of the *mantra* or mystic syllables. Likewise, Amogha's biography shows that he also had an interest in the use of the *mandala* and the *mantra*, predicted rain, and cured disease. Hyech'o's work with these great Indian monks must be seen in the light of the growth of the Tantric School. This was extremely popular in T'ang in the mid-eighth century and would have appealed to the Silla monk not only as a trend in contemporary Chinese Buddhism, but also as a parallel to the primal religion of Silla. Prediction of rain and the curing of disease are important elements in shamanistic ritual.

(d) Artistic and Cultural Achievements

The late seventh and eighth centuries were a time of great artistic development, a sign of the growth of an indigenous Buddhist culture in Silla. This era is the golden period of sculpture, bronze-casting (for figures of the Buddha), and architecture. Of the many possible examples, we will single out two temples which are worthy of comment, the Sach'ŏnwang-sa, and the Pulguk-sa and its attached grotto, the Sŏkkur-am.

The Sach'ŏnwang-sa or Temple of the Four Heavenly Kings was built in 679 on the advice of Myŏngnang to protect the nation against foreign invasion. The Four Heavenly Kings are the protectors of the four cardinal points of the universe and are part of the esoteric cult of Buddhism. The designation of the temple by the names of these figures indicates that the temple was intended to be a gigantic *mandala* and was laid out as such.

The function of protecting the nation through esoteric rites performed at the temple is congruent with the use of the *Jên-wang Ching* (Sutra of the Benevolent King) and other scriptures at the *P'algwan-hoe*. The utterance of the phrases of these scriptures was thought to offer spiritual or magical protection to the nation. These two practices – the use of the temple as a *mandala*, and the use of sacred formulas – are similar to the requests for blessings which are an important aspect of shamanistic rites. Furthermore, the temple as sacred space bears comparison with the *sodo* of the tribal period. The abbots of temples such as the Sach'ŏnwang-sa would be comparable to the great shamans who resided in the *sodo*. Nothing could be a clearer indication of the way in which primal religion had put on Buddhist clothes. Even as late as the eighth century, Korean primal religion had not been transformed by the foreign religion, but instead had transmuted the incoming religion into what was in practice a Korean religion.

No discussion of the Unified Silla period can neglect a discussion of the Pulguk-sa (Temple of the Buddha's Land) or the Sŏkkur-am (Hermitage of the Stone Cave). Both were built under the authority of Kim Taesŏng (701–74), the prime minister of Silla during the 750s. The Pulguk-sa is a temple of a most unusual design, being built upon a series of terraces, access to which is gained by passing over several stone bridges and stairs. The Buddha's Land referred to in the name of this great temple must be the Western Paradise of Amitābha, an indication that the precinct of the temple was meant to be a symbol of that spiritual realm. The physical passage into the precinct of the temple over an elaborate system of bridges must also have been meant to symbolize the passage into the Western Paradise. The sophistication of the construction techniques of the various terraces and the arched bridges of the Pulguk-sa has not been surpassed by any other temple in Korea.

The *Samguk yusa* recounts the story that Prime Minister Kim Taesŏng was widely believed to be the reincarnation of a pious farm boy who had lived in a village near Kyŏngju. The tale goes on to say that the Pulguk-sa temple was built as a great mortuary temple for the repose of the souls of his parents in both his previous and his current existences. This story draws our attention to the fact that the sending-off and propitiation of the souls of the dead were important concerns for the aristocracy during the Unified Silla period. The reader will recall that from the sixth century onwards rites were established which were meant to propitiate the souls of the deceased, such as the rites for Ich'adon, or the *P'algwan-hoe* ceremony for slain warriors. The designation of the Pulguk-sa as a mortuary temple was a continuation of the tradition of soul-propitiation which was deeply rooted in Korean shamanism. As we have seen, the name of the temple, the Temple of the Buddha's Land, implies that not only was the temple dedicated to Amitābha, ruler of the Western Paradise, but that the temple precinct was meant to be a symbolic representation of the Western Paradise itself. Prime Minister Kim must have entertained the pious hope that his several parents would be reborn to spend an eternity in the Abode of the Blessed as represented by this grand temple. The erection of the great Pulguk-sa is an indication of the strength of the Pure Land cult in the mid-eighth century and of the support which that cult found even in the highest circles of society.

The Sŏkkur-am, also created at the order of Kim Taesŏng, is one of the greatest artistic and engineering marvels of East Asia. Although presently subordinate to the Pulguk-sa, this grotto was originally built as a separate temple. Situated high on T'oham-san overlooking the East Sea (Sea of Japan), the Sŏkkur-am was constructed for the purpose of protecting the nation from invasion by sea. It is a completely artificial grotto, constructed in three separate sections: an entrance chamber, a connecting corridor, and the grotto itself. It is neither a natural cave reused nor a cave carved out of the living rock. It is a man-made, domed grotto covered over with earth to simulate a natural grotto and to the author's knowledge is unique in East Asia.

As an example of the calibre of engineering in Unified Silla times, the grotto demonstrates a very sophisticated technical knowledge. Measurements based on the T'ang *ch'ih* (0.3581 m.) show that the principal chamber is perfect in every proportion, and that the various dimensions are multiples of each other. In short, the grotto is a mathematical representation of a perfect universe. The sculpture decorating the three chambers shows a progression from a profane world through to a pure, perfect universe. The passage by the pilgrim through these three chambers has the same meaning as the passage over the bridges of the Pulguk-sa into the pure world of the temple precinct.

The outer chamber of the grotto contains a series of eight guardian figures on the north and south walls, with two muscular guardian figures or *vajrapāni* flanking the entrance to the connecting corridor. This second chamber has sculptures of the superior guardian figures, the Four Heavenly Kings, carved on the walls. The transition is completed with the passage into the innermost chamber by passing beneath an archway which is strikingly like the gates around the great *dagoba* at Sanchi in India. The sculptures of the grotto proper are of four types: the Indian gods Brahmā and Indra immediately flanking the inner entrance; then the Bodhisattvas Mañjuśrī and Ksitigarba, followed by sculptures of the ten chief disciples of the historic Buddha; and finally at the far back an exquisite sculpture of Ekādaśamukha, the eleven-headed Avalokiteśvara. In the centre of this perfect universe sits a Buddha figure of incomparable grace. Most Korean scholars believe this statue to be a representation of Amitābha sitting in the Western Paradise. However, it is possible to interpret this grotto as being a great *mandala* of immense power in the centre of which sits Vairocana, the Great Sun and Supreme Buddha, which is the view held by the author. Ekādaśamukha, Mañjuśrī, Ksitigarbha, and Vairocana are all major figures in the esoteric cults of Buddhism. Such an interpretation would be consistent with the use of temples, such as the Sach'ŏnwang-sa, as divine protectors of the nation. The appropriation of esoteric Buddhism for use in buildings of such artistic merit and sophistication in engineering techniques shows the degree to which Buddhism and the primal religion of Korea had become mixed. Esoteric Buddhism was acceptable at the very highest level of society.

3. The Emergence of the Ch'an Tradition

(a) The Ku-san: The New Orthodoxy

With the social and economic decline which overtook Silla in the ninth century, the growth and importance of the doctrinal schools declined. In an age when people began to question the certainties of a prior age, Ch'an Buddhism began to have an increased appeal. The period of the florescence of the Ch'an tradition in Silla was precisely the time when the political and social scene looked bleakest. This tradition in Silla was known as *Sŏn*, and we shall refer to it afterwards by that name when speaking of the meditational sects of Buddhism in Korea.

The growth of Ch'an Buddhism dates to the arrival of the Indian or Serindian monk Bodhidharma (c.470–543) in China in the early part of the sixth century. A dispute arose in the eighth century over the identity of the sixth patriarch of the school, which led to a split into Northern and Southern Schools of Ch'an. The Southern School, which emphasized the instantaneous and complete nature of enlightenment, became dominant in China. This school in turn broke up into two competing lines. One, the Lin-chi School, stressed the use of shock techniques to induce enlightenment, while the second, the Ts'ao-tung School, emphasized silent introspection under the guidance of a master. Ch'an stressed spontaneity of action, meditation, and the rejection of doctrine and scripture. This individualistic, spontaneous approach to religion was more in line with the temper of society in the late Unified Silla period than were the speculative philosophies taught by the *O-gyo*. Consequently, at the same time that Sŏn became important in Silla, the *O-gyo* entered into a state of decline from which they have never recovered. Esoteric Buddhism and the folk Buddhist tradition were not affected, however.

The roots of Sŏn go back to the reign of Queen Sŏndŏk of Silla in the mid-seventh century (see Fig. 8). Pŏmnang, the first monk known to have gone to

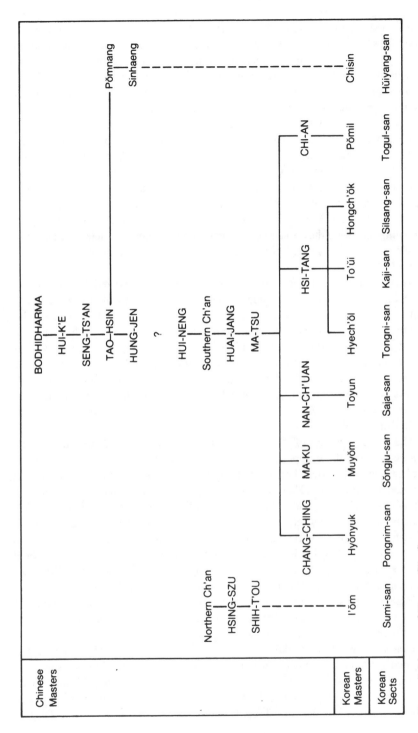

Figure 8 Lineage of Korean Sŏn Sects

T'ang to study the precepts of Ch'an studied under the fourth patriarch of the order, Tao-hsin (580–651). Pŏmnang returned home and settled in at Koho-san (or Hogo-san). His disciple, Sinhaeng, studied at Koho-san for three years and then went on to T'ang to study with the Chinese adept Chih-k'ung. Sinhaeng returned to Silla and set up monastic life at the Tansok-sa, where he died in 779. As Pŏmnang and Sinhaeng learned the doctrines and practices of the Ch'an school prior to the split into the Northern and Southern Schools, the roots of Silla Sŏn Buddhism may be traced back to the earliest form of the Ch'an tradition.

The first monk known to have brought the concepts of the Southern School to Silla was To'ŭi. He went to T'ang in 784, first staying at the K'ai-yüan Temple in Hung-chou, then going on to study with the monk Huai-hai at Pê-chang Shan. Upon returning to Silla in 821, he set up monastic life at the Chinjŏn-sa in Sŏrak-san. He died in 844. None of these three monks, however, had much of a following, nor were they able to establish schools to continue their practices. The development of formalized orders of Sŏn Buddhism was a phenomenon of the ninth century.

There were nine schools of Sŏn Buddhism which existed by the end of the Silla period. They were called the *ku-san* or Nine Mountains, each school taking its name from the mountain on which its central temple was situated. This practice reflected the Sŏn emphasis on removing oneself from the centre of social activity, on retreating from society. Each of these schools, although indigenous and based on the teaching and practice of a Silla monk, was rooted in the teachings of various of the popular masters of late T'ang times. The importance of these schools lies not in their individual establishments but in the fact that from this time on Sŏn Buddhism became the orthodox form of monastic Buddhism in Korea.

The nine schools of Sŏn Buddhism were established in fairly rapid succession, and there appears to have been little differentiation between them in their form or practice. The first to become established was the Silsang-san sect founded by Hongch'ŏk. He went out to T'ang sometime during the reign of King Hŏndŏk (r. 809–26) and returned during the first year of King Hŭngdŏk (r. 826–36). During his stay in China, Hongch'ŏk studied with the eminent monk Hsi-tang. The Tongni sect was founded by Hyech'ŏl, who went to T'ang in 814 and returned in 839. He had also been a student of Hsi-tang. The third school was the Kaji-san sect, founded by Ch'ejing. He went to T'ang in 837, but returned in three years time because he thought that he had no more to learn in China. Ch'ejing's Sŏn master was Yŏmgŏ, a disciple of To'ŭi who had received his training from Hsi-tang. Thus three of the nine sects in one way or another owed their origin to the teaching of Hsi-tang.

One of the most influential Sŏn teachers of this period was Muyŏm, who was originally a member of the *Hwaŏm-jong*. He went out to China to study the doctrines of that sect, but became convinced that he should study Ch'an instead. His teacher was Ma-ku, one of the key figures of T'ang Buddhism. Muyŏm was held in great esteem by the Chinese, who gave him the title of *Tung-fang Ta*

P'u-sa or the Great Bodhisattva from the East. Upon his return to Silla, he organized the Sŏngju-san sect.

Pŏmil left Silla in 831 and studied under the T'ang masters Ch'i-an and Wei-yen. During the persecution of Buddhism under the Emperor Wu-tsung he was forced to leave T'ang, and he returned to Silla in 846 or 847. Pŏmil was supposed to have taught for some forty years after his return from T'ang. The school he founded was known as the Togul-san sect. The sixth order of Sŏn Buddhism to be founded was the Saja-san order. Its founder Toyun studied in T'ang under Nan-ch'uan, but like Pŏmil he was forced to leave his master and come home in 847. His principal student was Chŏlchung, who eventually settled at Saja-san, from which mountain the order took its name. The Pongnim-san sect was based on the teaching of the monk Hyŏnuk (787–870), who went out to T'ang in 824 and returned in 837. During his sojourn he studied with the monk Chang-ching. Hyŏnuk established himself at Silsang-sa where he gathered many disciples around him. Hyŏnuk's principal disciple was Simhŭi, who, in order to avoid being called to the dissolute court of Queen Chindŏk (r. 887–97), fled to a wild and remote area. He finally settled at Pongnim-san near Kimhae where he established the order which was founded on the doctrines of his master Hyŏnuk.

All of the orders mentioned above can trace their origins back to the teachings of one of the disciples of the great Southern Ch'an master, Ma-tsu. The two remaining sects, however, had a very different origin. The Huiyang-san order traced its roots to Pŏmnang and Sinhaeng, the first Korean monks to bring the Ch'an philosophy to Silla. The monk Chisŏn claimed direct descent from these two monks, and gathered monks around him on Hyŏn'gye-san. His disciple Ch'imch'ung later moved the school to Huiyang-san, from which the sect took its name. The claim to descent from the earliest practising Sŏn monks evinces a certain element of nationalism, an attempt to show a more authentic Sillan ancestry. In examining the lives of monks from earlier periods, we have already noticed this trend, as when Wŏnhyo felt that he could learn nothing from T'ang masters which he did not know already.

The last of the Sŏn orders to be founded was the Sumi-san sect. The date of its foundation is so late that it is better, perhaps, to think of it as an early Koryŏ sect, rather than as a Silla sect. The Sumi-san sect drew on traditions which were different from those of the other orders, including the Huiyang-san sect mentioned above. The Huiyang-san sect claimed a connection, through Pŏmnang, with the Ch'an tradition prior to the split into Northern and Southern Schools. The Sumi-san sect, on the other hand, claimed descent from the Northern School of Ch'an, the only Korean Sŏn sect to do so. The order was founded by I'ŏm, who was born in 870 and travelled to T'ang in 894 to study Ch'an. He returned to Korea in 911 shortly after the collapse of T'ang. Initially, I'ŏm established himself in the Sŭnggwang-sa in Naju, in the state of Later Paekche. It was a sign of the times that in 934 he accepted the invitation of the founder of Later Koguryŏ to resettle in his territory. I'ŏm brought his disciples to Sumi-san near Kaegyŏng, the capital of the incipient state. His decision to relocate his disciples in an area close to the new capital reflects the rise and fall of the political stars of the various incipient states during that turbulent period. His move also hints at the future importance which Buddhism was to hold throughout the Koryŏ period.

We may sum up our discussion of Sŏn Buddhism in Silla by observing first, that there were three different streams of meditative monasticism, an indication of the complexity and sophistication of Silla Buddhism in its final phase. These three streams were the Ch'an tradition prior to the split into Northern and Southern Schools, and the traditions of these two later forms of Ch'an. Second, the tradition of the Southern Ch'an schools of T'ang dominated the Sŏn Buddhism of Silla, especially the practices of the disciples of Ma-tsu. Among these disciples, Hsi-tang seems to have been the most important in the formation of ninth-century Korean Sŏn traditions. This is interesting, because in the T'ang Empire itself Nan-ch'uan was by far the most prominent of Ma-tsu's disciples. Third, as with Ch'an Buddhism in T'ang, the rise of Sŏn was directly related to the political and social crises characteristic of the final phase of the T'ang world-order. In an epoch when traditional values were crumbling, old certainties disappearing, and the whole social and political order coming unhinged, it is no wonder that thoughtful men turned to a quietistic, meditative form of religion which put one beyond the hurly-burly of the times.

(b) Esoteric Buddhism

The reader must not be left with the impression that Sŏn was the only form of Buddhism current in late Silla times. Certainly, it was the most prominent form of Buddhism amongst the intelligentsia. However, the stream of esoteric Buddhism continued to flow unimpeded as it had in all previous periods. In fact, it might be argued that at this time some of these cults offered a compelling alternative to the other religious traditions.

Tosŏn (827–98), perhaps the last great monk of Silla, is an example of a monk learned in Buddhist philosophy who also studied deeply in esoteric subjects. We have seen this tradition as far back as Chajang and Myŏngnang in the seventh century. At the age of 15, Tosŏn left his family to enter the monastic life. By the time he was 19, he was said to be so full of wisdom and had had so many mysterious events attributed to him that he was worshipped by many as a god. Throughout his life, he travelled to various temples to study and meditate, without making any one temple a permanent home. His teaching emphasized such contradictory-sounding concepts as 'the explanation without explanation' (musŏl-sŏl) and 'the law without law' (mubŏp-pŏp). Tosŏn, however, is best known for his writings on geomancy, fortune-telling, and prognostication. He is said to have possessed great magical powers, and there are many stories told about him which are associated with the Tosŏn-sa temple in Sŏul. The grand sculpture behind the temple is said to have been the result of his magic.

Significantly, modern fortune-tellers look to him as the patriarch of their tradition in Korea.

The monk Wŏnp'yo (9th cent.) set out for T'ang in 841, just at the start of the persecution of Buddhism under the Emperor Wu-tsung. He was only able to stay in T'ang until 846, and then went on to India, where he toured the sacred sites before returning to T'ang. On his return journey, he had a vision of the *Simwang* (Ruler of the Mind) or *Tae-il yŏrae* (the Great Sun), which is a guise of Vairocana. This Dhyāni Buddha is a major figure in a long-established esoteric cult of Silla. Wŏnp'yo's vision of this figure is one more indication of the continuation of the shamanistic influence on Buddhism in Silla. Wŏnp'yo was not only the last important esoteric figure of Silla, he is also the last Korean monk who is known to have made the journey to India. These two facts are related, as we saw in the case of Hyech'o who went to India in search of a deeper knowledge of esoteric Buddhism. The cessation of pilgrimages to India in this period is related to the decline of Buddhism in its homeland at this time. Although doctrinal Buddhism seemed to rise and fall in importance, esoteric Buddhism and the search for truth in the holy land remained characteristic of Silla to the end.

(c) General Remarks on Early Korean Buddhism

The Buddhism of the Three Kingdoms Period and the Unified Silla Period must be seen as an extended process of the acceptance and adaptation of this foreign religion to Korean soil. In the first stage of contact we have seen how Buddhism was first brought to the Three Kingdoms by missionaries who were usually foreign propagandists of the faith rather than Koreans who had become converts to Buddhism in China. In this way, Buddhism first gained acceptance in the Korean states as a cult of the royal court. In the case of Koguryŏ and Paekche, early royal patronage and establishment as the national religion led to the widespread dissemination of Buddhism. Even in the case of Silla, once opposition to the introduction of Buddhism was overcome, the stage was set for the dramatic growth of the new religion. Internal growth was also clearly co-ordinated with attempts to spread Buddhism elsewhere, as is indicated by the involvement of all three states with the missionary movement in Japan. At an early stage the Three Kingdoms showed a sophisticated awareness of intellectual trends in China and in India. Direct contact was made with these centres of Buddhism by student-pilgrims who went there to enrich their knowledge of their religion.

Perhaps because the records are better for Silla, it would seem that the trend towards the mixing of Buddhism with Korean primal religion was strongest there. This is reflected in personal names, royal titles, geographical names, festivals and rituals, and in the art and architecture of the time. Even in some of the most sophisticated aspects of the culture, a unique blend of Buddhism and the primal religion may be noted. The development of esoteric Buddhist groups is especially characteristic of mid- and late Silla times. The growth of the doctrinal and Sŏn traditions of Buddhism followed intellectual and social trends in China, but such growth in Silla was never subordinated to those trends. The doctrinal schools, or *O-gyo* collectively, all had their roots one way or another in China, but the most popular schools there were not the most popular in Silla. Furthermore, those orders which were popular in Silla can be shown to have had some characteristics parallel to those of the primal religion. The growth of Sŏn Buddhism was a reflection of the decaying state of society and the development of an inward-looking individualism. From this period on, the dominant form of monastic Buddhism in Korea became the Sŏn tradition.

4. Late Silla Confucianism

We have noted that there were elements in the folk philosophy of the ancient Koreans which bore certain resemblances to Confucian thought. We have also seen how from the late fourth to the seventh century Confucian thought influenced Korean education and letters. In surveying these trends, we noted that a clearly defined tradition of Confucian philosophy had not yet developed. The roots of this tradition may be found in the late Silla period, beginning significantly enough after the successful conclusion of the wars for peninsular unification. In the year 682, King Sinmun (r. 681–91) of Silla established for the first time a national academy, the Kukhak, which was, in effect, to assume the function of the Hwarang Troop in the education of the aristocratic youth of the nation.

The Kukhak academy had a precise course of study extending over a period of nine years which led to examinations in one of three fields of study. It was open to the son of any aristocrat regardless of grade who was between the ages of 15 and 30. The course of study prescribed for the highest level of examination included study of the Book of Rites (*Li-ki* in Chinese, *Ye-gi* in Korean), the Book of Filial Piety (*Hsiao-ching* in Chinese, *Hyo-gyŏng* in Korean), the Analects (*Lun-yü* in Chinese, *Nonŏ* in Korean), and the Book of Changes (*I-ching* in Chinese, *Yŏk-kyŏng* in Korean). The works prescribed for the second-level examination were the *Tso Ch'uan* (*Chwa-jŏn* in Korean), the *Shih Ch'uan* (*Si-jŏn* in Korean), the Analects, and the Book of Filial Piety. Those required for the third-level examination were the *Shu Ching* (Book of History, *Sŏ-gyŏng* in Korean), the Analects, and the Book of Filial Piety. The Book of Rites, the Book of Filial Piety, the Analects, the Book of History, and the Book of Changes are all constituent parts of the canon of Confucianism. The *Tso Ch'uan* is a commentary on the *Ch'un-ch'iu* (Spring and Autumn Annals) and attributed to the philosopher Tso Ch'iu-ming (or Tso-ch'iu Ming, 4th–3rd cent. BC). The *Shih Ch'uan* is a commentary on another canonical work, the Book of Odes (*Shih-ching* in Chinese, *Si-gyŏng* in Korean), which was composed by the philosopher Mao Hêng (3rd–2nd cent. BC).

It will be seen that the common element in the system of education was the study of the Book of Filial Piety and the Analects of Confucius. At this period, the core of Confucian learning was seen as knowledge of the stories told about and the aphorisms of Confucius, and the practice of filial piety. The results obtained by the candidate in the examinations determined the level of placement within the civil service to which the examinee was entitled. Unlike previous eras, by late Silla times an established system of Confucian study had emerged which was linked to the civil service. The effect of Confucian education and philosophy was to raise up a class of literati scholar-bureaucrats which would help to break down the feudalistic nature of late Silla society. It particularly appealed to the scions of the lesser nobility. It was not, however, a democratic system. Unlike the Confucian system implemented in China, people who were not of aristocratic background were denied admission to the Korean civil-service examination.

The system of Confucian education underwent several refinements in the eighth century. The college was renamed T'aehak-kam during the reign of King Kyŏngdŏk (r. 742–64). In 788, during the reign of King Wŏnsŏng (r. 785–98), a new system of examinations was created to bypass some of the problems of factionalism and aristocratic prerogative. This new exam system was the *Sambun-gwa* (Three-part Examination), which granted the same level of pass to the examinee as if he had been a graduate of the T'aehak-kam. Most of the candidates for this exam came from the petty nobility. The exam became a necessity, as the best positions had tended to be reserved for the grand aristocrats. One interesting feature of Confucian education in late Silla times was its link with politics and political reform. One hundred years after the founding of the T'aehak by King Sinmun, there arose a significant bloc of Confucian scholars who objected to the autocratic nature of late Silla government and worked actively to alter it along Confucian lines.

One important development of the eighth century was the establishment of the National Confucian Shrine, the Mun-myo, during the reign of King Sŏngdŏk (r. 702–36), the first time in the history of any Korean state that a national shrine had been erected to the memory of Confucius and his seventy-two chief disciples. The inauguration of rites at this shrine marked the beginning of the official veneration of the spirit of the Sage which was to continue down to the early twentieth century. These national Confucian rites, however, did not replace the national Buddhist rituals, but were held in addition to existing rites.

Perhaps the most important feature of Confucianism in Unified Silla times was the development of a class of Confucian scholars – apart from the examinees for the civil service – who helped to create a tradition of Confucian philosophy and scholarship in Korea. Four men in particular were important in the development of scholastic Confucianism. Kang Su (?–692) was noted for his literary skill, especially in the drafting of diplomatic notes, an important task where style and form were as important as content. From his earliest days, Kang Su studied the Book of Filial Piety and other key Confucian documents. Later he went to T'ang to study, where he won fame for his interpretation and understanding of Confucian philosophy. His expertise in writing formal diplomatic documents was especially useful during the unification period.

The second great figure of the Unified Silla period was Sŏl Ch'ong (7th cent.), son of the Buddhist monk Wŏnhyo and Princess Yosŏk-kung. He is regarded as one of the towering intellectual figures of this period. Called one of the ten great scholars of the Silla period, he is said to have founded the Haedong Kyŏnghak, the first Korean school of Confucian philosophy. He is also thought to have used the Korean syllabic script *hyangch'al* to write poetry. His work, the *Hwawang-gye* (Story of the Flower King), is the first Korean narrative using a parable format. In this tale the peony or king of flowers chooses as a companion a flower which is not showy, indicating a Confucian emphasis on substance rather than appearance.

Kim Taemun (late 7th–8th cent.), the third great figure, was a prolific scholar of King Sŏngdŏk's time who produced five works – none of which have survived. Kim Pusik in the twelfth century knew them and used them in writing the *Samguk sagi*. They were the *Hansan-gi* (Record of Hansan), the *Kosŭng-jŏn* (Lives of Eminent Monks), the *Ak-pon* (Book of Music), the *Hwarang segi* (Tales of the Hwarang), and the *Kyerim chapchŏn* (Tales of Kyerim). The *Hansan-gi* grew out of his appointment as a magistrate of Hansan-ju (modern Kwangju of Kyŏnggi Province near Sŏul) and is one of the earliest pieces of local historiography.

The fourth figure of importance in Unified Silla times was the late ninth- to early tenth-century figure Ch'oe Ch'i-wŏn (857–?). At the age of 12 he was sent to T'ang to study, where he passed the civil-service exam at a high level and was appointed to serve as a magistrate. Later, he served in the Chinese government secretariat. When he returned home, Ch'oe was honoured with the style *Hallim haksa*, the composer of royal proclamations. He eventually retired to the Hae'in-sa temple in the Kaya Mountains. A few of his works survive in part, for example the *Chewang yŏndae-yŏk* (Chronology of Emperors and Kings), and the *Kyewŏn p'ilgyŏng* (Writings from the Cinnamon Gardens). Each of these works gives considerable insight into the thought and life of the time. It was upon the foundation laid by these four men that the Koryŏ Confucianists erected a genuine Korean Confucian tradition. It is important to note that in the early tenth century no overt conflict existed between Confucianism and Buddhism. All that lay in the future.

What were the principal characteristics of Confucianism in the Unified Silla era? Confucianism in this period had few metaphysical interests, inclining rather towards matters of more practical concern. As a system of scholarship, it emphasized the exegesis of the Confucian classical works and looked to preparing students for the civil-service exams and placement in government service. It shared many elements with primal Confucianism, especially its emphasis on ritual and propriety in human relationships. Chief of these human relationships were filial piety to one's parents, and brotherly love to mankind. Late Silla Confucianism was principally a system of ethics with little or no metaphysical underpinning, and was deeply concerned with the creation of a system of good government. In spite of national rituals offered to Confucius and his disciples, it was in no sense a religion as we normally conceive of the term.

Part II

THE KORYŎ DYNASTY

5

THE EARLY KORYŎ PERIOD
(935–1200)

1. The Historical Background

With the founding of the Koryŏ Dynasty in the first third of the tenth century, Korean history entered a new phase. The accumulated social and political trends of the last century and a half burst out to create the framework of a new society, Koryŏ. The start of the new dynasty may be dated to 935, when Silla's last king Kyŏngsun (r. 927–35) surrendered to T'aejo (r. 918–43), founder and first king of the new state. Later Paekche was conquered in 936, and the realm which had been Unified Silla was once again one nation (see Fig. 9).

The rise of Wang Kŏn (877–943), known by his regnal name as T'aejo, was a reflection of the increased strength of the local landholders and the mercantile class in contrast to the decline of the aristocracy. Under King T'aejo the boundaries of the state were secured and expanded. The importance of P'yŏngyang as a strategic centre was re-emphasized with the placement of a major garrison there. Defensive preparations were made against a possible invasion by the Khitan tribes to the north, and plans were laid to seize the northern territories which had belonged to the Kingdom of Koguryŏ. These plans indicate the importance of the former state of Koguryŏ to Koryŏ, which saw itself as the successor of both Koguryŏ and Parhae as well as the successor of Silla. This attitude resulted in a northward emphasis in foreign policy. Upon T'aejo's death in 943, the king left a testament, the *Hunyo sipcho* (Ten Injunctions), in which he set out ten guide-lines for his successors. These guide-lines reflected both the king's Buddhist piety and his shrewd understanding of politics and human nature.

The years immediately following the death of the founding king were consumed in a bloody rivalry for the succession to the throne. King Kwangjong (r. 949–75) ruthlessly suppressed the opposition and simultaneously set in motion a reformation of the government which limited aristocratic power and strengthened the authority of the monarch. Kwangjong also freed the slaves, which had the effect of both undermining the power of the aristocrats and vastly increasing the tax revenues of the government.

The institution of a Confucian-style examination system in 958 was linked to the reorganization and centralization of the government. Rank was indicated by

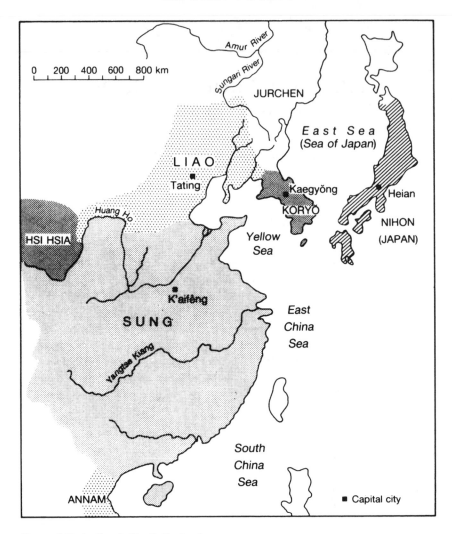

Figure 9 Early Koryŏ (Tenth Century)

type and colour of clothing. The process of the centralization of the government administration, initiated by King Kyŏngjong (r. 975–81), was taken further under his successor King Sŏngjong (r. 981–97) with the advice of the eminent scholar Ch'oe Sŭngno (927–89), and was completed under the reign of King Munjong (r. 1046–83). By the end of the tenth century, the political, social, and geographical basis of the state of Koryŏ had been created, upon which foundation a great Buddhist civilization was to be erected.

In the eleventh century, Koryŏ found itself confronted by the rising power of non-Chinese tribal peoples, in particular the Khitan. The Khitan attacked Koryŏ in 993, with the result that diplomatic relations were established in the following year with the Khitan state of Liao (907–1125) and were simultaneously suspended with the Chinese Northern Sung Empire (960–1127). This gave Koryŏ a chance to remove the Jurchen tribes from its border areas and to establish itself as far north as the Yalu River. However, Liao attacked Koryŏ in 1010, reaching as far south as P'yŏngyang, and attacked again in 1018, when the Koryŏ capital of Kaegyŏng was sacked, with the destruction of the royal palace, the library attached to it, and the national Confucian shrine. Because the last venture turned out to be a military disaster for Liao in spite of the wound it had inflicted upon Koryŏ, the two states re-established diplomatic ties. This event removed the threat of invasion from Liao, at least. None the less, the threat of invasion remained uppermost in the minds of the leaders of Koryŏ. In 1029 an outer fortification was placed around the ruined capital of Kaegyŏng, and a great stone wall was built in 1044 from the mouth of the Yalu River to Kwangp'o on the East Sea. Peace having once been established, the Koryŏ state entered into a period of prosperity.

Throughout the first two hundred years of the new state, two important social developments occurred: the emergence of a new aristocratic class, and the development of international trade. Before the establishment of the Koryŏ kingdom, the Bone Rank system of Silla had virtually disappeared, even though there had been various attempts to revive it. With the establishment of Koryŏ, the foundations of the Korean state were changed. A class of merit subjects – members of families who had been influential in the creation of the Koryŏ state – was created, which became the basis of the new aristocracy. Merit subjects were granted many privileges, including gifts of land and exemptions from certain taxes and levies. This class came to be called *yangban*, and that is the word used in Korea since then to designate the upper class. This class used its special privileges to amass even larger amounts of land and to consolidate its power in society, which in turn became a threat to the central government.

International trade at this time was most often carried out as part of diplomatic missions to the various neighbouring courts. That is, Koryŏ diplomatic envoys would have large retinues which included, in addition to diplomats bearing gifts, merchants who came to sell their wares and goods. Trading was conducted with all the nearby states, the Sung Empire, Liao, Japan, the Jurchen tribes, and even with the Arabs. This trade was for the most part in hard-to-obtain or luxury goods. The Arabs, for example, traded perfumes, dyes, and drugs for Korean silk and gold. Kaegyŏng, as the capital, naturally became the centre of this trade. There were several markets located within its boundaries, in addition to which there were important markets in the provincial centres.

The twelfth century saw the occurrence of numerous local rebellions against the central authority and a restiveness amongst the military which resulted in a *coup d'état* and effective rule of the kingdom by the military for nearly a century. These insurrections were directly related to the over-concentration of wealth in the capital and the opulent style of life of the aristocracy. During the reign of King Injong (r. 1122–46), the authority of the central government was challenged twice in attempts to overthrow the royal government. Following the suppression of the first attempt, the king came under the spell of a mysterious monk Myoch'ŏng (?–1135). The latter had devised a syncretic religion based on Buddhism, and suggested to the king that he should move the capital to the geomantically more secure city of P'yŏngyang, declare himself emperor, and fight against the rising power of the Jurchen Chin Empire (1115–1234). The king eventually did none of these things, which led Myoch'ŏng to declare the establishment of a new state. The rebellion, which took a whole year to suppress, was put down under the direction of Kim Pusik (1075–1151), the author of the *Samguk sagi* (History of the Three Kingdoms). The suppression of this second rebellion led to a generation of peace, during which time many important works of a cultural nature were completed, including the *Samguk sagi*, the most important early historical record of the Three Kingdoms Period. The peaceful appearance of these times, however, was misleading, as it was only a respite in the struggle for control of the central government.

In 1170, as a result of the injudicious treatment of the military, a royal escort slaughtered members of a royal entourage and took King Ŭijong (r. 1146–70) prisoner. Eventually he was deposed in favour of his brother, who became King Myŏngjong (r. 1170–97). This monarch presided over one of the saddest periods of Korean history. The military once having seized effective power then fought amongst themselves. Civilian officials were purged; military leaders were created, deposed, and new ones installed in their place. During this same time, the turmoil at the centre gave rise to rebellions and uprisings in the countryside which were utilized by one faction or another. Then in 1196, Ch'oe Ch'unghŏn (1149–1219) removed the most recent leader of the military government in what seemed to be a continuation of a generation of internal squabbling and fighting. However, the deposition of the military leader and the assumption of power by Ch'oe Ch'unghŏn ushered in an era of surprising stability.

Ironically, the troubled twelfth century was a period of cultural florescence. The development of printing and the growth of a literary tradition went hand in hand. By the mid-twelfth century the use of metal type was common, due to the need to replace lost copies of documents in quantity. Knowledge of sophisticated metal-casting techniques was based on technology known since Silla times. Printing in turn permitted the widespread dissemination of literature of all sorts. Vernacular poetry called *changga*, poetic drama, Confucian literature, historical writing, and music all flourished in this century. The intelligentsia of this time emerged as a unique Confucian class of literati with its own characteristic literature called *Hanmun-hak*. The rise of this class is some indication of the growth of Confucianism in the Koryŏ state as opposed to Buddhism. Buddhism's influence, whilst still strong though not predominant, began to decline from this period, while the influence of Confucianism waxed stronger. The two most important literary figures of the twelfth century were Confucianists, Kim Pusik and Yi Kyubo (1168–1241). Kim Pusik patterned his *Samguk sagi* after the

82

historigraphical treatise entitled the *Shih-chi* (Historical Record) by Ssu-Ma Ch'ien (145–93 BC). The classical music of this period derived from the ceremonial music of the Sung court, and was used in Koryŏ for the performance of Confucian rituals and ceremonies. In one form or another it has descended to modern Korea, where it is known as *A-ak*.

2. Early Koryŏ Buddhism

(a) The Tenth Century

The victory of Koryŏ over Silla and Later Paekche not only led to the creation of a new state, but also to the establishment of Buddhism. Before total assumption of authority throughout the Korean peninsula, T'aejo had assiduously cultivated Buddhist monks such as I'ŏm, founder of the Sumi-san order. Upon his deathbed, the founding king issued the *Hunyo sipcho* (Ten Injuctions) for the guidance of his successors. The first of the ten articles of this testament states that Buddhism and Buddhist places of worship should be maintained and protected. These words stressed the importance of the Buddhist faith for the life of the state, and are a continuation of the *hoguk sasang* (Ideology for the Protection of the Nation) which was typical of the Silla period. The second testamentary note would seem to contradict the first, as T'aejo advised his successors not to build any more temples. This, however, was only political acumen on the king's part. In spite of the king's piety, he knew that a wealthy church capable of interfering in state affairs would bring destruction upon the nation. In the sixth testamentary note the king advised his successors to neither add to nor subtract from the principal Buddhist ceremonies, the *Yŏndŭng-hoe* and the *P'algwan-hoe*. This request also was a shrewd warning against the development of an opulent, self-satisfied Buddhist church. With the encouragement of the founding monarch, succeeding generations of monarchs nurtured the association of the Buddhist church with the government and stimulated the growth of Buddhism as a key institution in Koryŏ society.

Shortly after the creation of the state civil-service examination based on the Confucian classics in 958, King Kwangjong ordered the creation of a parallel set of state examinations for Buddhist priests, the *sŭnggwa*. In part this may be seen as an attempt to control the Buddhist church, but its ostensible purpose was to create an institutional link between the central government and the church. There was a separate series of examinations for both the Kyo (doctrinal) and Sŏn (meditation) sects. Candidates proceeded through a series of six examinations and ranks, which culminated in the top ranks *sŭngt'ong* and *tae sŏnsa* for the doctrinal and Sŏn sects respectively. Members of the top ranks could be appointed as teachers to the state and were accorded a higher social rank than their Confucian counterparts.

The king could make two special appointments to a type of super-grade, the *kuksa* and the *wangsa*. The former, meaning 'teacher to the nation', was a distinction intended to honour monks of unusual ability. *Wangsa*, meaning 'teacher to the king', was an important political post, as this figure had the privilege of lecturing the king. The institutionalized connection between church and state laid the seeds for a long-standing war of attrition between the Buddhists and the proponents of Confucian government. In the very early part of the Koryŏ Dynasty, however, the statement of the Confucian scholar Ch'oe Sŭngno (927–89) was true that Buddhism was for spiritual education and that Confucianism was for the practice of government. Initially no inherent contradiction between the two traditions was felt to exist. To the contrary, there was felt to be complementarity between them as they dealt with different spheres of life.

Another important feature of Koryŏ Buddhism was the attempt made to unify the various Buddhist orders into a single sect. King Kwangjong, having once established order in the political sphere, wished to do the same with the various squabbling and bickering orders of the Buddhist church. This attempt was related, of course, to the movement for institutionalizing the relation of church and state. King Kwangjong thought that unity could be achieved through a union of the doctrinal and Sŏn sects in the *Ch'ŏnt'ae-jong*. However, not even royal authority was strong enough to make the monks come together, and this first movement for union died without any success.

During the reign of King Kwangjong, the Ch'ŏnt'ae School and its doctrines achieved an intellectual prestige which they had never had during the Silla period. Two monks, Ch'egwan (?–970) and Ŭit'ong (927–88), were key figures in the revived Ch'ŏnt'ae movement. Ch'egwan's story is instructive because it illustrates the prestige of early Koryŏ Buddhism. When an important Chinese official was unable to interpret a passage in a Buddhist text, he requested the Chinese T'ien-t'ai monks to interpret it for him. The official was told that the phrase in question came from a book which had been lost in China during the turmoil of the Five Dynasties Period (907–60), but that it survived in Koryŏ. Consequently, the official sent an emissary and some fifty monks to Koryŏ to learn if the book did in fact exist there and to have the Koryŏ monks interpret the passage of scripture for him. King Kwangjong instructed the monk Ch'egwan to go to Sung with various scriptures. Ch'egwan did so and wrote a short book of one *chüan* called the *Ch'ŏnt'ae sagyo-ŭi* (Four Doctrines of the T'ien-t'ai Sect). Ch'egwan spent ten years in China working to revive the T'ien-t'ai School and died there without returning to his homeland.

At the same time that Ch'egwan was in China, Ŭit'ong was there studying under various masters. Recognized as a superior monk, Ŭit'ong was elected the thirteenth (or sixteenth according to another reckoning) patriarch of the T'ien-t'ai School. The effect which both of these Koryŏ scholars had on the world of Chinese Buddhism demonstrates that Koryŏ held an unparalleled position of eminence in the realm of Buddhist thought. Kyunyŏ (723-73) was another early Koryŏ monk/scholar who was concerned with the unification of the different Buddhist schools. From 958, he was the supervisor of the *sŭnggwa* or state

Buddhist examinations through which post he was able to spread his views to both the meditational and doctrinal sects. He was an important scriptural commentator and was noted for his *hyangga* poetry. These writings were collected by his disciples in a work known by its abbreviated title as the *Kyunyŏ-jŏn* (Works of Kyunyŏ). Hyegŏ (?–974), another eminent monk of Kwangjong's reign, was simultaneously appointed as the first *kuksa* and as the first *wangsa*, a recognition both of his scholarship and of his political importance.

(b) The Eleventh Century

During the eleventh century, there emerged a class of aristocratic literati monks, the greatest of whom was Ŭich'ŏn (1055–1101). He was the fourth son of King Munjong (r. 1046–83). The influence of this monk, also known as *Taegak kuksa*, was augmented by the fact that he was a royal, and that his three elder brothers ruled in succession during his lifetime. At the age of 11, Ŭich'ŏn became a monk under the tutelage of the *wangsa*, and proceeded with the course of study for the Buddhist state examinations, passing the top level, *sŭngt'ong*, at the age of 15. In 1085 Ŭich'ŏn went to Sung to study, where during a year's sojourn he became conversant with most of the various Buddhist schools at the time, including Ch'an. In the end, he studied with the T'ien-t'ai School and felt that their interpretation was the correct approach to Buddhist faith and practice. In 1086 he returned to Koryŏ and established himself at the great Hŭngwang-sa temple in the capital. Whilst there, he became the director of the temple library and proceeded to amass a collection of Buddhist works from Sung, Liao, and Japan amounting to some 4,740 volumes. From the Hŭngwang-sa, Ŭich'ŏn eventually went to the Kukch'ŏng-sa, where he used his royal prerogatives to create a movement for the unification of Korean Buddhism under the *Ch'ŏnt'ae-jong*. In addition to this movement, Ŭich'ŏn was also involved with the dissemination of Buddhist literature. He caused the books which he had collected for the Hŭngwang-sa to be printed on wooden blocks and distributed widely. Ŭich'ŏn died at the age of 46 in 1101.

Ŭich'ŏn is interesting to us because he was the second member of the royal family to attempt to unify the various Buddhist sects under the banner of the T'ien-t'ai doctrines. The T'ien-t'ai School with its balanced emphasis on meditation and doctrinal study must have seemed a simple and natural means to unify the Buddhist church. The prestige of Ŭich'ŏn and the appeal of his movement did have a great effect on the structure of the Buddhism of his time. He was very influential in drawing many monks out of their own order and into his revitalized *Ch'ŏnt'ae-jong*. He drew especially heavily on the membership of the *Hwaŏm-jong* and the various Sŏn sects. At one point, in fact, it seemed as if he might become the head of the *Hwaŏm-jong*. The net result of his efforts, however, was to create three sects, the doctrinal, the Sŏn, and the Ch'ŏnt'ae sects. In retaliation for the losses suffered from defections to the *Ch'ŏnt'ae-jong*, the various Sŏn orders came together to form a unified order. The movement for union had only further divided the Buddhist world by the end of the eleventh century.

As we have mentioned, the eleventh century was a period of intellectual and cultural ferment. Buddhist literature also experienced growth during this period. Perhaps the greatest Buddhist literary achievement of this age was the creation of the first of several compilations of Buddhist scriptures made during the Koryŏ period. This first canon is known as the *Ch'ojo changgyŏng* (First Great Canon) or *Koryŏ changgyŏng* (Great Canon of Koryŏ). Started under the reign of King Hyŏnjong (r. 1009–31), the work was completed forty years later during the reign of King Munjong. The work was commissioned initially by King Hyŏnjong as an act of filial piety for the repose of the spirits of his deceased parents. At the time of the Liao invasion of 1010, the king made a further vow that if the nation were spared, he would ensure the completion of the compilation and printing of the Buddhist canon. The total work comprised some 6,000 *chüan*. The plates and text of this collection were placed in a repository in Puin-sa on P'algong-san near Taegu. Unfortunately this important collection was destroyed during the Mongol invasions of the thirteenth century. A portion of a copy of this canon is thought to be preserved at the Nanzen-ji temple in Kyōto, Japan.

The second important compilation of Buddhist scriptures to be made during the eleventh century was by Ŭich'ŏn, who had made a collection of rare works during the reign of King Sukchong (r. 1095–1105) and then caused them to be printed. Said to have numbered 4,740 *chüan*, this collection was seen as an addition to the *Koryŏ changgyŏng* and became known as the *Sok changgyŏng* (Supplement to the Great Canon). It too is believed to have been lost during the Mongol invasions.

(c) The Twelfth Century

Korean Buddhism in the twelfth century was dominated by the thought and work of one man, the monk Chinul (1158–1210). Chinul, also known as *Pojo kuksa*, was the son of Chŏng Kwangu, an official of the Kukhak or royal Confucian academy in the capital Kaegyŏng. Because of a serious childhood illness, Chinul's father vowed to the Buddha that if his son lived, he would be dedicated to the monastic life. The child did survive and joined a monastic community at the age of 7, receiving the precepts of monkhood at the age of 15. He passed the Buddhist examinations for the Sŏn order in 1182, but seems to have been greatly disturbed by the general state of corruption of the Buddhist world at that time. Consequently, Chinul and a few friends entered into a compact to form a *kyŏlsa* or religious society in order to pursue a pure religious life. At this time, it was not possible for Chinul and his friends to act on their convictions, and the matter was postponed.

In the same year, 1182, Chinul left Kaegyŏng and went to Ch'ŏngwŏn-sa in the Chŏlla region, where he had his first spiritual awakening, which confirmed him in the spiritual quest which he had set himself. Leaving Ch'ŏngwŏn-sa in

1185, he went to Pomun-sa in the Kyŏngsang region, where he had a second significant spiritual experience. This second experience convinced him of the ultimate similarity of the aims of meditative practices, *Sŏn*, and doctrinal studies, *Kyo*. These experiences were an outgrowth of his concern over the conflict between the two streams of Koryŏ Buddhism, the Sŏn and the Kyo sects. From then on, Chinul vowed that he would work for the union of these traditions. In the spring of 1188, Chinul moved to another temple, Kŏjo-sa, where he joined one of the original members of the spiritual compact of 1182. In 1190, along with several others, Chinul formed the *kyŏlsa* community of which he had dreamed for many years.

As the community continued to increase in size, Chinul and his associates decided to relocate in 1197. On their way to the new site, they stopped at a hermitage on Chiri-san where Chinul read the comments of the Chinese Ch'an monk Ta-hui Tsung-kao (1089–1163) on the practice of achieving sudden enlightenment. This practice, called *hwadu* (*hua-t'ou* in Chinese), was the method favoured by the Lin-chi order of the Southern Ch'an School. The enlightenment which he gained from reading this commentary became the third significant spiritual experience of Chinul's life. He spent three years at the hermitage on Chiri-san consolidating this experience. In 1200, Chinul went to Kilsang-sa, where he established the community which eventually became known as Songgwang-sa. He spent the remaining ten years of his life developing the community through which he hoped that he could both revitalize Buddhist spiritual life and unify the various orders into a single, co-operating community.

Often credited with the reformation of the corrupt Buddhist church of the twelfth century, Chinul was also an important writer on Buddhist philosophy and monastic practice. Among his most important works are the *Kwŏnsu chŏnghye kyŏlsa-mun* (Encouragement to Practice: The Compact of the Samādhi and Prajñā Community), the *Kye ch'osim hagin-mun* (Admonitions to Beginning Students), the *Susim-gyŏl* (Secrets on Cultivating the Mind), *Chinsim chiksŏl* (Straight Talk on the True Mind), the *Yŏmbul yomun* (Essentials of Pure Land Practice), the *Wŏndon sŏngbul-lon* (Complete and Sudden Attainment of Buddhahood), the *Kanhwa kyŏrŭi-ron* (Resolving Doubts about Observing Hwadu), his major work, the *Pŏpchip pyŏrhaeng-nok chŏryo pyŏngip sagi* (Excerpts from the *Dharma* Collection and Special Practice Record, with Personal Notes). The latter, written in 1209, was a commentary on a work by the fifth Hua-yen patriarch, Kuei-feng (780–841), and contains an extensive discussion by Chinul of the various forms of enlightenment and the types of meditation practice.

(d) Buddhism and Early Koryŏ Culture and Society

Buddhist influence on art and architecture was an important component of early Koryŏ culture. Typical of the art of this time are the elaborately carved stone pagodas which became the orthodox Korean expression of the pagoda-form.

Although many were of comparatively small size, similar to large stone lanterns, this was not true of them all. Especially magnificent is the 50-foot high pagoda of Wŏlchŏng-sa on Odae-san. It has an upturned lotus base, supporting nine elaborately carved tiers with bells at each of the eight points of the octagonal roofs, and it is capped by a six-tier wrought-iron finial. Placed in front of this pagoda is a richly carved human figure in the act of prayer, which some say is the Dhyāni Buddha Bhaisajyaguru (*Yaksa yŏrae* in Korean), the Buddha of healing. The sumptuousness of this pagoda is a vivid reflection of the cultural opulence of the time.

Cast-bronze Buddhist statues continued to be made during this period, and great carved stone figures of Maitreya (*Mirŭk* in Korean) were made, although the latter were crude by comparison with the sophistication of other types of sculpture. Some scholars feel that these great Mirŭk statues are shamanistic in origin, and were re-used or re-carved during the Koryŏ period. If this is true, it is yet one further example of the survival of traditional beliefs and practices in a more sophisticated guise.

Twenty years ago, many elegant Buddhist paintings of the Koryŏ period were discovered in temples in Japan. Previously, virtually all of this art was thought to have been destroyed during the various 'barbarian' invasions, but recent research has confirmed the existence of a substantial number of Koryŏ paintings. Initially labelled as of Chinese origin, internal evidence has indicated that they were of Koryŏ provenance. The most popular figures depicted in these paintings are the Buddha Amitābha and the Bodhisattvas Avalokiteśvara and Maitreya. The paintings of Amitābha are by far the most common, an indication that the Pure Land cult retained its strength and popularity with the laity throughout this period.

There were many Buddhist festivals celebrated during the early Koryŏ period, among which were *Wŏn-il* (First Day [of the New Year]), the *Yŏndŭng-hoe* (Festival of Lotus Lanterns), *Sangsa-il, Ch'op'a-il, Tano, Yudu, Paekchung, Ka'ŭi, Chungyang-jŏl,* and the *P'algwan-hoe.* Not all of these festivals and festive days were strictly Buddhist in origin as some of them were derived from popular culture. However, by this period all these festivals or ceremonies were influenced by Buddhism in one way or another and came to make up part of the Buddhist folk culture of Koryŏ. Particularly important were *Wŏn-il,* which was celebrated on the first day of the first lunar month as a New Year's Day festival; the *Yŏndŭng-hoe,* which was celebrated on the fifteenth day of the same month; *Ch'op'a-il,* on the eighth day of the fourth month; *Paekchung,* celebrated on the fifteenth day of the seventh lunar month; and the *P'algwan-hoe.*

The *Yŏndŭng-hoe* or Festival of Lotus Lanterns, which dated from Silla times, was the first major ceremony offered to Buddha in the New Year. It took its name from the custom of stringing up lotus-shaped lanterns in the temples. *Ch'op'a-il* was the celebration of the birth of the historic Buddha, and was a major urban festival as well an important temple celebration. *Paekchong* was the Buddhist feast for the propitiation of the souls of the dead, which had – and still has today

– shamanistic associations. Called *Manghon-il* (Day of the Dead Soul), it was celebrated on the fifteenth day of the seventh lunar in honour of the mother of the Buddha's chief disciple, Maudgalyāyana. The *P'algwan-hoe*, also a feast for the dead, we have met before in our discussion of Silla customs. It had a variable date of performance, being held in the Koryŏ capital Kaegyŏng on the fifteenth day of the eleventh lunar month, but one month earlier in the western capital P'yŏngyang. It will be seen immediately that many of these feasts had obvious shamanistic functions such as a sacrifice to a superior spirit, in this case Buddha, and various rites to propitiate the souls of the dead, as in *Paekchung* and the *P'algwan-hoe*. Several of the festivals clearly derived from popular religious practices and were related to the changing seasons and times of the year. *Tano* held on the fifth day of the fifth lunar month, *Yudu* held on the fifteenth day of the sixth month, and *Paekchung* were clearly of this type and had special seasonal foods associated with them. These festivals together with the popularity of the Pure Land cult illustrate the continued influence of the basic religious modes of belief typical of Korean primal religion.

One of the most important features of the Buddhist church during this period was the extent to which it developed its own economic system. The Buddhist church was wealthy, far wealthier and more deeply involved in the economy than it had been during its heyday in the Unified Silla period. Contrary to the founding monarch's wishes, numerous temples were built in the Koryŏ period, many of which were opulent, palatial structures rivalling in size the residences of the royal family. The great Hŭngwang-sa in Kaegyŏng, for example, was erected between 1056 and 1068 and enclosed a building area of 2,800 *kan* (= 9,270 sq. m.). The basis of the wealth of the church was its large, tax-free landholdings which were constantly added to throughout the Koryŏ period.

The temple landholdings produced marketable goods which were sold to provide capital for the various projects of the church. In addition to income-earning land, there were two types of capital resources, the *po*, and *changsaeng-go*. The former was a special type of fund, the interest from which was applied towards the financing of Buddhist feasts, for scholarships for monks, or for local relief work. The *changsaeng-go* was capital created from the sale of harvested goods which came from temple-owned land, and which in turn was applied to the maintenance of the Buddhist church.

The labour required for the support of the Buddhist economic system came in two forms, indentured serfs and worker-monks. The former were a category of peasants who had voluntarily donated their land to the church to avoid exploitation by the gentry. In return for their donation, the church gave them security of tenure, and gained valuable produce. Worker-monks – labourers integrated into the monastic system – belonged to temple societies which functioned much like medieval guilds. These labourers were organized into specialized groups dealing with the construction of temple buildings, and the creation of books, sculpture, paintings, and pottery. In addition, there was a class of warrior-monks who acted as a police force to protect the temples, and in times of war as an armed force against invading armies. By the eleventh century, the Buddhist church had become a state within a state, rivalling the functions of the central government. In the end, the church became a danger to the survival of the state and the nation. While apparently at its zenith, the Buddhist church had succumbed to secular ideals and had become corrupt.

3. Early Koryŏ Confucianism

Although Buddhism remained the dominant intellectual and religious force in early Koryŏ, Confucianism continued to increase in importance, especially in its influence upon the apparatus of government. Under King Kwangjong the *kwagŏ* or State Examination was officially instituted in 958. From the time of King Sŏngjong, Confucianism became the accepted philosophy of government, following the thought of Ch'oe Sŭngno. The slogan *Sungyu chu'ŭi* (Honouring Confucianism) became the force behind the resurgence of Confucian studies, which were known as *Kukhak* (National Studies) in Koryŏ. To further the study of Confucian thought King Sŏngjong ordered the creation of a national Confucian college, the Kukhak-kam, and the construction of two libraries to house collections of Confucian works – the first time that such a collection had been undertaken in any Korean state. These libraries were the Pisŏ-wŏn and the Susŏ-wŏn. The former housed certain government documents and Confucian works, while the latter contained historical materials.

The growth of Confucian institutes of learning began in the tenth century and continued throughout the eleventh century. Especially important was the creation of private schools of Confucian learning. Prior to this time, formal Confucian education had been the prerogative of the government. Upon his retirement in 1055, Ch'oe Ch'ung (984–1068), a former prime minister, created the first of the twelve private Confucian academies of Koryŏ. Other retired officials followed suit, and the resultant group of private foundations became known as the Twelve Kyŏngdo. These schools were considered to be very prestigious as their students had a very good pass rate in the *kwagŏ* examination.

The success of the private schools led the government to create official academies called *haktang* in the countryside. During the reign of King Munjong the Sŏjŏk-chŏm, a publishing house, was created to print the Confucian classics. Several measures were taken to reform the curriculum of the national college during the reign of King Yejong (r. 1105–22), particularly with regard to the preparation for undertaking administrative duties. In line with these changes, the title of the college was changed to Kukhak. King Yejong also created a scholarship fund called the *Yanghyŏn-go* to aid needy students during the course of their studies. Yejong was also responsible for the creation of the Pomun-gak (Pavilion of Precious Literature), a research institute for the government. During the reign of Yejong's successor King Injong, the national college was again restructured with the creation of six graded departments. Rural schools or *Hyanghak* were also created during King Injong's reign.

The Hallim-wŏn academy (Forest of Scholars Academy) was another important Confucian institution which directly influenced the conduct of government. Patterned after the Hanlin-yüan academy founded in T'ang China in 725, it was established during the reign of T'aejo, the first king of Koryŏ. Initially called the Yemun-gwan (Hall of Literature), it was renamed the Hallim-wŏn during the reign of King Hyŏnjong in the early eleventh century. In a Confucian system of government, the creation of documents written with appropriate forms of etiquette and the compilation of historical records were important bureaucratic functions. The Hallim-wŏn was charged with the execution of these two tasks. It was necessary that documents sent to China and to other nations should reflect the nature of the Confucian relationship which existed between them. The Hallim-wŏn scholars made certain that in these documents appropriate courtesies were observed. In addition, historical materials were compiled at the academy and scholars were assigned to examine them and to draw from them the appropriate historical and philosophical lessons. The latter function reflects the Confucian emphasis on learning from the past in order to govern the nation in the present. Critical philosophical study of the Confucian classics would also have been undertaken at the academy. Ideally, there were twenty positions in the academy arranged in hierarchical order according to governmental rank. Among the more important posts were the *haksa* (Academy Scholar), *sidok haksa* (Reader), and *sigang haksa* (Lecturer). Although Ch'oe Ch'iwŏn (857–?) of the late Silla period was styled as *Hallim haksa*, this term would appear to have been only an honorary title as the Hallim Academy does not seem to have existed in Korea during that period.

There were numerous Confucian scholars of note in the early Koryŏ period, among whom Hong Kwan (?–1126), Kim Injon (?–1127), Pak Sŭngjung (12th cent.), Kwak Yŏ (1059–1130), Chŏng Chisang (?–1135), and Kim Pusik (1075–1151) were the most significant. Hong Kwan was a noted calligrapher who served as an emissary to the imperial court of the Northern Sung Dynasty, during which service he gained a considerable reputation in China for his elegant brushwork. Hong was killed during the Yi Chagyŏm insurrection of the 1120s. Kim Injon was a scholar of wide interests who specialized in the study of the Analects of Confucius and *Yin-Yang* geomancy. Along with three other scholars, he compiled the *Haedong pirok* (Secret Records of Haedong), one of the earliest Korean works on geomancy. Pak Sŭngjung, who had been associated with Kim Injon in the compilation of the *Haedong pirok*, was a member of the Hallim Academy and specialized in the study of Confucian ritual and propriety. He was sent into internal exile as a result of the Yi Chagyŏm insurrection and died there.

Kwak Yŏ was a typical member of the literati class of the early Koryŏ period. He served in several governmental positions, but eventually retired to a scholar's retreat in his home village. From there he was called to the court of King Yejong, where he served as tutor to the crown prince. Even after he was removed from that position, it was said that the king enjoyed strolling over to Kwak Yŏ's home where the two would while away the evening hours composing poetry.

Chŏng Chisang, a scholar of considerable merit from P'yŏngyang, became involved with the intrigue of the monk Myoch'ŏng. Called by Myoch'ŏng one of the Three Holy Ones (*Samsŏng*), Chŏng urged the removal of the capital to P'yŏngyang and the declaration of the king as an emperor. Chŏng was killed during the suppression of the Myoch'ŏng revolt by Kim Pusik.

Kim Pusik and his two brothers Kim Pu'ŭi (1079–1136) and Kim Puil (1071–1132) were among the most important political figures of the literary class of twelfth-century Koryŏ. Kim Pusik was a member of the prestigious Hallim Academy and was the compiler of two official dynastic records, the *Yejong sillok* (Veritable Records of King Yejong) and the *Injong sillok* (Veritable Records of King Injong). Among other important posts, Kim Pusik was tutor to the crown prince during Injong's reign, giving him the opportunity to instil in the future king the essential concepts of Confucian kingship. As a Confucian, Kim Pusik valued historical records and the lessons to be learned from history. He not only compiled the veritable records of the reigns of two kings, but he also wrote the *Samguk sagi* (History of the Three Kingdoms), the oldest extant treatise on Korean history. In this book Kim Pusik, a descendant of the royal house of Silla, argues against northern expansionism, against the claims to the former territories of Koguryŏ in Manchuria. Fearful of the power of the various barbarian states, Kim Pusik saw such expansionist claims as threatening the survival of Koryŏ. Fear for the survival of the state also explains his ruthless suppression of Myoch'ŏng's rebellion. Kim Pusik may be taken to be a typical example of an early Koryŏ Confucianist – scholar, teacher, government official, and patriot.

Up to the middle of the Koryŏ Dynasty, we may say that Confucianism in Korea was largely an ethical and political philosophy, principally concerned with the governing of the nation. Confucianism also exercised certain cultural influences, encouraging, for instance, the creation of a historical literature. However, at this date the government was not thoroughly Confucian, nor did the Confucianists feel compelled to oppose the other major social force, the Buddhist church. It was the rise of Mongol power – which destroyed the independence of the state – along with the development of a metaphysical Confucianism which altered dramatically the relationship between Confucianism and society, and between Confucianism and Buddhism.

6

THE LATE KORYŎ PERIOD
(1200–1392)

1. The Historical Background

The history of Koryŏ in the latter half of the twelfth and in the thirteenth and fourteenth centuries was dominated by military *coups*, military dictatorship, and finally conquest by the Mongols (see Fig. 10). We have already seen how the peace of the mid-twelfth century was shattered by the military overthrow of the civilian government, and how the military leadership exercised indirect leadership over the royal government through various para-governmental institutions. When Ch'oe Ch'unghŏn seized power from Yi Ŭimin and installed himself as head of the *Chungbang* (Council of Generals), it seemed to be yet another chapter in the history of military *coups* and counter-*coups* which had typified a generation of Koryŏ history. Instead, Ch'oe created a dynasty of military rulers which maintained effective control of Koryŏ until the mid-thirteenth century. Ch'oe Ch'unghŏn had a ten-point programme of reform which he attempted to initiate shortly after assuming control of the *Chungbang*. Among other things, he stressed impartial taxation, return to the peasants of any land illegally confiscated, a prohibition on the construction of more temples, and an attempt to control conspicuous consumption. A *coup* attempt against Ch'oe in 1209 led to the creation of the *Kyojŏng togam* (Directorate of Decree Enactment), an institution which acted to detect hints of *coups* and unrest, and through which Ch'oe actually came to govern the nation. Ch'oe Ch'unghŏn was succeeded by his son Ch'oe U (?–1249).

Ch'oe U ruled Koryŏ at the time of the first Mongol invasions, and it was through his ineptitude that Koryŏ came to be subjugated by the warriors from the Central Asian steppes. In 1231, the Mongols quickly overran northern Korea and struck at the Koryŏ capital, Kaegyŏng. Ch'oe U refused to assist the royal government in the defence of the capital, with the result that it had to sue for peace on most unfavourable terms. In 1232, Ch'oe U ordered the royal government and the citizens of the capital to take refuge on the island of Kanghwa-do in the mouth of the Han River. Shortly afterwards, there was a second Mongol invasion, which was repulsed following the death in battle of the Mongol leader. This victory and the rapid retreat of the Mongols enabled Koryŏ to retake P'yŏngyang.

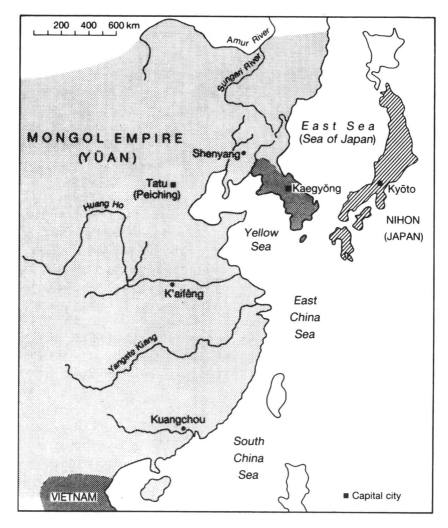

Figure 10 Late Koryŏ (Thirteenth Century)

Koryŏ was invaded again in 1235 when the Mongols went on a four-year rampage destroying everything in sight. There were four more invasions between 1235 and 1258, when Koryŏ finally surrendered to the Mongols. One of the great tragedies which occurred during these invasions was the sacking and total destruction of Kyŏngju, the magnificent former capital of Silla. The court on Kanghwa-do carried on much as it had in Kaegyŏng. It is some indication of the wealth upon which it could draw that the court could continue in such opulence and splendour amidst the general destruction of the nation. One of the greatest treasures created in this period was the *Koryŏ taejang-gyŏng* (Tripitaka

94

Koreanum), which was produced on Kanghwa Island using more than 80,000 printing blocks. Ch'oe U was succeeded by his son Ch'oe Ŭi (?–1258), whose assassination in 1258 led directly to negotiations with the Mongols and to the return of direct royal rule.

Although certain factions of the military remained in a state of revolt until 1273, by 1260 the entire nation of Koryŏ had effectively submitted to Mongol domination, a situation which was to continue for a century. Having once secured control of Koryŏ, the Mongols began to use the peninsula as a staging-ground for the assault on the last part of Asia which had not already submitted to them, Japan. The Mongols made two unsuccessful attempts to conquer the island empire, in 1274 and again in 1281, which imposed incredible strains on the economy of Koryŏ. In addition to the exactions which the Mongols had already placed upon the nation, the new war preparations created untold hardships for the people.

One lasting effect which the Mongol invasions had on Koryŏ was the establishment of the *Chŏngdong haengsŏng* (Eastern Expedition Field Head-quarters), an institution which co-ordinated all preparations for the invasion of Japan. After the failure of the last attempted invasion, this institution was not abolished but became the means by which the Mongols controlled the internal affairs of Koryŏ. It can be compared to the *Chungbang* of the military leaders of the twelfth century. This institution naturally distorted the functioning of the royal government, as did another institution over which the Mongols had control, the kingship of Shenyang. Although not the ruler of an actual kingdom, the King of Shenyang was given nominal authority by the Mongols over the Koreans resident in Manchuria. The existence of this pseudo-court functioned to weaken the authority of the King of Koryŏ, as the 'kings' of Shenyang were drawn from the deposed kings of Koryŏ or from princes of the blood who might have some reason for creating trouble for the current incumbent of the throne of Koryŏ.

By the fourteenth century, Koryŏ, a nominally independent state, had come totally under Mongol control, which affected every aspect of its social life. The crown princes of Koryŏ were held hostage at the Mongol court in Peiching, where they were under the daily observation of the Mongols. Often these princes were married to Mongol princesses, so that at the end of the Koryŏ dynasty, the royal family was little more than a Mongol clan. The Kings of Koryŏ were required to use regnal names which were inferior to Mongol titles and which included the character *ch'ung* (loyalty) to indicate their subservience to their Mongol overlords. The diminution of royal authority permitted powerful families, members of the royal family, aristocrats, and local magnates illegally to seize large tracts of land. This land seizure and the heavy exactions placed upon the nation by the Mongols created an intolerable burden on the mass of the people.

The Buddhist clergy were not exempt from the general corruption and debauchery of the fourteenth century. We have noted the remarkable growth of the Buddhist economy within the national economic system from the eleventh century onwards. The conspicuous consumption of the church in the fourteenth century stood in remarkable contrast to the poverty of the peasantry. The weakening of central authority, domination by a foreign power, and the corrupt use of power by the Buddhist church became the fuel which fed the growth of a new philosophy, Neo-Confucianism. The emergence of a Confucian literati class which was drawn from the petty gentry created a movement for governmental and social reform which would ultimately be responsible for the demise of Koryŏ. The emergence of this new class also initiated the struggle between Buddhism and Confucianism which was to characterize the Chosŏn Dynasty.

By the 1340s, Mongol power in China was waning, and armed revolts began to break out everywhere, most notably led by a quasi-Buddhist sect, the White Lotus Society. By the 1360s, effective Mongol power had been broken, and in 1368 a new empire called Ming (1368–1662) had established itself amongst the ruins of the Mongol Empire in China. During this turbulent period, King Kongmin (r. 1351–74) came to the throne of Koryŏ. Significantly, he was the first Koryŏ king for eighty years not to use the submissive character *ch'ung* in his regnal name. King Kongmin abolished the *Chŏngdong haengsŏng* and attempted to strengthen royal authority. Following the death of his queen, Kongmin increasingly came under the influence of a mysterious and controversial monk Sindon (?–1371). We have already seen how the influence of Buddhism was indirectly exercised at court by such figures as Ŭich'ŏn and directly by such figures as Myoch'ŏng. It was this power to influence the course of government which infuriated the believers in Confucian government and which set the stage for the conflict between the two forces. United aristocratic opposition resulted in the death of this monk, who had been entrusted with the implementation of the reforms by his monarch.

The death of King Kongmin led to a power vacuum, with a series of weak or puppet rulers who reigned until the establishment of the new Chosŏn Dynasty. A complicated battle for power took place during the last three decades of the fourteenth century. These dynastic troubles were worsened by the predations of the *wako* or Japanese pirates, whose raids were particularly frequent during this period. The political squabbling was not simply between Confucianists on the one hand and a collection of royalists, aristocrats, and Buddhists on the other hand. Feuding took place amongst the Confucianists as well. Confucianism ordains absolute loyalty to the monarch. Scholars such as Chŏng Mongju (1337–92) could not and would not join with the insurrectionists against the ruling family, however much he might agree with them. Yi Sŏnggye (1335–1408), a leading general, gathered around himself a collection of reform-minded military and civilians, including the Confucianist Chŏng Tojŏn (1337–98) and the Buddhist monk Muhak (1327–1405). In 1392, King Kongyang (r. 1389–92) was removed from office and General Yi was raised to the throne. Thus was the Buddhist Kingdom of Koryŏ swept away and the Confucian Kingdom of Chosŏn established.

2. Buddhism in the Late Koryŏ Period

(a) The Thirteenth Century

Probably the greatest cultural and artistic event of the thirteenth century was the creation of the *Koryŏ taejang-gyŏng* (Koryŏ Tripitaka, or Tripitaka Koreanum), known popularly as the *P'alman taejang-gyŏng* (Tripitaka on 80,000 Printing Blocks). The reader will recall that there had been several previous compilations of Buddhist scriptures. The first printing of a Buddhist canon was the eleventh-century collection entitled the *Ch'ojo changgyŏng* (First Great Canon), which was compiled at the instigation of King Hyŏnjong. Additional scriptural material to this canon was compiled and edited by Ŭich'ŏn in the twelfth century and is known as the *Sok changgyŏng* (Supplement to the Great Canon). Immediately after the Khitan invasions, the compilation of the Canon was undertaken in fulfilment of a vow by King Hyŏnjong, who had sworn that if the nation were spared he would place all of the known Buddhist scriptures on printing blocks in order to disseminate Buddhist knowledge. This vow paralleled the Silla belief that the recitation of the *Jên-wang Ching* (Scripture of the Benevolent King) would provide divine protection for the nation. During the Mongol invasions of 1232, the invaders reached Puin-sa temple north of Taegu, where the canon and its supplement had been housed, and set fire to the lot. This was not only an act of wanton destruction but also was a sign that Koryŏ could no longer count on this talisman for the spiritual protection of the state.

King Kojong (r. 1213–59), like his ancestor King Hyŏnjong, took a vow to create a new wood-block canon. Work was begun in 1236 under the direction of the monk Sugi (13th cent.), a noted scholar and linguist. Sugi was in charge of a committee of scholarly monks who examined and compared various canonical collections including the previous Koryŏ works, the new enlarged Liao canon, and the Sung canon known as the *Shu-pên*. They derived what is probably the best text for each of the works included, although many important materials were excluded. Among the latter were the scriptural commentaries which had been written by various East Asian authors and included by Ŭich'ŏn in his canonical supplement. The task of creating this enormous canon and placing it on wooden printing blocks took fifteen years (1236 to 1251). The canon was carved on blocks of seasoned *paktal namu* (a type of birchwood) which measured 2 feet 3 inches in length, 10 inches in width, and 1 inch in thickness. Both sides of the block were used, and each side could hold 23 lines of 14 characters. Illustrations and decorative materials were also included. This great collection consists of 81,258 wooden printing blocks divided into 1,512 books encompassing 6,791 *chüan*. The whole collection comprises nine categories of texts, including sutras, disciplinary rules, scriptural commentaries, and philosophical writings from both the Mahāyāna and Theravāda traditions. It is unquestionably the most complete single corpus of Buddhist writings in East Asia.

97

When the great canon was finished in 1251, a commemorative ceremony was held which was presided over by the king. At first housed in a gate by the royal palace on Kanghwa Island, the canon was later moved to Sŏnwŏn-sa on the same island, and from thence in the early Chosŏn Dynasty to Chijang-sa near Sŏul. In 1399 the canon was again moved, this time to its present location at Hae'in-sa. There it is housed in a specially designed building with vents which permit the proper circulation of the mountain air around the blocks to ensure preservation. The importance of this collection is not widely recognized, although it is the basis of many of the modern scholastic collections of Buddhist scriptures, such as the *Taishō Tripitaka* made by the Japanese in the 1920s and 1930s. This lack of knowledge about the *Tripitaka Koreanum* obscures not only its own cultural importance but the brilliance of the Buddhist culture of Koryŏ as well.

(b) The Fourteenth Century

Among the great monks of the final phase of the Koryŏ period were Po'u (T'aego hwasang, 1301–82), Hyegŭn (Na'ong hwasang, 1320–76), and Chach'o (Muhak taesa, 1327–1405). Each of these monks was influenced by the great Indian monk resident in China, Dhyānabhadra (Chih-k'ung in Chinese, Chigong in Korean, ?–1363), whose teachings had a tremendous influence on late Yüan China as well as on Koryŏ.

Po'u was the most influential Sŏn monk of the fourteenth century. He became a monk at the age of 13 and adhered for a while to the doctrines of the Hwaŏm Sect. In 1337, he became convinced of the value of the Sŏn methods as opposed to the doctrinal schools' teachings. In 1346, he went to Yüan to study Ch'an and became the first Koryŏ monk to become acquainted with the Lin-chi School. The Southern Ch'an order since the late T'ang period had had two principal schools, the Lin-chi and the Ts'ao-tung schools. Founded by I-hsüan (?–867), the former school favoured a form of 'shock therapy' to jolt the searcher for truth into an awareness of *nirvāna*. Thus, when a student asked a question of his master, the teacher-monk might reply by striking him with a stick, by making some sort of shocking or ribald statement, or by giving the student a seemingly nonsensical reply to his question. Although it seems improbable that early Koryŏ monks were unaware of the practices of the Lin-chi School, no Koryŏ monk before Po'u was known to have adopted their methods. Po'u founded the *Tong'guk imje-jong* or the Lin-chi School of Koryŏ. Upon Po'u's return to Koryŏ, the king created him *wangsa*, a post which he held until he fell foul of the monk, Sindon. He was confined to Songni-san, but upon Sindon's death in 1371 Po'u was restored to the office of *wangsa* and he held this dignity until this death in 1382.

During the period in which Po'u was active in Koryŏ, the Indian monk Dhyānabhadra was the central figure in Chinese Buddhism. Born as the third son of the ruler of a petty state in the Magadha region of India, Dhyānabhadra entered the monastic life at the age of 8. He studied at the famed Nālandā University, and at the age of 19 went to south India for further study. Some time afterwards he went to Yüan Dynasty China, and then in 1328 passed on to Koryŏ. During his sojourn in Koryŏ, he visited the famed Kŭmgang-san (Diamond Mountains) and made a pilgrimage to many important Buddhist sites on the Korean peninsula. He returned to Yüan, where many students sought him out, among them Hyegŭn, who learned the practice of Sŏn from the Indian master. Dhyānabhadra died in 1363, but was so revered by King Kongmin that some of his relics were brought back to Koryŏ. At first housed in the royal palace, the relics were later permanently installed in a reliquary at Hoeam-sa in Yangju. For nearly a thousand years, Korea had had direct contact with India, either through Korean monks who had made the journey to India or through Indian monks who had made the reverse journey to China and Korea. Even by the late Koryŏ period that connection had not been totally severed.

As a very young boy, Hyegŭn had the experience of seeing a young friend die. Gaining no explanation from his elders about where the human soul goes at death, Hyegŭn began a long search for Truth. This young man must have been of a very inquisitive disposition, because even the monks to whom he addressed his questions had to admit that they could not answer them. Eventually at the age of 20 he took monastic orders. In 1344 Hyegŭn went to Hoeam-sa, where he spent three years in meditation. He left Koryŏ in 1347 and went to the capital of Yüan, where he studied under Dhyānabhadra for two years. After having studied Sŏn under various masters in southern China, Hyegŭn returned to the capital and continued to study under Dhyānabhadra. He achieved such fame that the emperor, Shun-tsung (r. 1333–67), created him the abbot of a temple.

He returned from Yüan in 1358, and took up residence at Odae-san in 1360. In the following year, 1361, he gave lectures at the royal palace in Kaegyŏng. In 1371 he was made abbot of Hoeam-sa and simultaneously *wangsa* and head of the Sŏn *Chogye-jong* order. In 1376, he initiated a *Munsu-hoe* or Society for Worshipping Mañjuśrī, which caused so much confusion in Buddhist circles that Hyegŭn was sent down to the provinces; he died at Sillŭk-sa in the same year. Hyegŭn and Po'u were the two most important exponents of Sŏn Buddhism in late Koryŏ, yet it is interesting to note that even Hyegŭn had an interest in the esoteric practices of the cult of Mañjuśrī first popularized by Chajang.

Chach'o, or Muhak as he is more commonly known, entered the monastic life at the age of 18 and studied for many years under various masters. In 1353 he went to Yüan and studied under Dhyānabhadra. While he was there, he met Hyegŭn, who was studying under the same master. After leaving Dhyānabhadra and Hyegŭn, Muhak travelled throughout China, visiting among other places Wu-t'ai Shan, the abode of Mañjuśrī. Returning to the Yüan capital, Muhak spent several years in the company of Hyegŭn. He returned to Koryŏ in 1356, and when Hyegŭn also returned there, Muhak continued their close association and took up residence at Hoeam-sa with the senior monk. He assisted Hyegŭn in the creation of the Society for Worshipping Mañjuśrī. After Hyegŭn's death, Muhak wandered throughout Korea for many years and developed a close association with the circle of Yi Sŏnggye.

When the last king of Koryŏ was set aside and Yi Sŏnggye was enthroned as T'aejo, first monarch of the Kingdom of Chosŏn, Muhak found himself in the anomalous position of being the Buddhist adviser to the king of a Confucian dynasty ostensibly dedicated to the elimination of the pernicious influence of Buddhism. Muhak's appointment is some indication that at this period, in so far as the royal Yi family was concerned, personal faith and the affairs of state were two different matters. In the year of T'aejo's enthronement, 1392, Muhak was created *wangsa* and simultaneously head of the *Chogye-jong* order of Sŏn monks. In the former position he exercised considerable influence over T'aejo. For example, Muhak assisted in the selection of the site of the Chosŏn Dynasty capital. In 1393, Muhak accompanied T'aejo on a circuit of the kingdom, paying particular attention to Kyeryŏng-san near Kongju, and to the city of Hanyang. It was at Muhak's urging that Hanyang was selected as the new capital, now known as Sŏul. Apart from military and geographic considerations, the geomantic configurations of the land were most important, as it was vital that the capital of the new kingdom should have an auspicious location in order to ensure the longevity of the dynasty. In 1402 Muhak was appointed abbot of Hoeam-sa, but he was forced to relinquish the post in the following year. Muhak spanned two eras, the demise of Koryŏ and the establishment of Chosŏn. In doing so, he showed that Buddhist influence on those who had the direction of the state in their hands had not altogether died out. The tradition of private Buddhist devotion by the sovereign would continue for several more generations.

3. Late Koryŏ Confucianism

Throughout the Late Koryŏ period, even under Mongol domination, the government continued to give support to Confucian studies as it had in the early part of the dynasty. In 1296, during the reign of King Ch'ungnyŏl (r. 1274–1308), a section of the government was organized to supervise instruction in the Confucian Classics. During the reign of his successor, King Ch'ungsŏn (r. 1308–13), the Mun-myo or national Confucian shrine was greatly restored. With the advice of the great Confucian scholar An Hyang (1243–1306), the national Confucian college, the Kukhak, was reorganized, renamed and henceforth known as the *Sŏnggyun-gwan* (College of Perfection and Equalisation), the name by which its successor institution in the twentieth century is still known. At the further suggestion of An Hyang, the scholarship foundation to enable students to study at the National Academy was reinvigorated and renamed the *Sŏm hakchŏn* (Sufficient for Fees). These developments were not new trends but were a continuation of the traditional relationship between Confucianism, education, and governmental service. However, in this period a new form of Confucian philosophy began to emerge in China called *Hsing-li hsüeh* (Philosophy of Nature and Principle, *Sŏngni-hak* in Korean) or Neo-Confucianism. When imported into Koryŏ, it would not only threaten the foundations of the state but would also alter irrevocably the relationship between Buddhism and Confucianism.

Neo-Confucianism, also known in Korea as *Chuja-hak* (Philosophy of Chu Hsi), is a system of philosophy which developed during the late Northern Sung Dynasty (960–1127) and early Southern Sung Dynasty (1127–1279) in China, and was brought to its final form by the great philosopher Chu Hsi (1130–1200). Chu is considered by many to be the greatest Confucian philosopher after Confucius himself and Mencius (371–289 B.C). His philosophy synthesises aspects of the thought of Chou Tun-i (1017–73), Chang Tsai (1020–1077), Ch'eng Hao (1032–1085) and his brother Ch'eng I (1033–1107). Chou, effectively the pioneer philosopher of Neo-Confucianism, set out the essential parameters for the ethical and metaphysical concepts of Neo-Confucianism. In two works, the *T'ai-chi-t'u shuo* (Explanation of the Diagram of the Great Ultimate) and *T'ung-shu* (Penetrating the Book of Changes), he developed the idea of the inter-relationship between principle, nature, and universal destiny. Chou used the *T'ai-chi* (the Great Ultimate, *T'aegŭk* in Korean), the image of the *yin* and *yang*, to explain the origin of the universe, which evolved from the Great Ultimate into the *Yin-Yang* (*Ŭm-yang* in Korean), thence into the five elements (metal, wood, water, earth, and fire) and finally into the 'myriad things' of the universe. In terms of moral philosophy, Chou saw 'sincerity' as the basis of man's moral nature and the means through which one can discern good and evil. Chang, who was a rationalist and materialist in his philosophy, stated that the *yin* and the *yang* are the same as *ch'i* or material force and thus *ch'i* is the same as the *T'ai-chi* or Great Ultimate. Chang said that the universe is in a constant state of flux, of integration and disintegration following certain rational physical laws. The Ch'eng brothers, in spite of certain differences in their philosophies, were the first Chinese philosophers to build their system of thought on the concept of Principle, called by Ch'eng Hao as *T'ien-li* (Principle of Heaven, *Ch'ŏlli* in Korean). Principle underlies everything in the universe and governs everything. All individual principles in turn are part of Principle, and everything (the 'myriad things') is a manifestation of it. The Ch'engs understood that their philosophy encompassed both material and moral principles, thus creating a cosmological system of thought containing strong ethical considerations.

Chu Hsi synthesised these various ideas into a coherent philosophical system. He stated that the Great Ultimate (the *T'ai-chi*) is without form and comprises the totality of all individual principles in the universe. As it is the nature of principle to become actualised, Chu stated that the universe must be made up of two basic elements, *li* (principle, *yi* in Korean) and *ch'i* (material force, *ki* in Korean). *Ch'i* was necessary to bring into actuality the potential of *li*. On the one hand, *li* explains the reality and universality of things while *ch'i* explains the process of coming into being, and the facts of universal transformation and change. However, principle and material force are not to be seen as separate entities, but are to be understood as inseparably linked together. The universe functions because of the 'mind' of the universe, which is Ultimate Principle. Ultimate Principle in turn is reflected individually in the moral mind of man, representing his original nature, and the human mind, the individual manifestation of the moral mind formed by the individual circumstances of a person's physical endowment and desires. Believing that the actual differences amongst humans are caused by differences in individual *ch'i*, Chu Hsi felt that men could be brought to a higher moral state through education. Using philosophical elements drawn from Buddhism, Taoism, and Confucianism, Chu Hsi gave Confucianism what it had always lacked, a formalised metaphysical system. This cosmological system, however, linked together grand concepts about the nature of the universe with discussions of the moral nature and potential of individual persons. From now on, Confucianism was no longer just an ethical system but, in effect, a religious system as well. Moral living now meant moral harmony with the Ultimate Reality.

In addition, it was Chu Hsi who established the orthodox line of the transmission of Confucian thought from Confucius, through Mencius, to Chou Tun-i, Chang Tsai and the Ch'eng brothers. Also, in contrast to earlier Neo-Confucian thinkers who had a high regard for the *I-ching*, Chu viewed it as being only a book of divination and not a source for philosophical speculation. Importantly for Confucian education, Chu fixed the core texts of Confucianism as being the *Analects*, the *Mencius*, the *Ta-hsüeh* (the Great Learning, *Taehak* in Korean), and the *Chung-yung* (the Doctrine of the Mean, *Chungyong* in Korean). Collectively known as the Four Books (*Sa-sŏ* in Korean), they formed the basis for the civil service examination in East Asia from the fourteenth to the early twentieth century.

Although Chu Hsi's version of Neo-Confucian philosophy was first transmitted to Korea through the agency of An Hyang and later by Paek Ijŏng (*fl.* 1275–1325), it was in the latter part of the fourteenth century that Neo-Confucianism took significant hold on the world of thought in Korea. Offended by a century of Mongol domination and angered by the corrupt influence of Buddhism at the court, many young scholars who sensed the impending end of the Koryŏ kingdom turned to *Chuja-hak*. Among the scholars who were attracted to this philosophy were Yi Chehyŏn (1287–1367), Kil Chae (1353–1419), Yi Saek (1328–96), Chŏng Mongju (1337–92), and Yi Sungin (1349–92). The latter three men were known as the *Samŭn* or Three Hermit Scholars. Chŏng Tojŏn, associated with Yi Sŏnggye, was another brilliant scholar of this period who accepted *Chuja-hak*. He especially emphasized propriety with respect to one's deceased parents and ancestors. He urged the adoption of the three-year mourning period for deceased parents as binding on all members of society and the maintenance of ancestral shrines in each home.

Each of these scholars was a radical in his own way. Chŏng Tojŏn became associated with the founders of the new Chosŏn Dynasty, but was himself swept away within the first decade in a succession struggle amongst the sons of the founding monarch. Before he died, however, Chŏng Tojŏn created the legal code which was to be the foundation of the legal system of the new state. Against the opinions of men such as Chŏng Tojŏn stood two of the most eminent late Koryŏ scholars, Chŏng Mongju and Kil Chae. These scholars both refused to accept the advent of the new Chosŏn Dynasty because it contradicted the loyalty which a civil servant should have to his monarch. Confucian tradition made no allowance for a switch of loyalty to another king by revolt, and these honest men refused to be moved by political expediency.

Chŏng Mongju was the most distinguished thinker of late Koryŏ times. He was a member of the Yemun-gwan (Hallim-wŏn) and was several times an emissary from the Koryŏ court to foreign sovereigns. Because Chŏng Mongju's thinking emphasized *ch'ung-hyo* (loyalty to one's sovereign and filial duty to one's parents), he refused to accept the establishment of the Chosŏn kingdom. He was ardently concerned with Confucian education and with the creation of a corps of national leaders of rectitude. He helped found the *obu haktang*, the Five Confucian Academies located in the five wards of the capital, and was also instrumental in the movement for the establishment of Confucian academies and shrines in major provincial towns and cities. These combinations of academy and shrine were called *hyanggyo* (country school). Because he refused to lend his support to the new Chosŏn Dynasty, Chŏng Mongju was assassinated while crossing a bridge in the Koryŏ capital Kaegyŏng, on the orders of one of Yi Sŏnggye's sons, Yi Pangwŏn (1367–1422), who later reigned as King T'aejong (1400–18).

One young scholar who was strongly influenced by Chŏng Mongju was Kil Chae. Early on in his career, Kil Chae was made a member of the national college, the Sŏnggyun-gwan. His career there was cut short by his refusal to accept the new dynasty, following the lead of his mentor Chŏng Mongju. To avoid the fate which befell his teacher, Kil Chae fled to his home town of Kumi in Kyŏngsang Province, and for many years hid nearby in a cave near the summit of Kŭmo-san. Local legend says that his disciples would come secretly to bring food to their master. In later years, they founded an academy at the base of the mountain to perpetuate his memory.

Yi Chehyŏn was considered by later generations to typify the Confucian minister who loyally served his king. For his personal rectitude and unswerving loyalty in the king's service, a unique honour was conferred upon him. Upon the death of King Kongmin, the spirit tablet of Yi Chehyŏn was placed in the king's shrine and was reverenced during the ceremony at which homage was paid to the king's spirit. Yi Sungin and Yi Saek along with Chŏng Mongju were known as the Three Hermit Scholars. Yi Sungin had a distinguished career in government, but refused to accept the new dynasty and was executed at the behest of his erstwhile colleague Chŏng Tojŏn. Yi Saek was unique amongst late Koryŏ scholars of distinction in that he survived without compromising his principles. Yi Saek became an inspiration to later scholars such as Kim Chongjik of the Chosŏn period. Nearly unique amongst contemporary Confucianists, Yi Saek had a profound interest in and knowledge of Buddhism.

At the close of the Koryŏ period and at the opening of the Chosŏn Dynasty, it is clear that the philosophical motivation of society had passed from Buddhism to Confucianism. Whereas in the past there had been harmony and complementarity between Buddhism and Confucianism, there was now overt conflict. Confucianism in Korea had been transformed from a system of practical ethics into a metaphysical system with a vision of man's moral participation in the Ultimate. Thus ethics was no longer a matter of social mores but of ultimate religious concern. The Confucian scholars of the late Koryŏ period, regardless of the views which they held on the establishment of the new dynasty, were passionately concerned about the ultimate nature of society. Confucianism in Korea was now moving from being one among several political and cultural influences to being the primary social influence. In this climactic era, we stand at the dawn of a truly Confucian social system.

Part III

THE CHOSŎN DYNASTY

7

THE EARLY CHOSŎN PERIOD
(1392–1600)

1. The Cultural and Political Background

The revolution which swept aside the last king of Koryŏ and elevated Yi Sŏnggye to the throne of the new state was the culmination of a movement for governmental reform which dated back to the period of King Kongmin. The supplanting of Buddhism by Confucianism was part of this socio-cultural trend and continued throughout the first century of the new state. Although changes took place gradually rather than abruptly, by the end of the fifteenth century a new Confucian state and society had emerged (see Fig. 11). King T'aejo was responsible for several important changes. First, the new king moved the capital from Kaegyŏng to Hanyang, modern Sŏul. Second, he made it a major point of his foreign policy to develop a close relationship with the new Ming Dynasty (1368–1662) in China, a position which became known as *sadae chu'ŭi*, bending before the great. Third, he created a special class of merit subjects, or *kongsin*, who were lavished with grants of land, slaves, and various gifts. The Merit Subjects were a class of people who had been instrumental in elevating the new king to his throne. This process of creating Merit Subjects became a common means of honouring loyal subjects, although it also presented problems for governmental revenues.

In this period, the governmental system was brought into line with Confucian ideals, and the system of Confucian education which was supposed to supply a trained bureaucracy was also emphasized. The king in the new Confucian society was not an absolute monarch, because his ability to act was largely constrained by the Confucian advisers who surrounded him. Using historical precedent and philosophical discourse, these courtiers would endeavour to make the king's behaviour and decisions conform to the *wangdo* or Way of the King, an important Confucian ideal.

Although the new dynasty experienced a smooth transition to power, when T'aejo abdicated in 1398 a squabble broke out between the various sons of the retired king. The struggle for succession led to a series of clashes between the supporters of various contenders for the throne and to the execution or assassination of many people. The succession question was settled when

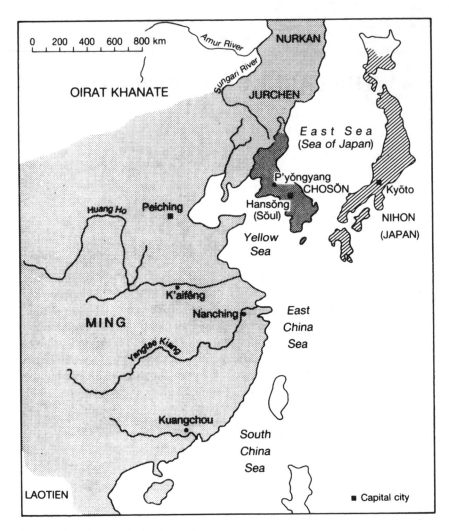

Figure 11 Early Chosŏn (Fifteenth Century)

T'aejong (r. 1400–18) ascended the throne. T'aejong was a vigorous and capable leader, even if he was ruthless in achieving his aims. He banned private armies, centralized the governmental structure, created the *Ŭijŏng-bu* or State Council of three senior councillors, and decreed that every male aged 16 years or more must carry an identification tag called a *hop'ae*. It was under T'aejong's reign that discrimination against the *sŏja* or the sons of concubines began. Unlike his father, T'aejong rigorously suppressed Buddhism. He closed all but 242 temples and confiscated the material and human property which had been held by the former temples.

T'aejong was succeeded by his third son, King Sejong (r. 1418–50), who is considered to have been the most brilliant and typically Confucian ruler of all the kings of the Chosŏn Dynasty. Sejong was not only a great administrator, but also a great patron of science and culture. He possessed one of the most enquiring and logical minds of any of the Chosŏn monarchs. Among the important projects which he sponsored was the reorganization of the *Chiphyŏn-jŏn*, or Board of Scholars. Sejong appointed a number of young scholars to posts in the *Chiphyŏn-jŏn* to do research on a variety of significant problems. It quickly became the research arm of the government and produced many important inventions.

Foremost among the inventions of the *Chiphyŏn-jon* was the *Hunmin chŏngŭm*, the Korean alphabet now known as *Han'gŭl*. This alphabet, originally containing twenty-eight letters, derived from comparative linguistic research, and remains a monument to the advanced state of Korean linguistics in the fifteenth century. After years of preparation, the alphabet was promulgated in 1446. A programme of instruction in the use of the new alphabet was given to prospective teachers who were to instruct the people in the use of *Han'gŭl*. In addition, a programme was fostered to encourage writing and translation in the new alphabet. The *Chiphyŏn-jŏn* also created a gauge for measuring rainfall, and formulated a tax system based upon the yield of different land and rainfall conditions. Astronomical, calendrical, mathematical, and chronological research was also undertaken. The *Chiphyŏn-jŏn* may be said to have been one of the earliest governmental think-tanks and was a reflection of Sejong's paternalistic and Confucian concern for his people.

Strangely, even though he had done more for the suppression and control of Buddhism than any previous Chosŏn Dynasty monarch, at the end of his life Sejong sought solace not in Confucian teaching but in Buddhist piety. Two years before his death, this most profound of Confucian monarchs built a Buddhist temple within the confines of the principal royal palace, and he died in the bosom of Buddhism in 1450.

Following Sejong's death, there was another succession crisis. King Sejong's crown prince became King Munjong (r. 1450–2), but was dead within two years. Munjong left the throne to his infant son, Tanjong (r. 1452–5), under the regency of the boy's uncle Prince Suyang. Prince Suyang quickly replaced his nephew – he later had him murdered – and assumed the throne as King Sejo (r. 1455–68). During Sejo's regency and the early years of his reign there were several rebellions aimed at placing Tanjong on the throne again. These were all ruthlessly suppressed. Sejo, however, proved to be a capable and good administrator. Later in life, he experienced great remorse for his bloody purges, and became the most devout Buddhist of all of the Chosŏn Dynasty kings. He instituted two major innovations in government, the *amhaeng ŏsa* and the *Chosŏn kyŏngguk-chŏn*. The first was a corps of secret inspectors sent *incognito* into the provinces to determine if provincial governors and magistrates were performing their duties justly. The second innovation was the creation of a single unified code of law, based upon the practice and proclamations of previous eras and providing for the first time a systematic presentation of the laws of the kingdom.

During this period, a four-tiered class society emerged, the four classes being the *yangban* or aristocracy, the *chungin* or professional middle class, the *yangmin* or peasantry, and the *ch'ŏnmin* or slave class. As the government was undergoing a process of Confucianization, Confucian thought was also reshaping the family system, determining the proper place for all members within the system. Linked with the development of a Confucian government and a Confucian family system was the growth of Confucian literary and cultural activity. Historical records, such as the *sillok* or 'veritable records' of each reign, and the *Koryŏ-sa*, a history of the previous dynasty, were important undertakings of this early period. Condensations of these records and various moralizing texts on good government for the edification of the sovereigns and their councillors were also produced at this time.

Scientific matters were investigated and recorded, and several books were written giving accurate information on methods of agriculture. Daily meteorological records were also compiled, as well as books of medicine and medical practice. These books were all printed and widely distributed.

Many literary works of this period were produced in *Han'gŭl*, including the *Yongbi ŏch'ŏn-ga* (Songs of the Dragons Flying to Heaven) compiled by the *Chiphyŏn-jŏn* in praise of the ancestors of the royal family, and the *Sŏkpo sangjŏl* (Episodes from the Life of the Buddha). The latter book was created by Prince Suyang on the order of King Sejong in 1447.

At the same time that science and literature began to flourish, poetry and music were also reinvigorated. The *sijo* form of poetry, known since Koryŏ times, took on greater importance. With the use of *Han'gŭl*, it became possible to write true Korean poetry without having to borrow clumsy, rhyming phrases from Chinese. Consequently, the long metrical phrases necessary for *sijo* could be written in the native script. Music, particularly music for Confucian ritual, was fostered, and musical scholarship was furthered. One result of these studies was the *Akhak kwebŏm* (Guide to Musical Studies), an important encyclopaedic record of classical and folk music in the early Chosŏn period. By the final quarter of the fifteenth century, Chosŏn was well on its way to being a thoroughly Confucian society.

After the brief reign of Sejo's son King Yejong (r. 1468–9), King Sŏngjong (r. 1469–94) was elevated to the throne as a boy of 12 years. He came under the influence of a group of scholars called the *Sarim-p'a*, who traced their origins to Kil Chae, the late Koryŏ scholar who had refused to recognize the new dynasty and had retreated to a cave on Kŭmo-san. The *Sarim-p'a* scholars became a radical Confucian force, biding their time in the countryside until they could formally assume power. They were imbued with a strong sense of Confucian idealism and morality, and accepted the interpretation of Confucianism propounded by the Chu Hsi School. The *Sarim-p'a* came to regard the ascension of Sejo to the throne as a usurpation, a heinous crime in Confucian thought. The leading scholar of this school, Kim Chongjik (1431–92), became a tutor to the boy king Sŏngjong. Through Kim Chongjik's influence the young king became thoroughly Confucian in his outlook. The last years of Sŏngjong's reign represented the height of Confucian idealism, but the result was a radical reaction against the *Sarim-p'a* idealists by the conservative aristocracy.

King Sŏngjong died suddenly in 1494, and his eldest son, Prince Yŏnsan (r. 1494–1506), came to the throne. He proved to be such a dissolute, immoral, and erratic leader that a group of scholars banded together and had him dethroned, deprived him of a royal regnal name, and raised his brother to the throne in his place. This young king was King Chungjong (r. 1506–44). During Prince Yŏnsan's reign, in 1498, the first purge of scholars took place. Until the end of the following century, much of Korean history was dominated by the factional squabbles amongst the Confucian literati.

King Chungjong, like his father Sŏngjong, came under the thrall of the radical *Sarim-p'a* and especially their leader, Cho Kwangjo (1482–1519). Cho was a renowned and uncompromising member of the Board of Censors, the government watchdog agency. Through the institution of a simplified governmental examination, Cho was able to fill the main organs of government with his supporters. With the control of government securely in their hands, the *Sarim-p'a* proceeded to further reshape the Chosŏn state into their image of a Confucian society. One of the most important measures which they undertook was the creation of a social contract for the villages, the *hyangyak*. Villages were encouraged voluntarily to adopt this code for governing social, village, and family behaviour. Virtually every aspect of social life was considered in minute detail. The administration of this contract was placed in the care of an organ of government which appointed the individual village leadership. The *hyangyak* became a prime means by which Confucian ideals, especially in the more radical *Sarim-p'a* version, came to filter down to the lowest level of society. Even the *ch'ŏnmin* came to pride themselves on their Confucian conduct. Although Cho Kwangjo and his clique held the ear of the king for many years, they eventually overreached themselves, and the king gave tacit approval to their opponents to begin a purge of the radicals. This purge resulted in the death of many people, including Cho Kwangjo himself. Following the purge, the remaining two decades of Chungjong's reign were quiescent.

This mood of quiet was shattered by the re-emergence of strong party strife during the reigns of King Myŏngjong (r. 1546–67), and King Sŏnjo (r. 1567–1608). In 1575, factional warfare broke out fiercely between two groups known as the Westerners and Easterners after the place of residence in Sŏul of their respective party leaders. The Easterners, following their victory, divided into Northerners and Southerners, of which the Northerners emerged victorious. This group then split into the Great Northerners and the Lesser Northerners. The Westerners also split up into the *Noron* and *Soron* factions. This made four major factions by the 1580s. The social fabric of the state was rent in pieces by this feuding, which left the nation totally unprepared for an invasion from outside.

Japan, now a unified nation after decades of internecine warfare, acquired a leader who was hungry to exercise his power in other parts of the world. In 1592, the Japanese warlord Toyotomi Hideyoshi (1536–98) invaded Korea, bringing great devastation to the unprepared and defenceless nation. During the six-year period before the Japanese were finally evicted from the peninsula, Admiral Yi Sunsin (1545–98) provided the only bright spot on the military scene. His armour-clad warships, the first of their kind in the world, successfully harried the Japanese navy. Even though the Koreans were able with the assistance of their Ming allies to repulse the Japanese, the ravages of the Hideyoshi Wars were to have a grave effect on the economy and society of seventeenth-century Korea.

2. Early Chosŏn Confucianism: The Golden Age

The creation of the new state of Chosŏn not only gave birth to a new Korean dynasty, it brought Confucianism to power. The government of the Kingdom of Chosŏn, more so than any preceding dynasty, was based on Confucian philosophy. As we have seen, at the end of the Koryŏ period there emerged two groups of Neo-Confucian scholars. One group included men such as Chŏng Tojŏn, who became members of the circle of Yi Sŏnggye, founder of the new dynasty, whilst the second group included men such as Kil Chae, who refused to recognize the usurpation of the Koryŏ monarchy. These ill-defined groupings of scholars gradually formed into schools of Confucian thought during the first century of the new dynasty, representing respectively two major trends in fifteenth-century Confucianism: a concern for administrative matters on the one hand, and an interest in metaphysical matters on the other. It should be stressed, however, that both these schools were concerned with the reformation of society in a way which no previous group of Korean Confucianist thinkers had ever deemed possible. From the fifteenth century, Confucian influence came to mean social influence as we have defined this earlier rather than merely political and cultural influence.

(a) The Fifteenth Century

Two of the principal representatives of the *Kwanhak-p'a*, or School of Administrative Philosophy, were Chŏng Tojŏn, whom we have met before, and Kwŏn Kŭn (1352–1409). Chŏng, who had the ear and favour of Yi Sŏnggye, was extremely influential in the formulation of the concept of the ideal society which it was hoped the new state would become. He envisaged a state freed from the pernicious influence of Buddhism and which conformed to the ideal precepts of *Chuja-hak*, the Neo-Confucian philosophy of Chu Hsi, also called *Sŏngni-hak* (in Chinese, *Hsing-li Hsüeh*, Philosophy of Nature and Principle). Chŏng's diatribe against Buddhism, the *Pulssi chappyŏn* (Various Criticisms of Mr. Buddha) comprising the ninth volume in his collected writings the *Sambong-jip*, set the tone for the official and scholarly attitude towards Buddhism during the Chosŏn Dynasty. He sets out some twenty arguments against Buddhism. From the stance of Neo-Confucian metaphysics, he attacks in particular the Buddhist ideas of the cycle of birth and rebirth and the concept of cause and effect. As he perceived Buddhism to be a worthless superstition inimical to both the state and society, he argued that it should be suppressed. Criticism of Buddhism may be found elsewhere in his collected works. Chŏng also strongly urged the legal prescription of the three-year mourning period for parents as binding on all members of the society and the maintenance of family shrines in all homes. In addition, he began the first summary history of the Koryŏ Dynasty, the *Koryŏ-sa*, and compiled the first codification of the laws of the previous dynasty, the *Chosŏn kyŏngguk-chŏn*. His interests exemplify the concern of the *Kwanhak-p'a* with the total reformation of society and the construction of a new state based on a sound, logical, and orderly basis.

Kwŏn Kŭn was one of the foremost administrators of his day. In 1375, at the age of 23, he and a group of young scholars including Chŏng Tojŏn and Chŏng Mongju advocated a policy of close ties with the emergent Ming Empire, and rejected the policy of greeting the envoys from the Mongol Yüan Empire. Kwŏn, who held many posts under the last days of the Koryŏ Kingdom, was later exiled and released. Unlike Chŏng Mongju, he successfully made the transition to the new state. He is best remembered for his *Sasŏ ogyŏng kugyŏl*, an introduction to the Confucian Classics, and the *Iphak tosŏl*, an elementary introduction to the work of Chou Tun-i and Chu Hsi. Rich in cosmological diagrams, it exercised a great influence on later scholars, such as Yi Hwang.

Eight of the most prominent early Chosŏn Dynasty philosophers, including Chŏng Tojŏn and Kwŏn Kŭn, were known collectively as the *P'al myŏngyu* (Eight Eminent Confucianists). The other six scholars were Pyŏn Kyeryang (1369–1430), Chŏng Inji (1396–1478), Kim Chongjik (1431–92), Sin Sukchu (1417–75), Sŏ Kŏjŏng (1420–88), and Kim Sisŭp (1435–93). Pyŏn Kyeryang, a native of Miryang, is best known for his work on the Veritable Records of the reign of King T'aejo, and for his revision of the *Koryŏ-sa*. Chŏng Inji was one of the finest scholars of his day. He was appointed early in his career by Sejong to the *Chiphyŏn-jŏn*, where he did research on astronomy, calendrical science, and music. He is credited with work on the revision of the *Koryŏ-sa*, the Korean alphabet, and the *Yongbi ŏchŏn-ga*.

Sin Sukchu was another bright young scholar elevated by Sejong. He travelled as a royal emissary to Japan via Tsushima in 1442 and held many appointments in the *Chiphyŏn-jŏn*. Whilst in the *Chiphyŏn-jŏn* he was directly responsible for the creation of the Korean alphabet. During that period, Sin Sukchu and one other scholar were sent to China to seek out the Ming scholar Huang Tsan (15th cent.) to question him on problems of linguistics and Chinese pronunciation. Sin met Huang on no less than thirteen different occasions. Although Sin held many high posts and was directly responsible for the creation of *Han'gŭl*, modern Koreans tend to dismiss him because of the support he gave to King Sejo when he usurped the throne. Sin edited the Veritable Records of King Sejo and King Yejong. He also prepared maps of Japan and the Jurchen Kingdom.

Sŏ Kŏjŏng's approach to life well exemplified the typical Confucian scholar's attitude. There is a story told in his home city Taegu that Sejong requested that the Talsŏng fortress, property of the Sŏ clan and the site of their ancestral-tablet hall, should be given to the government in exchange for an equal amount of land. Sŏ Kŏjŏng replied that as a simple scholar he should be given a hill in exchange, as the farmers needed the productive flat land. Stories such as this emphasize the fact that Confucian civilization was austere in nature, and that knowledge meant moral knowledge. The scholar was to concern himself with the moral and physical welfare of the people. Sŏ was a descendant through his mother of Kwŏn Kŭn. At the age of 6, he composed elegant poetry which earned him the title of *sindong* (divine child). He was a member of the *Chiphyŏn-jŏn*, held many governmental posts, and travelled to China as the king's representative, where he was well received. He was involved with the editing of the *Tongguk yŏji sŭngnam* (A Geographical Survey of Korea), which is a thorough record of the geography and customs of the eight provinces of Korea. Sŏ's knowledge of astronomy and geography was legendary.

By the middle of the fifteenth century, the Confucian world was torn apart by a controversy as great as that which had faced the Confucianists of the late Koryŏ Dynasty. The usurpation of the throne by King Sejo brought to prominence the second major party of the early Chosŏn Dynasty, the *Sarim-p'a*. These idealistic scholars traced their intellectual ancestry to Kil Chae, noted for his refusal to accept the establishment of the new dynasty. They believed loyalty to the monarch was absolute and unchanging. It was a total commitment.

Many of the members of the *Sarim-p'a* therefore refused to accept the authority of the usurper. Scholars who took this view towards King Sejo are recalled by modern Koreans as the *Sayuk-sin* (Six Dead Loyalists), and the *Saengyuk-sin* (Six Live Loyalists). The former group of scholars attempted to overthrow Sejo and to reinstate Tanjong and were executed along with seventy of their followers. The latter group of scholars refused to co-operate with the new king and withdrew from all active political life. The *Saengyuk-sin* found ingenious ways of avoiding governmental service, and even managed to avoid accepting gifts from the new king.

Kim Sisŭp, who is counted among the *P'al myŏngyu*, was one of the Six Live Loyalists who was so revolted by the king's murder of his nephew that he threw aside all affairs of the world and became a wandering Buddhist monk. This is especially interesting as it shows the extent to which this great *Chuja-hak* scholar rejected Sejo by turning to a religion which as a Neo-Confucianist he should have despised.

Perhaps the most influential Confucian scholar of the fifteenth century was Kim Chongjik, who may be termed the founder of the *Sarim-p'a*. A native of

Miryang, Kim early demonstrated his brilliance, and he held many important posts in the government. His scholarly thought emphasized the loyalty and faithfulness of sons, friends, students, and servants of the king. He summed up his thinking in the phrase *hyoje ch'ungsin* (Filial Piety and Loyalty). His work on the revision of the *Tongguk yŏji sŭngnam* was an important intellectual contribution. However, it is not for his pure scholarship for which he is remembered, but for his courageous stand during Sejo's era.

The usurpation of the throne by Sejo gathered into a common party all those scholars who looked to the tradition of Kil Chae. The *Sarim-p'a* bloc was not simply antagonistic to the *Kwanhak-p'a*, whom they saw as time-servers and toadies, but it was also dedicated to the creation of a thoroughly Confucian society. Kim Chongjik emerged as the leader of this band of disgruntled men and assumed the post of tutor to the boy-king Sŏngjong. Like the *Kwanhak-p'a*, the *Sarim-p'a* scholars were interested in the reformation of society, but in a more thoroughgoing manner. Rather than emphasizing immediate, practical matters, the *Sarim-p'a*'s interests were more philosophical and abstract. They had three principal philosophical concerns: a theory of the nature of the universe, a theory of knowledge, and a theory of morality. We have seen how in Sŏngjong's reign this Confucian theory was put into practice.

Sŏngjong's era saw the first significant attempt since the reign of King Sejong to create a totally Confucian society. This process was briefly interrupted by the rule of Prince Yŏnsan, but continued again under his brother, Chungjong. The movement for the Confucianization of society was carried forward vigorously by Kim Chongjik's disciple, Cho Kwangjo. Cho was the son of an important Chosŏn Dynasty official, and showed great promise at an early age. We have already seen how his party came to have great influence on the social and political events of his time. In this context it is not necessary to say more about his life, except that his importance cannot be overemphasized.

By now, the mainstream of Confucian influence had passed from the *Kwanhak-p'a* to the *Sarim-p'a*. Under Cho Kwangjo, the ideals of the *Sarim-p'a* concerning the nature and form of society were instituted in a way in which Buddhism had never been able formally to influence Korean society. The nature of Korean society was radically reshaped under the followers of Cho Kwangjo. Although they were defeated at the end of Chungjong's reign, the effect of what they had done was not significantly altered. The truly Confucian shape of Korean society began here, in the early sixteenth century. Subsequent actions taken by various schools in later generations only built on what the *Sarim-p'a* had accomplished. Later generations amended the achievement of the *Sarim-p'a*, but did not erase it.

Before we move on to the sixteenth century, we must mention one other group of scholars of the early fifteenth century, the *Ch'ŏngbaeng-ni* or Five Pure Officials. Like the Eight Eminent Confucianists, the Five Pure Officials became symbolic of the ideal Confucian scholar. These very titles show a Confucian penchant for singling out and categorizing historical persons and events for the moral lessons which they teach. The *Ch'ŏngbaeng-ni* were Ha Yun (1347–1416), Chŏng Kapson (?–1451), Hwang Hŭi (1363–1452), Hŏ Cho (1369–1439), and Yu Kwan (1346–1433). They were all noted for their purity, honesty, and simplicity of lifestyle.

Ha Yun, in particular, led an unusually austere life. An official of the late Koryŏ Dynasty, Ha was able successfully to make the transition to the new Chosŏn Dynasty. He was one of a group of scholars who urged the selection of Sŏul as the new dynastic capital. Scholastically, Ha is remembered for his knowledge of the *Yin-Yang* philosophy, medicine, astronomy, and geography. If Kil Chae and the *Sarim-p'a* scholars represented the Confucian ideal of loyalty to the monarch under all circumstances, the Five Pure Officials symbolized the purity of conduct which characterized the civil servant. Although the *Sarim-p'a* scholars and the Five Pure Officials might have political differences amongst themselves, both groups well represented the Confucian ideal of the scholar/ bureaucrat.

(b) The Sixteenth Century

The defeat of Cho Kwangjo and his followers in the first quarter of the sixteenth century did not mean the re-emergence of the *Kwanhak-p'a* as a significant intellectual force but rather the continuation of a clash between the entrenched aristocracy with landed interests and the idealist intellectual class who were also members of the aristocracy. The power of the idealist literati came to be preserved through the development of regional Confucian academies called *sŏwŏn* ('book garden', see Fig. 12). Like their predecessors the *shu-yüan* in the Sung period in China, these schools were more than just places of study, but were centres for political discussion and criticism and contained shrines to the founding scholar and his chief disciples. The first *sŏwŏn* to be established in Chosŏn Korea was the *Paegŭn-dong sŏwŏn* (White-cloud Valley Academy) which was founded in 1543 in P'unggi in North Kyŏngsang Province. Through a memorial sent to the throne by a later magistrate, Yi Hwang, the academy gained the epithet by which it is more popularly known, *Sosu sŏwŏn* (Academy of Received Learning). By preserving and developing a particular line of Confucian thinking and by creating a body of men dedicated to its political implementation, these academies served to develop the political power of the idealist Confucian literati. By the eighteenth century, the *sŏwŏn* had come virtually to replace the government-sponsored regional academies, the *hyanggyo*.

The intellectual field continued to be dominated by the descendants of the *Sarim-p'a*, who by the mid-sixteenth century had split up into two distinct schools of dualist philosophy, the *Churi-p'a* (Principle First School) and the *Chugi-p'a* (Matter First School). It is significant that at the same time that these intellectual trends emerged, rabid political factionalism arose which nearly destroyed the state during the invasions of the Japanese war-lord Hideyoshi. The

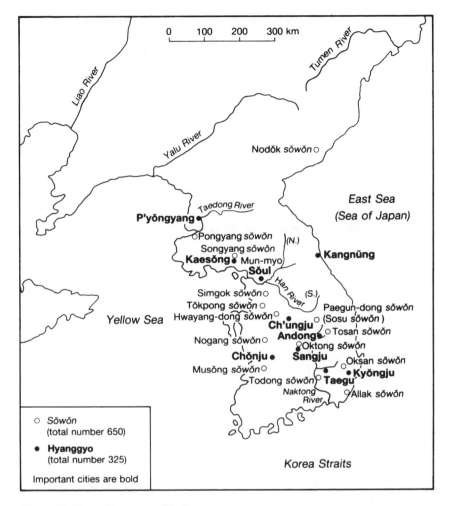

Figure 12 Sites of Important *Sŏwŏn*

sixteenth century was the great century of Korean philosophy as all the major trends of Confucianism which are unique to Korea arose during this period. In spite of the destructive party strife, the sixteenth century may be called the golden age of Neo-Confucian thought. We shall consider in turn the two main schools of Confucianism.

The *Churi-p'a* derived its concepts from the philosophy of the scholar Yi Ŏnjŏk (pen-name Hoeje, 1491–1553), whose followers founded the prestigious *Oksan sŏwŏn* (Jade Mountain Academy) near Kyŏngju. Although he was one of the most esteemed administrators of his time, he was twice relieved of his posts. In 1530, during his first period of retirement, he returned to his home area where he set up a scholars' retreat which became the basis of the later Oksan Academy. Yi was reinstated in 1537, and was banished again in 1547 to Kanggye in north Korea where he remained until he died. While he was in exile in north Korea, Yi Ŏnjŏk wrote many of his important writings, including a discussion of the *Ta Hsüeh* (Great Learning), the *Taehak changyu poyu*. His principal philosophical concept is called *Mugŭk t'aegŭng-non* (Philosophy of the Infinite Great Ultimate). Yi drew his thoughts not from Chu Hsi but from his predecessor Chou Tun-i, who utilized a diagram called the *T'ai-chi* composed of 250 characters which explained the origin of the universe. The Supreme Principle or *T'ai-chi* produces two elements, the *yin* and the *yang*, from which all else is derived. Hoeje borrowed these concepts and created two philosophical principles which he termed *mugŭk* (*wu-chi* in Chinese) or Emptiness and *t'aegŭk* (*t'ai-chi* in Chinese) or Supreme Principle. With these two basic principles Yi explained both the creation and the essence of the universe.

The foremost thinker of the *Churi-p'a* was Yi Hwang (pen-name T'oegye, 1501–70), who was greatly influenced by Hoeje. The Principle First School was so strongly affected by T'oegye's philosophy that it is often referred to as *T'oegye-hak* (T'oegye Philosophy). T'oegye founded the important *Tosan sŏwŏn* (Edification Mountain Academy) near Andong where he taught his disciples and from where they went out to spread their master's ideals. Accepting the basic premises of Hoeje's philosophy, T'oegye developed a system of thought called *Yigi yiwŏn-non* (Dualism of Matter and Form), the concepts of which were such an innovation in Neo-Confucian thinking that T'oegye became known as *Tongbang Chuja*, the Chu Hsi of Korea.

His original contribution to an interpretation of Chu Hsi's metaphysics is a theory called *Sadan ch'ilchŏng-sŏl* (Theory of the Four Beginnings and the Seven Sentiments). The concepts themselves are not original, as T'oegye found the concept of the four beginnings in the *Mencius*, and that of the seven sentiments in the Book of Rites. This aspect of T'oegye's thought is a philosophy of mind which demonstrates the relationship of the minds of individual persons to the fundamental elements of the universe. For T'oegye, the beginnings of the four cardinal virtues are generated by *yi* (*li* in Chinese) or Principle, while the seven sentiments of human emotion are generated by *ki* (*ch'i* in Chinese), Matter or Material Force. Thus the virtues and emotions of the individual mind are formed by the two basic elements of the universe, Principle and Material Force. T'oegye further believed that *yi* was the fundamental, prescribed element in the universe which led or directed *ki*, the material force or essence of matter. For this reason the school was called the *Churi-p'a*, the School of Yi Leading.

Yi Hwang's philosophy ran counter to another trend in Neo-Confucianism in Korea and led to a famous series of debates between him and Ki Taesŭng (1527–72) known as the *Yi-gi* debates. T'oegye's philosophy was the direct ancestor of the *Yŏngnam-p'a* of the eighteenth century, which included many members of the dissident Namin or Southerner political faction.

118

Yi Hwang's most notable disciple was Yu Sŏngnyong (1542–1607), who was prime minister during the latter part of the period of the Hideyoshi invasions. Yu was largely responsible for reinstating Yi Sunsin, who had been ousted in political wrangling. Yu is the prime example of a principled scholar-official of the sixteenth century. Yu attacked the philosophy of Wang Yang-ming (1472–1528) for its assumption of the unity of knowledge and action, which Yu felt threatened the active aspect of *yi*. Another disciple of T'oegye was Kim Sŏngil (1538–93), who was responsible for the dissemination of Yi Hwang's thought to Japan, where it came to play a significant role in the Confucian world of Tokugawa times.

The second of the two great philosophical schools of the sixteenth century was the *Chugi-p'a*, or Matter First School. The first scholar to suggest that Material Force, not Principle, was the fundamental element of the universe was Ki Taesŭng, who had been involved in a series of debates with T'oegye. More important than Ki Taesŭng, and second in importance only to T'oegye, was the scholar Yi Yi (pen-name Yulgok, 1536–84). Born in the great aristocratic centre of Kangnŭng, he was the son of an eminent lady philosopher and artist, the Sin Saimdang (1512–59). Yulgok's philosophy, which blended the interests of the *Kwanhak-p'a* and the early *Sarim-p'a* of the fifteenth century, was called *Yigi irwŏn-jŏk yiwŏn-nŏn* (Theory of Monistic Dualism). While T'oegye saw *yi* as a transcendent, primary force, Yulgok saw *yi* as one of the factors involved in *ki*. Thus the four beginnings were in effect a part of the seven sentiments of human emotion. As *yi* is generated by *ki*, Material Force, not Principle, is responsible for the generation, maintenance, and purification of the values held by the mind. This emphasis on the material force of the universe led Yulgok and his disciples to stress the importance of practical affairs. The school of Yi Yi gave rise in the late seventeenth and eighteenth centuries to the School of Northern Learning (*Pukhak-p'a*) which, more so than the *Sirhak-p'a*, was concerned with the technical and scientific aspects of social development.

Before leaving our consideration of the schools of dualism of the sixteenth century, we must point out that there were three common points in their thinking which reflect the philosophy of early Confucianism. Both the Principle First School and the Matter First School believed that there was a direct correlation between the order which exists in the material universe and the order which exists in human society. Both schools also believed that the essence of man was good, and that his character could be brought into a better if not a perfect state through the performance of ritual propriety and social virtues. Finally, both schools emphasized the importance of unity and harmony in all relationships.

Although dualism was the prevailing philosophical mode of Confucian scholarship of the sixteenth century, monistic thinking was also present. The leading exponent of monism was Sŏ Kyŏngdŏk (1489–1546), who advocated a materialistic monism. He argued that *ki* was the essence of the universe and the only thing which was real. This point of view was called *Mulchil pulbyŏn-non*

(Theory of the Immutability of Matter). Although Sŏ had several disciples, his philosophy never entered into the mainstream of Confucian thought in Korea.

The sixteenth century also saw the rise of the *Yehak-p'a* or School of Ritual Studies. Song Ikp'il (1534–99) and his disciple Kim Changsaeng (1548–1631) and his son Kim Chip (1574–1656) focussed their research and writing on the rituals associated with Confucianism not only for the correctness of ritual procedure but also for the rôle which ritual acts had in the moral discipline of the individual and society. Especially important was the study of a Chinese work called the *Chu Hsi Chia-li* (Chu Hsi on Family Rites, *Chuja karye* in Korean) compiled in the fourteenth century from Chu Hsi's writings on the four domestic rituals associated with Confucianism. The *sa-rye* or Four Rites were capping (a coming-of-age ritual when a youth first wore an adult's hat), marriage, mourning, and ancestral rites. Kim Changsaeng's most influential work was the *Karye chimnam* (Exposition of Family Rites). *Yehak* studies assumed particular importance amongst the *yangban* class during the succeeding seventeenth century and the growing interest in creating a society which conformed to Confucian moral values and ritual practices. The work of the *Yehak-p'a* scholars led to the subsequent rise of the *Kiho* School of Confucian studies.

3. Early Chosŏn Buddhism: A Tradition Displaced

As has been indicated in the survey of the history of the first half of the Chosŏn Dynasty, Buddhism entered into a long period of decline punctuated by several periods of revival. As in China, the development of Buddhism in Korea had always been dependent on patronage by the government or by the royal house. Consequently, with the advent of a revolutionary Confucian government, the fortunes of Buddhism were bound to decline. The attitude taken by Confucianists towards the Indian religion is indicated by a work of Chŏng Tojŏn, the *Pulssi chappyŏn*, which forms part of his collected writings, the *Sambong-jip*. In this tract he attacks the philosophical and ethical stance of Buddhism, comparing it highly unfavourably with Confucian thought. The arguments which he put forward against Buddhism became the basis for the suppression and rigid control of Buddhism which was to be the typical policy of Chosŏn Korea.

During the reign of the first king, T'aejo, a policy of strictly controlling Buddhism called *toch'ŏp-che* was instituted. A system of registering the names and residences of monks, the *toch'ŏp-che* policy set the tone for the official attitude towards Buddhism of virtually all the early kings of the Chosŏn Dynasty. On a personal level, the actions and attitudes of the kings were different. As we have seen, T'aejo had a close relationship with Muhak, one of the greatest Buddhist figures of the late Koryŏ period. T'aejo not only utilized this great monk as an adviser on various matters of state, but he also continued a Koryŏ practice by appointing Muhak as *wangsa* or royal preceptor. T'aejo also established two great national temples, the Hŭngch'ŏn-sa and the Hŭngdŏk-sa, and built a royal Buddhist shrine, the Naewŏn-dang, within the precincts of the

120

royal palace. Thus the pattern of the official governmental suppression of Buddhism and the personal piety of the monarch was established from the beginning. Although Buddhism's influence at an official level declined dramatically, Buddhism never totally disappeared as a force in society due to the tacit approval given to it by the royal house.

Under T'aejo's successor T'aejong, the official suppression of Buddhism was intensified. The titles of *wangsa* and *kuksa*, relics of the Koryŏ period, were abolished, and the number of temples officially permitted to operate was drastically reduced. All but 242 temples were closed during the reign of this king. Under Sejong, grandson of the founder T'aejo, the control and suppression of Buddhism was the greatest it had been at any time during the first century of the new dynasty. The various sects of Buddhism which had survived from the Koryŏ period into the new era were forced to combine into two large super-sects, the Kyo or doctrinal sect, and the Sŏn sect. In addition, only thirty-six temples of any significance were permitted to remain open. Eighteen temples were assigned to each sect; all other temples were forced to close their doors. This rigorous control of what was seen to be a decadent doctrine was symbolic of Sejong's devotion to the development of a Confucian society. However, Sejong had an enquiring mind and found that the metaphysics of Confucianism could not satisfy his search for the meaning of man's destiny. Although maintaining a formal policy of support for Confucianism, King Sejong turned to Buddhism in the hope of finding the answers to the mysteries of life. Within the precincts of the palace he erected a Buddhist shrine, the Naebul-tang, which caused an uproar amongst the literati in the capital. Sejong also wrote or sponsored several Buddhist works. Apart from the *Sŏkpo sangjŏl* (Episodes from the Life of the Buddha) which he caused his son Prince Suyang to write, Sejong wrote a collection of lyrical poetry with Buddhist motifs, the *Wŏrin ch'ŏn'gang-ji kok* (Songs of the Moon's Reflections on a Thousand Rivers). He also had Buddhist scriptures transcribed into *Han'gŭl* so that the common man could read them. These *Han'gŭl* translations were known collectively as *ŏnhae* (vulgar elucidations). Thus, the Korean alphabet, which is often cited as an example of the sophisticated research of Confucian scholars, came to be a means for the dissemination of Buddhism.

Sejong's son, King Sejo, was the first king of the Chosŏn Dynasty to actively support Buddhism. As we have seen, this was probably as the result of the remorse which the king felt for the murder of his nephew, Tanjong. It also may possibly have been due to the influence of his father's example. Although it had been the practice of previous Chosŏn monarchs to forbid the existence of temples within the precincts of the cities, especially the capital, Sejo built the great Wŏn'gak-sa in the middle of Sŏul, and erected a splendid thirteen-storey stone pagoda in its midst. This pagoda is probably the finest example of Buddhist art from the Chosŏn Dynasty. Although modelled on Koryŏ prototypes, it is exquisitely executed, each level being made to look like a four-sided building with a tiled roof. The various sections contain panels with intricately carved Buddhist figures. The pagoda still stands on its ancient site in Sŏul, which is now the modern Pagoda Park. Sejo also established the *Kan'gyŏng togam*, a government bureau for the publication of Buddhist scriptures. This support for Buddhism was reversed by Sejo's successors, King Sŏngjong and Prince Yŏnsan.

Sŏngjong was a very Confucian monarch, and under his reign Korean society became more Confucianized than at any previous time. Two notable edicts of his reign were the forbidding of persons to leave their families and join a monastic community, and the forbidding of the construction of any new temples. Although existing monks were not to be laicized, by forbidding people to leave their homes as an unfilial act the source of new monks to reinforce the monastic communities was to be dried up. Thus it was hoped that Buddhism would disappear in a generation. The suppression of Buddhism at the end of the fifteenth century was fiercest not under the rule of a Confucian monarch, but under the reign of a totally dissolute ruler, Prince Yŏnsan. The Buddhist examinations, which were meant to ensure the quality of Buddhist leadership, were suspended, and the major temples, the Hŭngch'ŏn-sa and the Hŭngdŏk-sa, were closed. The grounds of the Wŏn'gak-sa, which had been erected as a pious act by King Sejo, were used as a pleasure-ground for the revels of the king.

After the deposition of Prince Yŏnsan, the formal suppression of Buddhism continued under his successor King Chungjong. The Buddhist examination system, which had been suspended during Yŏnsan's time, was abolished altogether, and the formal social-standing of the Buddhist clergy was lowered to the bottom status shared by butchers, prostitutes, and slaves. The mendicant life of monks, however, was not forbidden, but this lifestyle only served to reinforce the impression that monks were the same as beggars.

Following the death of Chungjong, his successor King Myŏngjong (r. 1545–67) came to the throne as a child. Consequently, governmental authority was exercised by Myŏngjong's mother, Queen Regent Munjong (r. 1546–53). For the first time since the reign of King Sejo, the ruler actively supported Buddhism. During Munjong's era, the Buddhist examination system was revived, and the advice of leading monks was actively sought. For example, the principal monk of the time, Hyujŏng (Sŏsan taesa, 1520–1604) became an adviser and confidant of the royal entourage. However, when Myŏngjong attained his majority, the position of Buddhism was again reversed. The examination system was once again abolished, and Hyujŏng was sent into internal exile. It is a significant fact of early Chosŏn Buddhism that after Muhak, there was not a single Buddhist monk of note until Hyujŏng. The fortunes of Buddhism had so dramatically changed that the religion had lost its ability to influence the nation socially or culturally, and had lost its ability to produce scholarly monks. These facts were the result of the various policies pursued by the Confucian monarchy over a century and a half. Buddhist Korea was a thing of the past.

Hyujŏng was an original thinker who attempted to draw together the various Buddhist traditions in Korea into a coherent whole. Although he held to the superiority of Sŏn, Hyujŏng also stressed the repetition of the name of Amitābha, the *yŏmbul* formula, and the study of scripture as stages in the growth of Buddhist consciousness. He also developed a theory which stressed the ultimate similarity of the three great religions and philosophical traditions of East Asia, Buddhism, Confucianism, and Taoism. This appeal to unity was actually a sign of the weakened state of Buddhism by the mid-sixteenth century as it was an implicit appeal for the tolerance of Buddhism by the Confucian establishment. At the age of 72, Hyujŏng rendered a great service to his country during the Hideyoshi invasion by organizing bands of warrior-monks who assisted the regular troops.

Hyujŏng's successor and great disciple Yujŏng (Samyŏng taesa, 1544–1610) was also involved in the work of the warrior-monks. Such military action by these leading monks was a continuation of a tradition of defending the nation which had originated in the Silla period. The actions of these monks should be compared to the fifth law in the Code of the Hwarang Troop of Silla, which contradicted the Buddhist concept of reverence for life. Although the actions of Hyujŏng and Yujŏng might seem patriotic, they explicitly reject one of the core tenets of Buddhism – reverence for living things. As such, these actions may be seen as an attempt to gain favour with the Confucian establishment, and are a sign of the decadent state of early Chosŏn Buddhism.

8

THE LATE CHOSŎN PERIOD
(1600–1871)

1. The Cultural and Historical Background

The conclusion of the Hideyoshi Wars of the 1590s did not bring peace to the Korean peninsula. In the first place, the nation lay prostrate after a decade of fighting, and there seemed to be little hope of immediate recovery. Secondly, the whole system of governmental administration, which had been enfeebled by factionalism, had also been impaired by years of war. Thirdly, before the nation could recover from the attacks of one foreign adversary, it had to contend with invasion from another enemy, the Manchus.

In 1616, the Manchu king proclaimed himself emperor, a direct challenge to the Ming Empire, and thus signalled to the Chinese the beginning of a war the outcome of which could only be total victory for one or the other side. When the struggle with the Ming was enjoined, Korea was drawn into the fight. In 1627, Korea was invaded. King Injo (r. 1623–49) took refuge on Kanghwa Island, but was finally forced to recognize the Manchu state of Later Chin as an elder brother – a Confucian term to indicate the dominant relation of one state towards another. On a subsequent invasion in 1632, King Injo formally surrendered to the Manchus and was forced to abandon his vassal relation with Ming in favour of a similar relationship with Later Chin. This was especially hard for Korean intellectuals to accept, as the Manchus were viewed as being barbarians (see Fig. 13).

The seventeenth century also saw the revival of the political factionalism which had lain dormant due to the state of national emergency. The bitter feuds of the latter half of this century centred on the propriety of participation in mourning-rites for deceased monarchs by queen mothers who were only stepmothers of the kings in question. These squabbles continued throughout the remainder of the seventeenth century and centred on the rites for King Hyojong (r. 1649–59) and his wife, the mother of King Hyŏnjong (r. 1659–1674). The main tousling was between the Westerners and the Southerners, the former gaining ultimate victory. Upon emerging as the dominant political faction, the Westerners broke up into two factions, the *Noron* (Old Learning) and the *Soron* (Young Learning) factions. Their squabbles continued throughout the reign of

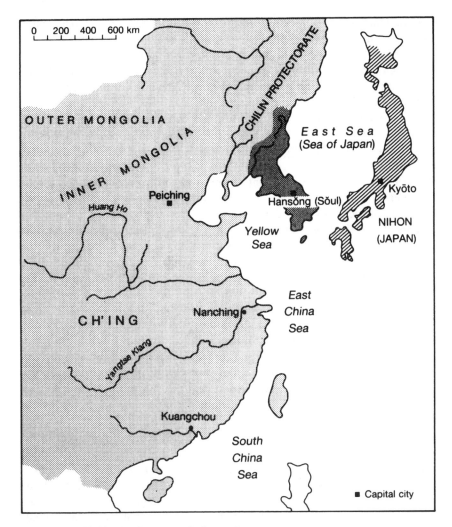

Figure 13 Mid-Chosŏn (Seventeenth Century)

King Sukchong (r. 1674–1720) until they were finally suppressed under the reign of the great King Yŏngjo (r. 1724–76).

While these political events were taking place, several economic changes occurred which were to have long-term effects on the dynasty. First, more and more persons began to find ways to enlarge their landholdings and to remove their lands from the tax register. Collateral members of the royal house could claim their land as tax-exempt, and an increase in such claims led to a significant decline in state revenues. This in turn led to a reform of the tax law. The local tribute, a yearly gift of local products to the court, was now to be paid in grain, some of which was to be used to purchase local specialities (tribute) to be sent to the court. This policy was implemented in various provinces over a hundred-year period beginning in 1608. The men who contracted to handle the collection of the 'tribute' from the provinces formed the basis of a mercantile class centred on three areas – Sŏul, Kaesŏng, and Ŭiju. The development of this mercantile class was also aided by the widespread use of coins as a means of exchange.

Along with these economic changes, profound intellectual changes were taking place as well. After 1600, Korea came into closer contact with Western ideas, especially through contact with the Jesuits resident at the imperial court in Peiching or through works written by these missionary priests. The influence of Western ideas which percolated into Korea was most pronounced on a group of scholars which have latterly become known as the *Sirhak-p'a* (School of Practical Knowledge). One of the earliest men to be singled out as a leader of this movement was Yi Sugwang (1563–1628), whose collected essays called the *Chibong yusŏl* (Collected Essays of Master Chibong) had a great impact on subsequent generations. It was an encyclopaedic work and showed close knowledge of the Western world and of Catholicism in particular. Another scholar of the early *Sirhak-p'a* was Yu Hyŏngwŏn (1622–73), who wrote a comprehensive summary of knowledge called the *Pangye surok* (Collected Essays of Master Pan'gye). Yet another intellectual figure of this period was Yi Ik (1681–1763), the author of the *Sŏngho sasŏl* (Essays of Master Sŏngho). These men all had a common desire for precise knowledge of a scientific sort which could be used to improve both the livelihood of the ordinary person and the state of the nation as a whole. The emergence of the *Sirhak-p'a* was an intellectual reaction to the depressed condition of the country and to the revived factionalism of the seventeenth century.

The eighteenth century was different from the previous century in that a comparative calm existed in the political sphere. The long reigns of two brilliant kings dominated Korean history for the better part of a century. The reigns of King Yŏngjo and his grandson King Chŏngjo (r. 1776–1800) represent the second peak of Confucian civilization in Korea before significant cultural impact from the West. During the eighteenth century many of the economic trends typical of the seventeenth century continued, especially the growth of commerce and the development of a mercantile class. By this stage, Korea had become an incipient capitalistic state.

It is, however, the cultural changes and developments of the eighteenth century for which the reigns of these two kings are best remembered. This cultural development was obviously facilitated by political stability and economic growth, but it was also a reflection of the intellectual leadership of these two monarchs. There were three main lines of scholarly interest: the *Sirhak-p'a*, which had its roots in the seventeenth century; the *Pukhak-p'a*, a development of the mid- and late eighteenth century; and nationalistic studies.

Typical of the later *Sirhak-p'a* scholars was Chŏng Yagyong (1762–1836), a member of a renowned family, who was banished to internal exile for seventeen years from 1801 to 1818. His philosophical goal was to create a just society with equitable distribution of goods to all members of the society. The flaw in his vision was that he wished to create a stable and unchanging agricultural society with strictly limited commercial aspects. In this regard, Chŏng and other *Sirhak-p'a* scholars were at one with the traditional Neo-Confucianists who scorned commerce.

Pak Chega (1750–1815), who wrote the *Pukhag-ŭi* (Discourse on Northern Learning), a description of flourishing commerce in Ch'ing China, stressed the need for Korea to learn the importance of commerce and trade from her northern neighbour. The *Pukhak-p'a* which gathered around Pak Chega, like the *Sirhak-p'a*, stressed the equality of all men and equal opportunity. However, the *Pukhak-p'a* scholars, unlike the *Sirhak-p'a* scholars, were more cognizant and accepting of the economic and commercial developments which were occurring at that time.

Linked with this interest in the social and economic development of the nation was a concern for its history. The interpretation of the past was a major Confucian concern, regardless of the school to which a scholar belonged. Ancient history was of particular interest, and it was in the eighteenth century that we may discern a renewed interest in Parhae, the successor state of Koguryŏ. Linguistic work and geographical research were also an indication of patriotic interests. *Han'gŭl* came to be used in literature at this time. Poetry was often written in a mixed script of Chinese characters and the Korean alphabet rather than solely in Chinese script. Among notable works were the *Hong Kiltong-jŏn* (Tale of Hong Kiltong), *Ku'un-mong* (Cloud Dream of the Nine), and the *Ch'unhyang-jŏn* (Tale of Ch'unhyang). Genre-painting emerged as a trend in this period, lending a distinctive Korean flavour to art works. The best known of these genre painters was Kim Hongdo (1745–post-1814), who tried to portray realistically the life of the ordinary people of his day.

The death of King Chŏngjo in 1800 marked a dramatic change in Korea's fortunes. For the better part of a hundred years social stability and some limited commercial progress had prevailed throughout the nation. The nineteenth century, however, was a time of remarkable decline in the affairs of the state. Factionalism, which had been under control, broke out again. Every king who came to the throne in the nineteenth century did so in his minority, the country being ruled through the agency of a queen regent. As according to tradition the eldest surviving queen mother had the right to decide the succession, factionalism broke out along clan lines. Of these feuding clans one clan, the Andong Kim clan, came to dominate Korean politics for most of the century.

Clan politics on a high level lent itself to corruption on the local level. Magistracies were openly sold and used by their incumbents to milk the countryside. The rapacity of these petty officials led to several peasant revolts, most notably the uprising of Hong Kyŏngnae (1780–1812) in P'yŏngan Province in 1812. The country in the first half of the nineteenth century was beset as well by various natural calamities – devastating floods, uncontrolled fires, and a prolonged outbreak of cholera. These conditions, when added to the corrupt state of the government, only increased the restiveness of the general population.

Korea was also unprepared for the advent of Western adventurism. For centuries since the Hideyoshi Wars, various governments had pursued a policy of complete isolation. From the 1830s onwards, Western commercial and naval vessels began to appear off Korea's coasts, demanding trade and diplomatic relationships. By the 1860s, all these developments had become acute. Popular uprisings were occurring with frequency; foreign vessels appeared more frequently off Korea's coasts; the traditional class structure was collapsing; and foreign ideas, especially Catholicism, were creeping in to undermine the traditional system of values.

At this point, the last great leader of traditional Korea came on the scene, the *Taewŏn-gun* or Prince Regent Yi Ha'ŭng (1820–98), who had manoeuvred to have his twelve-year-old son placed on the throne of Korea as King Kojong (r. 1863–1907). In many ways, the Prince Regent represented the best of traditional Confucian virtues, but his vision of a revived Korea was badly out of step with the times. He simultaneously concentrated on building up the strength of the nation and firmly closed her borders and coasts to the entrance of foreigners. The attempt by the Regent to stave off contact with the outside world was initially successful. Korean troops and naval batteries were able to repulse the foreign warships which appeared off her coast. However, the pursuit of this policy left the country unprepared to deal with the inevitability of foreign intercourse and the changed nature of international politics. Similarly, the Prince Regent's policies were unable to resolve the problems of the internal economic and social situation. It is at this point that Korea had significant contact with Protestant Christianity. Decades of social instability during the nineteenth century provided a fertile ground for the advent of new religious ideas.

2. Late Chosŏn Confucianism: Practical Confucianism

(a) The Seventeenth Century

If the sixteenth century is the golden age of Korean speculative philosophy, the seventeenth century is the era of practical philosophy. The sixteenth century ended with the virtual destruction of the state during the Japanese invasions. Further invasion under the Manchus, political factionalism, and a disrupted economy and agricultural system created a situation of social decay and personal frustration. Out of this chaos arose a unique Korean contribution to Neo-Confucian thought which drew on the philosophy of one of the sixteenth-century schools. The scholars who came to be called members of the *Sirhak-p'a* rooted their philosophies in the ideas of Yulgok and the *Chugi-p'a*. The School of Practical Knowledge concentrated on reform in two areas, agriculture and commerce.

The origin of the *Sirhak-p'a* may be traced to the writings of two men, Yi Sugwang and Han Paekkyŏm (1552–1615). Yi Sugwang's collected works referred to above, the *Chibong yusŏl*, was especially influential in stimulating younger scholars to confront the social and economic realities of their day. He had lived through the era of the Hideyoshi wars and had seen the social catastrophe which had followed in its wake. He was also familiar with Western scientific knowledge, and keenly felt the need for Korea to learn to use these scientific advances. Han Paekkyŏm's historical works created a sense of nationalism which aided in raising the consciousness of scholars to the crisis facing the nation. It is not surprising that the primary concern of the first generation of Sirhak scholars was agriculture. Agriculture was the basis of the national economy and without reform in this area the nation could not hope to recover.

Two early seventeenth-century thinkers, Yun Chŭng (1629–1714) and Yu Hyŏngwŏn, developed the ideas first suggested by Yi Sugwang. Yun refused government office and devoted himself entirely to the development of Sirhak philosophy. He is credited with the surprisingly democratic remark that the king could not exist without the people, but the people could exist without the king.

Yu Hyŏngwŏn's influence was even greater than that of Yun Chŭng, especially through his collected writings, the *Panggye surok*. Born in the capital to a family of scholars, Yu paid particular attention to the development of rural life and society. He passed the *chinsa* (Literary Licentiate) examination, but refused to spend his life in government service, instead led the life of a retired, country scholar. He finally settled in Pu'an County in north Korea in 1653, where most of his important writings were composed.

Although resident in Pu'an, Yu Hyŏngwŏn made several journeys throughout the country observing the condition of rural life. Influenced by Yulgok, Yu in turn influenced Yi Ik and Chŏng Yagyong. The key to the problems of agricultural development in Yu's opinion was the system of landholding. Consequently, he appealed for a ruling against the expansion of private estates at the expense of the ordinary farmer. Further, Yu thought that the system of taxation should be completely restructured so that it did not place a heavy burden on the general populace. Perhaps his most telling comment was that the system of education and appointment to the civil service should be based on merit and open to anyone regardless of social origin. Ever since the introduction of Confucianism to Koguryŏ, Confucian education in Korea had been restricted to members of the aristocracy, thus undermining the democratic principle of Confucian philosophy. Yu's remark was a call for a return to the original principles of Confucianism.

The leadership of the second generation of this faction of the *Sirhak-p'a* passed to Yi Ik (1681–1763). His collected works, the *Sŏngho sasŏl*, like Yu Hyŏngwŏn's *Panggye surok*, had a great influence on the young thinkers of his time. Son of the deputy head of the Board of Taxation, Yi had one of the most distinguished careers of his day. He was several times head or deputy head of the

Boards of Personnel or Punishment, and had also been governor of Kyŏnggi and Kyŏngsang Provinces. He was exiled twice, and was involved with the factional feuds of his time. It is, however, for his writings and his philosophy, and not for his career, that he is best remembered.

Widely versed in many areas of learning, from the physical sciences such as astronomy and geography to legal matters, Yi Ik was very concerned about the reform of agriculture and rural life. He advocated among other matters the abolition of slavery, the citizen's identification tag, the *kwagŏ* civil-service examination, and all practices which led to the creation of class barriers. He strongly advocated scientific research and study as a means of improving the rural economy. Yi Ik also urged the abolition of money and of the practice of money-lending, which he felt led to usury, and which in turn created misery in the lives of the people. Like his predecessors, Yi Ik did not envisage the development of a commercial economy, but instead abhorred the possibility of its emergence. All of the scholars of the *Sirhak-p'a* who followed these lines of thought envisaged the continuation of an essentially agrarian economy.

Other important figures in the movement for the reform of rural society were Yun Hyu (1617–80), Pak Sedang (1629–1703), and Hong Mansŏn (1643–1715). In particular, the latter two men considered not only the question of the reformation of rural society, but also the development and improvement of agricultural technology and techniques. In so doing, they went one step further than Yu Hyŏngwŏn or Yi Ik.

Pak Sedang is an excellent example of the seventeenth-century scholar/ politician. Son of a high official, Pak held many high positions in government, including deputy minister of the Boards of Rites and Punishment. In 1694, at the age of 65, he held successively the posts of Minister of Works, Rites, and Punishment. In 1703, at the age of 74, when he should have been enjoying a quiet old age, he wrote a blistering attack on the philosophy of Chu Hsi which caused him to be stripped of all his titles and imprisoned. He died in prison in the same year. The book which created such a furore is the *Sabyŏn-nok* (Thoughtful Elucidations).

Hong Mansŏn never held high office, but was distinguished by the sobriety of his conduct and his refusal to become involved in the partisan politics of the late seventeenth century. More importantly, Hong was extremely critical of Chu Hsi and emphasized the practical application of philosophy. He was noted for his knowledge of agricultural technology, medicine, and famine relief.

It should be emphasized that as the *Sirhak-p'a* scholars concerned themselves more and more with the practical matters of the reformation of rural society and of the nation itself, they came to sense the utter emptiness of the thinking of the school of Chu Hsi. Along with their practical interests and social criticism, these scholars created a fundamental critique of *Chuja-hak* itself. Pak Sedang and Hong Mansŏn led this critique. Yun Hyu set himself the goal of examining all known forms of philosophy, including despised Taoism. For the temerity to question the philosophical foundations of the Chosŏn state, critics such as these men were committed to long periods of internal exile, during which time many of them died.

(b) The Eighteenth Century

A second strand of the practical philosophy movement did not emerge until the eighteenth century. The first generations of Sirhak scholars had concerned themselves largely with agricultural matters. Beginning with Yu Suwŏn (1695–1755), many scholars began to seriously consider commercial, technical, and scientific matters. The first of these subjects, in particular, would have been anathema to Yi Ik. In his collected works, the Usŏ (Idle Jottings), Yu makes several sweeping suggestions, such as the elimination of tracing yangban ancestry, the abolition of the four-class social structure, the recognition of the equality of all work and occupations, and equal opportunity for specialized education in various occupations. He also suggested that the government should encourage capital accumulation for the development of commerce, and advocated the coining of money. This was the most radical break of all with orthodox Confucianism by any practical scholar and opened the way for the potential commercial growth of the nation. Curiously, although Yu argued for the equality of occupations and open access to education, he tacitly approved of rural slavery for the promotion of agriculture.

Yu Suwŏn was followed by a series of important eighteenth-century figures who interested themselves in commercial and technological development. These included Pak Chiwŏn (1737–1805), Pak Chega (1750–1805), Hong Taeyong (1731–83), and Yi Tŏngmu (1741–93). Because these scholars looked towards their northern neighbour Ch'ing China for new ideas, this group is often called the Pukhak-p'a, or School of Northern Learning.

One of the first scholars to emphasize learning from the 'barbarian' Ch'ing Dynasty was Pak Chiwŏn. The suggestion of learning from the Manchus was hard for many Koreans to accept not only because the 'barbarian' Manchus had conquered the legitimate Chinese Ming Dynasty, but because only practical matters of commerce and science could be learned from these 'barbarians'. In his Yŏrha ilgi (Diary of Travels in Jehol), Pak Chiwŏn described his journey in 1780 as a member of the entourage of the royal embassy sent to the imperial court. In this journal, he demonstrated both how far behind Korea had fallen economically and the necessity for her to catch up. Pak felt that the development of the Korean nation must involve improvements not only in the agricultural sphere but in the commercial sphere as well. He advocated adopting not only Chinese irrigation and metallurgical technology, but also improved transportation for trade. His later writings, such as the Yangban-jŏn (Tale of a Yangban), were a blistering attack on the corrupt nature of yangban society in the eighteenth century.

An important contemporary and disciple of Pak Chiwŏn was Pak Chega, who wrote the influential book Pukhag-ŭi mentioned before. Although Pak Chega never held high government posts, he was appointed four times as a member of the official diplomatic missions to the Ch'ing imperial court. It was these first-hand experiences of Chinese society and his position as a member of the *Kyujang-gak*, the palace library and research centre created by King Chŏngjo to further the development of practical Confucian studies, which shaped his critique of late Chosŏn society and culture.

In most respects, Pak Chega was like his mentor. Having had the opportunity to visit China, Pak became fully convinced that not only should Korea develop its own internal commercial structure, but that the government should promote international commerce by sending regular missions to Ch'ing China. He also urged the invitation of Western scholars to Korea to offer instruction in Western technology. In the *Pukhag-ŭi*, one of Pak Chega's most memorable statements is 'The consumer is the way to encourage production', which stresses the importance which he placed on commerce and trade as the engine which would drive the economy. It is also symbolic of how far the Pukhak scholars had moved away from the orthodox Neo-Confucian position which abhorred the very thought of trade.

Two lesser scholars of the reign of King Chŏngjo were Hong Taeyong and Yi Tŏngmu noted for their diaries both titled *Yŏn-gi* (Peiching Diary). Hong Taeyong had a great interest in commercial and military affairs. Like several other practical scholars, he went to Peiching and made contact with Chinese literati. He also had contact with two Catholic priests, Augustin von Hallerstein (1703–74) and Antonine Gogeisl (1701–71), from whom he learned about Catholicism and astronomy. Hong was also very much concerned with what we would now call universal education and suggested that children from the age of eight should all be sent to school. Yi Tŏngmu, like other members of the *Pukhak-p'a*, got his ideas about modernization from a visit to Ch'ing China. Along with Pak Chega, Yi was a keeper of the *Kyujang-gak* library.

Although the trend of practical thinking in the eighteenth century was largely focused on commercial matters, the last and perhaps the greatest of these scholars was Chŏng Yagyong, who devoted his years of internal exile to the study of agricultural affairs. One of a family of famous intellectuals and early Catholic believers and martyrs, Chŏng was influenced by the thought of Yi Ik through his own mentor Yi Pyŏk (1754–86). Chŏng passed the literary examination at the highest level in 1789 and intermittently held several influential positions in government during the next ten years. In 1790 he was denounced as a Catholic and exiled to Haemi in Ch'ungch'ŏng Province, but he was released after ten days. In 1794 he was appointed as a secret royal inspector for Kyŏnggi Province, in the course of which duty he exposed a corrupt official. From then on he held a variety of responsible positions, including Deputy Minister of Punishment. He was later assigned to the *Kyujang-gak*. In 1801 he was again denounced as a Roman Catholic and was sent into internal exile for seventeen years. Released in 1818, Chŏng retired to his home where he spent the remainder of his life as a country scholar. Chŏng Yagyong's philosophy reflects the influence of many of the various practical thinkers mentioned above, especially Yu Suwŏn and Yi Ik, as well as knowledge of the Chinese philosopher Wang Yang-ming whose ideas were considered to be a heterodox philosophy in Chosŏn Korea. It is still uncertain whether or not he remained formally a member of the Catholic Church, was a crypto-Catholic, or abandoned the faith entirely.

Among Chŏng's writings, the *Kiye-non* (Theory of Technology) and the *Ch'on-non* (Theory of Rural Society) are particularly important. In the former book, we can see the influences of the *Pukhak-p'a*, especially as regards the necessity for technological innovation. In Chŏng's opinion, technical education was essential for the progress of the nation. It is, however, in the *Ch'on-non* that we can see the ideal which he envisaged for a future society. The nature of this ideal society shows that although Chŏng was aware of the importance of commercial and technological development, he believed society as a whole should be based on agriculture. For a nineteenth-century figure this was not a progressive concept. Chŏng's concept of rural society was called *Yŏjŏn-je*. Village land was to be held and worked in common, the harvest being divided according to the amount of labour which a family unit supplied. A portion of the harvest was to be set aside as a form of tax in kind. This type of thinking was a precursor of the commune which developed in China more than a century later. If Chŏng's ideas had been accepted it would have meant the most radical reconstruction of Korean society since the introduction of agriculture itself. None the less, because it did not take note of the importance of commerce and industry, such a system would not have helped to advance Korea's position in the world. Fascination with rural life was a distinctive and lingering influence of Confucianism on the thoughts even of such radical thinkers as Chŏng Yagyong.

(c) The Nineteenth Century

The principal events which affected Confucian scholars during the early and mid-nineteenth century were factionalism at court and Western imperial encroachment. Late Chosŏn began to grapple with the issues raised by the advent of Western thought. There were four principal Confucian thinkers during the nineteenth century, three of whom belonged to the tradition of the *Churi-p'a*: Ki Chŏngjin (1798–1876), Yi Hangno (1792–1868), and Yi Chinsang (1818–85). The latter was the author of the *Yihak chongyo* (Epitome of the Study of *Yi*) in which he stated that Mind and *yi* are the same. This, in a sense, was the logical outcome of centuries of debate within the *Churi-p'a* of Korea. These three scholars generally took a more conservative and rejectionist view of Western thought and culture. The fourth scholar was Ch'oe Han'gi (1803–79) whose thought represents a continuation of the *Sirhak-p'a* in light of the impact which Western science and imperialism were making on East Asia. Ch'oe tried to relate traditional Confucian values to the question of modernization and especially the need to learn Western science and technology. He also urged the direct importation of Western technology to aid in the development of the nation.

(d) Common Trends in Chosŏn Dynasty Philosophy

In this discussion, the reader will have become aware of the extent to which later Confucian scholars had changed the nature of Confucian philosophical enquiry in Korea (see Fig. 14). Although sixteenth-century scholars debated strictly metaphysical matters, there is a straight line of descent from the *Sarim-p'a* of the fifteenth and sixteenth centuries to the *Sirhak-p'a* of the seventeenth and eighteenth centuries. Kim Chongjik and Cho Kwangjo were passionately concerned with the reformation of society, which they saw as the restructuring of the moral order of the nation. Through the philosophical developments of the *Chugi-p'a* and Yulgok's thought, practical matters more and more gained the attention of the Confucian scholars of the late sixteenth century. With the national devastation which occurred at the end of that century and during the early part of the next, philosophical enquiry turned to the very practical matters of commerce and technology, moving so far in that direction, in fact, that such concerns dominated the interests of the later scholars. This would have been an abomination to their intellectual ancestors of two centuries before. Pursuit of such precise practical concerns by Korean scholars was in contrast to the strictly academic and antiquarian pursuits of their counterparts in Ch'ing China. The *Sirhak-p'a* and *Pukhak-p'a* scholars were part of a unique trend in East Asian Confucianism, a movement for a practical philosophy embracing technical, commercial and scientific issues.

Nevertheless, the common thread within all the schools of Neo-Confucianism in the Chosŏn Dynasty was a concern for the reformation of society, whether it was the reformation of the moral order or the reformation of the economic order. Confucian thought in the Chosŏn Dynasty did not mean the institution of a form of government or a system of education. It meant the remaking of society into some ideal image. It is important, however, at this point to remind ourselves that intellectual trends do not mean political trends or even political influence.

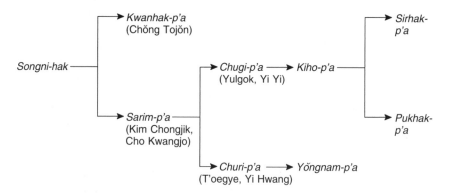

Figure 14 Lineage of Chosŏn Period Confucian Schools

134

Although most of the men of the seventeenth and eighteenth centuries whom we have discussed here are giants in the intellectual history of Korea, they were for the most part unable to institute the ideals which they advocated.

(e) Wang Yang-ming and Chosŏn Dynasty Thought

One must not leave a discussion of Confucianism in the late Chosŏn period with the sense that the field was held entirely by the *Sirhak-p'a* or even by the school of Chu Hsi. We have seen that the *Sirhak-p'a* implicitly rejected the social efficacy of Chu Hsi's thought, and also that certain critics such as Yun Hyu and Pak Sedang openly criticized the entire system of Chu Hsi's philosophy. In Korea, Neo-Confucianism meant Chu Hsi's philosophy, whereas in China there were alternative forms of Neo-Confucian philosophy, such as the system of Wang Yang-ming (1473–1529). As Wang Yang-ming had been born well after the founding of the Chosŏn state, it is not surprising that Chosŏn-period scholars were slow in paying attention to him. Moreover, T'oegye had examined Wang's system and had pronounced it to be unorthodox and consequently unworthy of further consideration. As a result, few Korean scholars examined Wang's philosophy seriously. Unlike that of Chu Hsi, Wang's system was not dualistic but monistic, placing emphasis on knowledge to gain enlightenment about the nature of the universe. *Li* (*yi* in Korean) and *ch'i* (*ki* in Korean) were unified in *li*, making the essence of the universe mental.

Among Korean proponents of Wang's philosophy were Ch'oe Myŏnggil (1586–1647), Chang Yu (1587–1638), and Chŏng Chedu (1649–1736). The latter scholar set up the tradition of the Kanghwa Island scholars who followed the thought of Wang Yang-ming. Chŏng Chedu was one of the most unusual, if not unique, figures of the late Chosŏn Dynasty. At an early age he studied Chu Hsi's philosophy and came to reject it, taking up Wang's thought instead. Although he had accepted a few minor government posts, he decided to devote himself entirely to philosophy and research. So assiduously did he pursue this course that he refused to accept some thirty significant government appointments which were offered to him. For Chŏng, the appeal of Wang's philosophy was its perceived unity of thought and action. Most scholars attribute the development of Wang Yang-ming's thought in Korea to the school which Chŏng started. In the politico-intellectual climate of the late Chosŏn period, this development amounted to the creation of an opposition movement to the prevailing 'orthodox' Confucian system.

(f) The End of a Confucian Polity

Although most important thinkers of the late Chosŏn Dynasty were stimulated by the advent of Western ideas and technology, there were a few scholars who rejected Western knowledge, most notably Sin Hudam (1702–61). Sin wrote the *Sŏhak-pyŏn* (Critique of Western Learning), a treatise strongly critical of

Western culture. While unusual in its rejection of Western knowledge, the *Sŏhak-pyŏn* does stand in the trend of nationalistic studies typical of the eighteenth century.

The burgeoning of scholastic studies which took place under the aegis of the *Sirhak-p'a* found expression in various other scholarly endeavours which reflected a nationalist bias, a trend which had begun with Han Paekkyŏm. Notable contributions were made in the areas of politics, foreign affairs, history and ancient history, geography and cartography, economics and commerce, medicine, natural sciences, linguistics, biographical studies, folklore, and music. Most of this work was done in the eighteenth century and reflected the generally advanced state of cultural affairs at that time. It was the last flowering of a Korean Confucian civilization before the impact of Western culture.

The end of formal Confucian influence on Korean society came dramatically in the seventh decade of the nineteenth century. King Kojong came to the throne at the age of twelve in 1864. As the king was still a minor, the actual affairs of state were carried out by his father, who was styled *Taewŏn-gun* or Prince Regent. The *Taewŏn-gun's* principal policy of government was to strengthen the power of the throne against any centrifugal forces which might weaken the power and authority of the central government. We have seen how from the sixteenth century onwards the *sŏwŏn* or private regional academies not only displaced the *hyanggyo* as the main seats of provincial education but also became major centres for regional politics which could challenge the central government. The judgements of one *sŏwŏn* in particular, the Hwayang-dong academy, carried especial weight in the world of nineteenth-century Korean Confucianism. The other threat to the central government from the *sŏwŏn* came from their entrenched privileges. The *sŏwŏn* not only held large numbers of slaves and great tracts of valuable agricultural land, they were also exempt from taxes and corvée labour. By the middle of the nineteenth century, the *sŏwŏn* had come to constitute a major political and economic threat to the central government.

Between 1864, the year in which he came to power, and 1871 the Prince Regent acted resolutely against the academies. In 1864 he banned their further reconstruction; in 1866 he abolished two special shrines to the last two Ming emperors; in 1868 he decreed that the *sŏwŏn* should be taxed. In 1871 the final blow fell when the Prince Regent closed all but forty-seven of the hundreds of academies in the country. This final act symbolized the demise of formal Confucian influence in Korean society. For Confucianism, it had the same effect as the mass closure of temples had had on Buddhism in the fifteenth century. What was different, however, was that the temple closures were carried out by a Confucian government against the Buddhist establishment, while the closure of the academies of the Confucian establishment was undertaken by a Confucian government. In my view, this final event in 1871 was so important in the religious and philosophical history of Korea that I have dated the beginning of the modern era of Korean religious history from the next year, 1872.

3. Late Chosŏn Buddhism: The Submerging of a Tradition

From the conclusion of the Hideyoshi wars to the end of the nineteenth century, Korean Buddhism reached the lowest point of its historical trajectory in terms of its social and cultural influence. It is significant that after Hyujŏng, there was not one monk of national distinction. The nation was dominated by Confucianism as in no previous period making itself felt in the political, cultural, and social spheres to the extent that Buddhism was virtually excluded. Social criticism came from Confucian thinkers and not Buddhists. Art and art forms were influenced by Confucianism. The social system conformed more or less to Confucian standards. The monastic life had an appeal only to those who wished to opt out of society. Those persons who wished to be socially and politically influential had to know the Confucian classics and had to take the Confucian state examinations.

Buddhism was not only socially and culturally in decline, it was actively suppressed by the government. This persecution had gone on before in the early part of the dynasty, but it was more vigorously pursued in the latter half of the Chosŏn period. During the early years of King Hyŏnjong's reign in the late seventeenth century, various Confucian scholars were concerned that a strong Buddhist church would weaken Confucian influence on the state and society. They urged certain measures to control or suppress Buddhism even more vigorously. In the latter part of 1659, to prevent large numbers of the peasantry from taking monastic orders, an edict was issued forbidding any novice from taking monastic orders. It was also decreed at the same time that persons discovered to have entered monastic life after the proclamation of the edict would be subject to arrest and returned to secular life.

In the following year, 1660, two small Buddhist academies were destroyed. The younger monks were laicized and the older monks were retired to a small home outside the capital city's walls. Shortly after this, a decree was issued forbidding any monk or nun from entering the walled city of Sŏul. Hyŏnjong, recalling that Chu Hsi was supposed to have converted a temple into a Confucian academy, attempted to use temple buildings as Confucian study-halls. In 1662, a report came from the governor of Chŏlla Province that Buddhist statues in various temples were sweating. This was explained as due to moisture affecting the wood of which the statues were made, although the populace was said to understand it to be the sweat of the Buddha. Because it was feared that a superstitious cult would spread, the statues were all destroyed.

King Sukjong (r. 1674–1720), Hyŏnjong's successor, continued the practice of the official suppression of the 'superstitious' creed of Buddhism. In 1675, the court suppressed a cult which had begun to develop around the son of a government official who had become a clandestine practitioner of esoteric Buddhism. Court servants secretly availed themselves of his curative powers. One of these servants made the astounding claim that the monk-sorcerer was actually the deceased crown prince, Sohyŏn (1612–45). A message written in the

Korean alphabet was produced which was supposed to prove the authenticity of the claim. The suppression of this cult, with its implications for the dynastic succession, was ruthlessly carried out and the principal participants were executed. Such events only confirmed Confucian scholars in their view of the superstitious and subversive nature of Buddhism.

King Yŏngjo's reign (r. 1724–76), though a brilliant period in the history of Korean culture, was also characterized by the repression of Buddhism. In 1749 the edict forbidding Buddhist clerics from entering the capital was reissued. In 1760, after receiving a report that a young nun was claiming to be a living Buddha, the king sent a secret inspector to investigate. Because it was feared that the minds of the peasantry would be polluted with gross superstition, the nun was beheaded and her head displayed as a warning to other potential cult figures. Among other edicts issued against Buddhism in Yŏngjo's reign was the forbidding of the building of temples in the vicinity of royal tombs. It had been an unofficial practice in the early Chosŏn period to build temples near royal tombs which could function as mortuary temples for the souls of the deceased.

Even though Buddhism reached its nadir during this 250-year period, and even though it was suppressed by the government, it did survive to enter the twentieth century. First of all, there were a few monks who did uphold the standards both of monastic discipline and of Buddhist learning. Among these men, perhaps Yŏnch'o (1676–1750) is the most important. Following the death of Hyujŏng, there emerged two strands of Buddhism, one of which was more inclined towards doctrinal study, whereas the other inclined towards the practice of Sŏn. Neither of these schools, however, excluded entirely the practices of the other school. Yŏnch'o hoped to revive Buddhism by creating a single order out of these two strands of late Chosŏn Buddhism. He went to Ŭnmun-sa temple near Taegu at the age of 13 and took orders there. His great work as a monk was the eventual reunification of the various divisions of Buddhism in his day, which he effected by demonstrating that the doctrinal and Sŏn strands were not only complementary but fulfilled each other.

Although it had always been official policy to suppress or control Buddhism, we have seen how in the early Chosŏn period members of the court and even the monarchs themselves were often Buddhists. Shortly before his death, the great Confucian monarch Sejong sought for the meaning of life in Buddhism. More than 300 years later King Chŏngjo, one of the three or four Confucian sage monarchs of the Chosŏn Dynasty, also practised Buddhism. This may seem odd in view of the vigour with which his grandfather Yŏngjo had persecuted the Buddhist church.

Chŏngjo was noted as being the most filial of all Chosŏn kings because of his unusual attention to his father's tomb. Chŏngjo's father was Prince Changhŏn (1735–62), Yŏngjo's crown prince who was tragically murdered as the result of court intrigue. When Chŏngjo came to the throne, he never forgot his father's distressed spirit and paid great reverence to it. He gave his father a royal regnal style, and his father's grave was moved to a more propitious place near Suwŏn. When Chŏngjo died in 1800, he and his government had been in the process of creating a new capital city at Suwŏn, so that the king could be near his father's grave. Near the tomb of his father, King Chŏngjo caused a great temple to be erected, the Yongju-sa (Dragon Jewel Temple), which was to serve as a mortuary temple for the repose of his father's spirit. That was in the year 1789. In 1790 Chŏngjo caused a stele to be erected in a temple as a thank-offering for the answer to his prayers, a son to succeed him on the throne. Chŏngjo was the first Chosŏn monarch to display Buddhist piety publicly since King Sejo in the fifteenth century. However, royal favour was granted to Buddhism for *raisons d'état* as well as for personal reasons.

Another factor in the continuation of Buddhism during the difficult period of the late Chosŏn Dynasty was its appeal to the populace. Court servants helped to provide a degree of protection to the faith through the indirect influence which they had with officials. At the popular level, Buddhism was a mixture of Korean folk religion and doctrinal Buddhism. By far the most popular cults were the worship of *Amitābha* and *San-sin*, the Mountain God. The former cult was linked to the desire to depart this life and live eternally in the glorious Western Paradise with its benevolent ruler, *Amitābha* (*Amit'a* in Korean). The cult of the mountain god was practised inside the temple precincts and was popular with women seeking male offspring.

Not only did Buddhism exercise an influence on the peasantry during the late Chosŏn period, it also had an influence *sub rosa* on the Confucian literati. We have seen how various monarchs privately supported or practised Buddhism. It is not surprising that many of the intelligentsia did the same. Most of the scholars who expressed an interest in Buddhism did so because it represented an alternative to the prevailing rigid orthodoxy of the philosophy of Chu Hsi.

Perhaps the best-known figure who took an interest in Buddhism is Kim Manjung (1637–92), noted for his novels *Sassi namjŏng-gi* (The Southern Journeys of Lady Sa) and *Ku'un-mong* (The Cloud Dream of the Nine). The *Sassi namjŏng-gi* is a disguised critique of the court intrigue which led to the downfall of King Sukjong's legitimate queen and her replacement by a concubine. This novel was largely responsible for her reinstatement and contains many Buddhist motifs. Buddhist elements are more obvious in the *Ku'un-mong*. The story centres around a young hero who falls in love with and lives with eight beautiful women. He attains great eminence as a military and political figure enjoying immense wealth and power. In the end, he realizes that everything which is prized highly in this world is transitory. The *Ku'un-mong* is the first of many novels stressing the transitoriness of this world and its glories, reflecting a certain *ennui* on the part of the Confucian literati. Such sentiments well demonstrate the inability of Chu Hsi's thought to speak to the longing of man's spirit for knowledge of a world beyond the present.

4. The Advent of Roman Catholicism

(a) Initial Missionary Endeavours

Prior to the middle of the nineteenth century, the history of the Roman Catholic Church in Korea may be divided into three broad periods: (1) a period of initial missionary endeavours; (2) a period of initial organization under local believers; and (3) a period of persecution and the growth of an underground church. The first period encompasses the late sixteenth century and the early seventeenth century and includes attempts by Catholics in Japan, China, and the Philippines to reach the population of the 'Hermit Kingdom'. With the success of Jesuit missions among certain of the feudal *daimyōs* of Japan, several Jesuit missionaries turned their thoughts to Korea. Among the earliest was Father Gaspar Vilela (1525–72), who had been in Japan since 1556. Around 1567 Father Vilela drew up comprehensive plans for the development of a Jesuit mission in Korea, but he was unable to implement them before he died in Malacca in 1572.

Ironically, the first Jesuits to come to Korea arrived in the company of the invading armies of Toyotomi Hideyoshi in 1594. Father Gregorio de Cespedes (1551–1611) and a Japanese Jesuit brother, Foucan Eion were attached as chaplains to the forces of the Christian *daimyō* Konishi Yukinaga (1556–1600). Because of a dispute with the other Japanese commander who was a Buddhist, the two chaplains were withdrawn. It would seem that neither Father de Cespedes nor the Japanese brother had any significant contact with the Korean population. One curious result of the Hideyoshi invasions was that many of the Koreans who were taken back to Japan as slaves became Christians through the efforts of Jesuit missionaries working in Nagasaki and other major cities. Father Louis Fröes (1532–97) stated in a report for the year 1596 that 300 Korean slaves had been instructed in Catholic doctrine in that year in the city of Nagasaki. During the suppression of Catholicism at the beginning of the Tokugawa shogunate in the early seventeenth century, at least thirteen of the 205 Catholic martyrs are known to have been Koreans. Among these was a young Korean known as Vincent Kwŏn (1581–1626) who had been captured by a Christian *daimyō*. Under the influence of this Japanese feudal lord, Kwŏn became a Catholic. From 1614 to 1626 when he was martyred in Nagasaki, Kwŏn made several attempts to re-enter his homeland in order to undertake evangelistic activities there.

While the Jesuits were attempting to enter the 'Hermit Kingdom' from Japan, the Dominicans in the Philippines were also considering plans for the evangelization of Korea. Father Juan de Domingo (?–1619) was selected to undertake this task and made two unsuccessful attempts to enter Korea in 1611 and in 1616. He finally went to Japan where he was martyred in 1619 while staying at the home of a Japanese believer in Nagasaki.

In China, a convert of the Jesuit missionary Matteo Ricci (1552–1610), the powerful minister of state Hsü Kuang-ch'i (1562–1634), petitioned the throne twice, in 1620 and in 1621, to be allowed to go to Korea, allegedly for oversight of various political and military problems. Although he was refused permission to enter Korea, it is known that his intention was to undertake propagation of Christianity there. He had collected a number of Jesuit pamphlets explaining Catholicism and had obtained the consent of Father Francesco Sambiasi (1582–1649) for his proposed journey. Although Hsü was unable to journey to Korea, Christians in China continued to think of ways to introduce their religion into the peninsula. Father Antonio de Sainte-Marie attempted to gain entrance in 1650, but was unable to do so and completed his ministry in the Shantung peninsula. Joannes Adam Schall von Bell (1591–1666), the head of the Jesuit mission in Ch'ing China, came into contact with Crown Prince Sohyŏn (1612–1645), who was a hostage at the Manchu court. The Crown Prince became interested in Catholicism, and upon his return to his homeland he took Christian books and religious objects with him. The Jesuits entertained high hopes that when he ascended the throne Prince Sohyŏn would permit the open propagation of Christianity. These hopes were dashed by his death in the midst of court intrigue a few months after his return.

The Catholic Church did have an indirect influence on many of the scholars of the seventeenth century through the pamphlets which the Jesuits wrote to explain Catholic belief and doctrine. The *Chibong yusŏl*, a work in twenty *chüan* by the Confucian scholar Yi Sugwang, contains the earliest known reference to the Catholic church and its doctrines. This information is clearly based upon Ricci's *T'ien-chu Shih-i* (The True Teaching of the Lord of Heaven), a copy of which had been given to him by his friend Yi Kwangjŏng (1552–1627), who had visited Peiching. Another Confucian scholar, Chŏng Tuwŏn (1581–?), went on a diplomatic mission to the Ming court in 1630 where he made the acquaintance of Father João Rodrígues (1561–1633). From this missionary, Chŏng obtained several works of a scientific nature which had been translated by the Jesuits into Chinese. Although aware of Catholicism, neither of these men appear to have taken more than an intellectual interest in the subject.

Before the middle of the eighteenth century, the dynastic records of the Chosŏn kingdom contain two curious references which have led some Korean scholars to think that there may have been some kind of Catholic presence in Korea before the official organization of the church in the late eighteenth century. In the dynastic record for King Sukchong for the year 1686, there is a mention of an edict to apprehend foreigners illegally in the country. Another later reference in the record for King Yŏngjo in the year 1758 states that many people in Hwanghae and Kangwŏn Provinces had ceased the performance of the *chesa* or ancestral memorial rites. It is felt that the latter remark in particular reflects Catholic teaching on the ancestral rites. There is, however, no specific evidence to support this conclusion.

(b) Indigenous Organization of the Church

The second or formative period of Korean Catholicism encompasses the last quarter of the eighteenth century. It is at this time that we first find definite evidence for the existence of a body of professing Christians and the beginnings of an organized church. This period of Korean Catholicism was dominated by Confucian scholars following the line of the *Sirhak-p'a*, and particularly those scholars who were students of the thought of Yi Ik (1681–1763). Many of these men were in turn connected to the Southern or *Namin* political faction, which was out of power at this time. Consequently, the formative stage of the church was dominated by the aristocracy and typified by intellectual and scholastic concerns.

From the middle of the eighteenth century onwards, various young scholars took a religious interest in Catholicism. Hong Yuhan (1726–85), a disciple of Yi Ik, lived the life of a Christian solitary, setting aside the seventh, fourteenth, twenty-first, and twenty-eighth day of the lunar calendar as a time for worship and prayer. More important than Hong, however, was a group of scholars who gathered in 1777 in the grounds of a Buddhist temple to study the religious tracts put out by the Jesuits. It is to this group that the Korean Catholic Church traces its origins. Gathered together by Kwŏn Ch'ŏlsin (1736–1801), the group also included Chŏng Yakchŏn (1758–1816) and Yi Pyŏk (1754–86). It was not until 1784, however, that this group began to act seriously on their interest in Catholicism. In that year Yi Pyŏk convinced Yi Sŭnghun (1756–1801), who was accompanying his father on an official mission to the imperial court in Peiching, to make contact with the Catholic priests there. Yi Sŭnghun was baptized, and upon his return to Korea he and Yi Pyŏk began to evangelize amongst their friends and neighbours. From the first the Korean Catholic Church has been a self-evangelized church.

The Catholic faith spread rapidly amongst the members of the circle of Yi Ik, and it is from within the ranks of that group that we notice the first criticism of Catholicism being raised by Yi Kahwan (1742–1801) who encouraged the young scholars to cease from pursuing their studies of the new (heterodox) doctrines. In 1785 the government, learning of the spread of this strange creed, issued an edict suppressing it, and in the following year issued another edict banning the importation of Catholic works from Peiching. In addition to members of the aristocracy, members of the *chungin* or middle bureaucratic class also became interested in Catholicism. It is from this latter class that the first Korean martyr came. This was Kim Pŏmu (?–1786), a government interpreter, who died in 1786 as a result of the torture which he underwent during his incarceration. Social pressure was also applied against many of the aristocratic members of the Catholic Church. In the face of his father's threat of suicide, Yi Pyŏk recanted his faith, but he died shortly afterwards in 1786 as the result of bodily weakness and a plague which he had contracted.

Following this initial clamour, the remaining members of Yi Ik's circle began to create a church based on what they knew of the church in Peiching. A bishop and priests were elected, and these appointments remained in force for two years until 1789. In that year, a letter written to the bishop of Peiching brought the response that what they were doing was illegal according to canon law. Another letter in 1790 discouraged Christians from participating in the ancestral ceremonies, which caused many people to drift away from the Church. In 1791 two cousins, Kwŏn Sangyŏn (1750–91) and Yun Chich'ung (1759–91), were arrested and executed for not performing the ancestral rites and for burning the ancestral tablets in their possession. These were the first executions for belief in Catholicism and set the pattern for the persecutions which were to typify the history of the Korean Catholic Church in the nineteenth century.

From the 1790s onwards we hear less about Catholics from the aristocratic class, and more about Catholics from the middle and lower classes. Also, it is in this period that we learn of the first Catholic missionary being sent to Korea, a Chinese priest, Father Chou Wên-mu (1752–1801), who arrived in Sŏul in 1795. He was denounced within six months and sought refuge in the home of an aristocratic lady, Kang Wansuk (1760–1801). When Father Chou arrived, there were some 4,000 believers which by the turn of the century had increased to 10,000 believers. The very growth of the sect caused grave concern in certain circles. With the sudden death of King Chŏngjo in 1800, the constraints against the open persecution of the church were removed. As his son Sunjo (r. 1800–34) came to the throne as a boy, his grandmother ruled as Queen Regent in his stead. Under her aegis began the Sinyu Persecution, the first of the great persecutions of the nineteenth century.

(c) Persecution and the Underground Church

The Sinyu Persecution is a watershed in Korean Catholic history, marking the end of the scholarly church of the aristocracy and the beginning of the persecuted underground church of the people. This was the third phase of Korean Catholicism since the sixteenth century. Part of the ferocity of this first persecution was due to an unwise letter sent by a young scholar, Hwang Sayŏng (1775–1801), who appealed for a Western navy and army to protect the fledgling church. The interception of this letter and the digestion of its contents were all that the authorities needed to prove that Catholicism endangered the Korean body politic. In the eyes of the ruling Confucian bureaucracy, Catholicism endangered the moral fabric of society by its refusal to perform the ancestral ceremony, the *chesa* rites, which were seen to be the centre-piece of Confucian morality. Added to this moral problem was concern for the political independence of the nation. Catholicism, it was thought, would draw Korea away from her traditional ties with China into the orbit of, or possession by, some other foreign power. The fact that many of the aristocratic Catholics belonged to a dissident political faction also did not help the position of the church.

The Sinyu Persecution of 1801 was the first of the major suppressions of Catholicism. It resulted in the execution of such leaders as Kwŏn Ch'ŏlsin, Yi Sŭnghun, Father Chou Wên-mu, Kang Wansuk, Hwang Sayŏng, and also of Yi Kahwan, who at first had tried to dissuade his friends from converting to

Christianity and in the end himself converted to the 'heterodox' creed. Until the middle of the second decade of the nineteenth century there were no further persecutions on a national scale, although local suppressions occurred continuously during the years 1811 to 1814.

In 1815 the Ŭrhae Persecution suddenly broke out, resulting in the execution of many who had fled to mountainous regions for refuge (see Fig. 15). This persecution was followed twelve years later by the Chŏnghae Persecution of 1827. After another quiet period of twelve years, a fourth major persecution broke out in 1839, the Kihae Persecution. This later persecution was the result of the discovery of foreign missionaries on Korean soil, which raised the fear of subversion of the Korean state by foreign powers. There was another smaller persecution of the church in 1846, but the next major national persecution was not until 1866. Known as the Great Persecution, this attempt to eradicate Catholicism and foreign influences from Korean soil lasted for five years until 1871. This suppression of Catholicism was triggered by Russian attempts to seize part of Korean national territory in 1866, and was fanned by the appearance of a French fleet off the Korean coast in the same year, attempts to desecrate the tomb of the father of the Prince Regent in 1868, and the appearance of an American fleet in Korean waters in 1871. In the periodicity with which these persecutions occurred one can see the authorities' concern for the potential subversion of traditional social mores and the threat to the sovereignty of the nation. Unwittingly, Korean Catholicism had become mixed up in the maelstrom of nineteenth-century European imperialism and suffered for it.

If the officially sanctioned persecutions constituted the social context of the church for the first two-thirds of the nineteenth century, the church leadership, however, was vitally concerned with the maintenance of a regular spiritual life and the extension of the membership of the church. With the death of Father Chou, there was no clerical oversight of the church until 1831. In 1811, a decade after the Sinyu Persecution, the lay leadership of the church wrote two anonymous letters pleading for a priest. And again, between 1816 and 1825, Chŏng Hasang (1795–1839), the son of Chŏng Yakchong, made ten secret trips to Peiching to plead the Korean church's cause. These actions were followed in 1826 by a direct appeal to the Pope. Finally, in 1831, Korea was created a Vicariate Apostolic, but its first missionary bishop, Bartholemy Bruguière (1793–1835) died en route. A Chinese priest Liu Fang-chi (19 cent.) did enter Korea in that year and five years later, in 1836, he was joined by Father Pierre Philibert Maubant (1803–39), and in 1837 by Father Jacques Honoré Chastan (1803–39). Bishop Bruguière's successor, Bishop Laurent Marie Joseph Imbert (1796–1839) arrived in Korea at the end of the latter year. For a generation the Korean church had been without proper priestly supervision, yet it had not disappeared but had survived.

Within three years of the arrival in Korea of the missionaries of the Société des Missions Étrangères de Paris, the size of the church had trebled to 9,000

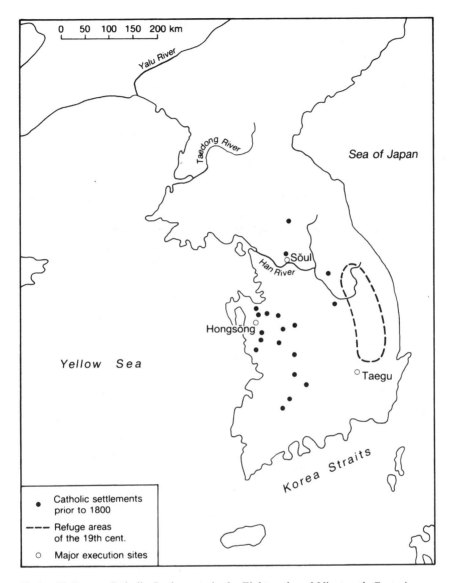

Figure 15 Roman Catholic Settlements in the Eighteenth and Nineteenth Centuries

members and three young Koreans had been sent to Macao to study for the priesthood. The hopes raised by this sudden growth were smashed by the Kihae Persecution of 1839 in which all of the French clergy were executed. Again the church was without clerical supervision until 1845 when Bishop Jean Joseph Ferréol (1808–53) and Father Marie Antoine Nicolas Daveluy (1818–66) were

145

brought in with the assistance of Kim Taegŏn (1821–46), one of the men sent to Macao for study. Kim Taegŏn's execution in 1846 deprived the fledgling church of its first native priest, and Bishop Ferréol's death from exhaustion in 1853 further weakened it. The bishop was replaced by a new papal appointment, Bishop Siméon François Berneux (1814–66) in 1856. In 1857, the bishop reported to Rome that the church membership numbered over 15,000, a remarkable figure when one considers the condition of persecution under which the church existed and the lack of clerical supervision for most of the first half of the nineteenth century.

These seemingly encouraging circumstances were again altered dramatically by the onset of the Great Persecution of 1866–1871, beginning with the withdrawal of Russian forces from Korea. This final persecution was a resolute attempt by the Prince Regent and the conservative faction of the Confucian bureaucracy to eradicate once and for all the pernicious influences of Western culture as symbolized by the strange Catholic doctrine. During this period nine French clergy and some 8,000 believers were executed making this the most severe persecution in the entire 500 year history of the Chosŏn Dynasty. When the Prince Regent was removed in 1871 and the persecution ceased, more than half of the membership of the church had suffered martyrdom.

Not surprisingly, the beliefs of the early Catholics reflected the difficult circumstances under which they lived. Analysis of printed materials used by the Catholic Christians reveals a preoccupation with divine judgement on one's actions, a rejection of the things of this world, and a devaluation of the body as opposed to the immortal soul. As we have noted previously, the membership of the Catholic Church after 1800 tended to be drawn from the poor and dispossessed members of Korean society. These people looked for a reward for their virtuous lives not in this life but in the next. Thus, life here in this world and the body were of little importance compared with the life hereafter. Examination of some of the prayers extant from that period reveals an emphasis on the Passion of Christ and the Sorrows of Mary, from which sorrows the early Korean Christians drew strength during their own periods of trial. Although there were many printed materials available concerning the Mass, and even a translation of *The Imitation of Christ*, there was no complete Korean translation of the Bible. This in part reflects the Roman Catholic Church's emphasis on the teaching function of the church, and partly the fact that the quiet conditions necessary for a scholarly translation did not exist. Portions of the Scripture would have been known, however, from the Chinese Missal in which appropriate sections of the Bible would be quoted during the course of the Mass. None the less, the church in Korea would have been ignorant of the whole content of the Christian Scriptures.

Part IV

KOREA IN THE MODERN ERA
(1872–2000)

9

DYNASTIC COLLAPSE AND
NATIONAL REBIRTH

Korea, like the other nations of East Asia, has been caught up in the web of Western imperialism. For centuries a 'Hermit Kingdom', in the late nineteenth century Chosŏn was forced to come to terms with the various nations which for their own purposes sought to bring her out of her isolation. After considerable dickering, the Japanese forced on the Korean government the first Western-style treaty, the Treaty of Kanghwa, in 1876. This treaty was followed by treaties with the United States in 1882, with the United Kingdom and the German Empire in 1883, and with other European nations shortly afterwards. The 1880s also saw the first Western settlements in Korea, initially in Inch'ŏn, and then later in the capital and the interior cities. These merchant settlements provided the locations for the first missionary settlements when the missionaries arrived in the mid-1880s. The Japanese settled in the ports, being especially numerous in Pusan. Japanese attempts to modernize and control Korea brought Japan into direct conflict with China, notably in the Post Office Banquet *coup* of 1884. The Chinese decisively maintained their position of privilege in Korea in these conflicts, but the Japanese became determined to defeat China and make her relinquish her nominal suzerainty over Korea.

At the end of the 1880s, none of the Western powers were as vitally concerned with Korea as were China and Japan, except possibly for Russia. Thus began a triangular battle which lasted until the Russo-Japanese War of 1904–5. In 1894 and again in 1895, there was a series of peasant revolts led by the local leaders of the *Tonghak* syncretic sect. When the Chinese came to the aid of the Korean government, the Japanese saw their chance to rid themselves of the problem of Chinese influence in Korea. They moved immediately against the Chinese forces and successfully routed them. The resounding Japanese victory in the Sino-Japanese War ended forever formal Chinese suzerainty over her Korean vassal and symbolized Japan's ascendancy over other powers in Korea. Under Japanese tutelage, the Korean government was encouraged to undertake the Kaehwa reforms of 1896. After the murder of his wife, King Kojong eventually sought refuge in the Russian legation whose councillors encouraged the king to declare his kingdom to be the Empire of Tae Han. For the next ten years the Russians and Japanese jockeyed with each other for supremacy on the peninsula. One important point to observe about the period from 1870 to 1900 is that all foreign powers treated Korea as a pawn to be moved about at will, which is some indication of the politically and physically weak state of the dynasty. The 500-year-old Chosŏn Dynasty was near collapse, as also was the traditional structure of society.

In the new century, Korea was the centre of the principal conflict between Russia and Japan which culminated in the Russo-Japanese War of 1904–5. Again, Japan's victory gave her a clear hand to proceed in Korea as she liked. A Japanese Residency was established in 1905, then Korea was created a Protectorate in 1907, and finally was forcibly annexed to Japan in 1910. Following annexation, Japan attempted to 'Japanize' Korea. Land was confiscated and given to Japanese colonials. Business laws were created which were deliberately harmful to Korean companies. Instruction in schools was to be in Japanese only. By the death of the retired King Kojong in 1919, strong emotions had become pent up to the point of explosion.

On the 1 March 1919, thirty-three Representatives of the People read out a declaration of independence from Japan in Pagoda Park in Sŏul. This deliberately non-violent, nation-wide demonstration was brutally suppressed by the Japanese. Over 7,000 persons were said to have been killed by government soldiers and more than twice that number wounded. Protestant missionaries were the first to smuggle out notice of these atrocities to the outside world. The Governor-General was replaced and the Japanese began to take a more conciliatory attitude towards the Koreans. Although the movement did not result in the independence of the nation, it did have the effect of unifying the people in their desire for independence and in their sense of being a distinct people. The modern history of Korea may be said to have begun in 1919. The nation was being reborn from the ashes of the Chosŏn Dynasty.

From 1919 to 1945, Japanese control of Korea went through various phases. During the 1930s, as a result of the militarization of the government of Japan and her military adventures elsewhere in East Asia, the colonial government began to take a harsher line towards Korea. Patriotic acts were required of the Korean people to show their loyalty to the Japanese government such as attendance at rituals held in local Shintō shrines. For Christians in particular this was offensive. Later, Koreans were required to take Japanese names, a calculated insult to a Confucian nation proud of its family lineages and clans. Many Koreans were taken as forced labourers to Japan and other parts of the Japanese Empire, particularly as the war in the Pacific expanded.

By the end of the Second World War, Korea lay prostrate from the hardship of thirty-five years of colonial exploitation. The land and the resources of the nation had been used for the benefit of the imperial master, especially during the years of the most intense warfare. The expectations raised by liberation from imperial Japan were dashed by the division of the nation into two spheres of interest, one American and the other Soviet. Said to be a temporary division while plans were laid for a period of trusteeship, the division hardened over the years to result in the creation of two separate states. Talks broke down between the two powers which had taken the Japanese surrender in their respective spheres, and administrative zones were set up in each sphere. The United States through the United Nations attempted to have nation-wide elections held to establish a new state. Refusal of entry into the northern part of Korea led to elections being held only in the south in May 1948. The Republic of Korea was established at the end of that month, with the seating of the first assembly. The Soviet Union announced the formation of the Democratic People's Republic of Korea in September of the same year. Thus was the temporary division of the peninsula turned into a permanent sundering of the nation.

Since the establishment of the DPRK in north Korea, its government has been dominated by Kim Ilsŏng (*nomme de guerre* of Kim Sŏngju, 1912–1994) and his family and associates. Recent archival evidence confirms the fact that Kim, with the support of Mao Tse-tung and Josef Stalin, was responsible for initiating the Korean War (1950–3) as a war of liberation. Since the end of the civil war, north Korea has used a series of multiple-year plans to build up the industrial infrastructure of the state. This centralist approach to economic and social development was affirmed with the proclamation in 1956 of the *Chuch'e* philosophy or philosophy of self-reliance. From then, the economy made strides with the heavy industry focus of Stalinist state planning. At the same time, governance came more fully into the hands of the Kim family and its associates. Kim Chŏngil (1941–), the son of Kim Ilsŏng, was proclaimed his father's successor in 1980. However, from the mid-1970s, the north Korean economy failed to keep pace with economic developments in the south. Following the death of Kim Ilsŏng in 1994, the economy began to come apart even more rapidly due to a combination of overly-centralised planning and years of natural disaster. By the end of the twentieth century, north Korea was in desperate straits economically, but yet gave little external sign of immanent political collapse.

The Republic of Korea in 1950 possessed a small army unprepared for war of any kind. On 25 June 1950 the north invaded the south, beginning a three-year war which ended in an uneasy truce and involved the armies of the United States and its United Nations allies on the one side and the Chinese and north Korean forces on the other. It was especially shocking because it was the first time in 1300 years that Korean had fought Korean. There were three scars left at the finish of hostilities – the psychological tragedy of a fratricidal war after liberation from Japanese rule, the appalling loss of life, and the shattering of the national economy. Even at the beginning of the twenty-first century, the border between the two states remains one of the most tightly closed borders in the world. The two Korean states, left prostrate after this fratricidal war, spent the next decade in recovering from it.

In the Republic of Korea, the 1950s were a time of reconstruction and economic hardship. The government, led by the rightwing patriot Yi Sŭngman (Syngman Rhee, 1875–1965) proved to be inept and corrupt. Lack of economic development was attributed to the policy of the Rhee regime of selling off property belonging to the former colonial government to its supporters and unemployment became widespread from the late 1950s. The regime held on to its power through constitutional manipulation in 1952 and 1954. Frustrations born of economic decay and political corruption were vented in the Student Revolution of 19 April 1960 which was sparked by fraudulent elections and the murder of a middle-school student in the provincial city of Masan. The student revolution led to the creation of the Second Republic based on a cabinet-style of government. However, continued student unrest and alleged government inefficiency gave the military an excuse to overthrow the new government on 16 May 1961. The Military Revolution of 1961eventually established the regime of General Pak Chŏnghŭi (Park Chung-hee, 1917–79), who was to rule the country for the next eighteen years.

The ostensible aim of General Pak and his military confreres was three-fold – to build up a self-reliant economy, eliminate corruption, and strengthen ties with the United States. A new constitution for the Third Republic was written and approved in 1962, and elections held in 1963 to elect the first president, who was now-retired General Pak. Even before the return to civilian rule, the Pak regime created an economic policy based on a series of five-year plans to rapidly develop the economy. Among the early goals for national reconstruction were population control, renovation of the agricultural sector, and the creation of major heavy industries. In 1965, Korea established formal diplomatic ties with Japan after twenty years of unofficial hostility. This treaty and Pak's subsequent attempt to have a final and third term in office sparked off unsuccessful student demonstrations in 1965 and again in 1967. President Pak won a resounding victory in the 1967 presidential elections. It would seem that the populace did not widely support the student demonstrations as they had done with the Student Revolution of 1960 and were favourably disposed towards the regime's policy of rapid economic change. The 1960s was the period when the phenomenal economic growth of Korea began. During these years, the Pak regime enjoyed enormous support.

The political climate changed in the 1970s. When the Pak regime in the south entered into conversations with the Kim regime in the north, the constitution of the Republic was abruptly altered. The creation of the *Yusin* (Revitalization) Constitution in 1972 entrenched Pak in permanent power. Beginning in 1973, moves for the repeal of the Yusin Constitution were instituted, which led to continuing, widespread demonstrations against the government, and calls for the return to a more democratic-form of government. One of the first of these demonstrations began following the Easter Sunrise Service on Nam-san mountain in central Sŏul. Tension increased with the assassination of President Pak's wife on 15 August, 1974 by a north Korean agent. From that time until the assassination of the President himself on 29 October 1979, student demonstrations and general popular unrest continued to characterize the political climate of the nation. However, the nation's economy continued to grow in spite of both the 'Oil Shock' of the mid-1970s, and this civil turmoil.

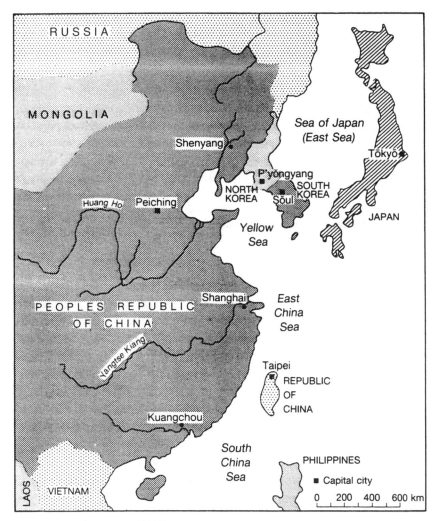

Figure 16 Modern Korea (2000)

Every goal of the five-year plans were met creating improved economic conditions throughout the nation. For people for whom the devastation of the Korean War and the hardships of the 1950s were still a vivid reality, many people found themselves hesitant to 'rock the boat' and thus to destroy the gains of the past two decades.

The assassination of the President in late 1979 brought to power his prime minister Ch'oe Kyuha (1919–), a career diplomat who gave the people a few brief months of genuine freedom. Neither the nation nor the economy came apart. Many people looked forward to the creation of a new constitution and a more

153

democratic government. These hopes were shattered by the entrance again of the military onto the political scene. On 12 December 1979, various military factions had a shoot-out in Sŏul in which the Chief of the General Staff was replaced. Continued social unrest gave the military an opportunity to step in and take control of the government. When the city of Kwangju in the south-west rose up against the brutal military suppression of a demonstration, the army reacted in force. The Kwangju Incident of 17 May 1980 became one of the defining events of modern Korean history. It was the first time since before the Korean War that the army was used to suppress a popular demonstration. The dead were certainly numbered in the hundreds, probably in the thousands. This incident also brought to power the regime of General Chŏn Tuhwan (Chun Doo Hwan, 1931–), and was one reason why, although Chŏn remained in power until the end of his term in early 1988, he had very little if any popular support. Widespread demonstrations embracing virtually every sector of Korean society rocked the nation in June 1987 when Chŏn presented No T'ae'u (Roh Tae Woo, 1932–) to the nation as his handpicked successor to the presidency. The popular demonstrations in June forced the government to make several concessions to the popular will, including meeting the demand for the direct election of the president.

The failure of the two principal opposition leaders, Kim Yŏngsam (1927–) and Kim Taejung (1925–), to join forces to present a single opposition presidential candidate led to the defeat of the opposition. Although they collectively polled nearly 60 percent of the vote, the division of the opposition vote led inevitably to the election of No T'ae'u as Chŏn's successor. The election in early 1988, however, of an Assembly dominated for the first time by opposition politicians dramatically changed the appearance of the Korean political scene. In 1990, Kim Yŏngsam led his party into a merger with the party headed by President No, which although it shocked many people, paved the way for Kim's election in 1993 as the first president not to have a military background since the election of President Pak in 1963. Kim Yŏngsam who had been a leading dissident politician during President Pak's time had his reputation tarnished by the various scandals which rocked the latter years of his presidency. He was succeeded in 1997 by the other veteran opposition leader Kim Taejung. Shortly after his election, the nation was shaken by the economic crisis of December 1997 which led to the rapid devaluation of the wŏn, the national currency. Many major industrial conglomerates found themselves with considerable debts and having to lay-off substantial numbers of workers, to close down or sell off corporate assets and subsidiary corporations. By the end of the last decade of the twentieth century, the economy had shown signs of recovery but was still in an unhealthy state. Perhaps the most significant development was the visit by President Kim Taejung to the capital of north Korea, P'yŏngyang, in July 2000 where he met and held lengthy discussions with the north Korean leader Kim Chŏngil. This event seemed to presage a thaw in the relations between north and south Korea and raised hopes for the eventual re-unification of the two parts of the nation.

10

THE ADVENT OF PROTESTANTISM

1. The End of the Chosŏn Dynasty

The transmission of Protestant Christianity, the imposition of Japanese colonial rule, and the Korean War are the three most important influences on Korean history in the last hundred years. The modernization of Korea owes much to the advent of Protestantism there. At the time when Protestant Christianity came to Korea, the power of the Korean state was crumbling and the culture was in a state of flux. Young, progressive aristocrats were looking for new solutions to questions of national development and the creation of a healthier economy. It was in this critical period that Korea had direct contact with Western civilization, and this contact was provided largely through the agency of Western missionaries who were both evangelical in theology and deeply concerned with the material plight of the people amongst whom they worked. The discussion of this Protestant century may be divided conveniently into three periods, namely, the end of the Chosŏn Dynasty (1872–1910), the period of Japanese colonial rule (1910–45), and the post-liberation period (1945–).

Prior to the arrival of Protestant missionaries in the mid-1880s, a small body of Protestant Christians already existed inside the boundaries of the Kingdom of Chosŏn. From the first third of the nineteenth century onwards, various attempts had been made to enter the 'Hermit Kingdom'. In 1832 Karl Friederich August Gützlaff (1803–51) made an exploratory trip along the Manchurian and Korean west coasts. He seems to have made contact with some Catholics, and he did distribute copies of the Scriptures in Chinese. Robert Jermain Thomas (1839–66), taking the advice of Alexander Williamson (1829–90), who represented the National Bible Society of Scotland in North China, was aboard the American trading vessel the 'General Sherman' in September 1866 when it ventured up the Taedong River to P'yŏngyang. The recklessness of the captain led to the destruction of the ship and the death of all aboard including the young Revd Thomas. While dying, Thomas attempted to distribute copies of the Chinese Bible. Alexander Williamson himself attempted to discover something about the situation in Korea and in 1867 made a visit to the customs barrier with

Korea known then as the Corean Gate or the *Kao-li Mên*. None of these attempts had any long-lasting impact on Korea.

The first missionary to have any impact on Korea was the Revd Dr John Ross (1842–1915) of the United Presbyterian Church of Scotland mission to Manchuria. Although Ross was assigned to Shantung, immediately upon his arrival in Chihfou he took the advice of Alexander Williamson and went to Manchuria. He settled in at Yingk'ou, the port at the mouth of the Liao River. One of Williamson's interests had been the development of a mission to Korea, an enthusiasm which Ross took up. Ross made two trips to the Corean Gate in 1874 and 1876, where he made the acquaintance of a man who became his Korean-language teacher. In 1877, Ross published the first primer of the Korean language in a European tongue, followed in 1879 by the publication of the first English-language history of Korea. In 1882, the first portions of his Korean translation of the New Testament were printed and circulated. By 1887, the entire New Testament had been translated and was bound and distributed as a single volume.

Ross's converts were responsible for the establishment of Christian communities in north-western Korea, in the capital, and in the Korean communities along the northern bank of the Yalu River, which was nominally Korean territory at that time. It was Ross's idea that Christianity spread best through the agency of convinced converts rather than through the efforts of the foreign missionary. The emergence of Christian communities in Korea before the arrival of foreign missionaries is an eloquent testimonial to Ross's conviction. It is also important to note that this process of indigenous evangelization took place through the distribution of Scripture. This is all the more amazing in that the Ross Translation is a dialectical translation which seemed curious to most Koreans even then. The significance of the Ross Translation is twofold: (1) it was the only complete Korean translation of the New Testament until 1900, when the translation of the New Testament done by the Korean missionaries was completed; (2) it introduced key theological terms which are still in use. With regard to the latter point, it is significant that it was Ross who selected the term for God, *Hananim*, a pure Korean word for the Ruler of Heaven. Even in cases where later usage altered some of Ross's choices of terms, the most recent translations of the Bible done by Korean scholars have often gone back to the words which were selected by Ross.

From the mid-1880s on, various attempts were made to introduce Protestant Christianity into Korea. Yi Sujŏng (1842–86), a Korean aristocrat who had become a Christian whilst sojourning in Japan, sent out a plea to Western churches in 1884 for the evangelization of his homeland; a Japanese Christian representing the National Bible Society of Scotland came to Korea in 1883 to distribute Scriptures; Dr Horace Newton Allen (1858–1932) of the Northern Presbyterian Church came to Korea as a medical missionary in 1884 and was attached to the American legation; Dr Robert Samuel Maclay (1824–1907) of the Northern Methodist mission in Japan came on an exploratory trip in the same year. These uncoordinated efforts eventually resulted in the arrival of the first official Protestant missionaries on Easter Sunday, 1885, the Revd Horace Grant Underwood (1859–1916) of the Northern Presbyterian mission and the Revd Henry Gerhard Appenzeller (1858–1902) of the Northern Methodist mission. Although these men hold the palm for first setting foot in Korea, they were followed almost immediately by various other missionaries. By the end of the ninth decade of the nineteenth century, a foreign-mission enterprise was well under way.

Due to uncertainty about Korean government permission for the direct evangelization of the population, the first generation of missionaries concentrated initially on work in institutions such as hospitals and schools. It should be stressed, however, that this social emphasis was as much due to the uncertainty of the times as to the missionaries' Christian concern for the welfare of the Korean people. By the end of the 1880s, the foundations had been laid for several of modern Korea's major institutions. Dr Allen helped found the first Western-style medical institution, the Kwanghye-wŏn, which was followed in short order by a similar Methodist institution and the Methodist hospital for women. Paejae Boys' High School and Ewha Girls' High School were founded at this time by the Methodists, and there was a similar though abortive attempt to follow suit by the Presbyterians. Royal approval of the Methodist schools is indicated by the fact that the king and queen selected the names for the boys' and girls' schools respectively. In this same period, the Religious Tract Society for the distribution of Scriptures and religious materials was created and the Tri-Lingual Press, the first Western-style publishing operation, was inaugurated. In 1887, two years after their arrival, the missionaries had organized a committee to produce a Korean translation of the Scriptures which would replace the dialectical Ross Translation.

In the 1890s, the number of missions increased to include the Australian and Southern Presbyterians; the Southern Methodists; and the High Church wing of the Church of England, the Society for the Propagation of the Gospel. The Canadian YMCA also took an interest in Korea at this time and sent out missionaries. The Southern Methodist mission owes its origins to Yun Ch'iho (1865–1945), a Korean aristocrat trained at a Methodist college in the American South who had become a Methodist. Yun wrote to the board of missions upon his return that if they would send a missionary, he would make arrangements for his support and work. This is another example of the self-evangelized nature of Korean Christianity.

The 1890s was a period of growth in the numbers of converts and also a very productive literary period. In this decade, missionaries produced a number of works including dictionaries, manuals of the Korean language, and translations of devotional works, such as the *Pilgrim's Progress*. It is also interesting to note that the missionaries in Korea entered into the same debate which had exercised their brethren in China several years before, namely the question of the proper term for God. The term which had been selected by Ross, *Hananim*, a variant of the indigenous name for the rul-er of Heaven, finally came to have currency amongst all the Protestant groups, except the Anglicans who chose to use the term selected by the Catholics, *Ch'ŏnju*. In the early 1890s, John L. Nevius (1829–93), a Presbyterian missionary in Shantung, China, was invited to come to Korea to explain to the first missionaries his mission methods (called the Nevius Method) of creating self-propagating, self-governing, and self-supporting churches. This became the universally accepted policy of all missions in Korea. By 1900, the prospect for Protestant Christianity seemed especially bright. The young progressives looked to Christianity and the missionaries in particular as harbingers of progress and development; there was no body of organized opposition to Christianity; and the missionaries had the respect and tacit support of the King of Korea and his family.

The final decade of Korean independence, from 1900 to 1910, evinces considerable numerical gains in the membership of the church. The outstanding event of this decade was the Great Revival of 1907 in P'yŏngyang, the effect of which quickly spread everywhere in the peninsula, and even into Manchuria. This revival undoubtedly had its roots in the unstable political and cultural circumstances of the time. The power released in this unusual event became the energy for the evangelization of the nation by the Koreans themselves. By 1910, one per cent of the population was Protestant. The Japanese Protestant Church today, with a longer history, has yet to achieve this figure. There were mission stations in every corner of Korea, and everywhere schools were created and medical work carried on along with pure evangelism. One important result of the missionaries' social outreach was that the Korean Christians came to see that they too should found Christian schools for their people. Many schools in Korea today claim a Christian, but not a mission, foundation due to the efforts of Korean Christians in this decade.

Much of the success of the Protestant churches in the first twenty-five years after the arrival of the missionaries was due to the association of Christianity with the 'progressive' West, and to the emphasis which the first generation of missionaries placed on the responsibility of local Christians for the growth and support of their churches. The view held by many late nineteenth century Koreans that Protestantism would contribute to the revitalisation of the nation has been explored recently by Kenneth Wells in his book *New God/New Nation: Protestants and Self-reconstruction Nationalism in Korea*. By the end of this first decade of the new century, the first seminaries had been founded, the first seminary graduates had graduated, and the first class of Korean ministers had been ordained. In 1908 all Protestant missionaries, except the High Church Anglicans, had agreed upon a comity arrangement dividing the peninsula into spheres of interest to avoid competition so that there would be only one denomination in one area (see Fig. 17). A vote taken at the same time by the missionaries to create a United Church of Christ in Korea was, sadly, rejected by the home churches in North America. None the less, the comity agreement, the use of a single translation of the Bible, a common hymnal and other

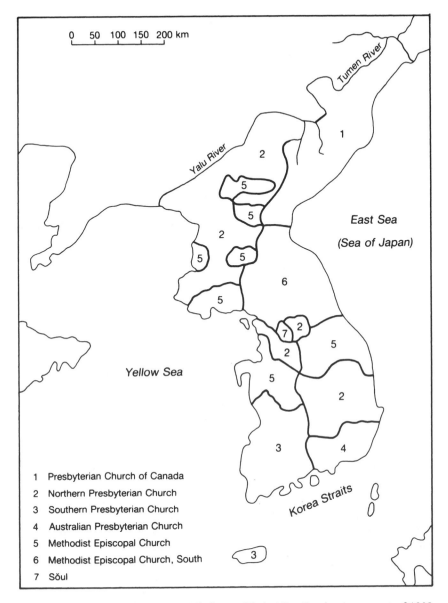

0 50 100 150 200 km

Tumen River

Yalu River

1

2

5

5

East Sea

(Sea of Japan)

2

5

5

6

Yellow Sea

5

7 2

2

5

5

2

3

4

1 Presbyterian Church of Canada

2 Northern Presbyterian Church

3 Southern Presbyterian Church

4 Australian Presbyterian Church

5 Methodist Episcopal Church

6 Methodist Episcopal Church, South

7 Sŏul

Korea Straits

3

Figure 17 Allocation of Protestant Missionary Work After Comity Agreement of 1908

pan-denominational activities helped to create a communal sense of Christianity. Before the absorption of Korea into the Japanese Empire, the Protestant churches were thriving institutions supported and sustained locally and with the beginnings of an indigenous clergy. The churches also had the only complete

159

system of Western-style education in Korea prior to the development of the Japanese government schools. The background was set for a bitter struggle between the church and the new colonial government.

2. The Church under Japanese Colonial Rule

In the second decade of the twentieth century, Korean Christians began more and more to take a prominent place in the affairs of the church and in society as a whole. One indication of this prominence was the Conspiracy Trial of 1912. 124 persons were accused of attempting to assassinate the Governor-General, Terauchi Masatake (1852–1919). Of these men, ninety-eight were Christians. The Japanese must have seen the Christians as the one well-organized group which could challenge their total domination of Korea. The inability of the Christians to accept Shintō mythology as historical fact would have been a major point of conflict. Eventually all but six of the alleged conspirators were acquitted. Among the six imprisoned 'conspirators' was Yun Ch'iho, the Korean aristocrat who had helped to organize the Southern Methodist mission. The trial and its outcome highlighted the growing link between Korean nationalism and Christianity.

The pent-up frustrations of a subjugated nation are well demonstrated by the conflict which arose from the attempt of the colonial government to impose its own system of 'patriotic' schools on the Korean nation. In addition to Sungsil College (Union Christian College), which had been founded in 1905 in P'yŏngyang, the missions founded two more colleges in Sŏul, Ewha Woman's College in 1910, and Yŏnhŭi College (Chosen Christian College) in 1915. Besides the mission-related colleges, Korean Christians continued to found more high schools and other institutions. To control this situation, the Government-General in 1915 announced regulations which not only required the use of Japanese as the national language, but which also, if fully implemented, would have forbidden both religious instruction and worship in private schools. The threat of the implementation of these regulations caused considerable consternation not only amongst the mission community, but amongst the Korean Christian community as well. This issue was one of many which led to the movement to repeal the act of annexation and to re-establish Korea as a sovereign state.

Growing nationalism made itself felt even in the conduct of church affairs. The missionaries more and more had visibly to demonstrate their support for the Korean desire for a state independent of Japanese rule. In 1913, the Northern Methodist missionary bishop, Merriman C. Harris (1846–1921), a former missionary to Japan, nearly caused a revolt amongst Koreans present at the annual conference of that year because of his pro-Japanese sentiments.

The March First Movement of 1919 which declared Korea's right to be independent of Japan was entirely the work of the religious leaders of the nation. Of the thirty-three signatories to the declaration of Korean independence, fifteen were Christians. More importantly, it was the Christians' insistence on non-violence which gave the uprising its unique character. It is not surprising that the Japanese were correspondingly harsh with Christians. There were many examples of churches being burned by Japanese troops, the execution of numbers of Christians, and in one spectacular incident the herding of villagers into the local church which was then set aflame. Missionaries were the first to smuggle out reports about these atrocities, and it was the mission boards at home which forced Western governments to condemn Japanese brutality. Events such as these showed that the Korean church was not an agent of imperialism, but had become linked in the minds of both Japanese and Koreans with Korean nationalism.

One after-effect of the suppression of the March First Movement was the clear emergence of two strands of Protestant Christianity, one which was both more theologically liberal and more socially active, and another which was both more theologically conservative and more concerned with purely 'church' affairs. The period of the 1920s was a quiet time of growth when great numerical though not percentage gains in church membership were made. It was also the period in which the more conservative, churchly party began to take command of the churches. During this time, with the expansion of Japanese military power on the Asian continent and the take-over of the Japanese government by the military, xenophobic Shintō patriotism emerged as a key cultural factor in both Japan and Korea. With the creation of the principal Shintō shrine for Korea in 1925, the stage was set for a battle which was to continue for nearly two decades.

The Shintō Shrine Controversy became the major theological issue facing the Korean church during the 1930s. Formally, the colonial government said that attendance at rites held at State Shintō shrines was merely a 'patriotic' act. But for Korean Christians the issue was a two-fold problem; performance of the rituals would be contrary to their own sense of nationalism as Koreans, and idolatrous as Christians. The colonial regime applied pressure incrementally to obtain adherence to attendance at shrine worship. The final act was the forcing of the General Assembly of the Presbyterian Church in 1938 to pass a resolution that shrine worship did not contravene Christian faith. Shortly afterwards, all other churches and church organisations were likewise forced to conform. Some two thousand people were arrested for refusal to comply and between 1938 and 1945, there were at least fifty people who died as a result of incarceration and torture for refusing to comply with demands for attendance at State Shintō rites. Following Liberation from Japanese rule, a conflict arose about who had and who had not conceded to the Japanese authorities which continues to have a lasting impact on the Korean Protestant churches. Missionaries were deported for their refusal to support the shrine edicts, while at the same time the Presbyterian missions closed their schools rather than concede on this issue. Methodists, on the other hand, turned their schools over to Korean control, which more often than not meant compliance with government regulations.

The Japanese authorities also attempted to gain control over the various annual church meetings, the conferences of the Methodist Church and the presbyteries of the Presbyterian Church. These actions resulted in ever-stricter control of the local churches. Various attempts were made to 'Japanize' the churches in an effort to vitiate their influence. The Korean Methodist bishop was forced to forbid the use of the Old Testament or the Revelation of St John the Divine because of their prophetic revelation of God's condemnation of the powers of this world and the dream of a just future world. Various Methodist churches were closed and their property sold. One Methodist church was even made into a Shintō shrine. That latter act well demonstrated the combined fear and scorn with which the Japanese authorities regarded the Christian churches. When war was declared with the United States in 1941, those missionaries who had not already left or been deported from Korea were arrested and subsequently deported. The final act of Japanese dominance over the Korean churches was the forced merger of the various denominations into a united church on 25 June 1945, scarcely two months before the surrender of Japan to the United States.

3. The Post-Liberation Church

Immediately following liberation from Japanese rule, the church had to face a complex set of interrelated problems, namely, the different attitudes taken by the governing authorities towards religion which were the result of the division of the nation into Soviet and American spheres of influence; questions of complicity in Japanese rule and repentance for such involvement; and the legacy of the Japanese-imposed church union.

The Russians, having made plans to impose their influence in Korea, began to systematically suppress and uproot Christianity. After Liberation in 1945 and the creation of the Soviet zone of influence, two political parties emerged which were led by Christians, the *Kidokkyo sahoe minju-dang* (Christian Social Democratic Party) and the *Kidokkyo chayu-dang* (Christian Liberal Party). Seen as opposing the establishment of a communist nation, these parties were eventually suppressed. By 1946, Christians found themselves in conflict with the emerging communist regime over two issues. The first was the desire by Christian leaders to hold a commemorative ceremony for the uprising of 1 March, 1919, a movement which was seen by the communists to be bourgeois and contrary to revolutionary history. The second event was the holding of elections for a People's Assembly on a Sunday, which ran counter to the strong sabbatarian views of many Korean Christians. Control or suppression of the Christian community in the north was important not only because Christians represented a different voice on social and political matters, but because of the size of the Christian community. At this time, the centre of Christianity in Korea was in the north, not the south, an irony of history considering the current size of the Christian Church in south Korea. These practices were objected to by the Joint Presbytery or governing body of the still-unified Protestant church, and were countered by the authorities with the formation of the *Kidokkyo kyodo yŏnmaeng* (Federation of Christians), to which all church officers were required by law to join. This counter-church was organised both on the national and local level. All those who refused to join, such as the leaders of the Joint Presbytery, were arrested for belonging to an illegal organisation and were imprisoned. Churches and other church properties were confiscated and put to secular uses. Those who could escape, fled to the south, while those who remained in the north were rounded up shortly before the onset of the Korean War and executed *en masse*. Little was heard about the state of Christianity in the north until the mid-1980s when it was announced that a hymnal and a translation of the New Testament had been published in 1983 and a translation of the Old Testament in 1984. In the late 1980s, delegations of North American and European churches reported taking part in worship in the homes of individual Christians. In 1988, the government of north Korea announced that it had built and opened a new Roman Catholic and a new Protestant church for use by the respective religious communities. Subsequently, officials designated as leaders of the Christian community in north Korea have met with various Western and south Korean church leaders to discuss national unification. However, the church organisations in north Korea are not freely formed associations but essentially the creatures of the government, their representatives being government-approved personnel. This was confirmed to me in the mid-1980s when I was told by a Korean Christian resident in China that they were amazed upon meeting a representative of the north Korean church that they knew nothing of the Bible.

In southern Korea, on the other hand, the Americans had made no preparations to take over the running of the country and consequently had no formalized policy towards religion. The American commander, Lieutenant-General John Reed Hodge (1893–1963), took the *laissez-faire* policy of allowing the church to handle its own affairs. Consequently, all of the pent-up emotions which had developed under Japanese rule were released in the south during the brief five-year period prior to the Korean War.

In both the northern and southern halves of the peninsula, representative members of the united church gathered in late 1945 to decide whether to continue the union or not. In both cases, a bloc of Methodists bolted to re-form the Methodist church structure as it had existed prior to union. Conflicts arose over the questions of complicity in Japanese rule, attendance at Shintō rituals, and the perversion of Scripture. The conflict dragged on from 1945 until 1947, when in southern Korea a manifesto was issued accusing those who were pressing for the continuation of the union of having been collaborators with the Japanese. The Presbyterians likewise split over the refusal of certain church leaders to approve a call to repentance for tacit acceptance of worship at Shintō shrines. The resultant Koryŏ Group, the descendant body of a group of people who had contracted a covenant against shrine worship, took a hard line against any one attending shrine rituals. It is considered to be the most conservative of the four major groupings of the contemporary Presbyterian denominations.

Another point of conflict arose over the nature of the church union, as well as the manner in which it was accomplished. The church was organized along

Presbyterian lines with a system of lay leaders called elders who held their posts for life. This was different from the Methodist system of elected leadership, which was meant to act as a safeguard against entrenchment of power by a single person. All these internal conflicts were brought to an abrupt end by the outbreak of civil war on 25 June 1950.

The three-year conflict ended with an armistice and a very uneasy truce. The aftermath of this devastating civil war led to a decade of national poverty and destruction in which the church shared. Much of the 1950s was spent in repairing damage to churches and church-related institutions and in an attempt to provide various needed social services. Housing, transportation for refugees, emergency medical aid, distribution of clothing and food, and the establishment of orphanages were all undertaken in the immediate post-war period. Much of this was done or assisted by foreign church mission bodies, but the local Korean church played a very significant role as well. Foreign mission boards also provided money for the maintenance of such mission-founded institutions as Yonsei University, Severance Hospital, and Ehwa Woman's University. The numerical size of the church continued to grow throughout the 1950s, but owing to continued increase in the population, the percentage of Christians within the national population remained at about 3 per cent.

We may trace the rapid development of the church to the 1960s when 'Church Growth' (*kyohoe sŏngjang*) became a key concept amongst the clergy and laity. This decade also saw an enlargement of social and evangelistic outreach symbolized by such projects as work with prostitutes and with labourers, foreign mission work by Korean ministers, provision of relief supplies to foreign nations, and the establishment of a nation-wide radio network, the Christian Broadcasting System. Support for the futherance of education and higher education continued until by the end of the century, there were thirty-one universities and 225 schools which claimed a Christian foundation. The 1960s saw a doubling of the size of the membership of the Protestant churches until they represented more than six per cent of the population. From that point, reached at some time in the late 1960s, the church has continued to grow phenomenally until the end of the century when more than one quarter of the national population is Protestant. Throughout the 1970s, in addition to the continued emphasis on church growth and on social involvement, Christian political movements emerged, particularly for a more democratically-based system of government. While the membership of the Korean Protestant denominations has grown enormously, perhaps the most characteristic feature of the church is the physical presence of recently constructed churches of cathedral-like proportions. These great churches are often filled to capacity every Sunday, commonly with two or three services a day plus evening services. In the cities, foreign visitors are often surprised at night by the number of red neon crosses signifying congregations worshipping in their own buildings or in a borrowed storefront building. However, the physical presence of the Church is obvious not only in the urban areas but also in the countryside. Although

Christianity is primarily an urban phenomenon, virtually every village in the rural areas has at least one church.

The rapid development of the church is due in part to the adoption of the evangelistic methods of the Church Growth School of evangelical Protestantism. While it has been a great success-story in one way, Church Growth has created enormous problems for adequate Christian nurture and education. Furthermore, these great congregations may last no longer than one generation, as too often attendance is dependent upon the appeal of the minister. Particularly in conservative circles, the minister tends to be a charismatic figure. Much of the content of the preaching is centred on belief in *kibok*, a wish for blessings in this life. Joint, out-loud congregational prayer (*tongsŏng kido*) is impressive not only for its volume but also for its fervent nature. Attendance at church and fervent prayer are believed to create a spiritual condition in which the believer will be blessed (often understood to be material blessings), a clear reflection of the shamanistic religious traditions of Korea. Another danger of Church Growth has been the weakening of denominational and co-operative ties. It is at this point that the clan-nature of Korean society reveals itself in the emphasis on the growth and work of the local church as opposed to denominational effort. Churches of the same denomination in the same area will enter into intense competition for members, while support for denominational projects are often set aside for projects of the local church such as the construction of a grander church edifice.

The Church Growth movement in Korea has been strongly related to the development of two characteristics of modern Korean church life, the *kido-wŏn* and the *puhŭng-hoe*. Although the *kido-wŏn* is literally a hall of prayer and the *puhŭng-hoe* a revival meeting, both have strong connections with faith-healing practices. Virtually any large church will have a *kido-wŏn* located in the hills surrounding its town or city. Ostensibly for religious retreats and other religious functions, these halls are often used for faith-healing services. There are also independent *kido-wŏn* which specialize in curative practices. Some of these are so large that they maintain pastors who specialize in particular diseases. The *puhŭng-hoe* has been a feature of Korean church life ever since the Great Revival of 1907 in P'yŏngyang to which has been attributed the great evangelical and proselytising fervour of the Protestant churches. However, it is only recently that the *puhŭng-hoe* has become associated largely with the curing of disease. When the author attended a revival service with the Christian scholar Ch'oe Kilsŏng, Dr Ch'oe pointed out how the atmosphere of the service, the use of hypnotism, the manner in which the revivalist spoke to the afflicted person, the use of the laying on of hands, and other features paralleled Korean shamanistic practices.

Although the Protestant churches are often criticised for not showing sufficient accommodation to local Korean culture, this is not strictly speaking the case. Centuries of Confucian influence on society stressing filial piety and its ritual expression through the performance of the ancestral or *chesa* ceremonies led to a conflict for Christians between the need to ritually express filiality and the fear of participating in idolatrous rituals. From the beginning of Protestant missions, Christians often placed great emphasis on the fifth of the Ten Commandments to honour your father and your mother reflecting their innate attitude of filial piety. As a result of this thinking, by the 1920s Christianised ancestral memorial rituals were being performed which, in varying formats, have now found their way into the books of liturgy of every Protestant denomination. These rites, called *ch'udo yebae* (service of recollection), are different from the Confucian *chesa* rites in that they are normally performed for one's immediate relatives such as parents and grandparents, although there is no formal prohibition against going further back.

It is an interesting feature of modern Protestant churches that although there is a strong sense of identity with the individual church and the particular denomination, the actual formal difference between Methodist and Presbyterian churches is slight and there has been a general assimilation of practices between both major Protestant traditions. Methodism world-wide usually adheres to the principal of 'itinerancy' where clergy are moved at frequent intervals to different churches to pastor rather than the Presbyterian system of appointment of a pastor to a church for as long as the incumbent is supported by the congregational leadership. In the Korean Methodist system, however, the Presbyterian system of appointment now holds true. Likewise, Methodism traditionally elects stewards to serve for fixed periods whereas Presbyterianism appoints lay elders effectively for life. In Korea, Methodism now has lay elders or *changno* like Presbyterianism. A unique feature of world Methodism is the class meeting, called *sok-hoe* in Korean, a gathering for study and spiritual support, a practice which has been adopted by Korean Presbyterians as the *kuyŏk-hoe*. All Protestant churches have a three-tiered structure of lay workers consisting of *changno* (elder), *kwŏnsa* (lay deacon), and *chipsa* (class leader), the only difference being that Methodism has male and female elders and lay deacons, whereas in most Presbyterian groups the elders are male and the lay deacons are female. Adding to these features the fact that the churches all use a common Bible translation and a common hymnal, and have a very similar liturgical order, it would be very easy for a Korean Christian to move from one denomination to another without feeling the degree of discontinuity which is felt by many Europeans attending a church outside of the denomination in which they were brought up.

It is curious that until the mid-1970s there was no movement for the creation of an indigenous Korean theology. Overseas Korean Christians in the United States and imprisoned theologians in Korea began this task, from which emerged *Minjŭng sinhak*, or the Theology of the People. This theology has much in common with Latin American Liberation Theology and places stress on the role of Christianity in giving hope to the dispossessed members of society. However, *Minjung* theologians are quick to point out that unlike Liberation Theology their theology has no connection with Marxism, perhaps a reflection of the anti-communist political climate of south Korea. Instead, these theologians argue that

God is working out Universal Destiny by His commitment to the poor and the oppressed. This theology has two key concepts, the *minjŭng* (the people) and *han* (enmity, grudge). *Minjung* theology proclaims that the people, the *minjung*, are the proper subject of history and that understanding history means to understand God's work in overcoming the *han* which the people feel in their conditions of oppression. It is an important contribution of this theology that the hope offered by God is a direct response to the suffering of the mass of the people. This Christian hope for freedom from oppression is often compared to the liberation of the Hebrew slaves in Egypt.

The liberal, politically active strand of Protestantism which had lain nearly dormant throughout recent decades emerged again in the late 1960s. While most liberal Protestants in Korea would be more theologically conservative than their corresponding Western brethren, these same people have been very much in the forefront of the political scene. It is these liberal laymen, not the formal leadership of the Protestant churches, who have called clearly for the restoration of democracy, for justice and for fairness in dealings with the workers of the new industrial state. The liberals attempted in 1973 to organize a petition for the repeal of the Yusin Constitution which had entrenched Pak Chŏnghŭi in power. Many of these Christians were imprisoned and tortured for their opinions. Opposition leaders, largely drawn from the Christian community, have often expressed their resistance to the military regimes of the past twenty years in terms of Christian belief. Catholics have joined with their fellow Christians since the 1960s in this battle but, curiously, Buddhists have been noticeably absent from expressed political dissent until the late 1980s.

A major social clash from the 1970s to the 1990s effectively was between Christian laywomen on the one hand and conservative men and the *Yudo-hoe* (Confucian Association) in particular over the issue of the basic equality of men and women before the law in family matters. This involved three issues, viz, the legal right of persons bearing the same clan name but otherwise unrelated to marry, the legal right of women to inherit property, and the legal right of a woman to be designated as the head of a household. The leader in this fight was the Methodist laywoman, Yi T'aeyŏng (Lee Tai-young, 1914–1998) who founded the Korean Legal Aid Center for Family Relations. In 1979, the Family Law was revised stipulating that a wife should inherit a share of the family estate equivalent to that of the eldest son. The section of the Family Law forbidding intra-clan marriage was abolished in the late 1990s. All of these revisions had been opposed because they were perceived to be contrary to Korean tradition.

In 1984–5, the churches celebrated the centennial of the arrival of foreign missionaries with a series of conferences, commemorative services, and rallies. On Easter Sunday, 1985 in Inch'ŏn, the port where the missionaries Underwood and Appenzeller first came ashore, there was a re-enactment of the arrival of Dr Underwood, who was portrayed by one of his great-grandsons.

In the early 1990s, some newly-formed eschatological sects began to preach the immanent end of the world. Two groups in particular caught the national headlines. From 1991, a charismatic 18-year old, Ha Pangik, who founded the Daverra Church, predicted the coming of the *parousia* (*hyugo* in Korean) or the assumption of all believers into Heaven at the end of the world. The failure of the prediction of the end time in October 1992 led to the disbanding of this group. Yi Changmin, founder of the Tami (Coming Days) Missionary Church, was arrested at the airport on 22 September, 1992 trying to leave Korea carrying the church's funds with him. He was forced to admit that he did not know when the end of the world would occur. This group too disbanded when its prediction of the end of the world on 28 October, 1992 failed to occur. At the time of its disbanding, the church claimed ninety branches and a membership of 8,000 persons. These events are one indication that new religious movements in Korea after 1945 are often Christian in inspiration in contrast to the situation in Japan where they tend to be of Shintō/Buddhist inspiration.

The 1980s and 1990s also saw the development of both dialogue and conflict between Christianity (primarily Protestant Christianity) and Buddhism. From the 1980s, a number of Roman Catholic and Protestant theologians, among whom one of the leaders was Pyŏn Sŏnhwan (1928–1995), gathered together with some leading Buddhist monks and laity for a series of seminars on inter-religious dialogue. These meetings were criticised by the more conservative quarters of the churches which led to accusations of heresy against some of these theologians such as Pyŏn that they were rejecting the core teaching of the Church about the uniqueness and divinity of Christ. This conflict was a reflection of larger tensions between Christianity and Buddhism. By the 1990s, both religious bodies had become strongly evangelical, inevitably bringing them to a sense of competition or conflict with each other. On the Buddhist side there were accusations by some that arson attacks on temples were committed by Christians. Whether these accusations, which have not been legally tested, are true or not, they reflect the climate of competition and distrust which exists between the two groups. On the other hand, there has never been any evidence of an organised programme of Christian violence, either by individuals or formal Church bodies, against Korean Buddhists or their places of worship. Rather, the attitude of Protestants to Buddhists has been one of either indifference or avoidance.

By the final decade of the twentieth century, the Christian churches, especially the Protestant churches, were the predominant religious fact of modern Korean history. Numerically, Christians of all groups constituted more than one quarter of the south Korean population. They had proved themselves adequate to the task of self-support, self-governance, self-development and survival under extremely harsh conditions of foreign colonial and local military rule. Protestantism in particular has exercised an extraordinary influence on the other religious traditions in helping to create a more outward-looking attitude amongst Catholics, by providing both a sense of competition and a model for growth which aided in the revival of Buddhism, and has been the source of inspiration for various new non-Christian religious movements. There has been extraordinary Christian influence on the development of modern education. Forty universities and 293 schools claim a Christian origin, including three of the five top universities in the country. Having achieved such outstanding numerical, physical and social success, the churches face the challenge of adapting themselves to this success without losing their commitment to the essence of Christianity. Moreover, it is curious to note that although the church has been successful in many ways, it has had little cultural impact. It has made little attempt to create Korean hymns, build churches in a Korean style, and in general adapt Christianity to Korean culture by removing unnecessary Western cultural structures and forms. It is the author's opinion that this must be done if the church is to have a lasting influence on the nation. Although the Christian churches are the predominant religious fact of early twenty-first century Korea, the direct Christian influence on Korean society and forms of cultural expression is disproportionately less than one would anticipate. Why is it that this church has not created Korean forms of Christian art, music, and architecture? At a similar stage in its history, Buddhism had a proportionately greater influence on the culture, art, and mores of the nation.

Although the Eastern Orthodox tradition of Christianity is unrelated to the historical development of Protestant Christianity, which is after all a branching off from Roman Catholic Christianity, it is useful to discuss here the history of the small Korean Orthodox community as its beginnings are in the same era as the origins of the Presbyterian and Methodist missions and reflect some of the same political influences. A Russian Orthodox chaplain had been associated with the Russian legation almost from the beginning of Russo-Korean diplomatic relations. At the end of the nineteenth century, a number of Koreans who had settled in eastern Siberia because of the better farming and political conditions there were baptised as Orthodox Christians. Some of these Koreans returned to Korea and got in contact with the Russians in Sŏul. As a result, in 1900 the Holy Synod in Moscow created a mission under the authority of the Archimandrite Chrysanthus Shchetkovsky. In 1903, King Kojong made a grant of land to the legation for the erection of a church, St. Nicholas, which was placed under the care of the Archimandrite. Various liturgical materials were translated into Korean around this time. The first Korean priest, Kang Hant'ak (1877–1939) was ordained in Tōkyō in 1912. Missionary activity ceased following the Russian Revolution in 1918, and the community survived as a mixture of local Korean Christians and expatriate White Russians. Various small congregations were created in the area north of Sŏul which were closed by 1930, although a small congregation existed in P'yŏngyang for ten years until 1939. The last Russian priest left in 1947 when the small church passed entirely into Korean hands. During the Korean War, Greek soldiers discovered the struggling community and helped to re-invigorate it. The Korean Orthodox Church then became a part of the Greek Orthodox Church and is now under the jurisdiction of the Archdiocese of New Zealand. In 1965, the St. Nicholas Orthodox Church was moved to a site in the Map'o area of Sŏul where a new edifice was erected in 1968 in the form of a Byzantine cross, and consecrated in 1978 following completion of the elaborate interior decorations. In 1994, the Korean Orthodox Church reported that it had 2,000 adherents, six priests, and eight churches.

11

ROMAN CATHOLICISM
From Ghetto to Society

1. The End of the Chosŏn Dynasty

The modern century of Korean Catholicism may be divided into the three main periods of secular history: the final phase of the Chosŏn Dynasty (1872–1910), the Japanese colonial period (1910–45), and the post-liberation period (1945–). The most striking characteristic of the first two phases of recent Catholic history is the effect which the century of persecutions had on the outlook of the ordinary believer. A ghetto mentality was inculcated in the mind of the average Catholic, which persisted down to the late 1970s. Even at that late date one could still hear the phrase 'Old Catholics' and 'New Catholics', referring respectively to those people who could trace their ancestry to families which had lived through the period of persecutions, and those who were recent believers and could not trace their spiritual ancestry back to the period of the martyrs. Another characteristic of the first two phases of recent history is an emphasis on the growth and development of the institutional church with little concern for social outreach or for the historical events which were transpiring around the church. This attitude, too, was the result of the ghetto mentality which came to characterize even the clergy and the ecclesiastical leadership.

Even during the period of the Great Persecution, plans were still being laid for the further evangelization of the peninsula. Between 1868 and 1874, a conference was held under the authority of the new bishop Félix Clair Ridel (1830–84) in Ch'a-kou, a village in the Liaotung Peninsula in southern Manchuria. In 1876, five years after the cessation of the Great Persecution, two priests returned to Korea, and they were joined in the following year by Bishop Ridel. It was during the latter part of the 1870s that the Catholic Church achieved tacit recognition of its right to exist in Korea. Although the bishop and another priest were deported in 1878 and 1879, by 1881 the government had ceased officially to harass priests carrying out their religious functions. This was undoubtedly the result of Korea's opening to the outside world and the moves to establish diplomatic relations with the various Western powers.

From the 1880s onwards, the institutional growth of the church was very marked. By 1882, there were 12,500 believers, an increase since the period of the Great Persecution of nearly 3,000 persons. By the time of the annexation of Korea by Japan in 1910, the number of believers had grown to 73,000 persons. A seminary was re-established in 1885, which by 1900 had produced ten Korean priests. By 1910, there were fifteen Korean priests in addition to which there were fifty-six foreign clergy. During this same time, various orders of nuns were established and charitable projects were undertaken.

Probably the most significant symbol of the new era of freedom from persecution was the erection of the first two permanent church edifices, the Yakhyŏn Church and the Cathedral of St Mary, both in Sŏul. The former was erected in 1893 and the latter was completed and dedicated in 1898. Both of these churches were built as memorials to the Catholic martyrs of the nineteenth century. The Yakhyŏn Church is situated on a hill above the execution ground outside the Sŏso-mun or Little West Gate, and the cathedral is on the site of the home of Kim Pŏmu, the first Korean martyr, in Myŏng-dong. Unlike the Protestant church missions, the Catholic Church seemed initially to have little interest in general social outreach as in this period they did not erect modern schools or hospitals as did their Presbyterian and Methodist counterparts.

2. The Church under Japanese Colonial Rule

At the start of the colonial era, on 3 May 1911, two Vicariates Apostolic were created in Sŏul and Taegu, indicating the growing size and independence of the Catholic community with a third vicariate being added in Wŏnsan in 1920. Statistics also indicate continued growth throughout this period. By the end of the ten-year period ending in 1920 there were 292 churches and ninety thousand communicants. By 1932, this had become 323 churches and 110,000 communicants served by 141 priests of whom 55 were Koreans; by the early 1940s, this had become 183,000 communicants served by 308 priests of whom 139 were Koreans. However, even though there was continued numerical growth, there was not a significant percentage increase of the Catholic community within the national population which remained at about 0.05 percent. This compares unfavourably with Protestant statistics during the same period. There was also less of an emphasis on institutional mission work, such as in the area of education. By 1932 there were no Catholic institutions of higher education, whereas in the same year there were seven such Protestant institutions.

It is facts such as these which have led Catholic scholars such as Min Kyŏngsuk to conclude that the Catholic Church continued to divorce itself from the mainstream of Korean society, to maintain a kind of 'ghetto' mentality towards the world outside the Church itself. Furthermore, they point out that the bulk of the converts continued to be drawn from the dispossessed sectors of society with the Church having little attraction to the intelligentsia. For the most part the colonial era was a period of tranquil development until the last five-years of Japanese control, the period of the Pacific War. There are two reasons for the attitude of the Catholic Church under Japanese rule. The first was the signing of a Concordat between the Office of the Sacred Congregation of the Propaganda Fide with the Japanese Government. On 25 May, 1936, it was announced by the Vatican that it accepted the Japanese Government's interpretation of State Shintō rites as being 'patriotic' rituals and consequently permitting Catholics to attend these rites without fear of committing an act of idolatry. The Concordat gave the Roman Catholic Church in the Japanese Empire, including Korea, a legal status and provided a framework for religious activities. This framework in turn would have constrained any criticisms of the colonial regime. Secondly, the Church leadership in Korea would have remembered the sufferings of the first century of the Church and would have feared the onset of another persecution. Consequently, during the late 1930s and early 1940s, when many Protestants were incarcerated and killed over their refusal to participate in State Shintō rituals, there was no Catholic reaction against these rites until 1944 when the first priest was arrested for his refusal to take a part in them. This passive acquiescence in a 'pagan' rite seems strange in light of the strong stand which the church had taken against participation in the *chesa* ancestral rites and is one indication that during this period the church had not yet outgrown its ghetto mentality.

Though the colonial regime does not seem to have been as harsh with the Catholic Church as they had been with Protestant bodies, in part a result of the Concordat, as the war effort in the Pacific intensified, the Catholic Church also was abused. The cathedral in P'yŏngyang was taken over in December, 1940 for military use, while missionaries were moved to the outskirts of the city. Following the attack on Pearl Harbor, French and American missionaries were arrested and the Americans were forcibly repatriated. In line with the attempts to 'purify' the Protestant churches of foreign influences, the government attempted to create a 'Japanese' Catholic Church in Korea by encouraging the appointment of Japanese priests in Korea. In 1942, Father Hayasaka Kubei (1887–1946) was appointed Bishop of Taegu, and Father Wakida Asagorō Bishop of Kwangju. As the war began to draw to a close, the Japanese Government took even more drastic measures, including the forced induction of priests and seminarians into the armed forces and the placement of other priests in conditions of involuntary servitude for the duration of the war. Church buildings were desecrated by being used as barracks for the Japanese army. This harsh treatment came to an abrupt end with the surrender of Japan on 15 August, 1945.

3. The Post-Liberation Church

The political division of the peninsula immediately following liberation from Japanese rule had the effect of instituting two different policies regarding the practice of religion. In southern Korea, foreign priests who had been held in prison by the Japanese were released and Japanese priests who had been in administrative positions in the Korean church resigned. The death of the Japanese bishop of Taegu in 1946 permitted the appointment of a Korean in his place. Catholic publications which had been suspended by the Japanese were again published and new ones were created. For example, the *Kyŏnghyang chapji* resumed publication as did *Catholic Youth*. A new newspaper, the *Kyŏnghyang sinmun*, began publication during this period. Religious works were also published, among them a Korean translation of the French martyrology *Martyrs coréennes* in 1946 and Yu Hongnyŏl's *Ch'ŏnju kyohoe-sa* (History of the Catholic Church [in Korea]). The picture which seem bright in south Korea was very different in north Korea and Manchuria. At the beginning of the Russian occupation of Manchuria in 1946, the army shot two priests who worked in the Kuan-tung area in which many Koreas resided. In 1947, the Russians arrested the bishop and thirty-nine priests, monks, and nuns. This same policy was applied in northern Korea where clergy in rural areas, for example, were rounded up and summarily shot.

With the establishment of two separate Korean governments in 1948, these differences in policy became even more accentuated. In the south Korea, no legal or bureaucratic impediment was placed in the way of Catholic evangelism. The Korean Church sent Chang Myŏn (1899–1966) as a special envoy to the Pope; a new Apostolic Delegate was created to oversee the life of the Korean Church; and a monument was erected in Sŏul in February, 1950 as a memorial to Catholic martyrs. In north Korea, on the other hand, more than a year before the outbreak of the civil war, the regime began to persecute the Church in earnest. In May, 1949, Bishop Bonifatius Sauer (1877–1950) and the members of the Benedictine abbey at Tŏgwŏn were imprisoned. The Catholic agricultural college was confiscated and renamed for the north Korean leader Kim Ilsŏng (1912–93). Korean parish priests were arrested in such numbers that many parishes fell inactive for lack of supervision. Bishop Hong Yongho (1906–?) of P'yŏngyang sent a letter of protest to Kim Ilsŏng, but was himself arrested for this act and is believed to have died whilst in prison.

With the outbreak of the Korean War on 25 June, 1950, the remaining priests who were at liberty in the north were arrested and imprisoned, many of whom were later found to have been killed. As the northern army advanced into the south, they took into custody and later killed numbers of priests, monks, and nuns, and took others back to P'yŏngyang for interrogation. This harsh treatment was not confined to Catholic religious alone but was also characteristic of the way in which the communist regime dealt with the Protestants as well. In 1953, at the time of the cessation of hostilities, the total number of Catholics in south Korea, including many refugees from the north totalled 166,000 which is ninety per cent of the number of Catholics in all of Korea in 1945, which was 183,000. How many secret believers still remained in the north at the time of the truce is not known. However, the statistics do give a dramatic indication of the magnitude of the loss of life during the conflict.

In south Korea in the decade following the Korean War, Catholicism experience a period of great growth. Two tertiary-level colleges were founded, Hyosŏng Women's College in Taegu in 1952, and Sŏgang College (now Sogang

University) by the Jesuits in Sŏul in 1960. The six dioceses in 1953 had become fourteen dioceses in 1963. The 166,000 communicants in 1953 had significantly increased to 575,000 by 1963. In 1962, the Vatican gave further approval to the growth of the Korean Church by creating the first ecclesiastical hierarchy in Korea, meaning that the Korean Church now had direct control over its affairs and was not subordinate to another body other than the Vatican itself. Thus the former vicariates of Sŏul, Taegu and Kwangju became archdioceses with dioceses subordinate to them. In the next decade from 1963 to 1974, further recognition was given to the rapid growth of the Church when Archbishop Kim Suhwan (1922–) was created a cardinal by Pope Paul VI (1897–1978) in 1968. More dioceses were created to a total of fourteen in order to accommodate the increased number of churches; communicants had risen to over one million people. More importantly, Catholics became more visibly involved in social outreach than at any time in the past. Unlike the situation in the 1930s, Catholic clergy and laity during the 1970s and 1980s also have been in the forefront of the criticism of the undemocratic, military-style governments of the Pak Chŏnghŭi and Chŏn Tuhwan regimes, most notably the Cardinal Archbishop himself. More so than Protestants, Catholics have been noticeably involved in social movements concerned with the welfare of the industrial worker in Korea's rapidly changing society which is undoubtedly a reflection of the roots of the church in the poorer sector of society. This involvement stands as a condemnation of Protestant concern with Church Growth. By the end of the twentieth century, the Roman Catholic Church in Korea had a membership of 2,950,730 adherents. Symbolic of the Catholic Church's increased social engagement since the 1930s is the number of educational institutions which have been founded, including nine universities and sixty-eight schools related to the Church.

In May 1984, Pope John-Paul II (1920–) paid a visit to Korea to take part in the bicentennial celebration of Korean Catholicism. At that time, a million Catholics attended a mass on Yŏ'ŭi-do Island in the Han River in central Sŏul at which the Pope canonized 103 Korean martyrs as saints of the church. This was not only the largest number of persons ever canonized at any one time, but the first time that a ceremony of canonization had been held outside Rome. The ceremony was a significant international recognition of a church which had struggled for decades to achieve the right to exist.

As an outgrowth of the preparations for the bicentennial of its foundation, the Catholic Church has created several martyrium, or martyr memorial churches or monuments, to commemorate the deaths of the thousands of official and unofficial Catholic martyrs. Chief among these is the *Chŏltu-san* ('Beheading Hill') church with its associated martyrs' museum built in 1967 on the cliff above the spot on the north bank of the Han River in Sŏul where the majority of executions of Catholics was conducted during the persecution of 1866–71. A memorial church was also built at Saenamt'o on the northern bank of the Han River in Sŏul in 1984. This was the place of the execution of many of the missionaries including the first priest Father Chou Wên-mu. Likewise, a memorial was erected in the park in the Little West Gate area of Sŏul which was the site where some forty-four executions were carried out. An important part of the consciousness of modern Korean Catholics is the memory of the thousands of people who died for their faith.

Like their Protestant counterparts, Catholic missiologists single out the church in Korea as being the national church which has experienced the most rapid numerical growth in the last quarter of the twentieth century. As we have indicated, this trend began at some time in the late 1950s or early 1960s. There were two principal reasons for this sudden change. The first was the dramatic increase in the size of the Protestant churches. At some time after 1945, these churches achieved a size greater than three per cent of the national population. From that point on, their increase in numbers and percentage representation within the national population has continued largely unabated. This high visibility of a sister form of Christianity unquestionably removed the quaintness or even stigma surrounding Christian belief. By the 1950s, a general national consensus had been reached that Christianity was not only acceptable, but a good thing. This consensus in turn affected the self-conception of the Catholic believer, broke down the ghetto mentality which had been built up through decades of persecution, and encouraged the ordinary believer to evangelize for his faith. The second factor influencing Catholic self-understanding was the Second Vatican Council (1962–65). The liberality of this council and its ecumenical emphasis not only affected the theology of the Korean church, but also changed its attitudes towards other Christian churches. Donald Baker points to two further reasons for the change from a church with a 'ghetto' mentality to a socially active, evangelical church, namely the increasing Koreanisation or localisation of the clergy, and the increasing urbanisation of the membership of the church. Taken together all these factors suggest that from the 1960s Korean Catholicism had not only joined the mainstream of Korean society, but had also joined the mainstream of Korean Christianity. In 1994, the Roman Catholic Church in Korea reported that it had a membership of 3,209,494 adherents, and 2,174 priests. The Church consisted of three archdioceses and sixteen dioceses and 947 churches. The 1995 National Household Census, however, revealed that there were 2,950,730 persons who self-identified as Catholics.

12

CONFUCIANISM
The Residue of a Great Tradition

1. Recent History

The first major event of the modern century of Korean Confucianism may be said to be the Kabo Reforms of 1894. The Confucian state examinations were eliminated, and a modern system of government and a modern, Western system of education were instituted. Throughout the Chosŏn Dynasty, Confucianism had exercised supreme influence on society in the political, cultural, and social spheres. The state examinations were the key prop to the system of government, as passes in these exams determined the examinees' fitness for governmental service. Neo-Confucianism was the dominant mode of philosophical reflection, which in turn exercised a tremendous influence on art, letters, and music. With regard to the social system, Confucianism exercised supreme influence both on the structural and on the cognitive level. Until the end of the Chosŏn period, Korea was the most thoroughly Confucian society in East Asia. This all began to change with the formal commencement of modernization, represented by the Japanese-influenced reforms of 1894.

Although the Korean government abolished the system of Confucian examinations and the Confucian system of government, the monarchy continued to support the Confucian ritual-system. Confucian ritual had been a prime means for expressing the moral and ethical system which was at the heart of the Confucian *weltanschauung*. King Sejong had eliminated the great rite offered to Heaven on the grounds that it was appropriate only for the Emperor of China to perform such a rite. When the Kingdom of Chosŏn became the Empire of Tae Han in 1897, this rite was restored and a special altar was created for its performance. As a sign of the submissive relationship between Korea and Japan, by 1908 all rituals but the rites offered to the dynastic ancestors and Confucius had been eliminated. These latter ceremonies survive to the present day.

The Japanese Government-General recognized, however, the importance of Confucianism to Korea and maintained it in an attempt to gain popular support for Japanese colonial rule. This policy of supporting Confucianism was also used in Manchukuo during the 1930s to provide a foundation for Japanese authority in northern China. Japanese support for Confucianism in Korea meant the retention and support of the memorial-rites for the royal ancestors, the rites for Confucius and his principal disciples, and special ceremonies which indirectly supported Japanese rule. Upon the marriage of the future Emperor Hirohito (1901–89) in 1924 and upon his ascension to the throne in 1928, Confucian-style ceremonies were authorized which would lend respectability to Japanese rule in Korea.

Following liberation, various Confucian associations were formed or re-instituted, which took over on a private basis the maintenance of the various Confucian shrines and the rituals performed in them. There are two types of shrines supported by these groups. One type of shrine is the *Mun-myo*, the principal national Confucian shrine, which in Korea is located in Sŏul (see Fig. 18), and the other type of shrine is the *hyanggyo* or regional Confucian academy and shrine. *Hyanggyo* are located in most of the important provincial cities. Rites are performed in both types of shrines to Confucius and his principal disciples twice a year in the second and eighth lunar months. The total number of spirits venerated has varied in recent years. Until 1949, a total of 138 spirits were venerated. In that year the number was reduced to twenty-five spirits, but in 1952 fourteen figures were reinstated. Korean Confucianism is a tradition which conserves so well the principal characteristics of Confucianism and Confucian ceremony that it has had an impact on Confucian ceremonies in Taiwan. For example, when the National Classical Music Institute troupe of Korea was on tour in Taiwan in 1967, their music and ceremonial propriety inspired the Chinese to re-examine their own ceremonial music. A discussion of Confucian ritual may be found in the next section.

With the disestablishment of the Confucian-style system of education, the principal academic institution, the Sŏnggyun-gwan, fell into disuse. In 1911, a group of scholars created the Kyŏnghag-wŏn, an institute for the study of Confucian thought and the Confucian classics. This institute was later raised to the status of a 'college' and was known as Myŏngnyun College until 1945. Shortly after liberation, the college was given the status of a university and renamed after the Sŏnggyun-gwan. Consequently, the university traces its ancestry back to the Confucian institute founded in 1288 in the Koryŏ capital of Kaegyŏng and is noted for its College of Confucian Studies which includes musical arts as well as philosophical studies. The university library preserves the largest collection of ancient Confucian documents and texts in Korea. In spite of the development of a modern Confucian university dedicated to the preservation of the cultural influence of Confucianism in Korean society, the primary mode of philosophical discourse in Korea is now Western philosophy.

Although Confucianism no longer holds a formal pre-eminence in the sphere of politics and culture, Confucianism still influences Korean society in the social sphere on both the structural and cognitive levels. It is ironic that the social implications of Confucianism which penetrated into Korean society well after the political and cultural aspects had been adopted have survived the demise of the Confucian system of government. It is for this reason that the author feels

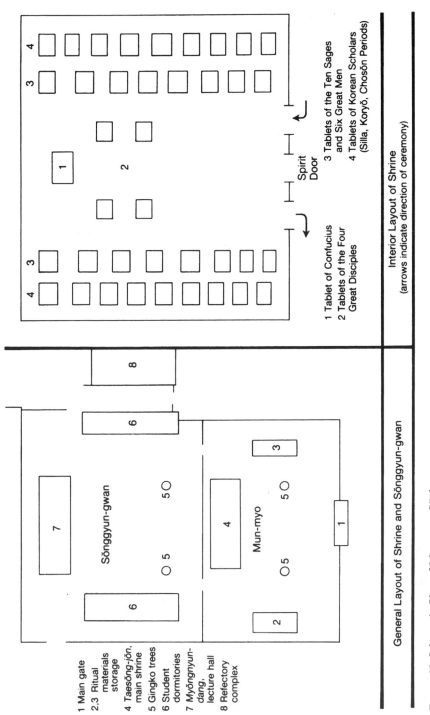

Interior Layout of Shrine
(arrows indicate direction of ceremony)

1 Tablet of Confucius
2 Tablets of the Four
  Great Disciples
3 Tablets of the Ten Sages
  and Six Great Men
4 Tablets of Korean Scholars
  (Silla, Koryŏ, Chosŏn Periods)

Spirit
Door

Sŏnggyun-gwan

Mun-myo

General Layout of Shrine and Sŏnggyun-gwan

1 Main gate
2,3 Ritual
  materials
  storage
4 Taesŏng-jŏn,
  main shrine
5 Gingko trees
6 Student
  dormitories
7 Myŏngnyun-
  dang,
  lecture hall
8 Refectory
  complex

Figure 18 Schematic Plan of Mun-myo, Sŏul

that even in the early twenty-first century, Korea may still be called a Confucian society. The Korean people have developed from a tribal society which was highly stratified and based on an extended-clan system of kinship. Confucianism did not create stratification, social distinction, or the importance of the clan in Korean society. These ideas were already there. Confucianism only reinforced these tendencies of Korean culture. After the middle of the Chosŏn period, through the efforts of the radical *Sarim-p'a* and their successors, the social characteristics of Korean culture were refashioned according to a rigid Neo-Confucian pattern.

On the structural level, the living patterns of modern Koreans, the importance of the extended-family group, the continued performance of the *chesa* or ancestral rites, all owe their continuity to the social influence of Confucianism. On the cognitive level, attachment to one's family, loyalty to one's friends, and respect for one's teachers all owe their existence to the continuation of Confucian social influence on Korean culture. Although formally Confucianism would seem to be a dead letter in Korean culture, something only of historical interest, its influence is pervasive and powerful, if ineffable. Several years ago, at a seminar held on the contemporary influence of Confucianism in which the author participated, virtually all the Korean participants denied the importance of Confucianism in modern Korea. Later, the comments of a participating scholar about the role of his son in the family and the relationship of a student to his teacher prompted the author to remind the speakers that these views were very Confucian. Similarly, the Confucian Association has fought hard over the past decades to preserve the social characteristics of 'traditional' Korean society including the forbidding of intra-clan marriage regardless of the distance of actual relationship, the right of women, mothers and sisters, to inherit property along with their sons and male siblings, and the right of a woman to be registered as the legal head of a household. These views have been opposed largely by Christian women's groups.

Modern Koreans' view of the world, and particularly of the relationship of the United States to Korea, attitudes to political leadership and criticisms of it, attitudes towards the family, friends, and the opposite sex are all influenced by Confucianism. For a number of years, it appeared that the United States had taken the place of China as the elder brother in many people's minds. Criticisms of American policy with regard to Korea seemed to be framed by a Confucian understanding of family relationships extended into the international sphere. Likewise concepts of governmental authority appear to stem from concepts of authority in the family. Criticisms of governmental leaders also seem to be framed by an understanding of the fulfilment by the leader of the role of family head. Young radical students, disdainful of the authority of older generations, naturally defer to the 'elder brother' leaders within their groups. The ministers of state, who are appointed by the President of the Republic of Korea, are more often than not professors of politics, law, education and other subjects reflecting the idea that scholars should be the ones to run the government ministries.

Because the Korean *weltanschauung* is still dominated by Confucian concepts of filial piety, loyalty, formal propriety and the value of education, Korean society may yet be called a Confucian society.

2. The Confucian Ritual System

The ritual system of Confucianism was a very rich and elaborate complex of rites and ceremonies. There were several layers of Confucian ceremonial, but broadly speaking they may be divided into two types: the clan-oriented rites called *chesa* addressed to near or distant relatives, and the royal ritual system. Both of these ritual systems survive, albeit in a reduced form. Recent research continues to show the surprisingly high level of performance of the *chesa* rites, even in an urbanized setting. In spite of recent government attempts to eliminate or curtail *Ch'usŏk*, the harvest festival held on the fifteenth of the eighth lunar month, virtually all Koreans, rural and urban, kept this festival. The government in the end was forced to recognise the importance of this festival and designated it a national holiday. At *Ch'usŏk*, families will visit their ancestral graves, sweep them clean, and offer up the *chesa* rite on a large or small scale. This fact alone attests to the tenacity of Confucian tradition.

The *chesa* or ancestral rite is usually performed on the anniversary of the death date of the relative. The largest and most elaborate rites are the three annual rites following the person's death. Usually, the last of the three rites is the grandest, as it is then that the spirit is presumed to go permanently to the next world and this rite thus concludes the formal period of mourning. After that, annual but less elaborate rites will be observed.

In preparing for the ceremony, an appropriate room is selected and the ritual materials laid out. A folding screen is set up, and immediately in front is placed the table for the ritual offerings. On this table is placed either a tablet with the name of the deceased or a photograph. In front of this are placed the various rice, vegetable, fish, meat, and confectionery offerings. In front of the offering table is the smaller table for the incense burner. In recent years, there has been a tendency to shorten the form of the ritual. Whether the ritual is performed in the traditional or modern fashion, the basic elements of the *chesa* are the welcoming of the spirits, the sharing of the prepared food offerings, the escorting out of the spirits at the conclusion of the rite, and the consumption of the food by those present. Obviously, the *chesa* rite is based on the idea of an elaborate banquet to entertain distinguished guests, the family ancestors. The ritual remembrance of one's forebears is such an important feature of Korean culture that there is a Christian memorial-rite, called *ch'udo yebae,* dedicated to one's parents and other relatives which in terms of form and function is similar to the Confucian *chesa* rite.

The system of royal Confucian rites reflected Korea's place in the cultural firmament of Chinese civilization (see Table 1). There were certain rituals which could not be performed because they were more appropriately conducted by the Emperor of China. Also the scale of certain ceremonies differed depending upon

Table 1 Confucian Sacrifical Rites

Ritual	Type of Spirit Addressed	Type of Ritual
Great Rites		
Wŏn'gu-je	Heaven (not performed in Korea)	Heavenly
Sajik	Earth and Grain	Earthly
Chong-myo and *Yŏngnyŏng-jŏn*	Royal Ancestors	Human
Ch'ilsa	Seven Sacrifices	uncertain
Kongsin	Merit Subjects	Human
Medium Rites		
P'ungunnoeu	Wind, Clouds, Thunder, and Rain	Heavenly
Sanch'ŏn	Mountains and Streams	Earthly
Sŏnghwang	Tutelary Spirit	Earthly
Akhaedok	Mountains, Seas, and Streams	Earthly
Sŏnnong	Agriculture	Human
Sŏnjam	Sericulture	Human
Usa	Elements and Grain	Human
Sŏkchŏn	Confucius	Human
Yŏktae sijo	Dynastic Founders	Human
Small Rites		
Myŏngsan taech'ŏn	Famous Mountains and Great Streams	Earthly
Yŏngsŏng	Star of Grain Cultivation	Heavenly
Noinsŏng	Star of Longevity	Heavenly
Majo	Star of Horse Spirits	Heavenly
Sŏnmok	First Horse Domesticator	Human
Masa	First Equestrian	Earthly
Mabo	Horse Injury	Earthly
Ma-je	War	Human (?)
Yŏng-je	Supplication for Clear Weather	Earthly
Sahan	Water	Human
Tuk-che	Military Banner	uncertain
Yŏ-je	Unsettled Spirits	Mixture
P'o-je	Crop Calamity	Earthly

Source: based on information provided by Dr Robert C. Provine.

whether they were performed in the capital or in a provincial centre. The royal ritual system consisted of five general categories of rites: (1) *Kil-lye* (Auspicious Rites), (2) *Ka-rye* (Congratulatory Rites), (3) *Hyung-nye* (Mourning Rites), (4) *Pil-lye* (Guest Rites), and (5) *Kul-lye* (Military Rites). The greatest number of rituals fell into the first category. These rituals, also called sacrifices, were addressed to a wide variety of personages and spirits and were performed on three degrees of scale, great, medium, and small. The type, quantity, and colour of ritual offerings were strictly regulated according to the type and scale of ceremony. Within each scale of ceremony, the rites were further differentiated according to whether the spirit being venerated was heavenly, earthly, or human.

An example of an auspicious rite on the great scale would be the *Sajik* rite offered twice yearly to the spirits of grain and harvest. This was, of course, an earthly rite. A human rite on the same scale would be the royal ancestral rites performed twice yearly at the Royal Ancestral Shrine, the *Chong-myo*. There was no heavenly rite on a great scale, as this was appropriately performed only by the Emperor of China. An example of a medium-scale heavenly rite would be the ceremony to the gods of Wind, Clouds, Thunder, and Rain, while an earthly rite would be the one to the spirits of mountains and rivers. The *Sŏkchŏn* ceremony, held at the *Mun-myo*, dedicated to Confucius and his premier disciples is an example of a medium-scale human rite. The *Noin-sŏng* ritual to the Star of Longevity is an example of a small-scale heavenly rite. Small-scale rites were not accompanied by music as were great- and medium-scale rites.

The great- and medium-scale rituals were composed of ten stages, each of which was accompanied by ritual music. The stages were: (1) Welcoming the Spirits, (2) Ritual Cleansing of the Hands, (3) Ascending into the Shrine, (4) Offering of Tribute, (5) Offering of Sacrificial Food, (6) First Offering of Wine, (7) Second Offering of Wine, (8) Final Offering of Wine, (9) Removal of the Ceremonial Vessels, and (10) Ushering Out the Spirits. From this it will be seen that there was a very formal structure to the service which again was based upon the idea of entertaining important ceremonial guests in one's home. Ritual propriety has always been an important characteristic of Korean Confucian social life, both in the family and in society at large. The type and structure of these ceremonies well indicate this cultural preoccupation of Chosŏn-period society.

13

BUDDHISM
Decline, Revival, and Conflict

1. Reasons for the Revival of Korean Buddhism

By the end of the Chosŏn Dynasty, less than a hundred years ago, most contemporary observers felt that Korean Buddhism was spent and would shortly disappear. Charles Allen Clark (1878–1961), a Presbyterian missionary who wrote sympathetically of Buddhism in the first third of the twentieth century, frequently refers to the decayed condition of the temples, the lack of fiscal support, the lack of unity within the Buddhist church, and generally the gross ignorance of the majority of the clergy. He was one among many who expected Buddhism to vanish from the Korean scene. As a glance at any of the recent government statistics will show, this has not happened. Buddhism in Korea has revived greatly. How are we to explain this phenomenon?

There were several factors at work. First of all, the opening of Korea to diplomatic and trade contacts with the Western world also meant a lifting of the restrictions against the practitioners of all religions. There could no longer be an official policy of the suppression of religion, including Buddhism, if there were to be sustained contacts with the Western world. Second, the sudden and rapid development of Christianity had a competitive influence on the more progressive elements within the Buddhist order. In time there came to be a movement for Buddhist evangelism and the creation of institutions such as high schools, colleges, hospitals, and student societies in imitation of similar Christian institutions. The third influence was Japan. Japan in the late nineteenth and early twentieth centuries was a state which was as heavily influenced by Buddhism as Korea was by Confucianism. With the absorption of Korea by Japan in 1910, the Japanese sought to implant their institutional form of Buddhism in Korea. Ostensibly done for the reform of Buddhism in Korea, this assistance was unquestionably motivated by political reasons. The Christian Church counted among its members a large number of the young progressive patriots and thus support for Buddhism could become a countervailing force against Christianity. Although many monks fought against this use of Buddhism for purposes of colonial rule, there is no doubt that such assistance was in some measure responsible for the institutional revival of Buddhism.

184

2. Four Key Figures in the Revival of Buddhism

Although there are many monks in the past hundred years who have exercised a beneficial influence on the development of Buddhism in Korea, four are of especial importance, Sŏngu (1849–1912), Yongun (1879–1944), Hyobong (1888–1966), and Kusan (1909–83). Sŏngu and Yongun are recognized as the most influential representatives of the traditionalist and modernist strands of modern Korean Buddhism, while Kusan was the most eminent modern exponent of Buddhist evangelism and overseas missions.

Sŏngu, better known by his literary name Kyŏnghŏ, was born as Song Tonguk into a peasant family living near Chŏnju in 1849. Following the death of his father he entered the Ch'ŏnggye-sa temple near Suwŏn at the age of 9. From there he went to Tonghak-sa on Kyeryong-san near Kongju, where he studied doctrinal Buddhism under the master Manhwa (also called Wŏno, 19th cent.). In 1871 Kyŏnghŏ was awarded the style of sutra master at the age of 23, which implied that he was the most astute of his master's disciples. Kyŏnghŏ continued along the path of traditional scholarship until at the age of 30 in 1879 he had an experience which changed the course of his life. On his way back to the Ch'ŏnggye-sa he was caught in a violent wind and rain storm and was forced to seek shelter in a nearby village. However, no one would admit him to their home. He learned that the reason for this was the fear of a deadly plague which was then spreading around the vicinity. Kyŏnghŏ suddenly realized that through learning alone he could not achieve release from life and death. Returning to the temple, Kyŏnghŏ went through a period of withdrawal and contemplation. From this experience he emerged determined to revive the tradition of Sŏn in Korea.

In the years 1884–5, Kyŏnghŏ made an extensive tour of the temples in Korea urging the upgrading of monastic standards. Among the temples which he visited were Hae'in-sa and Pŏmŏ-sa. He exercised a powerful influence on the monks of his day, reviving the monastic discipline of Sŏn Buddhism. Kyŏnghŏ's thought, judging from his surviving writings, suggests that he was influenced by the T'ang Ch'an master Hui-nêng (638–713) and the Koryŏ Sŏn masters Chinul and Po'u. Kyŏnghŏ acquired a reputation as a lecturer and was much in demand. He used these opportunities to propagate his vision for a revived and purified Buddhism. Kyŏnghŏ also helped initiate lay groups dedicated to the study of Buddhist doctrine and the practice of meditation. He died at the age of 63 in 1912, having laid the foundations for the growth of a revived form of traditional Buddhism.

If Kyŏnghŏ was the source of revived traditionalism, a much younger contemporary Yongun was the source of the movement for modernization. Yongun, better known by his literary name Manhae, was born Han Pongwan in Hongsŏng in Ch'ungnam Province in 1879. It is interesting to note that this area had been a major centre of Roman Catholic activity and social discontent. Han Pongwan was educated in the Confucian classics and while a young boy saw first hand the Tonghak Rebellion which attempted to bring about better conditions for the peasantry. Being disappointed with the outcome of the rebellion, Yongun went to Ose-am hermitage in the Sŏrak range where he studied for a while.

In 1905 Yongun took Buddhist orders at the Paektam-sa, a Sŏn temple. In 1908 he was one of fifty-two delegates to a conference which created the *Wŏn-jong* order of Korean Buddhism with its head temple at the newly founded Wŏnhŭng-sa in Sŏul. This was one of several abortive attempts to unify and revive Korean Buddhism in the early part of the twentieth century. After that, he went to Japan to visit temples there. His nationalism was aroused by the annexation of Korea by Japan in 1910. Manhae left Korea to visit the independence groups in China, returning to Korea in 1913 after visiting similar groups in Manchuria and Siberia. In that year he wrote a book, *Pulgyo taejŏn*, which explained the essence of Buddhism in terms of the *Prajñāpāramitā-sūtra*. Also in 1913, he wrote a treatise on his ideas for the renovation of Korean Buddhism, the *Chosŏn pulgyo yusin-non* (On the Revitalization of Buddhism in Korea) and in 1916 he was part of a group which initiated a Buddhist monthly magazine, *Yusim* (Mind Only). Up to this point, Yongun's life was typical of the patriotic members of the literary class. From 1919 onward, his thought was to be dominated by the need for national independence.

Manhae, one of the thirty-three *minjok taep'yo-ja* (Representatives of the People) who signed the 1 March 1919 declaration of Korean Independence, was imprisoned for three years by the Japanese. It is interesting to note that of the signatories, only three were Buddhists, the others being nearly equally divided between Christians and members of the Ch'ŏndo-gyo syncretic religion. Manhae was opposed to measures to absorb Korean Buddhism into Japanese sects and became involved with some of the political movements of the time, including the reaction to the Kwangju High School incident of 1929.

Manhae was also active in the area of literature at this time. He brought out a collection of his poems called *Nim-ŭi ch'immuk* (Silence of the Beloved), which expresses his love for his country in romantic and patriotic imagery. In 1931 he helped to reorganize the Buddhist youth association and undertook the publication of a Buddhist magazine *Pulgyo* (Buddhism). His most famous novel, *Hŭkp'ung* (Black Wind), was published in 1935. In 1937 he became implicated in a patriotic Buddhist secret society called *Mandang* and was arrested. He died in Sŏul in 1944 of a paralytic stroke at the age of 65. Manhae's image amongst the younger generation was that of a progressive, patriotic, Buddhist monk, and he was held in high esteem by many of the laity. His image among the clergy was however, very different. One leading monk was recently reported to have said that he did not feel that Manhae could be considered to have been a Buddhist.

Hyobong, a native of the P'yŏngyang area of northern Korea, was originally a lawyer who became the first Korean appointee to the judiciary under the Japanese administration of Korea. He was often troubled by the fact that he had to pass judgement on his fellow Koreans who had been arrested for patriotic activities. After serving ten years on the judiciary, he was forced to mete out the death penalty. This act so distressed him that he secretly left his work and home, and wandered for three years in the countryside as a peddler of Korean *yŏt*, a toffee-like candy. During this period, he reflected on life and decided, at the age of 39, to enter the monastic life. For the next six years he practised an austere form of meditation and monastic life, at one point sealing himself up in a hermitage cell for one and a half years. During the final thirty years of his life, he became one of the mostly highly regarded modern interpreters of traditional Buddhism. Hyobong took up residence in the Songgwang-sa temple near Sunch'ŏn, and it is there that the young Kusan sought him out. Hyobong was finally appointed as *chongjŏng* (patriarch or spiritual head) of the Chogye Order and passed away at the age of 78 in 1966.

Kusan, perhaps the most important disciple of Hyobong, was born in 1909 into a peasant family who lived near Namwŏn in south-western Korea. Kusan's life was much like that of any young peasant of the better-off class of his time. He attended the local school, which taught the Confucian classics, until he was 15; he married and helped work his family's farm. At the age of 29, he abandoned all this and set out on a journey which took him to eleven different temples searching for a teacher of Truth. When he arrived at Songgwang-sa, he sought out Hyobong and instantly felt that this was the man who could help him on his path. After eight months, Kusan was ordained and took up residence at Songgwang-sa.

For several years, Kusan practised meditation both in the meditation halls and in lonely hermitages, at times experiencing what seemed to be preliminary forms of enlightenment. In 1946, at a hermitage near Hae'in-sa, Kusan had his major experience of enlightenment, a period of such intense meditation that for two weeks he lost any sense of the world beyond his own sphere of concentration. It was said that Kusan was so unaware of the outside world that birds came and plucked stuffing from his clothes and he was not conscious of it. Kusan then went down from his cell and gave his discourse on the Law to the monks at Hae'in-sa.

For several years afterwards, Kusan alternated between long periods of meditation and holding important posts in the organization of the Buddhist order. In 1962 his teacher Hyobong asked him to come out of his retreat, and until 1967 Kusan was abbot of the important temple T'ongdo-sa, which preserves a relic of the Buddha. In that year he returned to his former temple Songgwang-sa, and in 1969 he was appointed as the *pangjang* or spiritual director of the monastic community. Kusan held this appointment until his death in 1983.

From 1966, Kusan began to travel extensively throughout Asia and the world. In 1966 he made his first trip outside Korea, journeying to Thailand, Vietnam, India, and Nepal. One result of that trip was his conviction that Buddhism could be propagated in the West, and he began to gather at Songgwang-sa a group of foreign monks whom he trained in the practices of Sŏn. In 1972 Kusan established a Sŏn centre in California and created the International Meditation

Centre at Songgwang-sa. Throughout the 1970s he vigorously pursued the tasks of building up a core of monks who could bring Buddhism to the West and creating Sŏn centres in various nations. Kusan also lectured widely in the United States, France, Denmark, and Switzerland.

3. The Organizational History of Modern Buddhism

The history of Buddhism in Korea during the past century has been dominated by several problems: the question of the unification of the various strands of Buddhism; the problem of how to deal with a colonial authority and its edicts; and the question of the need for the reform and revival of the Buddhist order. Korean Buddhism's modern century may be said to have begun with the edict issued in the early part of 1895 which revoked the long-standing order forbidding Buddhist clergy to enter the walled city of Sŏul. Although this took place more than ten years after the establishment of Protestant missions in Korea, it was a sign of the continued liberalization of government policy and attested to the end of the persecution of the Buddhist church. In 1899 the first of many moves was taken to unify Korean Buddhism with the construction of the Wŏnhŭng-sa outside the Great East Gate of Sŏul. It was intended that this temple should be the head temple for all of Buddhism within the nation.

In 1902, at a meeting at Wŏnhŭng-sa, a unified temple law of thirty-six sections to govern the administration of temples was deliberated and accepted, only to be abandoned two years later. In 1906, at another meeting, it was decided to reorganize the structure of the Buddhist church by creating the Wŏnhŭng-sa as the head temple and establishing various famous provincial temples as branch head temples. In the following year, some fifty representatives of the provincial temples met and created a Buddhist Research Society (*Pulgyo yŏn'gu-hoe ch'onghoe*). In 1908, at yet another meeting at Wŏnhŭng-sa, fifty-two representatives of the provincial temples met to create a single unified order, the *Wŏn-jong*. Yi Hoegwang (Sasŏn, 1840–1911), was elected as the first *Taejong-jong* (Supreme Patriarch) of the new order.

Sasŏn travelled to Japan in 1910, the year in which the Japanese annexed Korea, in order to urge the union of the *Wŏn-jong* with the Japanese Zen order, the *Sōdōshū*. Manhae, who had initially been favourably inclined towards the Japanese, and other priests were strongly opposed to the merger of Korean and Japanese Buddhism and created a counter-order, the *Imje-jong*, in 1911. The headquarters of this new sect was established at Songgwang-sa in Sunch'ŏn. Thus, fifteen years after the removal of traditional restrictions against Buddhism, the Korean Buddhist order was confronted by problems of factional feuding and by the threat of absorption into the Buddhist institutions of Japan.

Ostensibly to bring order into this chaotic situation, the Japanese Government-General issued edicts in June and July 1911 creating a system of thirty head temples (*ponsa*), eliminating the executive branch of the *Wŏn-jong*, and creating in its place a committee of representatives from the thirty *ponsa*.

Although this system may not seem substantially different from the previous arrangement, it was introduced so that the Buddhist church was more effectively under the control of the Government-General. In reaction to these actions, another counter-organization was created in 1912, the *Chosŏn pulgyo sŏn'gyo yangjong ch'ongmu-wŏn* (Administrative Council of the Chosŏn Buddhist Joint 'Sŏn and Kyo' Order), a free association of Buddhist leaders centred at Kakhwang-sa in Sŏul. The on-going struggle between monks working for an independent Korean Buddhism and those who accommodated themselves to Japanese rule became a feature of the second decade of the twentieth century.

Korean Buddhism was not solely characterized by political problems and factional feuds. Cultural activities proceeded apace. In 1912 the *Nŭngin pot'ong hakkyo* was founded and Yi Nŭnghwa (1869–1945) was created first principal of the school. Yi, a brilliant scholar fluent in many foreign languages, is a symbolic figure of the cultural renaissance of Korean Buddhism during this period. In the 1910s, he helped initiate several magazines for the advancement of Buddhism and began to do research on and to publish his massive studies of Korean religion and folklore. His works include *Chosŏn pulgyo t'ongsa* (A Complete History of Korean Buddhism), *Chosŏn kidokkyo-gŭp oegyo-sa* (A History of Korean Foreign Relations and Christianity), *Chosŏn musok-ko* (Records of Korean Shamanism), and *Han'guk togyo-sa*. (A History of Korean Taoism). In spite of national political turmoil, the roots of Korean Buddhism's cultural revival may be traced to this period.

It is interesting to note that in the aftermath of the March First Movement of 1919, the Buddhist lay movement began to emerge, perhaps as a reaction to the YMCA which was flourishing at this time. This lay movement was in contrast to the condition of clerical Buddhism, which contemporary observers tended to disparage. James Bissett Pratt (1875–1944), a sympathetic observer who had made extensive journeys to several Buddhist countries, found the monks in Korea ignorant of Buddhist doctrine, confusing Buddhism with a mixture of folk religion and esoteric Buddhism. He also found that the standards of monastic discipline and personal behaviour were not high. The revival of Buddhism in the twentieth century must be attributed to movements founded by the laity and not primarily to the efforts of the clergy.

Many of these lay movements were founded in the 1920s under the inspiration of or with the assistance of Manhae. In June 1920 the *Chosŏn pulgyo ch'ŏngnyŏn-hoe* (Chosŏn Buddhist Youth Association) was founded, followed two years later by the creation of two lay associations, the *Chosŏn pulgyo-do ch'onghoe* (Association of Korean Buddhists) and the *Chosŏn pulgyo hyŏpsŏng-hoe* (Korean Buddhist Co-operative Society). In September of the same year, Manhae and others founded the *Pŏppo-hoe* (The Society of the Precious Law) for the purposes of modernizing Buddhism and translating the Buddhist scriptures. More societies of a lay nature continued to be founded, such as the *Chosŏn pulgyo sonyŏn-hoe* (Chosŏn Buddhist Young People's Association).

The phenomenon of the growth of Buddhist lay groups continued well into the 1930s. The 1928 Buddhist Youth Conference was followed by a Pacific Area Buddhist Youth Conference held in Hawaii in 1930. In 1931, under Manhae, the Buddhist youth group was reorganized and styled a federation of youth. There were other cultural activities occurring, including the publication by the Government-General of the *Tripitaka Koreanum* at Hae'in-sa in 1936, known to the scholarly world as the *Taishō Tripitaka*. There was a national meeting of Buddhist laity during the same year. While none of these events is sufficient in and of itself to show the vigour of Korean lay Buddhism, taken together they do show an increasing momentum characterizing the lay Buddhist world. These events were also in striking contrast to the general opinion of clerical Buddhism, the weakened standards of which were further shaken by the proclamation in October 1926 which permitted monks to marry and to eat meat. Although the possibility of doing this had already existed in the temple law promulgated under Governor-General Terauchi Masatake in 1911, the later edict made it officially plain and permissible. Unquestionably the growth of the lay associations must be seen as a reaction to the decay of the discipline of clerical Buddhism.

In the 1940s, perhaps the most important development was the attempt to structurally reorganize clerical Buddhism. In June 1941 the Buddhist order was reorganized and called the *Chogye-jong*, a term which can trace its usage back to early Koryŏ times referring to the place where the Chinese Ch'an patriarch Hui-nêng had an important spiritual experience. It was felt that the long historical association which this word had with the Sŏn tradition in Korea would aid in the reformation of clerical Buddhism. It is interesting to point out that this was happening at the same time that the Government-General was attempting to unify Korean Christianity in order to more effectively control the church during the years of the Second World War. The T'aego-sa in central Sŏul was selected to be the head temple of the order, and Pang Hanam (1876–1951), a disciple of Kyŏnghŏ, was chosen to be the first Supreme Patriarch.

The Chogye Order came in for further reorganization with the defeat of Japan and the establishment of an independent Korea. T'aego-sa was again selected as the head temple, and a regulation was promulgated creating thirty-one *ponmalsa* or district head temples. It is interesting to note that the most far-reaching reformation in modern Korean Buddhism was the result of actions taken by the first president of the Republic of Korea, Yi Sŭngman (1875–1965), who was a Methodist. In 1954, during the course of several visits to Buddhist temples, the president was shocked at the practice of clerical marriage and other aspects of Korean Buddhism which he thought reflected decadent Japanese influence. Apparently, President Yi's sense of patriotism as well as his sense of religious purity was strongly offended, and he initiated a national movement for the purification of clerical Buddhism. The result was the continuation of the *Chogye-jong* as a celibate order and the creation of the *T'aego-jong* as an order of married clergy. These two orders constitute the two largest branches of organized, orthodox Buddhism in contemporary Korea. In 1994, the *Chogye-jong* claimed an adherency of 9,125,991 members, 10,056 clerics, and 1,725 temples. In the same year, the *T'aego-jong* claimed an adherency of 4,083,926 members, 4,972 clerics and 2,578 temples. This gives a total adherency of 13,209,917 persons. However, the 1995 National Household Census revealed only a total of 10,321,012 persons who self-identified as Buddhists. The head temple of the *Chogye-jong* is the former T'aego-sa in central Sŏul, now renamed the Chogye-sa, and the head temple of the *T'aego-jong* is the Pongwŏn-sa located near Yonsei University in western Sŏul.

Since the 1960s, Buddhism has grown considerably, largely through the development of freely formed lay associations. A survey done in 1988 showed that at that time there were 298 associations of which 226 were focussed on youth, students or children. Consequently, many of these organisations have operated as a means for Buddhist evangelism as well as for fellowship and spiritual development. These organisations are usually not associated directly with the Chogye Order itself, nor do they receive funding from the Order. They have often been involved, however, with moves for the modernisation of Buddhism, including the translation of the Buddhist canon into contemporary Korean and the use of more contemporary music in Buddhist liturgical music. Another form of lay association is exemplified by the *Purir-hoe* (Buddha Sun Association) founded by Kusan at Songgwang-sa temple in 1969. Although this association is similar to the associations discussed above, it differs from them in that it is a nation-wide grouping of local lay associations which are linked to the monastic community at a particular temple, the Songgwang-sa. There are other associations like the *Puri-hoe* which tie local groups to a particular temple thus allowing the mountain-based monastic communities to have a direct connection with urban Korean believers in all parts of the country. Another way in which the temple communities connect with the laity is high school study groups which are led by a particular monk. These groups often meet at the same time on a Saturday afternoon when a similar Christian group would be meeting with a pastor at a church. These lay associations and youth groups all reflect Protestant influence on the religious culture of Korea where a Protestant model has been adapted to Buddhist usage. This adaptation can also be seen in the setting of tunes from well-known Protestant hymns to the religious songs sung by these lay groups.

The significant expansion of Buddhism from the mid-1980s to the end of the twentieth century is indicated by increased institutional work and by Buddhist missionary work overseas. At the end of the century, there were two major Buddhist media networks, BBS (Buddhist Broadcasting System founded in 1990) and the Buddhist cable TV network founded in 1995. At the same time, the Buddhist Order supported or had connected to it three universities and twenty-eight schools, and – importantly for the development of Buddhist clergy – sixteen 'seminaries' or training centres located within designated temples. The modern Buddhist missionary movement begun by Kusan is another indication of the growing strength of contemporary Buddhism. At the end of the twentieth century, there were 148 Korean-founded Buddhist temples in fifteen countries of which 104 were in the United States.

The mountain-based monastic communities are still the most visible and most important part of the practice of modern Korean Buddhism. It is here that are found the largest monastic communities practicing the ascetic life in search of enlightenment. It is also here that the lay groups and associations will come on private or temple-sponsored pilgrimages or for periods of study and reflection. In some of the more remote hermitages high up in the mountains which are frequented by tourists, specially selected and trained monks will reside there who will engage the ordinary Korean weekend or holiday tripper in conversation about the more ultimate issues of life.

The temples in the mountains (see Fig. 19) are generally laid out on the following pattern. The entrance to the precinct of the vast temple grounds is marked out by a large tile-roofed gate called the *ilju-mun* which is supported on two large carved tree trunks. On this gate will be a signboard giving the name of the mountain on which the temple is located, the name of the Buddhist order, and the name of the temple itself. After a long walk into the forest, the traveller will come to the *sach'ŏnwang-mun* (Gate of the Four Heavenly Kings) which contains the ferocious images of the guardians of the four cardinal points of the universe. This marks the entrance into the precinct of the temple compound itself. Usually directly in front of the visitor will be the great *Tae'ung-jŏn* (Great Power Hall) named after one of the ascriptive titles of the historic Buddha. This hall will contain the principal Buddha image (usually of the historic Buddha, called *Puch'ŏ-nim* in Korean) and two bodhisattvas (*posal* in Korean) flanking the figure on either side. The walls of the hall will have subsidiary altars in front and be covered with Buddhist paintings. Here will be performed the regular monastic rituals for the community, individual acts of devotion by visitors, and ceremonies such as weddings.

Surrounding this main hall will be one or more of the following buildings. The *Myŏngbu-jŏn* (Hall of Hell) contains the images of the kings of the ten levels of Hell who surround the ruler of Hell, the Bodhisattva *Ksitigarbha* (*Chijang posal* in Korean). Here may be enshrined the paper tablets set on a paper lotus flower of deceased relatives accompanied by a photograph draped in black. Memorial rituals may be carried out in front of these tablets, which constitute a Buddhist form of the Confucian *chesa* rites for the ancestors. This practice dates back to the fourth century in China. A similar type of hall is the *Kŭngnak-chŏn* (Hall of Paradise). There will be other halls for devotions, perhaps one of the more common being the *Nahan-jŏn* (Hall of Arhats) which will contain five hundred white images of the chief disciples of the Buddha called *arhats*. Other buildings, which are strictly for the use of the monastic community, would include aside from their living quarters, the *Pŏp-tang* (Dharma Hall) in which the monks or nuns will receive lectures and study the Buddhist scriptures. The *chong-gak* or bell tower contains the large bronze bell, wooden fish-shaped gong, and drum which will be used to summon the

1. *Ilchu-mun:* Gate marking entrance to temple grounds. Large pillars of rough logs
   support elaborate tile roof with temple name plaque.
2. *Sach'ŏnwang-mun:* Gate of the Four Heavenly Kings. This marks the entrance
   to the temple precinct proper.
3. *Pŏp-tang: Dharma* Hall. Hall for lectures.
4. Monastic quarters
5. *Chong-gak:* Bell tower.
6. *Tae'ung-jŏn:* Principal shrine
7. Pagoda
8. *Myŏngbu-jŏn:* Hall of Judgement with
   Ten Kings of Hell and Ksitigarbha
9. *Nahan-jŏn:* Hall with 500 *arhats* (*nahan*),
   Buddha's chief disciples.
10. *Sansin-gak:* Mountain God Shrine.
11. Hermitage.

Figure 19 Plan of Typical Buddhist Temple

community to their times of practice or study. Almost without exception, a
Buddhist temple will have to the rear of the *Tae'ung-jŏn* a *Sansin-gak* (Mountain
God shrine). This is occasionally styled a *Ch'ilsŏng-gak* (Seven Star shrine) or
Samsŏng-gak (Three Star shrine), referring to the Pole Star. Inside will be

protraits of a grandfatherly figure with a long, white beard and seated under a pine tree leaning on a tiger who is San-sin (a guise of Tan'gun), of Ch'ilsŏng-nim or Samsŏng-nim (the Polar Star Spirit), and perhaps of Toksŏng (Lone Star Spirit). This shrine represents the accommodation of Buddhism with the folk religion and is a ubiquitous feature of temples in Korea.

Not only has Buddhism made an accommodation to the local religion of Korea, but it is also the case that the folk religion has accommodated itself to Buddhism. Laurel Kendall, an anthropologist who has spent years studying Korean shamanism, has remarked that people who were assisting her in her research would often introduce her to their friends as a student of 'Buddhism'. This was seen to be a more sophisticated subject of study than the common folk religion of Korea. The use of the name of Buddhism to lend sophistication to the folk religion can be seen in a more formal way as well. Surrounding a major shamanistic shrine in Sŏul the *Kuksa-dang*, which is close to the site of the Great West Gate, are a number of 'Buddhist' temples. These buildings each have the form and layout of a small Buddhist temple including the use of the same pictoral images and Buddhist statues found in a 'standard' temple. They are, however, shamanistic shrines which have been created in a Buddhist format. The first clue to the true use of the buildings is the fact that the name board outside each of them does not identify the Buddhist order to which it belongs, because there is none. These shrines are in fact privately run venues for shamanistic rites. They are an indication of the increased prestige of Buddhism in recent years and of its recovery from the nadir of the late Chosŏn period.

14

ISLAM IN KOREA
A New World Religion

Islam, meaning 'submission [to God]', was founded in the early seventh century by the Arabian prophet Muhammed (570–632) based on a series of revelations which he believed that he had received from Allah ('God'). The religion taught by the Prophet Muhammed was a doctrinally simple monotheism requiring the believer to perform five acts, known as the Five Pillars of Islam. These acts are the *shahada* or profession of faith ('There is only one God, and Muhammed is His Prophet'), *salat* or regular worship (five daily prayers and attendance at Friday communal worship), *zakat* or the giving of alms to the needy, *saum* or fasting during the holy month of Ramadan, and, if possible, the making of a *hajj* or pilgrimage to Mecca. The Islamic scripture, the *Qur'an* ('recital'), is seen to be the veritable word of God as revealed through Muhammed and recorded in Arabic for posterity. It is considerable to be sacred and untranslatable, although translations have been done of the scripture which are considered in effect to be commentaries on the scripture itself.

From its beginning in Medina and Mecca, Islam rapidly spread out of the Arabian peninsula to the Mediterranean world and beyond. It was brought to China probably at some time in the middle or late seventh century, during the early part of the T'ang Dynasty. The diffusion of Islam into the Far East is attributable to Arabic and other Islamic merchants and traders who traversed the land-routes from Persia through Central Asia to China bringing with them their religious beliefs and practices. Islamic traders had contact with the Korean kingdom of Silla from at least the late seventh century onwards. Records show that these trading relations did not disappear with the advent of the Koryŏ kingdom, for in the twelfth century there are several mentions of Arabian ships plying their way to Yesŏng, the port for the Koryŏ capital of Kaegyŏng. It is believed that these trading links with Korea existed up to the fifteenth century. Undoubtedly as a result of these commercial ties there would have been Near Eastern merchants who chose to settle down in Korea and establish a family there. At least one major Korean clan, the Chang family with its seat at Tŏksu, claims to be descended from a Muslim family. During the era of the Mongol Yüan Empire (1234–1367), the Mongol overlords of China depended on Muslim civil servants to run the empire and so those Koreans who visited China would have been aware of the religion practised by these strangers from the Near East or Central Asia. None the less, in spite of such contact between Korea and the Islamic world, there is no record of indigenous Korean Muslims before the end of the nineteenth century.

From the latter part of the nineteenth century onwards, impoverished Korean farmers and others crossed over the Yalu River to settle in the rugged valleys of eastern Manchuria. At that time land up to 90 *li* (36 km.) north from the river was nominally Korean territory and functioned as a barrier between Chosŏn Korea and Ch'ing China. Subsequently, Koreans came to settle in the major urban centres in Manchuria such as Mukden (Shenyang) which already had substantial communities of Muslims, descendants of Central Asian traders who had made their way to the Manchu homeland. Sections of these cities were set aside as Muslim quarters in which mosques were to be found. In Mukden alone, the Muslim quarter had five mosques. It was in the cities of Manchuria that Koreans first came to accept Islam as their religion. Following the conclusion of the Second World War, some of these people made their way back to Korea bringing their faith with them.

During the Korean War, Turkish troops serving with the United Nations forces in the conflict became aware of a small indigenous Korean Islamic community and obtained military permission for these people to worship with them under the guidance of the *imam* or spiritual leader who ministered to the troops. This was the beginning of formal Islamic worship on Korean soil. In 1955, the Korean Islamic Society was founded and a Korean *imam* was elected and a small house obtained for use as the first mosque in Korea. In 1959, two representative leaders of the Korean Muslim community visited Pakistan and Saudi Arabia in order to inform Muslims there about the situation of Islam in Korea and to gain support for its development. In 1962, the first cohort of students was sent on a six-month course of training as *imam* in scriptural studies and liturgy to a Muslim college in Malaysia. In 1967 the Muslim association was registered as a 'juridical person' with the Korean government as the Korean Muslim Federation. In 1976, with the assistance of the government of Saudi Arabia and other Islamic nations, the Central Mosque in Sŏul was completed and dedicated. Situated in the It'aewŏn section of Sŏul, it covers an area of 5,000 square metres. In 1980, the first Korean pilgrims went on a *hajj* to Mecca. During the past twenty years, a further five mosques have been built including the mosques in Pusan (1980), in Kwangju near Sŏul (1981), in Anyang near Sŏul (1986), in Chŏnju (1986) and more recently in the Manch'ŏn-dong section of Sŏul. It can be seen from this list that four of the six mosques are located in the Sŏul metropolitan region. In 1994, the Korean Muslim Federation claimed an adherency of 33,640 members and five clerics. It is thought that the majority of recent converts to Islam are young men who have served with Korean construction companies in the Near East or who have worked for commercial enterprises there. Although there are growing numbers of Muslims in Korea, the rate of growth is not substantial when compared with that of other religious groups. Some scholars have explained this slow growth by arguing that the Muslim religious cycle of daily prayers and a holy day on Friday rather than on Sunday raised practical problems which prevented large numbers of people converting to Islam.

15

CH'ŎNDO-GYO

The First Syncretic Religion

1. History of the Sect

At the end of the nineteenth century when it seemed as if Korea might be absorbed by the Western Powers and that her religious traditions might be supplanted by Catholicism, a young scholar from Kyŏngju proclaimed a new religion synthesizing important aspects of Korean traditional religion. Originally called *Tonghak* (Eastern Learning), this movement came to be known as *Ch'ŏndo-gyo* (The Religion of the Heavenly Way). Ch'oe Che'u (1824–64), the son of a well-known local scholar, had lost both parents by the time he was 16. From that time on, he tried various ways to earn a living, and later sought to find a way for national and personal salvation.

In early 1860 he was stricken by some strange disease which physicians were unable to cure. Suddenly, while he was resting one day, Ch'oe Che'u had a vision of a spirit who called himself *Sangje* (*Shangti* in Chinese), the Ruler of Heaven. This spirit instructed the infirm Korean to go and proclaim a special doctrine to the world. Ch'oe Che'u then asked Sangje if he was to teach *Sŏhak* (Western Learning = Roman Catholicism). Sangje replied in the negative and gave Ch'oe Che'u a piece of paper with a cryptic passage of twenty-one characters on it. Ch'oe was then instructed to use the mystic phrase to cure people's diseases. Sangje assured Ch'oe Che'u that constant use of this talisman would assure him of long life. Ch'oe then swallowed the paper and was instantly cured of his disease. His family, who up to this time had opposed his various philosophical ruminations, were converted upon drinking a mixture of water and ashes made from a piece of paper with the original talisman phrase written on it.

During the period of the early 1860s when Catholicism was experiencing its most severe persecution, Ch'oe Che'u went about quietly propagating his new teaching, which gradually began to spread throughout southern Korea. In 1864 he was arrested on charges of being a secret Catholic believer. Although he defended himself as being a proponent of *Tonghak*, he was executed in Taegu on charges of treason and of seducing the people with a superstitious doctrine. The leadership of the new sect fell to his nephew Ch'oe Sihyŏng (1827–98), who led the *Tonghak* group as an underground movement until the 1890s. In 1888 Ch'oe

198

Sihyŏng, fulfilling a vow he had made to Ch'oe Che'u, compiled several texts which have become the scripture of the *Ch'ŏndo-gyo*, the *Tonggyŏng taejŏn* (Great Compendium of Eastern Scriptures).

Oppressive rule and corrupt practices by local magistrates in the southern provinces during the years 1894 and 1895 caused local insurrections which were led by the leaders of the *Tonghak* cult. At this point, the direction of the movement had passed to Chŏn Pongjun (1853–95), while Ch'oe Sihyŏng went into hiding. The final suppression of this rebellion led to the death of many leaders including Chŏn and Ch'oe. The leadership of the movement then passed to Son Pyŏnghŭi (1861–1922), the chief disciple of Ch'oe Sihyŏng, in 1898 in a secret ceremony of transmission. This was reconfirmed in 1899 by other *Tonghak* leaders following the death of Ch'oe. In 1901, Son went to Japan where he stayed almost continuously until the spring of 1906. The leadership of the *Tonghak* movement in Korea was placed in the hands of Son's chief lieutenant, Yi Yonggu (1868–1912). A schism in the movement resulted, Yi eventually calling his group *Sich'ŏn-gyo* (Religion of Serving Heaven). In 1905, Son Pyŏnghŭi changed the name of the movement from *Tonghak* to *Ch'ŏndo-gyo*. Although Yi Yonggu at first had some success in drawing the membership away from Son Pyŏnghŭi, his movement was not in the end successful. Following Yi's death, his schismatic sect also broke up with the formation of another sect called *Sangje-gyo* (Religion of Sangje) led by Kim Yŏn'guk another disciple of Ch'oe Sihyŏng. This group was also called *Kwi'am-gyo*, Kwi'am being the literary name of Kim Yŏn'guk. Upon the death of Son Pyŏnghŭi in 1922, there was no one to succeed to the leadership of the mainline group. After several years of uncertainty, a conciliar system of administration was set up allowing local autonomy with the general affairs of the sect being run by a committee.

Following the end of colonial rule and the division of Korea into American and Russian spheres of influence, *Ch'ŏndo-gyo* found itself in two different political contexts. In the north, where the majority of *Ch'ŏndo-gyo* believers were now to be found, the sect's political arm was one of two non-Communist parties recognized by the Communist government. On 1 March 1948, the *Ch'ŏndo-gyo* spearheaded a Second March First Demonstration which was to begin a national, non-violent movement for the unification of the country and the creation of a unified government. 10,000 persons were apprehended, of whom eighty-two were given significant prison terms and five were executed. The *Ch'ŏndo-gyo* maintained itself as an underground movement until just before the outbreak of the Korean War, when its leaders were rounded up. There are reports that there is a *Ch'ŏndo-gyo* church which has been built recently in the capital P'yŏngyang. This would be on the pattern of the Roman Catholic and Protestant church buildings which were erected in the late 1980s.

While freer than in the north, the situation in the south has led neither to more significant political influence nor to greater development as a religious body. In the 1970s and 1980s, it was common to see pictures in the newspapers of

Ch'ŏndo-gyo believers at government-sponsored rallies supporting a nationalistic cause espoused by the current regime. This kind of activity undercut the sect's appeal to younger people who are both nationalistic and anti-government in attitude. Its religious appeal has also declined dramatically. In the mid-1960s the sect claimed a membership of 600,000 and in 1994, a membership of 1,220,623 persons. The 1995 National Household Census, however, revealed a self-identified adherency of 28,184 persons. Such discrepancies in the size of the membership raises serious questions about the survival of this group beyond the middle of the twenty-first century.

Before passing on to the beliefs of this syncretic religion, we must say a few words about Son Pyŏnghŭi. Born in Ch'ŏngju in 1861, Son became the leader of the *Tonghak* Rebellion in the Kyŏngsang and Ch'ungch'ŏng Provinces and became the third patriarch of the *Tonghak* Sect in 1898. Highly patriotic, he at first thought that reform could be brought about through Japanese assistance. After securing the development of the *Tonghak* Movement, he spent five years abroad from 1901 to 1906, principally in Japan. He subsequently changed his views and became actively involved in the movement to liberate Korea from Japanese domination. It is not an exaggeration to say that it was his patriotism which has given *Ch'ŏndo-gyo* its nationalistic character. He was responsible for the foundation of two schools, the *Posŏng chŏnmun hakkyo* and the *Posŏng chung hakkyo*, which later became Koryŏ University and Chung'ang High School respectively. Like many Christians, Son Pyŏnghŭi saw education as a patriotic means to achieve the goal of liberating his country. In 1919 Son was one of the key members of the committee which wrote the Declaration of Independence from Japan, and it was he who read the document aloud in Pagoda Park. Son died in 1922 as a result of his imprisonment by the Japanese authorities.

2. Beliefs and Practices of Ch'ŏndo-gyo

The principal characteristics of *Ch'ŏndo-gyo* are three fold: the belief in a Supreme Being, the identity of the believer with this deity, and the belief in curative magic. The core system of belief is clearly based upon the primal shamanistic religion of Korea with various additions and emendations drawn from Taoism, Buddhism, and to a certain extent from Christianity. Let us first examine the character of Ch'oe Che'u's experience.

Ch'oe's experience was wholly shamanistic in character. First of all, there was the call by a great spirit. It is normal that when a spirit selects a man to be his intermediary or shaman, that person becomes ill. Ch'oe was ill with a mysterious disease which no one could cure. The disease was not an ordinary malady but the result of the call by a spirit. Second, shamanism holds to a belief in a Supreme Being, and it is important to note that the spirit who called Ch'oe Che'u was Sangje, the Taoist Ruler of Heaven. Third, it is common for a spirit who has called a person to be a shaman to bestow a secret formula upon his devotee. We have seen this to be the case with Silla monks such as Chajang. When the Silla monks encountered Mañjuśrī, they would receive from the Bodhisattva a secret formula or a talisman. In Ch'oe's experience of Sangje, this grand spirit gave him a talisman which would cure disease, and a set of secret instructions. Thus Ch'oe Che'u's experience was essentially the experience of one who has been called to be a shaman and is the first clue which we have that Ch'ŏndo-gyo's basic elements are shamanistic.

As has been stated, the belief in the Ruler of Heaven is one of the core beliefs of Korean primal religion. However, it is interesting to note that in Ch'oe Che'u's vision, this great figure did not identify himself by a purely Korean name but by a name hallowed by Chinese and Taoist usage. It is also interesting to note that the new doctrine which this being taught Ch'oe was a doctrine of magical cures and long life. These doctrines and the use of talismans are an aspect of Korean primal religion, and are also found in religious Taoism. The curing of disease is one of the three major functions of Korean shamans, perhaps even their most common function.

Ch'ŏndo-gyo also teaches that man can identify with Sangje through the reverencing of this spirit (kyŏngch'ŏn) and the repetition of the sacred twenty-one-character phrase revealed to Ch'oe Che'u by Sangje. This unique concept is called in-nae-ch'ŏn, meaning that man and Heaven, man and God, are identical. Man must come to the realization of this fact by bringing his thoughts and actions into harmony with Heaven. This belief has obvious correlations with early Korean and with Taoist thought. Finally, Ch'ŏndo-gyo believes in the building of a paradise or perfect world in this time and place, and possesses a very patriotic and nationalistic character. It is no wonder that of the thirty-three signatories of the Declaration of Independence in 1919, fifteen were members of Ch'ŏndo-gyo.

There are certain ceremonies in which all members of the sect are asked to take part. First, members are asked to have private prayer every day at 9 p.m. An altar should be laid out in the direction of the Pole Star, on top of which a bowl of clear water is placed. In front of this, the worshipper will do a full Korean bow on the floor, repeating the sacred phrase and adding any special petitions. This sacred phrase, reminiscent of a Buddhist *mantra*, consists of the following characters:

chi-gi kŭm-ji
wŏn-wi tae-gang
si-ch'ŏn-ju cho-hwa-jong
yŏng-se pul-mang man-sa-ji.

God-head being present now,
I desire his great descent.
Serving the Heavenly Lord, I am.
Never forgetting, I know all things.

An interesting aspect of this 'shamanistic' prayer is its use of the word *Ch'ŏnju* (Lord of Heaven), the Roman Catholic term for God, to refer to the Supreme Being.

A service of public worship, called *Si-il*, is conducted on Sunday in buildings much like Protestant churches. The service itself is also similar to a Protestant service, including the use of hymns set to well-known Protestant tunes, silent prayers, and an exposition of the *Tonggyŏng taejŏn*. Ch'oe Che'u created a hymnal for use in propagating his doctrines, the *Yongdam yusa* (Hymns from the Dragon Pool), which is still used. Traditionally these services would conclude with selected members taking water from the altar in spoons and drinking it. Some special ceremonies are also celebrated: *Ch'ŏn-il*, on the fifth day of the fourth lunar month, the date on which Ch'oe Che'u had his revelation; *Chi-il*, on the fourteenth day of the eighth lunar month, in honour of Ch'oe Sihyŏng; and *In-il*, on the twenty-fourth day of the twelfth lunar month, in honour of mankind.

Ch'ŏndo-gyo is a uniquely Korean syncretic religion based upon shamanistic concepts of man and Heaven, and the curing of disease. Intellectually, it has been influenced by Taoism and to a lesser extent by Buddhism. Christian influence has been less of an intellectual than a practical influence, although *Ch'ŏndo-gyo* does use the Catholic word for God, *Ch'ŏnju*. It is Protestantism, however, which has most influenced its form of worship and style of religious architecture during the early twentieth century. This influence of Protestantism indicates that Protestant Christianity was the most dynamic religious force in early twentieth-century Korea and consequently the model which was to be imitated.

16

SINHŬNG CHONGGYO
Korean Syncretic Religions

1. What are the Syncretic Religions?

The process of religious syncretism is not, of course, a new phenomenon in Korean history. We have seen how the process of merging a foreign religion with Korean primal religion has been taking place since the late fourth century, since the advent of Buddhism in the Korean peninsula. Also we have seen how certain unorthodox, syncretic movements grew up in both the Koryŏ and the Chosŏn periods at critical times. What is new in the last century is the widespread development of the phenomenon of syncretism linked with the desire for national salvation or the emergence of some utopian state. The first modern Korean syncretic movement was the *Tonghak* Movement, later called *Ch'ŏndo-gyo*. The *Ch'ŏndo-gyo* movement fits perfectly Anthony F. C. Wallace's concept of a revitalization movement as 'a deliberate, conscious effort by members of a society to construct a more satisfying culture'.[1] As such it may be compared with the T'aiping Movement in China several decades earlier. The development of the *Tonghak* Movement and the advent of Protestant Christianity acted as a catalyst to other spiritually-minded people who created new movements which mixed various religious traditions to form a new synthesis. These religions are known collectively to Korean scholars as *sinhŭng chonggyo*, literally newly emerged religions, or *sin chonggyo* (new religions).

Whatever their differences, the *sinhŭng chonggyo* all share certain common features. Firstly, they are syncretic religions, religions which have brought together Buddhist, Taoist, Confucian, Catholic, and Protestant beliefs and practices with Korean primal religion (particularly the shamanistic elements), to create a new system of belief. Secondly, these religions are based primarily on shamanistic concepts to which the other elements have been added. Thirdly, the *sinhŭng chonggyo* may be divided into various traditions, those which are primarily Buddhist, Christian, Confucian, or shamanistic in their structure or format. Fourthly, in varying degrees, these new religions evince a strong element

---

1 Anthony F. C. Wallace, 'Revitalization Movements', *American Anthropologist*, 58 (1956), 265.

of nationalism in their doctrines and methods of propagation. Finally, the *sinhŭng chonggyo* look towards a utopian condition in this world, or in some manner offer hope to their members for a better life.

The development of religious syncretism in the previous century and a half may be divided into three stages. The first stage would begin with the emergence of the *Tonghak* Movement in the 1860s and other new religions of a revitalisation type as defined by Wallace which developed up until the annexation of Korea by Japan. The second stage would constitute those syncretic religions which emerged during the Japanese period (1910–1945), while the third stage would include all those new religions which emerged in the period following the Korean War. As we have discussed the phenomenon of *Tonghak* (*Ch'ŏndo-gyo*) in a previous chapter, we shall not say anything further about it here.

The second stage is particularly interesting, as many of these new religions established themselves in or around Kyeryong-san mountain near Taejŏn, congregating particularly in a village called Sindo-an or Sindo-nae (Inside the New Capital). This mountain and the village are associated with a prophecy that a new dynastic capital would be built on that spot after the fall of the Chosŏn dynasty. The development of new religions during the Japanese period must be seen against the background of the Japanese colonization of Korea and the wide-side aspirations of the Korean people for national liberation. There were a large number of groups, at least sixty-six identifiably separate organisations, which had emerged at this time. The research report on Korean new religions by the Government-General of Chōsen, the *Chōsen-no ruiji shūkyō* (The Pseudo-religions of Korea) classified them into six groups: 1) those which traced their origins to the *Tonghak* movement (seventeen groups), 2) those groups which traced their origins to *Chŭngsan-gyo* (eleven groups), 3) groups in the Buddhistic tradition (ten groups), 4) groups worshipping Korean mythical or historical figures such as Tan'gun or Kija (sixteen groups), 5) groups in the 'Confucianist' tradition (seven groups), and 6) groups of miscellaneous or uncertain roots (five groups). What is especially interesting to note is the absence of any groups which could be placed in a pseudo-Christian tradition.

The third stage in the development of Korean syncretic religions began with the period following liberation from Japan and the conclusion of the Korean War. During that critical decade, many new religions grew up offering hope to a people living in a divided, destitute land. It is interesting to note that in this latter stage, when Christianity had begun to attract large numbers of converts, many of the syncretic religions which emerged during that time and subsequently were of a Christian type. This development is yet another measure of the important rôle which Christianity has had in development of modern Korean culture. Records from the late 1990s show that there were sixty-nine new religions which had registered with the government. Of these, eight were of the Ch'ŏndo-gyo tradition, nine were of the Chŭngsan-gyo tradition, twelve claimed an association with Tan'gun, and four were of a Buddhistic tradition. Thirty-six groups, or over half the numbers of registered groups were not listed as being of any identifiable tradition.

2. The *Chŭngsan* Tradition

Kang Ilsun (1871–1909), whose literary name was *Chŭngsan*, founded a religious movement which came to be known by various names including *Hŭmch'i-gyo* (Teachings of the Open Mouth), *Chŭngsan-gyo* (Teachings of Chŭngsan) or *Chŭngsan-do* (The Way of Chŭngsan). It is said that Kang's birth was preceded – as is the case with most founders of a new movement – by several auspicious portents. Thirteen months before his birth, Kang's mother had a vision of Heaven opening up and of being surrounded by a heavenly light. At his birth, Kang's father dreamt that fairies guarded the baby during the birth ordeal. Kang Ilsun is said to have been an unusual child while he was growing up, and at an early age sought for truth in various books. He became an avid reader of Confucian, Buddhist, and Taoist books as well as various occult works. While in his early twenties, Kang witnessed the *Tonghak* Rebellion and its failure, and resolved to find a way for the affairs of the world to be ordered according to the Divine Plan. For several years he wandered the countryside seeking out various people known to have occult powers. In 1900, when he was 29, he entered into a nine-day period of intense meditation at Taewŏn-sa temple near Chŏnju. He had a vision in which he was visited by five dragons who gave him the power to rid the world of the Four Evils, avarice, lust, anger, and stupidity. Kang also came to realize that he had the power to communicate with the spirit world, that he could predict the future, and that he had the power to understand the *Ch'ŏnji undo*, the divine plan of the movements of the universe.

Following his experience at Taewŏn-sa in 1900, Kang Ilsun began to propagate his doctrines and to perform various 'miracles' which established his reputation as a sorcerer of great power. In 1902 he declared that he himself was the 'Lord of the Nine Heavens' who had descended to earth to order the public affairs of mankind. With the hopes that had been raised by the *Tonghak*s and through belief in the occult book of prophecy the *Chŏnggam-nok* (Record of Chŏng Kam),[2] many people came to feel that Chŭngsan might become a national

---

2 The *Chŏnggam-nok* (Record of Chŏng Kam) purports to be the record of a conversation between a man called Chŏng Kam and Yi Tam, who wrote down the conversation. The book claims to reveal the names of successive dynastic founders and the location of their new capitals following the fall of the Chosŏn kingdom. The Yi family will be followed in turn by the Chŏng, Cho, Pŏm, and Wang families on the throne of Korea. Apparently, neither Chŏng Kam nor Yi Tam are historic personages. In addition, the book also contains purported prophecies of the Silla monk Tosŏn, the Koryŏ-Chosŏn monk Muhak, and the Chosŏn-period seers T'ojŏng (Yi Chiham, 1517–78) and Kyŏgam. Said to date from the 16th century, there is no firm evidence for its existence prior to 1785 when the first copy was 'discovered'. This work is not the only book of prophecy. The tradition of prophesying on world and national affairs and fortune-telling began formally with Tosŏn. Throughout the Chosŏn period, numerous prophetic works were written. Besides the *Chŏnggam-nok*, the best-known of these is the *T'ojŏng pigyŏl*, which claims to be the writing of Yi Chiham. The *T'ojŏng pigyŏl* is used primarily to determine the fortune of an individual throughout the succeeding year.

saviour and gathered around him. Twenty-four persons came to be recognized as his principal disciples, among whom were Kim Hyŏngnyŏl and Ch'a Kyŏngsŏk (1880–1936). Chŭngsan subsequently married Ch'a Kyŏngsŏk's widowed sister-in-law, Lady Ko and also Kim Hyŏngnyŏl's daughter. The reputation which Chŭngsan had as a sorcerer and the following which he had attracted made the Japanese authorities, newly in control of Korea, very suspicious of him. He was arrested in company with twenty of his followers on 25 December 1907 and was incarcerated for forty days. The arrest and incarceration of Kang Ilsun led many of his followers to doubt his power to reorder the affairs of the world if he could not even prevent his own arrest by the police. His personal appeal waned until his death on 24 June 1909. His funeral was sparsely attended, a sign of the disrepute into which he had fallen. However, from the 1990s, there has been a revival of interest in Chŭngsan's teachings and study groups of Kang Ilsun's thought (called *Chŭngsan-do*) have been formed on university campuses.

After Chŭngsan's death, various of his followers created movements which traced their origins to him and to his prophecies. On 19 September 1911, while Lady Ko was celebrating the memorial date of her husband's birthday, she fell into a trance. It was later said that the spirit of Chŭngsan had come upon her and continued to speak through her. A group gathered around Lady Ko which became the nucleus of the *Tae'ŭl-gyo* sect. Subsequently her brother-in-law Ch'a Kyŏngsŏk set her aside and took control of her followers. These developments led to the eventual creation of the *Tae'ŭl-gyo* (Teachings of the Great East) and the *Poch'ŏn-gyo* (Teaching of Universal Heaven) sects. The re-established *Tae'ŭl-gyo* sect continued to be led by Lady Ko, while the *Poch'ŏn-gyo* sect was led by Ch'a Kyŏngsŏk. After this, other disciples of Chŭngsan created their own movements, which in turn have split up until there is a myriad of sects which in one way or another trace their origins back to Chŭngsan. Throughout the Japanese period the *Poch'ŏn-gyo* sect was the largest of the groups in the Chŭngsan tradition, although it has currently dwindled to insignificance. According to the 1995 National Household Census, the largest group in the Chŭngsan tradition is the *Taesun chilli-hoe* with 62,056 members.

Yi Sangho (1880–1967), effectively the re-founder of *Chŭngsan-gyo*, created the first scripture for the sect in 1926 under the title of *Chŭngsan ch'ŏnsa kongsa-gi* (Record of the Works of the Heavenly Teacher Chŭngsan). This work contains biographical information about the life of Kang Ilsun, his thoughts on a variety of subjects, and the 'wonders' which he performed. In this work, Kang is referred to as *Uju-ŭi chujae-sin* (Creator God of the Universe) and the *Ch'ŏnsa*, or Heavenly Teacher who descended to earth. He is described as performing *kongsa* or miraculous works to create a paradise on earth, referred to as *Huch'ŏn sŏn'gyŏng* (Paradise of the Later Heaven). The term *sŏn'gyŏng* (*hsien-ching* in Chinese) refers to the land of the Taoist Immortals. With supplementary material, this book was published as *Taesun chŏn'gyŏng* (Scripture of the Great Circuit).

To say that Kang Ilsun was an eclectic, eccentric thinker is to understate the case. It is difficult to find any systematic thinking in his pronouncements, nor is there a definitive statement of his doctrines or beliefs. There are, however, some basic concepts which may be extracted from his statements. Kang Ilsun's doctrines are of a highly polytheistic, shamanistic type. He believed that there were three eras, the past, the future, and the present era of *kairos* in which the other two eras meet. Destiny is determined by the spirit world, especially by the Lord of Heaven who works in concert with mankind. Chŭngsan saw himself as the incarnation of the Lord of Heaven, also known as the Lord of the Nine Heavens, who had come to earth to reorder the public affairs of men. The incarnated Lord had three goals on earth: (1) to save mankind from the anxieties, troubles, and diseases of this life, (2) to re-establish the sovereignty of the Korean state, and (3) to redeem the people by purifying the religions of man of their endemic evils. Chŭngsan himself used and taught his disciples to use various incantations and talismans to cure the diseases of the people and to help them achieve their wishes. In some cases amulets were carried with the believer for protection, and in other cases talismans were burned and the ashes eaten in order to cure or prevent disease.

The Chŭngsan tradition is essentially a shamanistic system. It is also a revitalization movement in the sense in which Anthony F. C. Wallace has defined that term. Chŭngsan's birth is surrounded by various auspicious portents; Chŭngsan encountered great spirits who gave him a mission and spiritual powers; Lady Ko is seized by a spirit who speaks through her body; Chŭngsan claims both to cure disease and to be able to order the affairs of this world and of the spiritual universe; incantations and talismans are used. What is unique about Chŭngsan's proclamations is that, unlike Ch'oe Che'u, the founder of *Ch'ŏndo-gyo*, Kang Ilsun did not claim to have been selected by the Lord of Heaven but to be the Lord of Heaven himself. Thus, while many of the elements of his doctrines reflect shamanistic or Taoist influences, Kang Ilsun's basic proclamation about himself is a reflection of an essential Christian doctrine, the incarnation of God Almighty in Jesus Christ. Christian belief, however, concerns the incarnation of a monotheistic god, while Kang Ilsun's Lord of the Nine Heavens is the supreme ruler of a polytheistic universe. Chŭngsan's movement is also a revitalization movement in that Kang Ilsun ascribed to himself the ability both to restore Korea to its rightful place in the world and to reorder the political affairs of the world in this time and in the future. Chŭngsan claimed to be able to save the people both physically and spiritually, while also being able to create a new world order.

3. *Chŏndo-gwan*: The Olive Tree Church

The *Chŏndo-gwan* (Evangelist Hall) movement founded by Pak T'aesŏn (1915–) was the fastest growing and largest of the Korean syncretic religions during the 1950s and 1960s. Throughout the countryside one could see white churches with crenellated front towers with crimson crosses painted on the top. These were the churches of the *Chŏndo-gwan* movement, and their ubiquity was an indication of the extent to which the movement had penetrated into the rural areas of Korea. Today, these same churches lie abandoned, often used as village store-houses but no longer as places of worship. The movement is now largely insignificant and may pass away shortly. The *Chŏndo-gwan* movement is a Christian syncretic movement emphasizing faith-healing.

(a) History of the Sect

Pak T'aesŏn was born in North P'yŏngan province in 1915. His father was seldom at home and his mother died when Pak was nine. From that time, Pak said that he attended the local Presbyterian church and a local elementary school. Later, he made his way to Japan where he worked and put himself through a technical high school. In 1944 Pak T'aesŏn returned to Korea and began to attend the Namdaemun Presbyterian Church. Pak also began his own precision machinery company at the same time. In 1954 he was made an elder of the Chang-dong Presbyterian Church, from which election he has drawn his most common Korean appellation, Elder Pak.

In April 1955, Pak was one of the principal speakers at a massive revival rally held on Nam-san mountain in southern Sŏul. Suddenly, he had a vision of fire and water descending from Heaven which cleansed him and gave into his hands great power. He then came off the rostrum and began to massage the head of a cripple. After Elder Pak's treatment the man got up and claimed that he, who had been a cripple for thirty years, could now walk. Thus began the *Chŏndo-gwan* movement. In 1956 the local presbytery expelled him on charges of heresy, but Elder Pak himself made no objection. He claimed at that time that he was a better Christian than the Christians who had denounced him. He was imprisoned briefly in 1959 under Yi Sŭngman's regime and later in 1960 by the government of Prime Minister Chang Myŏn, who succeeded Yi. The charges were for embezzlement of money, injury or death of believers through faith-healing practices, and promiscuity. Until the mid- or late 1960s, it seemed that the *Chŏndo-gwan* movement might surpass or even supplant orthodox Christianity. This has subsequently proved not to be the case. Beginning in the early 1970s, various scandals connected with Pak T'aesŏn and his immediate family created mass defection from the church. It is now largely a shell of what it had been as a movement.

The *Chŏndo-gwan* movement is best known for its attempt to create a new society, a new Zion in Korea. For example, two Christian communities were created near Sŏul which were linked to industrial estates which Pak Taesŏn owned. These were total communities with all the facilities which the members would need. One of the most famous products of these factories is the Zion blanket which was considered to be of very good quality. Some of the charges of financial misappropriation of church funds come from claims about abuse of church labour and the mishandling of company funds.

(b) Doctrines and Beliefs

The followers of Pak T'aesŏn place implicit faith in his statements that he is a prophet of God who is to usher in a new society in Korea. Pak identifies himself with the mysterious figure mentioned in two passages of Christian scripture. In Isaiah 41:2, the prophet speaks of a mysterious, ever-victorious figure who comes from the East. Pak claims to be this personage, who will lead his people to a better future. In the eleventh chapter of the Revelation of St John the Divine in the New Testament, there is a reference to two prophets who are called olive trees. These figures, at first defeated by the forces of this world, will be proven victorious and assumed into Heaven. Pak claims to be one of these trees and it is for this reason that his movement has been known popularly in English as the Olive Tree Movement.

The power which Pak was given is the power of healing, called by believers *anch'al*. Pak would vigorously massage the believer's head through which action a mysterious power was said to pass from Pak's body into the believer's body, effecting a cure. Objects which had touched Pak's body were believed to have magic properties. Some of the faithful believed that even drinking the water in which Pak T'aesŏn had washed himself would cure any disease. This belief is, of course, an example of contagious magic.

4. *T'ongil-gyo*: The Unification Church

'The Holy Spirit Association for the Unification of World Christianity', also known as the Unification Church in English or simply *T'ongil-gyo* in Korean, is the best known of Korea's syncretic religions and the most controversial. It was formally founded in Sŏul by Mun Sŏnmyŏng (1920–) in 1954, although its roots date back to the early 1940s. The movement claims to be the fulfilment of God's plan for the universe, and it emphasises the belief in the coming of the Lord of the Second Advent.

(a) History of the Sect

Mun Sŏnmyŏng, born in Chŏngju in north Korea in 1920, was brought up in a Presbyterian home. He left home to attend Waseda University in Tōkyō, where he majored in electrical engineering. He was at that time unremarkable amongst his fellow students. In 1945, following liberation from Japanese rule, Mun began to set up a movement in the P'yŏngyang area to reform Christianity. He based this movement on a claim that he had been given the authority to reform the churches in an experience which he had had of the Supreme Being when he was 16. His claims caused dissension amongst the local Christians in P'yŏngyang, which was then the centre of Korean Christianity, and Mun was imprisoned by the Communist authorities in 1948. He was liberated by the United Nations troops in 1950 and made his way south to Pusan. There Mun met Yu Hyowŏn, who subsequently became his most important assistant in the formation of the Unification Church. In May 1954, Mun and Yu announced the creation of a new religious body, the Holy Spirit Association for the Unification of World Christianity.

In July 1955, Mun was imprisoned for gross immorality, but was subsequently released. In the following year, his church was registered with the government as a religious body. From that point on, the Unification Church began to grow in membership within Korea and began to propagate its beliefs in foreign countries. In 1959 the first Unification Church missionary was sent out to the United States. In succeeding years, missionaries have been sent to the USA, Japan, Europe, Great Britain, the Near East, and Latin America. In the early 1970s, Mun moved the centre of his operations from Korea to the United States, at which time he combined his evangelistic efforts with a campaign against Communism. The Unification Church seminary was organized during the mid-1970s in Tarrytown, New York, and the first students graduated in 1977. In 1983 Mun was tried on charges of tax evasion and was sent to gaol. Some organizations, such as the American Civil Liberties Union, supported his defence. The Unification Church in the United States during the mid-1980s began a massive campaign to prove that it was the object of extensive religious persecution.

The most spectacular growth of the *T'ongil-gyo* has been outside Korea. The church numbers its membership in the millions at the present time, but it has aroused considerable criticism from orthodox Christian churches as well as from various humanitarian groups. The criticism of the church is along four lines: (1) criticism of its heretical doctrine, (2) criticism of its methods of attracting members and of the education of these members, called by some persons 'brainwashing', (3) criticism of the affluent style of living of the church's leadership, and (4) criticism of the extensive business holdings of the church. The Unification Church has not only been successful as an international religious organization, but it has been very successful as a business conglomerate. Through its various holdings and organizations, it owns in Korea among other companies the Ilhwa group (a major producer of Korean ginseng products), a company manufacturing the M-16 rifle, and newspapers. The church sponsors cultural activities such as the Seminar on the Unity of the Sciences and the Little Angels Dance Troupe. In Europe and in North and South America, the church owns hotels, newspapers, publishing-houses, and various other business enterprises. The church has received most criticism, however, for its methods of recruiting members, and for the way in which its leaders, particularly Mun, live. For example, in the late 1970s the Church of Scotland created a committee to investigate the harmful personal and social effects of the propagation methods used by the church. In the United States and Western Europe, parents and church leaders, including the Roman Catholic hierarchy, have formed organizations to return young members to their families. Though not numerically strong in Korea, the church has found great appeal amongst young Western intellectuals.

In 1994, the Church claimed a membership of 550,000 adherents in Korea, with 1,216 clerics and 502 churches.

(b) Doctrines and Beliefs

The Unification Church belief is that God, the eternal creator of the universe, is attempting to restore the state of perfection in the world which existed at the time of the Garden of Eden. Sin, it is said, came into the world through the violation of God's commands. Eve is believed to have had sexual relations with Satan in the form of a serpent, and it is thought that sin has been transmitted physically through Satan's blood to succeeding generations. Jesus, son of God but not God himself as in orthodox Christian theology, failed in his mission to save mankind because he did not marry and produce sinless children. Thus, physical sin continued to be transmitted to later generations. Jesus's death on the cross only brought spiritual salvation, but not physical salvation. For there to be a complete restoration of the world, its physical salvation is necessary as well.

In the *T'ongil-gyo* schema, Jesus is the True Father and the Holy Spirit is the True Mother of spiritual salvation. Jesus having failed in His task, it was necessary that Another should come to fulfil God's mission, Someone who would marry a perfect woman and so restore mankind physically as well as spiritually. This person who is to come is called the Lord of the Second Advent. His marriage, which will restore humanity, is called the Feast of the Lamb. Mun Sŏnmyŏng has been identified as the Lord of the Second Advent and his wife as the Mother of the Universe. Mun's identification as the Lord of the Second Advent has been justified on the basis of a reading of Revelations Chapter 7 verse 2 which speaks of an angel of God coming from the East, which is interpreted to mean Korea. Korea's place in this schema is often explained as a parallel to the history of Israel. As the Israelites wandered in the desert for forty years, so too Korea suffered under forty years of Japanese colonialism. Mun and his wife receive special courtesies such as bows from the believers, as do their children who are believed to be sinless. As one of the most important functions of the Lord of the Second Advent is the physical restoration of mankind, Mun selects suitable marital partners for the faithful and conducts sacred ceremonies of marriage in large groups. It should be noted with regard to the purging of physical sin that Mun has been accused of acts of gross immorality which are denied by Church authorities.

The principal text of the *T'ongil-gyo* is the *Wŏlli kangnon* (Exposition of the Divine Principle, or simply, The Divine Principle), which has gone through various editions and alterations. This book, some 556 pages in length, consists of seven principal chapters and an extensive section of appended material. The chapters discuss in turn Creation, the Fall, the Eschaton, the Advent of the Messiah, Resurrection, Predestination, and Christology. The appended material consists of a further six chapters. These chapters develop themes which are in the main text, especially the role of the Patriarchs of Israel such as Adam, Noah,

211

Abraham, and Moses. The sixth chapter is perhaps the most important as it is there that the Second Advent and its Lord are fully discussed.

5. *Wŏn pulgyo*: Revitalized Buddhism

(a) History of the Sect

Wŏn pulgyo does not fit into any neat schema. It is rejected by the clerics of the orthodox Chogye and T'aego orders as an unorthodox form of Buddhism, and yet its basic premises are clearly in line with traditional Buddhist concepts. It is a syncretic religion in that some of its precepts and practices may be shown to have been inspired by ideas and forms of worship from other traditions. None the less, it is unlike other syncretic religions discussed in this chapter in that neither does it have a shamanistic substratum, as do most of the *sinhŭng chonggyo*, nor has it abused or taken advantage of its followers, as many of the new religions have done. It must be seen as a genuine reform of Buddhism, but a reform movement which started outside the traditional orders.

In the period in which *Wŏn pulgyo* emerged two social factors are relevant to an understanding of the initiation of the movement. First, the general trend towards the reformation of the traditional Buddhist organizations from within through the agency of the Buddhist lay and youth movements. Second, the rapid development of Christianity, essentially a lay movement, which emphasized the unity of Godhead and the involvement of the believer in local church activities several times during the week. These factors, however, cannot be viewed as causes, but only as inspirations or catalysts for the *Wŏn pulgyo* movement.

The *Wŏn pulgyo* movement was founded by Pak Chungbin (1891–1943), better known by his religious style Sot'aesan, the third son of a farmer in South Chŏlla Province in the south-west of the peninsula. This province is part of a region in which there had been a large number of early Catholic believers and which later became an area of intense activity for some of the new religions such as *Chŭngsan-gyo*. From an early age Pak Chungbin was said to have been concerned with metaphysical questions. From the age of 10 to 15, he tried to have an encounter with the Mountain God through sincere and strenuous meditation. He spent a further six years in search of a wise or enlightened man to teach him, but was unable to find anyone who could help him in his search. In April 1916, in his twenty-sixth year, Pak had an overwhelming experience when he sensed the freshness of the dawn of that day and marvelled at the stars, which were still visible. The feeling which was engendered by that experience of the dawn was deepened by listening to a discussion by two Confucian scholars and through his own contemplation. Pak Chungbin gathered around him some key disciples who became the nucleus of his new movement. He taught that all things had the same origin and partook of the same nature.

Following his enlightenment, Pak Chungbin began a four-year study of the scriptures and writings of the three great traditions of East Asia, Confucianism,

Taoism, and Buddhism. Pak saw an essential unity in all of these traditions and took over what seemed relevant from them all. However, he felt that his system was closest to Buddhism, but did not reveal this fact to his disciples until 1919. Pak declared that his form of Buddhism was to be a Buddhism practised by the ordinary person and not by the monk. He taught his followers that they were not to worship the Buddha by reverencing images but by reverencing him everywhere, because the Buddha-nature is everywhere. He summarized his ideas by saying that the *Dharmakāya* (the Body of Truth) was the ineffable reality behind all things. This reality, which Pak called *pulbŏp-sin irwŏn-sang (Dharma body as one circle)*, could be represented by a circle or *wŏn*. For this reason Pak Chungbin's form of Buddhism is called *Wŏn pulgyo* or Wŏn Buddhism. For the next four years, Sot'aesan completed the formulation of his doctrines and developed a system of lay discipline. In 1924 he moved his headquarters to Iri City and founded the *Pulbŏp yŏn'gu-hoe* (Society for Research on the *Dharma*), which constituted the formal organization of *Wŏn pulgyo* as a movement. From 1924 to his death in 1943, Sot'aesan refined his concepts and concentrated his efforts on the training up of a leadership for the new order and on the propagation of the faith. Wŏn Buddhism began to spread beyond the Iri area and new temples were founded in various parts of the country.

When Sot'aesan the first *chongbŏp-sa* or patriarch of *Wŏn pulgyo* died, he was succeeded by one of his first nine disciples, Song Kyu (1900–62), who is better known by his religious style, Chŏngsan. The second patriarch steered the new movement through the difficult years at the end of the Second World War and during the Korean War. In 1946, Chŏngsan changed the name of the order to *Wŏn pulgyo* and emphasized the education of the laity and the importance of acts of charity as a part of the religious life. Wŏn'gwang University, the Wŏn Buddhist university in Iri, traces its origins to an institute which was founded by Chŏngsan in 1945, just after Liberation from Japanese rule. Chŏngsan was succeeded in 1962 by Kim Taegŏ, known by his religious style as Taesan, who in turn, was succeeded as patriarch by Yi Kwangjŏng known as Chwasan. In 1994, Wŏn pulgyo claimed a membership of 1,237,408 persons, 9,806 clerics and 500 temples. The 1995 National Household Census on the other hand found only 86,823 persons who self-identified as members of the order. This statistic raises the question of the eventual viability of the group.

(b) Doctrines and Practices

1. *Irwŏn-sang*: The circle or *wŏn* which gives its name to the sect symbolizes that everything in the universe has its origin in the *Dharmakāya* or Buddha Body of Truth. This is a traditional Mahāyāna concept adopted by Pak Chungbin, which is akin to both the monism of Chosŏn Dynasty Confucianism and the monotheism of Christianity.

2. The Gate of Faith: Sot'aesan argued that there are four positive factors, the *sa'ŭn* (Four Graces), which make human life possible, and four negative factors,

213

the *sayo* (Four Essentials), which are responsible for human suffering. The four factors enabling life are Heaven and earth, human parents, fellow humanity, and religious and civil law. Life is not possible without the *sa'ŭn*, and thus these factors are manifestations of the *pulbŏp-sin* or *Dharmakāya*. In order to be delivered from the bitterness of this life, one must realize what are the four essential causes of suffering. The *sayo* are lack of self-reliance, lack of good leaders for society, lack of education for all people, and the absence of a sense of public service. Unlike the traditional Buddhist orders, *Wŏn pulgyo* is concerned with the present world and its improvement. This is because the Body of Truth is manifested in this world, and in this world the believer may find happiness and release from suffering. The teaching of the Gate of Faith is summed up in the phrase *Ch'och'o pulsang; sasa pulgong* (everywhere are images of the Buddha, the Buddha is worshipped everywhere).

3. The Gate of Discipline: Sot'aesan not only analysed the nature of human life, he also provided a formula for the discipline of the lay believer. This is summarized in the phrases the *Samhak* (the Three Teachings) and the *P'alcho* (the Eight Branches). The three teachings train the believer to discipline his spirit in preparation for enlightenment, the realization of the universal origin of all things. These teachings are the cultivation of the mind to be free from desires and attachments, the examination of the facts of existence to see which ones lead to happiness or suffering, and the correct choice of a moral course of action. The eight branches have a positive and a negative aspect. The branches are the criteria which help the believer to discipline his spiritual life. The positive criteria are faith in oneself to accomplish one's goal, the courage of one's convictions, an inquisitive spirit about the nature of things, and sincerity or devotion to one's task. The negative criteria are the obverse of the above and the result of not following the path which leads to salvation. These criteria are faithlessness, greed, laziness, and foolishness. The Gate of Discipline is summed up in the phrase *Musi-sŏn; much'ŏ-sŏn* (practicing *Sŏn* without reference to time; practicing *Sŏn* without reference to place).

4. Practices: The manner of worship and the social organizations of *Wŏn pulgyo* are strikingly Protestant. The temples of *Wŏn pulgyo* are located in the towns and cities, unlike the temples of traditional Buddhism, and function much like a parish church. The congregation gathers on Sundays and on Wednesday evenings, as do Protestant congregations. The interior of the temples, while often Oriental in style, feels more Christian, particularly as the nave-like main hall focuses on a table at one end behind which will be a representation of the *wŏn*. As in Christian churches, there are societies for children, students, youth, and older persons, in addition to which there are various service organizations.

5. Scripture: The principal text of *Wŏn pulgyo* is the *Wŏn pulgyo kyojŏn* (Scripture of *Wŏn pulgyo*), which contains the writings of Sot'aesan, called the *Chŏng-jŏn* (Main Canon), and a record of the sayings and actions of the first patriarch, called the *Taejŏng-gyŏng* (Supreme Scripture). In addition to the *Kyojŏn, Wŏn pulgyo* also uses the *Chŏngsan chŏngsa pŏbŏ* (Religious

Discourses of Master Chŏngsan), a collection of the teachings of the second patriarch, Chŏngsan.

(c) Final Observations

Although *Wŏn pulgyo* is clearly an orthodox Buddhist movement, this reform movement owes much to the indirect influence of Christianity. Firstly, the emphasis which Sot'aesan placed on the *Dharmakāya*, the ineffable phenomenon which is the essence of the universe, was in part a reaction to the swift development of Christianity. The concept of the *Dharmakāya* is clearly Buddhist in origin, none the less its appeal to this creative religious thinker at the beginning of the century must have been a reaction to the proclamation of unified Godhead by the strange, foreign religion Christianity.

Secondly, the form of the service of worship, the time at which it is held, the arrangement of the interior of the temple, the importance of the laity as opposed to the clergy, the type of organizations associated with the local temple, and the emphasis on social outreach and charity are all a reflection of Protestant Christian practice which would have seemed dramatically different to traditional Buddhist practice at the beginning of the twentieth century. *Wŏn pulgyo* is an example of a Buddhist reform movement which was stimulated by the advent of Protestantism without wholly losing its Buddhist character. It is a syncretic religion, without being a hopeless mass of assorted and weird doctrines.

17

MUSOK-KYO

Folk Religion in Modern Society

1. The Historical Background

We have seen that when Buddhism first made contact with the ancient states of Korea, the Indian religion tended to absorb many of the characteristics and forms of Korean primal religion, which we shall now refer to as *Musok-kyo* (literally, shamanistic religion). Some scholars refer to the folk religion as simply *musok* (shamanistic customs) or more descriptively as *minsok chonggyo* (folk religion). I prefer the term *musok-kyo* because it emphasises the fact that while Korean folk religion is more than just shamanisim, the folk religion's most diagnostic characteristic is shamanism. The emergence of an eclectic and esoteric form of Buddhism in the seventh century did not mean the end of a separate tradition of Korean primal religion, as from this period onwards, the primal religion became the religion of the folk, the ordinary man. Traces of this folk religion may be found throughout the history of the late Silla, Koryŏ, and Chosŏn periods.

Scholars are generally agreed that during the Koryŏ Dynasty, there were three types of local ceremonies which were a continuation of the practice of the primal religion.[1] These were (1) the *sanch'ŏn-je*, ceremonies offered to the spirits of the mountains and rivers; (2) the *chosang-je*, or non-Confucian ancestral rites; and (3) the *ki'u-je*, or shamanistic petitions for rain. From the records remaining from the period, Ryu Tong-shik (Yu Tongsik) discerns five features of the folk religion of that time. First, there was a designated altar or shrine where ceremonies were held. Second, these rites were offered to a great spirit called either *Chesŏk* or *Ch'irwŏnsŏng-gun*. The term *Chesŏk* occurs in the Tan'gun legend (see Appendix A), where this word, originally referring to the great Hindu god Indra, was used to represent the Ruler of Heaven, *Hanŭllim*. *Ch'irwŏnsŏng-gun* is the Seven Star Spirit now more frequently called *Ch'ilsŏng-nim*, and also a guise of the Lord of Heaven. Third, the practitioners of Korean folk religion in the Koryŏ dynasty used wine, song, and dance as a

---

1 Yu Tongsik, *Han'guk Mugyo-ŭi yŏksa-wa kujo* (Sŏul, Yonsei UP, 1975), pp. 115–28.

means of inducing ecstacy and so permitting the spirits to enter into their bodies. Fourth, following the entrance of the spirit a message was conveyed from the spirit world to the earthly world. Fifth, these ceremonies were attended without discrimination by members of all classes and sexes who paid for the privilege of holding the ceremony. These Koryŏ rituals would seem to be a continuation of ancient traditions and are obviously parallel to the shamanism of modern Siberia. Hyun-key Kim Hogarth notes that historical records indicate that the *mudang* performed rituals with the following distinct characteristics – healing, divination and the conveying of oracles, descent of the spirit and possession of the shaman, and cursing. Except for the latter element, all these features are characteristic of contemporary shamanism.

Yi Nŭng-hwa, Ryu Tong-shik and others find that the folk religion of the Chosŏn period had similar characteristics to the Koryŏ period. They find that the historical records from this period show that there were three general classes of rites: the *sanch'ŏn-je:* the *ki'u-je*; and the *sŏnghwang-je*, or rites to the spirit of the city wall or the local village tutelary spirit. Ryu says that many of the rites addressed to the spirits of the mountains and rivers were petitions for prosperity or for the curing of disease, a common shamanistic emphasis. He and Kim Hogarth have also observed that *mudang* were frequent if unwelcome visitors to the royal palaces throughout the Chosŏn period. Although there are records of conflict between Confucian officials and the *mudangs* and that the latter were often forbidden access to the palace, it is also plain that the entrance of shamans to the royal residence was the generally accepted practice throughout the entire history of this most Confucian of dynasties. Not only were shamans permitted access to the palace, but a selected few were permitted the right to use one or two buildings within the palace precincts which had been specially prepared for them. These structures existed up to the end of the dynasty and were used for performing curative ceremonies. Shamans who gained access to the palace or who were resident in the halls prepared for them were called *kungmu* or national shamans. The ambivalent attitude to shamans is indicated by the fact that in both the Koryŏ and Chosŏn periods, shamans were taxed, that is, their existence was admitted officially if grudgingly. As a sign of the disdain in which the shamans and their rituals were held, official government documents from the period refer to *kut* or shamanistic rites as *ŭmsa*, 'obscene rites'.

Thus, historical records from the Koryŏ and Chosŏn periods show, that in whatever regard the shamans and their ceremonies were held, the primal religion of Korea did not disappear but became transformed into a folk religion which existed as the substratum of Korean religious experience. What is the nature of this folk religion at the present time? In the following sections, we shall discuss the modern practitioners of this folk religion, the spirits which they worship, and the ceremonies and rituals which they perform.

2. The Practitioners of *Musok-kyo*

(a) Shamans

Encompassing all the aspects of modern Korean folk religion, the practitioners of this folk cult may be divided broadly into three types, namely, shamans, ritual leaders, and diviners. There are two kinds of shamans in Korea, female shamans called *mudang*, who predominate, and male shamans called *paksu*. The first thing to observe about these terms is that they are not Chinese words but pure Korean words. Ryu Tong-shik has attempted to show that these terms are related to words used by various of the Neo-Siberian tribes in contemporary Siberia. Whatever the validity of Ryu's comparisons, it is certainly true that the practice of shamanism does not derive from a Chinese source but from a source common to both Korea and Siberia. A more respectful term for a female shaman is *mansin* (ten thousand spirits), referring to the number of spirits which she could call upon. Female shamans could be further divided into two types, the *kangsin-mu* (spirit-possessed shaman) who are possessed by their familiar spirits who then speak through them, and the *sesŭm-mu* (hereditary shaman) who receive their authority to shamanise not through a unique experience with a spirit, but by inheritance through the female line.

As with shamans in many nations, people become *mudang* through the encounter or possession of a spirit or spirits. This event usually happens when the potential *mudang* is in a dream or trance-like state, most frequently when the person is very ill. The illness which the potential shaman experiences at that point is called the *sinbyŏng* (spirit disease) or *mubyŏng* (shaman's disease). The experiences contained in these illnesses, referred to by Kim Hogarth and others as pre-shaman possession illness, are formalised in an initiation rite called the *naerim kut* (descent rite). A full-fledged initiation rite might consist of as many as sixteen sub-rituals and take as long as three days to complete. The ceremony's sub-rituals consist of three main sections, those sub-rites concerned with preparing the spiritual atmosphere of the core ceremonies, the core ceremonies consisting of trials and tests given to the potential shaman of which the *naerim kut* proper and its own sub-rites form the largest section, and the rite proclaiming the status of the candidate as a new shaman.

Another characteristic of Korean shamans is that they possess features which pertain to both the autochthonous aboriginal tribes called loosely the Palaeo-Siberian tribes and the more 'recently' arrived Neo-Siberian tribes. Like their Palaeo-Siberian counterparts, the Korean shamans wear the clothing of the opposite sex when performing the shamanic rituals. Like the Neo-Siberian shaman, the *mudang* and *paksu* dress in a garb which is covered with dangling, clanging objects. Palaeo-Siberian shamans are usually women, whereas Neo-Siberian shamans are males having more cultic functions. Korean shamans incorporate all of these characteristics. As with virtually all Siberian tribes, Korean shamans use the drum in order to perform their ceremonies.

Ornithological motifs, especially common among Neo-Siberian tribes, are a principal means for describing the Korean shaman and her experience. For example, the possession of the shaman's body by a spirit is described as if the person's soul had been seized by an eagle. Unlike most Siberian shamans, the soul of the Korean shaman does not ascend to the spirit world, but rather spirits enter into the shaman's body. Korean shamans are both hereditary, which is the general Neo-Siberian practice, and selected by a certain spirit, which is the Palaeo-Siberian practice. Thus it is plain that Korean primal religion represents a blending of the traits of Palaeo-Siberian and Neo-Siberian tribal groups, and that this blending must have taken place at the time of the arrival of the Tungusic tribes in the Korean peninsula between 1,000 and 600 BC.

In 1971, leading shamans and their supporters founded the *Tae Han sŭngkong yŏngsin yŏnhap-hoe* (Korean Victory over Communism Federation of Shamans). The association was formed to promote the interests of shamans, and in particular to help to remove the stigma of superstition and ignorance which surrounded them and their practices. The rather unusual name of the group indicates both the anti-communist climate of Korea in the 1970s and the shamanists' fears for their persecution under a communist social and political system if north Korea were to be victorious over south Korea. In 1994, this group claimed a membership of 120,000 persons, of whom 80,000 were women and 40,000 men.

(b) Ritual Leaders

Ritual leaders called *chegwan* are selected on a one-off basis to function as the celebrants of certain village ceremonies. Usually three men are selected by the head of the village to perform one of the village rites. From the period of selection to the conclusion of the ceremonies, these men must remain ritually pure, that is, they must avoid contact with menstruating women, with women who have recently given birth, and with corpses. They are also forbidden to have sexual intercourse or to quarrel with anyone. After selection by the village head, they live apart from their family and undergo ritual lustrations in order to purify their body in preparation for the village ritual. Some of the intercessory functions of the temporary ritual leaders or *chegwan* are similar to those of the Palaeo-Siberian shamans connected with the family cult, another point of contact with ancient Siberian shamanism. However, in modern times these *chegwan* seem to relate more to a Confucian world-view, although this probably represents Confucian influence rather than a Confucian origin.

(c) Diviners

There are several classes of diviners in Korea, the *chŏmjaengi* or fortune-teller, the *chigwan* or geomancer, and the *ilgwan* or selector of propitious days. In addition to the *chŏmjaengi*, there is a special class of blind fortune-tellers, the *p'ansu*. The *chŏmjaengi* as such is only concerned with fortune-telling, whereas the *p'ansu* has the additional function of exorcism. There are three principal ways in which divination may be practised: by the use of dice boxes, by the use of coins, and by the use of certain books of divination. The three types of divination are effective for all purposes, so the choice of method is unrelated to the purpose. The dice-box method consists in matching the results of the three throws of the box with a store of aphorisms which the *chŏmjaengi* proceeds to interpret. The box contains eight strips with symbols called *p'algwae* (the eight trigrams of the *I-ching*). With each throw one strip or die will be shaken out, and the results of the three throws will be recorded and correlated. Divination by coins takes place in the following manner. The fortune-teller will shake eight coins three times dropping one coin at each throw, or he will cast all eight coins three times. Either way, the coin faces are read, matched, and an aphorism found to suit the situation. The third and most prestigious method is divination by a book. The hour, day, month, and year of one's birth is matched with the content of the book which the diviner carries. After matching these essential facts, the fortune-teller proceeds to answer the client's questions. Methods of fortune-telling are keeping abreast of the times. The author has seen fortune-tellers who have set up on the street using a personal computer equipt with a specialised programme called *Tojŏng pigyŏl*!

In Sŏul, fortune-tellers used to be grouped around the base of Nam-san in the southern part of the old city, but recently have been forced by city plans to move away. Most of them have now congregated near the Mi'a-gogae pass in the northern part of the city. In other cities, fortunetellers are found in and around parks and markets, wherever people congregate in large numbers. A somewhat upmarket version of a fortuneteller's place of business is the *ch'ŏrhag-wŏn* or hall of philosophy, signs for which may be found in front of houses in many residential areas. There is a cluster of these *ch'ŏrhag-wŏn* near Sinch'on railway station in Sŏul. The term probably reflects the prestige of the *I-ching* (*Yŏk-kyŏng* in Korean) as a quasi-philosophical text in Confucianism. Signs for the *ch'ŏrhag-wŏn* often incorporate the reverse swastika, the symbol of Buddhism in East Asia.

The *p'ansu* in addition to fortune-telling performs exorcism. Among the types of exorcist ceremonies which a *p'ansu* may perform are the following rites: (1) *okchu-gyŏng* (exorcism of insanity spirits), (2) *ch'uksa-gyŏng* (exorcism of disease spirits by prayer), (3) *chisin-gyŏng* (exorcism of evil spirits in a house), (4) *sŏngsin-gyŏng* (exorcism of disease spirits at a distance), (5) *mansin-gyŏng* (ceremony for strengthening the ties between the *p'ansu* and his attendant spirits called *mansin*), (6) *susin-gyŏng* (exorcism of outcast spirits), and (7) *pangsin-gyŏng* (the freeing of lesser spirits imprisoned by greater spirits for their misdeeds). It will be seen that the rites are of two general types, rituals for the curing of disease by the ejection of spirits by other spirits, and rituals for the strengthening of ties between the *p'ansu* and the spirit world. The relation of the *p'ansu* to the spirit world is one of control through superior magical practices, while the *mudang* and *paksu* are humans who had been selected by the spirits to be their intermediaries on earth.

The *chigwan* or geomancer is a special category of diviner whose task is to select propitious sites for buildings and tombs. It was believed that the character of the terrain would affect the prosperity of those who utilized it. Geomancy or *p'ungsu chiri* (*fêngshui* in Chinese) is the art of determining a propitious site. The *chigwan* would use a special spyglass and a compass marked off into 24 directions called a *yundo* to determine the contours of the land, which in turn would be interpreted according to passages in the geomancer's handbook, the *Ch'ŏn'gi taeyo* (Great Digest of Heavenly Indications). Another method involved the use of a cosmic diagram called the *kugung* or nine palaces. The *ilgwan* or selector of propitious days likewise uses books to determine a propitious time to undetake an activity, such as a suitably auspicious day for a marriage, a trip, or some other important event. Among the books used are the *Ch'ŏn'gi taeyo* and the *T'ojŏng pigyŏl* (Earth Pavilion Secrets). Fortunetelling involving the knowledge of the birth year, month, day and hour of an individual by the lunar calendar is called *saju p'alcha* (four pillars and eight characters) referring to the four sets of two-character terms used to describe one's birth date in the sixty-year lunar calendar. Fortunetelling by physiognomy is called *kwansang* and by palmistry, *susang*.

3. The Spirits

(a) Hananim

The spirit world of Korean *Musok-kyo* may be divided into six classes: the Supreme Being, the gods of the air, the gods of the land, the gods of the water, nameless lesser spirits, and the ancestral spirits. The Koreans from the earliest recorded period have worshipped a high god who resided in the heavens from where he exercised his rule. He has been known in Korean variously as *Hananim, Hanallim, Hanŭnim*, or *Hanŭllim* – the Ruler of Heaven. Everything in the universe was attributed to him, the lives of the people, their harvest, the rain and other natural phenomena. However, as is the case with other high gods amongst tribal peoples, there was only occasional, if any, worship directly offered to him. He was the invisible and ultimate cause of everything. Worship was given to those spirits to which he had delegated authority.

Another spirit of the heavens whose shrine is frequently found behind the principal hall of Korean Buddhist temples is *Ch'ilsŏng-nim* or the Seven Star Spirit, the Pole Star. We have encountered references to his worship in Koryŏ times, along with that of *Chesŏk. Ch'ilsŏng* together with *Chesŏk* and *Ch'ŏn-sin* are the guises of or the alternative names for the Ruler of Heaven, *Hananim*. As *Ch'ilsŏng*, he is the Ruler of the Pole Star, the central and pivotal constellation of the northern hemisphere. In primeval times, Ursa Major was probably thought to be the residence of the supreme ruler. From this belief developed the cult of this star cluster and its powerful spirit. The shrine dedicated to *Ch'ilsŏng*, the *Ch'ilsŏng-gak*, is invariably a small, tile-roofed structure usually situated to the left and rear of the principal temple building. The interior often contains only a simple altar with a painting of the deity who is often depicted as a Bodhisattva.

(b) Gods of the Air

1. *Obang changgun*. Immediately beneath the Ruler of Heaven are his highest subordinates, the Generals of the Five Cardinal Points, the *Obang changgun*. Although the belief in these spirits is found amongst the Chinese as well, the source for their cult may not be China itself but Central Asia and Siberia. Tribal groups as distant from the Chinese world as the Samoyed and the Yenesei Ostyak in the far west of Siberia propitiate the rulers of the five directions. The worship of the guardians of the cardinal directions is not unique, as we also find the cult of the *Sach'ŏnwang* or Four Heavenly Kings in Buddhism. What is distinctive about the *cultus* of these five spirits is the designation of the centre as a point of the compass. The use of the number five indicates that the origin of the cult may well be autochthonous to Siberian peoples as they use a five-directional division of the world.

Each of the directions is associated with a particular colour. Thus the *Ch'ŏngje changgun* (Azure General) governs the East, the *Paekche changgun* (White General) governs the West, the *Chŏkche changgun* (Red General) governs the South, the *Hŭkche changgun* (Black General) governs the North, and the *Hwangje changgun* (Yellow General) governs the Centre.

These five great spirits resemble the Siberian master spirits who rule or govern a portion of the cosmos. The division of the spirit world into five grand hordes is also reminiscent of the great tribal hordes which swept across the plains of Central Asia and Manchuria. Neo-Siberian peoples, such as the Mongols, often conceived of their spirits as being divided into hordes under the authority of a superior spirit.

2. *Sinjang*. These spirits are subordinate to the *Obang changgun* and may be thought of as the *aides-de-camp* of the generals. There have been estimates that there may be as many as 80,000 of these spirits. Beneath them in turn are minor spirits such as the *saja* which constitute the heavenly troops. This orderly hierarchy again reminds one of the hierarchy of the Central Asian hordes. The *sinjang* or *mansin* are important because it is they who are the confidants of the shamans and the *p'ansu*, the blind fortune-tellers and exorcists.

(c) Spirits of the Earth

1. *San-sin*. Without question, the most important of the earthly spirits is *San-sin*, the Mountain God. His cult is celebrated in two places, in small shrines behind the principal hall of a Buddhist temple, or in front of the village altar. We have seen that the cult of *Ch'ilsŏng* or *Samsŏng* (Three Star Spirit, another guise of

Ch'ilsŏng) is also celebrated in such shrines. More common than the shrines dedicated to either *Ch'ilsŏng* or *Samsŏng* is the *Sansin-gak* or Mountain God Shrine. These plain shrines have only a simple altar behind which hangs a painting of the god. In this painting he is depicted as a benevolent, white-bearded figure of great antiquity seated on a tiger beneath a pine tree. Often to the side there is a small boy offering him a sŏndo (*hsien-tao* in Chinese) or Peach of Immortality from the Taoist land of the Immortals.

The unique characteristic of *San-sin* is that he is not the god of a particular mountain, but the god of all mountains, and the founder of the first Korean state. According to the myth, as the grandson of the Ruler of Heaven, Tan'gun was born on a mountain, and after completing his reign on earth he became the God of the Mountains. Historically, the worship of *San-sin* is very ancient. The oldest known stele in Korea is dedicated to this spirit and is dated to AD 85.

The association of the tiger with *San-sin* is significant in that the Tungus tribes of Siberia worship a master of the hunt, an old, white-bearded man who rides on a tiger. This spirit, *Bainaca*, is propitiated on mountain passes and river banks. So too with *San-sin*; Koreans to this day will place a pebble on a pile of stones at the summit of a mountain pass in order to propitiate this great spirit. The depiction of Tan'gun, the conception of his role, and the manner in which he is commonly propitiated would indicate that he belongs to the class of spirits known in Siberia as master spirits, rulers of aspects of nature.

Apart from the worship accorded to *San-sin* at the shrines in Buddhist temples and on mountain passes, the cult is practised in the villages, especially on *Tae porŭm*, the evening of the fifteenth day of the first lunar month. On that night, all the village elders or heads of households will gather before a plain stone altar or shrine erected beside the most ancient tree in the village. Written petitions for prosperity and health in the new year will be set on fire and allowed to float upwards to Heaven to be received by *San-sin*. Thus, *San-sin* is the benevolent protector of the household and of the village as a whole. There is one other simple rite which is offered to this god. Women who are barren or who have not produced male offspring will journey to some famous temple or revered rock deep in the mountains to offer up their petition for a child.

2. *Ch'on-sin.* The *Ch'on-sin* is a minor spirit of the land which is responsible for the fertility of the soil. It used to be common for farmers to offer a portion of their noonday meal to this spirit. The cult of this spirit is no longer widespread.

3. *Changsŭng.* In front of the entrance to most villages in pre-modern Korea, there were two standing posts frequently made of wood but in some areas made of stone. These posts, called *changsŭng* (which many early writers mistakenly called totem poles, or devil posts) were crudely carved in the shape of male and female figures and were labelled *Ch'ŏnha tae changgun* (Great General Beneath Heaven) and *Chiha tae changgun* (Great General Beneath the Earth). These spirits are the tutelary spirits of the village and are situated so as to block the entrance of malevolent spirits into the village precinct. The duality of male/female, sky/earth characteristic of the *changsŭng* is a primeval statement of the *Yin-Yang*

Theory. In our discussion of Confucianism in the Three Kingdoms period, we have noted that Yi Ŭrho holds that prior to the advent of Confucian philosophy there was already in Korea a folk philosophy which had many of the characteristics of formal Confucian thought. The *changsŭng* are one important reflection of this folk philosophy. On the volcanic island of Cheju off the southwest coast, these tutelary spirits are represented on statues of carved lava called *Harubang* (Grandfather) and *Halmang* (Grandmother) in the local dialect.

4. *Sŏngju* and other household spirits. There is a variety of guardian household spirits worshipped in the home, among which are *Sŏngju*, the chief guardian of the home; *Samsin halmoni*, the guardian of childbirth; *T'oju taegam*, the guardian of the house site; *Chowang*, the Kitchen Spirit; and *Pyŏnso kakssi*, the guardian of the toilet. Although a minor spirit in the Korean celestial hierarchy, *Sŏngju* is the supreme guardian of the home. He makes his residence in a packet of pine needles tucked away up on the central beam of the *maru* or central, wooden floor room of the home. Worship is offered to *Sŏngju* at harvest, when a new home is erected, when there is a new male head of the household, and on other occasions. If members of a household feel that *Sŏngju* is punishing them for some infraction or that he is not performing his duties well, this spirit will be specially propitiated. *Samsin halmoni* resides in an earthenware jar of rice grains kept in the inner room or woman's quarters of the house. Conceived of as a grandmother or matriarch, this spirit protects women during the ordeal of childbirth. *T'oju taegam* patrols the precinct of the household, while the Kitchen Spirit and the Toilet Maiden reside in those places guarding against the predations of evil spirits.

(d) Spirits of the Water

There is a variety of water spirits, all of which are conceived of as dragons. The *yong* or dragons live in the rivers and streams, in the springs and wells, and in the seas and heavens where they control the rains. The worship of these spirits is very ancient and similar in many ways to the practice of the modern Tungus groups. Stories in the *Samguk yusa* record various legends told about dragons during the period of the Three Kingdoms. One legend tells us that the construction of a royal palace was halted because of the presence of a dragon. Upon completion, the palace was named the *Hwangnyong-sa*, the Temple of the Yellow Dragon.

The most grand of all the dragons is the *Yong-wang* (Dragon King), also known as *Hae-wang* or King of the Sea, who is the ruler of the sea and all that moves within it. There are many legends about the Dragon King and his relations with the human world. The Hae'in-sa temple has a magnificent portrait of the *Yong-wang*, showing him dressed as a Korean king in state with a ferocious dragon-face and surrounded by his watery realm. Villagers propitiate the dragons at times of drought, while fishermen worship them before venturing out to sea. In addition to the normal village shrine, fishing villages will often have separate shrines dedicated to the *Yong-wang*.

(e) Nameless Spirits

Beneath the spirits discussed above come a host of spirits, ghosts, imps, and such which constitute the lowest level of the Korean spiritual realm. Some of these spirits are benevolent, such as the kitchen spirit and the spirit which inhabits the rice storage jar. There is also a class of malevolent spirits full of vengeance towards humanity. These spirits are often the souls of those who have died before fulfilling themselves, such as drowned persons, young boys, and unmarried girls. Another class of spirits would be the *tokkaebi* or imp-like creatures which delight in mischievous acts such as mislaying household items or cracking the kitchen crockery. All of these spirits had to be appeased to ensure harmony in the home.

(f) Ancestral Spirits

The Confucian cult of the ancestral spirits has been discussed above in relation to the *chesa* ceremony. It needs only to be stressed here that ancestor worship is indigenous to Korea. Confucianism only codified and organized a pre-existing practice. The Myth of Tan'gun, which dates back to the tribal states period, is one early indication of the importance of the cult of the ancestors. In this case, the ancestors worshipped are the progenitors of the royal family, and by extension the ancestors of the nation as a whole. In Siberia to this day there are ancestral cults presided over by shamans. In Korea there is a parallel to this in the shamanistic ancestral ceremonies which are unrelated to the Confucian ritual system, as well as the non-shamanistic, non-Confucian rituals.

4. The Ceremonies

(a) Purak-che, The Village Ritual System

Ch'oe Kilsŏng (1940–) classifies village rituals into two general types, the *tong-je* or community rituals and the *pyŏlsin-gut* or household rituals. Each of these classes of rituals has a Confucian ritual system and a corresponding or complementary shamanistic system. Ch'oe holds that these two systems form the parts of a harmonious whole and cannot be understood apart from each other. He points out that the Confucian ritual system emphasizes lineage structure and occurs at regular intervals, whereas the shamanistic rituals propitiate a host of polytheistic spirits at irregular intervals.

The following are some characteristic differences between the various ceremonies. First, the Confucian ritual system utilizes only members of the lineage, whereas shamanistic rituals will even draw on people from beyond the village. Second, with the Confucian system, the household and village rituals differ in that the former worship the lineage ancestors back to four generations, whereas the latter assume that the ancestors of a particular lineage are in fact the ancestors of all the village members. Third, Confucian ritual, as one might suspect, is more concerned with the worship of ancestors than is shamanistic ritual. Confucian ritual tends, also, to focus on one spirit, whereas shamanistic ritual offers worship to a whole range of spirits including Buddhist demi-gods. Fourth, the performance of Confucian and shamanistic ritual is different. In any Confucian rite, the celebrant is a non-professional. In Confucian household rites close kinsmen offer the rituals, and in the Confucian village ceremonies, the *tong-je*, it is the *chegwan* or elected elders who do so. In contrast to these temporary, non-professional officiants, the shamanistic ceremony is offered up by the *mudang*, sometimes in concert with selected village elders. Also, Confucian rituals tend to be simple in form and lack complexity in contrast to the shamanistic rites, which are complicated and lengthy. Fifth, as has been pointed out before, Confucian rituals occur regularly, usually twice a year in the spring and autumn, whereas the shamanistic rites may occur as frequently as every two years or as infrequently as every ten years, or simply irregularly.

(b) Household Ceremonies

The Confucian household ancestral ceremony or *chesa* has been discussed in a previous chapter and need not be mentioned further here. The corresponding shamanistic ceremonies are the *sanogu-gut* and the *ogu-gut*, which are performed for persons at their request somewhat like the mortuary services of the Middle Ages. The *sanogu-gut* is performed for persons still alive, while the *ogu-gut* is for deceased persons.

One elaborate example of the *sanogu-gut* was reported to have taken three days and nights and to have consisted of six separate sub-rites. These sub-rites were: (1) the *pujŏng-gut* or purification rite, in which the *mudang* invites the descent of the spirits, (2) the *kolmaegi-gut* addressed to the tutelary spirits of the village, (3) the *ch'omangja-gut*, addressed to the spirits of the recently deceased, (4) the *paridegi-gut*, the principal element of the *sanogu-gut*, (5) the *yŏngsan maji-gut*, which sends the spirits of the deceased into the next world, and (6) the *kŏri-gut* addressed to various malevolent spirits.

The main purpose of the *paridegi-gut* is to transform the spirit of the deceased into an ancestor, which does not occur automatically upon a person's death. It is interesting to note that in the story which is described in the *paridegi-gut*, the sons of the heroine of the story become the seven stars of the constellation Ursa Major, thus making a connection between the cult of the ancestors and the cult of *Ch'ilsŏng*. One interesting characteristic of the *yŏngsan maji-gut* is the pushing of ancestral tablets along a white strip of cloth, symbolizing the movement of the ancestors along the road to Paradise. Thus, ancestral ceremonies of the shamanistic type are elaborate, lengthy, and rich in symbolism by comparison with the more lineage-oriented, austere Confucian rites.

(c) Community Ceremonies

The *tong-je* or Confucian community rituals are held twice or even four times a year. A committee of ten village elders selects the *chegwan* who, in the manner already described, prepare themselves for the ritual. The ritual area becomes *tabu* and is marked off by a rope. Soil is also sprinkled around the shrine proper to show the sacredness of the area. The ceremony is offered to the spirits of the village who are treated as though they were the ancestors of the village. The ritual itself is very simple, consisting of a food-offering of rice, soup, wine, pork, fish, fruit, and *ttŏk* or Korean rice-cakes. A petition is made to the spirits, and sheets of paper are burned. A bright flame indicates that there will be good fortune. The ceremony concludes with the *chegwan* drinking cups of wine.

In contrast to this simple and dignified ritual is the *pyŏlsin-gut* or shamanistic village ceremony. A village ceremony offered to the spirits of a fishing village was observed to have had as many as nine different sub-rituals. These were (1) the *mun-gut*, which opens the ceremony on the evening before the principal events, (2) the *chesa* or Confucian rites offered to village ancestors, (3) the *pujŏng-gut* or purification rites, (4) the *tang maji-gut*, during which an elder holds a pole down which the shamans invite the spirits to descend to earth, (5) the *sejŏn-gut*, which emphasizes prosperity and the acquisition of wealth, (6) the *Sim Ch'ŏng-gut*, which stresses the importance of healthy eyes, crucial for seafaring people, (7) the *Ch'ŏnwang-gut*, which emphasizes harmony between the sexes and between wives and concubines, (8) the *Yongwang-gut* offered to the *Yong-wang* and also separately to each villager who has died at sea, and (9) the *kŏri-gut*, which is to appease malevolent spirits which might have been attracted to the ritual site. Thus a *pyŏlsin-gut* is in itself a complete ritual system offering worship to a wide variety of spirits in order to ensure the prosperity and happiness of the entire village.

(d) Non-village Ceremonies

We have seen that there are a number of *kut* or shamanistic ceremonies which are offered in the village at the household or village level. There are also a number of *kut* which are offered to spirits for personal reasons and which may be classified as non-village rites. Ryu Tong-shik classifies these *kut* as having one of three purposes or functions, the curing of disease, petitions for prosperity and other wishes, and the sending-off of the dead to the next world. Homer B. Hulbert at the beginning of the twentieth century discussed eight types of *kut*,[2] which we will classify according to Ryu's schema.

1. Curative Rites. The first *kut* of this type is a simple ceremony performed by the *mudang* in order to rid the patient of the disease spirit or spirits. It may be

---

2 Homer B. Hulbert, 'The Korean Mudang and P'ansu', *Korea Review*, 3 (1903).

made more elaborate according to the wealth of the client. This *kut* is called a *pyŏng-gut* (disease rite) and is the most common of all shamanistic rituals. The second type of curative rite which Hulbert described was a special *pyŏng-gut* addressed to the Smallpox Spirit, the only disease spirit to have such a specialized rite.

2. Petitionary Rites. In this category are a variety of *kut* which have the function of offering up a number of different types of petitions to several different spirits. First, there is the *yongsin-gut* (dragon-spirit rite) type, of which we have already met the rite addressed to the Dragon King. Among the various *yongsin-gut* are rites offered as village petitions for rain, for the protection of merchant vessels, for the protection of fishing vessels, for the protection of ferries, and finally for the protection of warships and sailors.

Another type of petitionary rite are the rituals offered to *Sansin*. In this category, Hulbert placed all those rituals which were offered by a supplicant to the Mountain God for long life and children. We have already seen how a woman might offer prayer at a temple or at a designated rock to the Mountain God for a male heir, which is the most common type of petition addressed to this august spirit. There was a third and special type of *kut* which was offered up to San-sin until 1894 by the servants of envoys going on diplomatic missions to Peiching. Although frowned upon by the Confucian envoys themselves, the retainers felt such worship a necessity to ensure the safety of the journey and the success of the mission.

3. Mortuary Rites. Hulbert described three types of rituals which could be classified in this category. The first is a pre-burial *kut* which was offered between the period of the death of a person and the actual burial of his body. This ceremony offers the spirit of the deceased, which lingers near the home, the opportunity to give his valedictory remarks to the assembled members of his family. A second type of *kut* is a post-burial rite which is offered immediately upon the burial of the body and invokes a spirit called the *saja*, who is implored to conduct the soul of the departed quickly and safely to the next world. A third type of *kut* in this category is an elaborate ceremony which is held a month and a half after the death of the person and which invokes the *Si-wang* or *Sip-wang* (Ten Judges of Hell). This is done to ensure that the deceased's soul makes the proper connections with important people in the next world. The deceased in his turn will then be in a better position to assist his relatives in this world. The belief that family and personal social connections enable a person to achieve a desired goal clearly reflects the reality of the Korean social system. Hulbert adds that once the line to the spirit world is open, attendants at the *kut* often call up other spirits and have quite 'an afternoon tea with the dead'.

There are other ceremonies than those which have been listed here, and for each type one may find variations in complexity and form according to the region or locale. It will seen from what has been said that the Koreans in pre-modern times were concerned, as Ryu has rightly pointed out, with health, happiness, prosperity, and the care and propitiation of ancestral spirits.

(e) Material Aspects of the Kut

The use of various colours in the costumes, and particularly the flags used by the shamans in their ceremonies, have specific meanings which in part derive from a broad East Asian tradition and which additionally have a distinct meaning within the context of *Musok-kyo*. In shamanistic ceremonies white refers to the Lord of Heaven, red to San-sin or the Mountain God, yellow to the ancestors, blue to the General or *Taegam,* and black to all miscellaneous spirits. The meaning of colour in the ceremonies applies to the shaman's flags, costumes, the colour of the ritual foods, and other ritual items.

Sacrificial items offered to the spirits during a *kut* consist of libations and food. Liquors of all traditional sorts are offered up while foods consist of rice, *ttŏk* (steamed rice cakes), fruits, nuts, vegetables and various kinds of meat. One item conspicuous by its absence is any type of *kimch'i*, the spicy accompaniment to any Korean meal. The central object on the sacrificial table is either a pig or an ox head.

Music is used to aid the shaman to enter into a state of trance and is thus a necessary accompaniment to any *kut*. The principal instruments used by the musicians who accompany the shaman are drums and brass percussion instruments. The characteristic drum for a *kut* is the *changgo* or hourglass-shaped drum; the *puk* or barrel-shaped drum is also used. Percussion instruments used are the *chegŭm* or brass cymbals, and gongs of various sizes. The *muga* or shamanistic songs are of four-broad types – long, epic-like mythic tales, tuneful singing supposedly sung by the spirits possessing the shaman called *t'aryŏng*, chanting for purification and the invitation of spirits, and incantations for driving away evil spirits, usually performed by male shamans.

The costumes worn by the shaman reflect the spirit possessing them, such as generals, kings, Buddhist spirits, figures appearing in the *muga* narrative, and other narrative characters. The shaman will use a *pangul* or brass bell rattle to achieve a state of ecstasy, fans, tridents, swords, knives, double knifeblades mounted on a block of wood for walking on, flags representing the *Obang changgun* or Generals of the Five Directions, paper cut-out objects in a wide variety of forms, boats to send off the souls of the dead to the next world, life-sized dolls for ghost weddings, and mirrors engraved with the images of the Sun, Moon and Pole Stars.

CONCLUDING REMARKS

1. Some General Observations about Korean Religions

Now that we have completed this general survey of Korean religions, examining in some detail the complex historical relations between the various religious traditions and several social and political factors, it will be salutary to step back for a moment and to consider two final points. First, what sort of general observations may we make about religions in Korea, and second, what importance may we attach to the academic study of Korean religion?

There are three general themes which we can discern in the history of the several religious traditions of Korea.

1. *The influence of the primal religion*. The primal religion of Korea is the original and most ancient religious tradition in Korea. Characteristic of the tribal groups of the Korean peninsula and southern Manchuria prior to the advent of Chinese civilization, this primal religion was of a type known commonly as shamanism. Among the functions of the clan or tribal leader during the ancient period was the intercessory rôle which he played between his people and the realm of the spirits. As in other societies with a shamanistic type of primal religion, shamans interceded on behalf of ordinary mortals for the purpose of obtaining blessings, the curing of disease, and the propitiation of the spirits of the dead. The primal religion of the ancient period did not disappear with the advent of Buddhism in the fourth century. Rather, it became the substratum of all Korean religious experience and has shaped the development of all religions and philosophies which have been transmitted to Korea, including Buddhism, Confucianism, and Roman Catholic and Protestant Christianity.

2. *Periods of religious dominance*. The history of religion in Korea, irrespective of the periods of political history, may be divided into four broad periods. In each period one particular religious tradition formed the dominant or most dynamic religious force in the society at that particular time. The four eras would be (i) the era of primal religion, (ii) the era of Buddhist dominance, (iii) the era of Confucian dominance, and (iv) the post-Confucian era. The first era would encompass all Korean history from primordial times to the advent of Chinese civilization in the fourth century. As indicated above, Korean primal

religion was to form the spiritual basis which would influence the reception and development of all later religious traditions. The second era, the period of Buddhist dominance, would extend generally from the fourth to the fourteenth century. During this period of Buddhist spiritual sway, the spiritual, intellectual, and aesthetic culture of the Koreans was formed along Buddhist lines, largely to the exclusion of other traditions. The greatest works of Buddhist art, for example, come from this period and not later. The third era, the period of Confucian dominance, witnessed a complete reversal of the positions of Buddhism and Confucianism, with the result that Korean culture for the next five hundred years was formed by Confucian concepts and values, almost to the exclusion of other traditions. The fourth era, the post-Confucian period, shows the decline of formal Confucian influence on society and the revival of Buddhism and the rapid growth of a new religion, Christianity. It is the author's opinion that the most dynamic religious force during the past hundred years has been Christianity, which has significantly influenced both Buddhism and the new religions. Whether it will become the dominant religious tradition in this new era, as Buddhism and Confucianism have been in the past, is an open question.

3. *Conservative nature of Korean religious experience.* It is the author's opinion that Korean religious experience on the whole tends to be conservative in nature. Once, when we were discussing the way in which Koreans have come to accept various world religions, a close Korean friend – who is a philosopher – commented to the author that it took Koreans a long time to accept new ideas or beliefs, but that once they had accepted innovations Koreans kept them. This remark has long stayed uppermost in the author's mind when considering the history of Korean religions, for it indicates that Korean religious experience has a strongly conservative element in it, and a tendency to avoid a significant degree of syncretism.

This conservative tendency may explain why the folk religion, the primal religion, has survived tenaciously for such a long period without forming itself into a new religious body, as did the folk religions of China and Japan, which eventually became religious Taoism and Shintō respectively. It may also explain why, in comparison with the popular forms of Chinese and Japanese Buddhism, popular Korean Buddhism has not experienced the same degree of syncretism, and why Sŏn Buddhism, which is after all an attempt to return to the original or primal form of Buddhism, has been the dominant and typical form of monastic Buddhism in Korea for a thousand years. Likewise, Confucianism in Korea has meant only the thought of Chu Hsi, to the exclusion of all other forms of Confucianism or Neo-Confucianism, and especially the philosophy of Wang Yang-ming. Christianity has also shared in this tendency. It is a remarkable feature of Korean Christian experience that even the most sophisticated and liberal Christians would be considered to be conservative in comparison with their Western counterparts. There is a clear tendency to preserve the doctrines and practices of Christianity as they were received more than a hundred years ago.

2. The Importance of the Study of Korean Religions

If it is true that there are at least three principal themes in the history of religion in Korea – the continued influence of the primal tradition, the tendency for one tradition to dominate the others, and the general conservative nature of Korean religious experience – we next need to ask in what ways a deeper knowledge of the history of Korean spirituality will contribute to comparative religious studies. I would suggest that there are three general reasons why the intensive study of Korean spirituality is important. These are (i) the need to elucidate certain problems in the history of world religions, (ii) the need to examine the causes for the dynamism of religions in contemporary Korea, and (iii) the contribution which the study of Korean religions or Korean spirituality can make to inter-religious dialogue.

1. *The elucidation of historical problems.* In examining the religious history of East Asia, there are several issues which could be illuminated by an analysis of Korean religious history. A number of books have been written in English and other European languages about the Buddhist and Confucian traditions of Japan. The question of the transmission of and the accommodation of these traditions to Japanese culture has not been adequately examined. In particular, the rôle of Korea in the transmission of Buddhism and Confucianism to Japan has been treated only cursorily. Most materials on Japan available to the general reader give the impression that the Korean kingdoms were some sort of passive conduit for the transmission of Buddhism for only a very short period of time. The reality of the situation was that Korean Buddhists were actively involved in the development of Buddhism in Japan for over 150 years. Likewise, the rôle of Korean scholars in the transmission and development of a Confucian tradition in Japan has not been researched to any extent.

The large question of the significant part which Korean Buddhists played in the life of the Buddhist world of China has not been given the academic consideration which it deserves. Two examples will suffice to illustrate the importance of this point. From a very early period, Korean Buddhists were active in China as students, teachers, and pilgrims. To date virtually nothing has been done to develop a connected history of the impact of these men on the Buddhist communities of their time. Such knowledge would greatly increase our understanding of the growth of Chinese religion as a whole. To give another example, we know that the *T'ien-t'ai* traditions in China went into a period of decay and that they were subsequently revived through the work of the Korean monk Ch'egwan, who spent the final ten years of his life at that task. As mentioned in the initial section of these concluding remarks, it has been a curious tendency in Korean religious history that Koreans have tended to preserve cultural traits which have been lost or distorted in their homeland. Other examples of this phenomenon should be examined in detail to clarify this cultural process.

Although much has been written about *Zen*, the meditative tradition of Buddhism in Japan, very little research has been done on the history of its

Korean equivalent and antecedent, *Sŏn*. *Sŏn* has been the predominant form of monastic Buddhism in Korea since the tenth century and possesses some interesting features. In Korea, doctrinal schools as we know them in China failed to take hold. Rather, the predominant Korean tradition from the tenth century has been one of meditation, with a secondary emphasis on doctrinal and scriptural studies. Examination of the reasons for the historic pre-eminence of Sŏn Buddhism in Korea and the unique symbiosis of the approaches of meditation and study would greatly extend our knowledge of the types of Buddhist meditative practice in East Asia.

It is an interesting fact that in no other society in East Asia did Confucianism take as strong a hold on the culture as it did in Korea during the Chosŏn Dynasty. China as a continental nation with a cosmopolitan society always had many cultural factors present in it which would mitigate against the development of a monolithic society. Consequently, although Confucianism originated in China, it never had the overall impact on Chinese society that Neo-Confucianism had on Korean society. In Japan, Confucianism was primarily a concern of the ruling élite and the associated scholarly class. It is only in Korea that we find a society in which the predominant political, cultural, and social influences were – and are still to an extent – Confucian. Moreover, the Confucianism latterly accepted in Korea was not just Neo-Confucianism, but the thought of one great thinker, Chu Hsi. Unlike the situation in China, other sources of Confucian thought, such as the thinking of Wang Yang-ming, were not acceptable to the Korean literati. Why was this so? How did Neo-Confucian thought as an ideology and as a practice shape Chosŏn society? In order to make valid comments about Confucian social and cultural influence, we need a more rigorous examination of the character of a Confucian society. The study of Korea during the Chosŏn period would contribute to this end.

Korea is an ideal historical laboratory to use to compare the introduction of the two main branches of Western Christianity, Roman Catholicism and Protestantism. A consideration of the reasons for the different ways in which these two forms of Christianity developed, and especially of the later influence of Protestantism on Catholic church growth, would help us to understand the twin processes of the transmission and growth of missionary religions. Research into the transmission and growth of Christianity in Korea could then be compared with the history of Christianity in China, Japan, and other parts of East Asia.

2. *The causes for the religious dynamism of modern Korea*. When examining the contemporary religious scene in Korea, the most significant question to ask may be why contemporary Korean Christianity and Buddhism are so vital a part of modern culture. This is a question of interest especially to the comparative researcher. In Japan, monastic Buddhism would seem to be on the decline, while lay Buddhism would appear to be growing. In Korea, by contrast, monastic Buddhism and lay Buddhism are both strong, to the extent that there are various programmes for Buddhist missions to foreign lands. In Japan, it would seem that Christianity has made only insignificant gains in numbers of converts, while the

churches in Korea are growing at a phenomenal rate. Why is it that in one East Asian industrial society, religious practices would seem to be on the decline, while in another near neighbour they are flourishing? What kind of cultural, social, and economic factors might be involved? These and other questions might be resolved by further research into the contemporary Korean religious scene.

The peculiar significance of the strength of Christianity in Korea also raises the important question of its influence on the revival of Buddhism. Most foreign observers in the early part of this century felt that monastic Buddhism was dying. As indicated in the chapter above on modern Buddhism, Buddhism has not only not died, but it has revived significantly. To understand the process of the revival of Buddhism and the growth of lay Buddhist movements, it would be helpful to know more about the direct or indirect influence of Christianity on this process. Did or did not the 'modernizers' see themselves as consciously appropriating practices which were Christian in origin? Examination of this question would deepen our general understanding of the impact of Christianity on those cultures in which it has been implanted.

A final question which ought to concern the student of religion is the continued social and cultural influence of Confucianism on Korean society long after the loss of effective political influence. Confucian thought still dominates the thinking of the majority of the Korean people and it exercises a degree of influence on the folk religion, Buddhism, and Christianity. If this influence is more than a simple residual cultural influence, how are we to account for its persistence? What does this continued if indirect influence on contemporary society tell us about the effects of prior concepts and beliefs on religious traditions which are transmitted at a later date? Again, examination of the Korean experience would greatly benefit the comparative researcher looking at the general processes of religious life.

3. *The contribution to inter-religious dialogue*. The academic study of religions is undertaken not only for reasons of simple academic curiosity, but also for the understanding which may be gained about the beliefs of members of religious traditions to which one does not belong. Basic religious convictions are often the most strongly held of all beliefs, and as such it is imperative that believers of one body of faith should understand the faith of other religions. Recently, there have been a number of conferences for the purpose of encouraging dialogue between Buddhists and Christians in Korea. For the most part, these conferences are gatherings of those committed to the academic study of religion and as such, they are at a fairly high level of enquiry and are generally committed to a large measure of tolerance for the other side. This kind of academic dialogue may be compared with the kind of daily dialogue which takes place in the multi-racial, multi-cultural societies of modern North America and Europe. The Christian, formerly the dominant member of the society, now daily rubs shoulders not only with the Jew, but also with the Muslim, Sikh, Buddhist, and members of other groups. Some of these people whom he meets may even

be converts from Christianity. The dialogue which takes place on this daily basis may be characterized neither by the high level of academic commitment nor by the large measure of tolerance which would seem to be a part of academic inter-religious dialogue.

The study of Korean religions may play a significant rôle in the development of religious dialogue for several reasons. Clearer concepts of the historical development of a religion and its doctrinal convictions will always help the believer in one religion to understand more certainly why believers in other religions believe, think, and act as they do. It is because Korean religions and philosophies have played such an important rôle in the development of Buddhism and Confucianism in East Asia, because Korean society has been uniquely dominated by Confucianism, because Buddhism and Christianity remain vital and mutually competitive, because Christianity has had a disproportionate influence on the other religious traditions in the past century, because of these and other reasons Korea is a unique religious laboratory to which we may turn to seek facts about religious belief and the relation of religion to culture and society. An examination of Korean religions will not only tell us more about Korea itself but will clarify our knowledge about the religions of East Asia. Popular knowledge derived from this research will contribute to mutual understanding and to the formal and informal dialogue which goes on between believers of different religions. It is the author's hope that research into Korean religions might ultimately contribute to mutual understanding and world peace. Therefore, I hope that the reader of this book will be encouraged to delve more deeply into the riches of the religious laboratory which is Korea.

APPENDICES

Appendix A

FOUNDATION MYTHS OF THE ANCIENT STATES

Introduction

Each of the ancient states and clans had a myth which described the birth of the progenitor and his exploits in establishing the state or clan. A common feature of these myths is the divine nature of the founder. Tan'gun is the offspring of the son of the Lord of Heaven and a Bear Woman. Other figures are born from eggs and arrive in the tribal area by sea or from the heavens. Bright lights, strange vapours, and acclamation by animals usually accompany the birth of the hero. Often, the setting is in a mysterious forest, which in reality is the clan *sodo* or shaman's grove. Clearly, the clan founders were seen to be not only divine but to be intercessors or grand shamans for their people. Clan names have shamanistic characteristics. Pak Hyŏkkŏse derived his surname Pak (gourd) from the egg or gourd from which he was born; Kim Alchi derived his surname Kim (gold) from the bright light surrounding his birth. Certain elements indicate that some clans may have claimed an animal as their prime ancestor. In the Tan'gun myth, the founder Tan'gun is the offspring of a bear, while in Sŏk T'arhae's story the surname is related to the magpie. The narrative features and structures of many of these early Korean myths are typical of the folklore of eastern Siberia, but are different from Chinese folklore. However, there are some motifs which are similar to ancient Chinese myths, such as referring to gods by feudal titles such as 'earl', 'marquis', or 'lord'.

The following myths are drawn entirely from the *Samguk yusa* and are fresh translations done by the author. At the end of each myth, I have stated its source within the text of the *Samguk yusa* and provided a few words by way of commentary. Anyone wishing to have a fuller commentary on the tales, and to see the various versions of the foundation myths should refer to my recent book *Myths and Legends from Korea: An Annotated Compendium of Ancient and Modern Materials*. In the translations given here, I have tried to stay as close to the words of the original text as possible in order to give something of the flavour of the language of the myths. Where it was not possible to do so without writing very peculiar English, I have included words within square brackets to indicate that these words are my own. The editor/compiler of the *Samguk yusa*, Iryŏn (1206–89), added comments of his own to the manuscript sources which he used. I have removed most of these comments, but I have indicated his remaining insertions into the text by enclosing the words in parentheses.

1. The Myth of Tan'gun

It is written in the [*Tan'gun*] *kogi*,

'In ancient times, Hwanin (this means Chesŏk) had a *sŏja* [called] Hwanung. He desired to descend from Heaven and to possess the world of men. His father, realizing his son's intentions, descended to the three great mountains and saw that mankind would benefit [from his son's actions]. He gave his son the three *Ch'ŏn puin* and commanded him to go and rule [over mankind].

'Taking with him three thousand [spirits], Hwanung descended upon the summit of T'aebaek-san beneath the tree by the Sacred Altar. That area was called the Sacred City. He was known as Hwanung *ch'ŏnwang*. Together with the Earl of Wind, the Master of Rain, and the Master of Cloud, [Hwanung] supervised agriculture, the preservation of life, the curing of disease, punishments, the difference between right and wrong, in all some three hundred and sixty kinds of work for mankind.

'At that time, there was a bear and a tiger which lived together in a cave. They constantly petitioned Sinung [Hwanung]. They wanted to be transformed into men. Then the god gave them a piece of Sacred Mugwort and twenty pieces of garlic saying, "If you eat this and do not see light for one hundred days, you will receive a human form." The bear and the tiger took [the plants] and ate. They fasted for three times seven days. The bear received a woman's body. The tiger was not able to fast and did not receive a human body.

'As there was no one with whom the woman Ungnyŏ [Bear Woman] could marry, she went daily to the base of the tree by the altar to pray for a child. Hwanung changed [his form] and married her. She became pregnant and had a son. He was called Tan'gun wang'gŏm. In the fiftieth year of the Emperor Yao, in the reign year *Kyŏngin*, Tan'gun established a city at P'yŏngyang and called the nation Chosŏn. He later moved his city to Asadal on Paegak-san which was also known as Kunghol-san and also as Kŭmmidal. He governed [the nation] for 1,500 years. King Hu of Chou in the reign year *Chi-mao*, enfeoffed Kija with [the state of] Chosŏn. Tan'gun then transferred to Changdang-gyŏng. Later, he returned to Asadal, hid himself, and became the Mountain God. [At this time,] he was 1,908 years of age.'

Samguk yusa, Part 1.1, *Ko Chosŏn, Wanggŏm Chosŏn.*

Analysis of the Myth of Tan'gun

This myth is a complex foundation myth describing the origin of the people, the state, the ruling house and the culture of the people but assumes the pre-existence of the world and of mankind. There are four ancient versions of this myth, two from the thirteenth century (in the *Samguk yusa,* and the *Chewang un'gi*) and two from the fifteenth century (in the *Ŭngje-si*, and the *Sejong sillok*). The five scenes plus one redacted scene in the myth form a coherent narrative structure consisting of the following structural elements – discussion betweeen father and son in Heaven, descent of the son to earth, trial of the bear and tiger, union of heavenly and earthly spirits, creation of the state of Chosŏn, change of dynasty / origin of the Mountain God cult. The motif of the descent of the son of the Ruler of Heaven, Hwanin, in the first scene shows that the political, social and cultural characteristics of the nation are the result of Hwanin's gracious act of sending down his son. Descent of the spirits is a typical element in modern Korean shamanistic ceremonies. The myth implies that the royal house which gave the people their civilization was descended from the Ruler of Heaven and therefore had a special relationship to Heaven. This shamanistic feature is reinforced by the geographic setting of the tale. T'aebaek-san, on the border of modern China and north Korea, is depicted in the myth as a univerisal axis linking Heaven and earth. Likewise the motif of the tree by the Sacred Altar is also a symbol of a link between Heaven and earth. These motifs are similar to descriptions in the ancient Chinese work the *Shan-hai Ching* which depicts shamans ascending to and descending from Heaven on top of the Kun-lun mountain range in China. The compiler of the Tan'gun myth, a Buddhist monk, refers to Hwanin the Ruler of Heaven as Chesŏk, who is Indra, one of the three great deities of Vedic Hinduism and the sustainer of existence. In the Myth of Tan'gun, the son is described as a *sŏja*, a second son or secondary son, a child who stands little chance of succeeding his father, thus explaining his desire to leave Heaven. The three *Ch'ŏn puin* (Heavenly seals) which the father gives to his son are not described but clearly symbolise the authority of the son to rule. In the second scene, Hwanung is depicted as the great culture bearer with a vast retinue of assistants, the chief of whom are given feudal titles such as 'earl' or 'master' (= lord), a descriptive feature of many ancient Chinese myths. Hwanung is referred to by a sacred title, 'Heavenly King' or *ch'ŏnwang* and his place of residence is called a sacred city. In the third scene, a conflict between various clans over the kingship is symbolised by the trial of the bear and tiger and the marriage of the former clan with the solar clan (represented by Hwanin) in the fourth scene. The foods given to the bear and the tiger are clearly sacred while the use of the numbers 'three' and 'seven' is a ritualised formula. In modern Siberia, animals such as the bear and tiger are said to be the progenitors of clans, a feature shared in this myth with the use of the term Ungyŏ or 'Bear Woman' for Tan'gun's mother. The final scene in this redacted myth explains how the Tan'gun dynasty, a sacred royal line, fell from power and was replaced by another line, additionally explaining how the cult of the Mountain God, the master of all Korean mountains, originated. In this final scene, we move from mythic time to history symbolised by the use of Chinese dynastic chronology. Thus, the Myth of Tan'gun, the quintessential Korean foundation myth, is rich in symbols drawing on ancient Chinese, Buddhist and shamanistic elements to explain the origin of the culture, nation and political system of Ancient Chosŏn.

241

2. Foundation Myth of Northern Puyŏ

It is written in an old book,

'According to the *History of the Former Han Dynasty, Ch'ŏnje* [heavenly ruler] descended to the Hŏlsŭnggol Fortress riding in a chariot driven by five dragons. This was in the third year of the reign era *Shen-jue* of the Emperor Hsüan-ti, the eighth day of the fourth month of the year *Jen-wu*. He made himself king and established his capital [there]. The name of the nation was Northern Puyŏ. The king took the name Hae Mosu. The king had a son whose name was Puru and who took Hae as his own surname. The king, hearing the command of Sangje [Chinese, Shang-ti = Supreme Ruler], moved the capital to Eastern Puyŏ. The ruler Tongmyŏng became king and established the capital at Cholbon-ju. The nation became known as Cholbon Puyŏ, and Tongmyŏng was the first ancestor of Koguryŏ.'

Samguk yusa, Part 1.12, *Puk Puyŏ.*

Analysis of the Myth

This simple myth uses the motif of the heavenly descent of the primal ancestor of the ruling family to explain the origin of the political system of the nation while at the same time providing divine authorisation for the removal of the nation to another geographical spot. A voice from Heaven speaks directly to the king who responds. As with the final scene in the Myth of Tan'gun, the time setting has been fixed within a Chinese dynastic chronology.

3. Foundation Myth of Eastern Puyŏ

Aranbul, prime minister of the King of Northern Puyŏ had a dream in which *Ch'ŏnje* descended [to earth] and said to him, 'My descendants will establish a nation in this place. Go to another land. By the East Sea, there is a land called Kasŏbwŏn which is very fertile, go and establish your royal city there.' Aranbul told the king [of his dream] and he moved his royal city to the place [which the god had commanded]. The nation became known as Eastern Puyŏ. When King Puru was old, he was [still] without a son. Every day, he prayed to [the gods of] the mountains and rivers. One day when the horse the king was riding reached Konyŏn, it stopped, looked at a large stone and began to shed tears. The king thought this strange and ordered a servant to turn over the stone. There was a boy in the form of a golden frog. The king was happy, saying, 'Heaven has blessed me with a son.' The boy was called Kŭmwa [Golden Frog]. When Kŭmwa became a man, he was made crown prince. After Puru died, Kŭmwa became king. [After Kŭmwa], the throne passed to the crown prince, Taeso. In the third year of *Ti-huang*, in the year *Imo*, Muhyul called Taemu *sinwang*, King of Ko[gu]ryŏ, invaded [the nation], killing Taeso. The nation [of Eastern Puyŏ] was destroyed [then].

Samguk yusa, Part 1.13, *Tong Puyŏ.*

Analysis of the Myth

This myth like the previous two myths contains the motif of the descent of a divine being which, unlike in those myths, is used to explain not the origin of the nation and its ruling family, but to explain why the nation had to move its location. The story, as before, is set within a Chinese chronology. The succession to the kingship is determined by an act of divination and the discovery of a strange child, Kŭmwa. His name implies that the ruling clan may have claimed the frog as their primal ancestor. The use of the title *sinwang* or 'holy king' to describe the King of Koguryŏ implies that he is of divine descent.

4. Foundation Myth of Koguryŏ

When Kŭmwa had been traversing through the southern side of the T'aebaek Mountains, he came across a girl at the Ubal River and spoke with her. She said that she was the daughter of Habaek [Earl of the River] and that her name was Yuhwa. The girl told Kŭmwa that one day when she was playing with her younger siblings, a man came to her and said that he was Hae Mosu son of *Ch'ŏnje*. She said that he had taken her to a house on the Yalu River just beneath Ungsin-san [Bear Spirit Mountain], committed adultery with her, and had not returned [since that time].

'My parents scolded me for having relations with a man without a go-between, and banished me to this place.' Thinking this very strange, Kŭmwa secluded [the girl] in a room, but the sun's rays shone in. The light caressed her body, she became pregnant and gave birth to an egg which was said to be five *sŭng* [4.75 litres] in size. The king threw the egg away, giving it to the dogs and pigs, but they would not eat it. He put it out on the road, but the cows and horses avoided it. The king threw it out on the field but the birds and the beasts would not tread on it. The king tried to smash the egg but was unable to do so and gave the egg back to its mother. The mother wrapped [the egg] up in cloth and placed it in a warm spot. A child broke open the shell and came out. His physique and outward appearance seemed unusual and full of wisdom. When the child was seven years old, he was precocious and unlike ordinary children. By himself he could make his own bows and arrows. If he shot a hundred times, he hit the target a hundred times. He was called Chumong, which in the language of that people means good shot.

Kŭmwa had seven sons but none were the equal of Chumong. The eldest son, Taeso, said to the king that Chumong was not a human child and that if he were not done away with now there would be problems later. The king would not listen to this advice and commanded Chumong to raise the horses. Chumong knew a fine horse and gave it little to eat making it thin. He gave the duller horses more to eat and made them fat. The king rode the fat horses while he gave the lean horses to Chumong. Chumong's mother learned that several of the king's sons and officials wished to kill him. She said to him, 'People wish to kill you.

Since you are resourceful, there isn't anywhere you couldn't go and live. Go, flee quickly.' Chumong took O'i and two other friends and fled to the River Ŏm. He announced to the waters, 'I am the son of the Ruler of Heaven, the descendant of the Earl of the River. Today I must flee; my pursuers are nigh; what shall I do?' Then the river fishes and terrapin formed a bridge over which he crossed. They then dispersed and the pursuers were unable to cross [the river].

Chumong came to Cholbon-ju and established his capital there. He had to build his royal residence but there was no time to do so. He built a house above the River Piryu and resided there. The name of the nation was Koguryŏ and Chumong took 'Ko' as his surname. (His original surname was 'Hae', but as he claimed to be the son of the Ruler of Heaven because of being born through the agency of sunlight, he took the surname Ko.) At this time, when he was twelve, he became king. This was in the second year of the *Chien-chao* reign era of the Emperor Hsiao-yüan of Han, or the year *Kapsin*. At this time, Koguryŏ consisted of 210,508 households.

Samguk yusa, Part 1.14, *Koguryŏ*.

Analysis of the Myth

This myth does not utilise the motif of descent of the god to explain the origin of the royal family, but instead uses the motif of oviparous birth to imply that their origins are in fact divine. Here the progenitor of the nation shows himself early on to be a hero by performing great feats such as the breaking open of his egg, and being a prodigious shot. This myth bears some resemblance to heroic tales told in the Mediterranean area where the hero is forced to flee his natal place. Unlike those myths where the hero returns to wreak his revenge, in the case of the Myth of Chumong the hero goes off with his followers to establish a new nation.

5. The Myth of Pak Hyŏkkŏse, Progenitor of Silla

On the first day of the third month of the first year of the reign era *Ti-chieh* of the Former Han Dynasty, the year *Imja*, the ancestors of the six clans took their descendants to a rock above the Ai River and began to discuss. They said that their people lacked a prince to govern them. Everyone did as he wished. It was necessary to find a person of virtue, create him king, found a nation, and establish a seat of royal residence. From the height they looked south to the Na-jŏng well at the base of the mountain Yang-san. They saw a strange vapour and a flash of light shining by the ground. There was a white horse nearby which seemed to be bowing. They went to that spot and found a red egg (some say a blue egg). The horse upon seeing the people gave a great cry and flew up to Heaven. Breaking open the egg, a finely formed, beautiful child emerged. Filled with wonder, they took the child to the Tong-ch'ŏn stream and gave him a bath whereupon a light shone from his body. Birds and beasts followed them dancing;

the heavens and earth shook; the sun and the moon shone brightly. The people called him King Hyŏkkŏse. His reign title was *kosŏlgan*.

The people contended in their praises [of the boy] saying, 'Now a *ch'ŏnja* has descended. He should marry a *nyŏgun* of virtue.' On that day, in the Aryŏng-jŏng well near Saryang-ni village, a *kyeryong* appeared and gave birth to a girl from her left side. Her head was beautifully formed, but her mouth was like the beak of a chicken. When the people took her to bathe in the Puk-ch'ŏn stream near Wŏl-sŏng fortress, the beak fell off. So they called the river P'al-ch'ŏn.

A palace was erected by the base of Nam-san and the sacred children were raised there. The egg from which the prince had been born was like a gourd. Because the local people called a gourd *pak*, the prince was given the surname of Pak. The princess took her name from the well from which she had emerged. When the two holy ones became thirteen, in the first year of the reign era *Wu-feng*, the year *Kapja*, the boy became king and the girl became his consort.

The country was called Sŏrabŏl or Sŏbŏl, and was also known as Sara or Saro. It is said that because the king was born from the Kye-jŏng, the nation was called Kyerim-guk. This was also suggested because he was born from a *kyeryong*. According to one tradition, in the time of King T'arhae when the king took in Kim Alchi, a cock crowed in the forest and for that reason the nation's name was changed to Kyerim. In a later time, the name of the nation was changed to Silla.

After reigning for sixty-two years, King Hyŏkkŏse ascended to Heaven. After seven days, his ashes fell from Heaven and scattered on the earth. His wife followed him. The people attempted to bury the couple in the same tomb but a great snake came out and prevented this. The remains were divided into five parts, separate funerals offered, and the O-nŭng [Five Tombs] was built to bury the remains. The tombs were also known as the Sa-nŭng [Snake Tombs]. This is precisely the Pung-nŭng [North Tombs] of the Tamŏm-sa temple. The crown prince, Namhae, succeeded [his father] as king.

Samguk yusa, Part 1.18, *Silla-jo, Hyŏkkŏse-wang.*

Analysis of the Myth

This myth explains both the origin of kingship in Silla, and the origin of the initial ruling clan. Hyŏkkŏse's oviparous birth is signalled by heavenly signs – strange lights, vapours and a horse which flies up to Heaven. Further proof of the divine selection of the child who is found inside the egg is given by the universal acclamation by Nature to his arrival. This story is unusual in that it also provides a separate narrative about the origin of the first royal consort. The king-to-be is called a *ch'ŏnja* [heavenly child] while the consort is called a *nyŏgun*, a princess. They are both said to be the offspring of a kyeryong [chicken-dragon = flying dragon], born near sacred wells. The reference to a forest (and sacred wells) in this tale and in the tale of Kim Alchi is to the clan sodo or forest glade where the clan shaman resided. As with other Korean foundation myths, the narrative of

245

this myth ties the events of the tale into Chinese historical chronology and provides extensive etymologies about the origin of the clan name, as well as the etymology of the name of the nation.

6. The Myth of Sŏk T'arhae, Sŏk Clan Progenitor

This is the story of T'arhae nijilgŭm. In the time of King Namhae, a boat came to the shores of Karak-kuk. King Suro and the people [of Karak-kuk] beat drums to encourage the boat to stay but it sailed on and stopped at the port of Ajin-p'o near Hasŏji-ch'on village in eastern Kyerim. On the shore was an ancient woman, Ajinŏisŏn who caught fish for King Hyŏkkŏ[se]. She thought to herself that it was strange that although there was no rock in the sea, magpies had gathered and were crying out. She took her boat and went and investigated. She found the magpies atop a boat in the middle of which was a box which measured 20 ch'ŏk [6.14 metres] in length and 13 ch'ŏk [4 meters] in width. She took the boat to a grove of trees. As she wished to know her fortune, Ajinŏisŏn prayed to Heaven for good luck. She opened the box and found a well-formed boy, seven treasures, and male and female slaves.

After they had been entertained for seven days, the boy said, 'I am a man of Yongsŏng-guk. Our nation has had twenty-eight dragon-kings, all of whom were born of the wombs of humans. At the age of five or six they became kings and instructed the people in virtue. Because [we follow] the eight characteristics of descent, they became kings without election. My father, King Hamdalp'a, married the daughter of the King of Chŏngnyŏ-guk. As he had wanted a son for a very long time, he prayed for a son. After seven years, a great egg was born. The king said to his advisors that as neither in the past nor in the present could one hear of a human giving birth to an egg, it was undoubtedly a bad omen. He ordered a boat constructed, placed me in it along with the seven treasures and the male and female slaves, and set it out on the sea. He hoped that I might go to a land of destiny, found a nation, and make my home there. Then a red dragon appeared and led me to this place.'

No sooner had the boy said this, than he took up a walking-stick and led his slaves to the top of T'oham-san mountain where he built a cave. From there for seven days he looked over the city [of Kyŏngju] seeking for a suitable place to live. He found a house shaped like a crescent moon and decided it would be a fine place to live. He went down [the hill] and discovered that it was the home of [the nobleman] P'ogong. The boy decided to play a deceitful trick, He buried a whetstone and some charcoal by the side of the house and on the following day went to the door of the home and announced that it was the home of his ancestors. P'ogong said that it was not so, and as they could not resolve their dispute, they went before a judge. When the judge asked the boy what evidence he had that it was his ancestors' home, the boy replied, 'My ancestors were traditionally blacksmiths. While they were away in the country, someone else came in and began to live in their house. If you dig up the ground there will be evidence [of what I say].' When they dug up the ground, a whetstone and charcoal were found, and so the boy was able to live there.

King Namhae knew of T'arhae's cleverness and married his eldest daughter to him. This was Lady Ani. One day, T'arhae went up the mountain Tong-gu and on the way down ordered his wife to fetch him some water. Lady Ani fetched the water but on the way back took a drink herself. The fish-shaped cup stuck to her lips. Her husband scolded her for doing this and when she had promised not to taste [the water] before [giving it to her husband], the vessel fell from her lips. Because she was frightened, the girl never again tried to fool [her husband]. There is a well on Tong'ak mountain called Yonae-jŏng which is precisely the well of this story.

In the sixth year of the *Chung-yüan* era of Emperor Kuang-hu, in the sixth month, in the year *Chŏngsa*, King Norye died and [T'arhae] became king. Because he had said that a home which was not his belonged to his ancestors and thus stole someone's home, T'arhae took the surname Sŏk [ancient]. It is also said that as it was the presence of magpies which had led to the opening of the box, T'arhae took the character for magpie and removed the character for bird in it to make the surname. It is [also] said that as he came out of a box and was born from an egg, T'arhae took the name T'arhae [to throw off]. In the fourth year of the *Chien-ch'u* reign era, in the year *Kimyo*, T'arhae died after reigning for twenty-three years. He was buried on Soch'ŏn-gu hill. Afterwards, there was a spirit voice which said, 'Bury my bones with care.' The circumference of his head was 3 *ch'ŏk* and 2 *ch'on* [99 cm.] and the length of his body was 9 *ch'ŏk* and 7 *ch'on* [2.98 metres]. The bones had become hardened and joined into one. Truly, he was a titan under Heaven. They washed his bones and made a clay image of T'arhae which was kept in the palace. Again, the spirit came and spoke, saying, 'Remove my bones to the hill Tong-gu', which was done with reverence.

Samguk yusa, Part 1.21, *T'arhae wang*.

Analysis of the Myth

This myth uses the idea of the oviparous birth of the hero and his expulsion by boat from his homeland to explain how he and his descendants became rulers of the Kingdom of Silla. These two motifs are commonly used in myths along the south coast of Korea to explain the origin of ruling families, along with the motif of the descent from Heaven. For the first time in a Korean foundation myth, we also see that the hero is a trickster, using his wit to gain a place in society, and subsequently to obtain the right to succeed the king on the throne. The narrative is also rich in details about ritual propriety in dynastic succession and the relationships between husband and wife. Unusually, we twice see the use of the motif of a voice from Heaven giving instructions to humans, in this case with regard to the placement of the deceased king's body, which reinforces the divine character of the king. The character *sŏk* literally means old or ancient and must refer to an attempt by the clan members to indicate the antiquity of their line, possibly *vis-à-vis* the Kyŏngju Pak clan, the putative founders of the state. The gloss in the text about removing the right-hand side of the character for magpie indicates the family must also have claimed the magpie as their primal ancestor. As birds are a shamanistic motif, it may be assumed that the Sŏk clan founder was a great shaman. The magpie is also an auspicious bird. Even today, Koreans say that when starting out on a journey if one first sees a magpie the journey will be successful, that one will receive blessings.

7. The Myth of Kim Alchi, Kyŏngju Kim Clan Progenitor

On the fourth day of the eighth month of the third year of the reign era *Yung-p'ing*, the year *Kyŏngsin*, P'ogong was travelling some four *li* [2.2 km.] from Wŏl-sŏng at night when he saw a strange light coming from Si-rim (also called Kye-rim). There were purple clouds descending from Heaven, and in the middle of the purple clouds there was a golden box which was at the base of a tree. Beside the box wreathed in clouds, there was a white cock which was crowing. All of this P'ogong told to the king. The king went to the forest and opened the box. Inside there was a boy lying down who woke up. Recalling the story of Hyŏkkŏse, the king called the boy Alchi, which means in our language a young boy. The king embraced the boy and carried him back to the palace while animals and birds followed behind dancing for joy. The king selected an auspicious day and created the boy crown prince. Later [Kim Alchi] gave way to P'asa and never himself became king. Because he came out of a golden box, he took the surname Kim [gold]. Alchi begat Yŏrhan, who begat Ado, who begat Suryu, who begat Ukpu, who begat Kudo, who begat Mich'u who became king. Thus, the Kim clan of Silla began with Alchi.

Samguk yusa, Part 1.22, *Kim Alchi, T'arhae wangdae*.

Analysis of the Myth

This brief foundation myth is rich in mythic depiction containing all the familiar motifs found in Korean myths such as strange lights, strangely coloured vapours or clouds, golden boxes, shining birds, trees, and the acclamation by Nature of the hero. Although at first explaining the way in which the clan progenitor was divinely approved for kingship, the myth also explains why the progenitor did not actually succeed to the throne. This narrative well illustrates the struggle between different clans to obtain the rulership, which eventually became settled in the Kim clan which produced the greatest number of Silla's kings.

Appendix B

RELIGIOUS STATISTICS
AND COMMENTARY

The National Population Household Census for 1995 (Table 1) reveals that the respondents who self-identified themselves as being members of the religious population of Korea accounted for only about one-half (approximately 50.7 per cent) of the entire national population. Among the features of the religious section of the census questionnaire are the designation of certain religious organisations to appear among the questions asked, the provision of an open-ended response for religious bodies which are not amongst the designated organisations, and the request for information about the religious affiliation for children beginning from the age of year '0'. The way in which this part of the Census was conducted and its results reported leaves open a number of questions.

Table 1 Summary of the 1995 National Population Household Census

Type of religion	Total adherents	% of population	Male adherents	% of population	Female adherents	% of population
Buddhism	10,321,012	23.2	4,870,853	10.9	5,450,159	12.2
Protestantism	8,760,336	19.7	4,087,356	9.2	4,672,980	10.5
Catholicism	2,950,730	6.6	1,339,295	3.0	1,611,435	3.6
Confucianism	210,927	neg.	113,951	neg.	96,976	neg.
Wŏn Buddhism	86,823	neg.	39,555	neg.	47,268	neg.
Ch'ŏndo-gyo	28,184	neg.	13,215	neg.	14,969	neg.
Taejong-gyo	7,603	neg.	3,642	neg.	3,961	neg.
Taesun Chilli-gyo	62,056	neg.	28,916	neg.	33,140	neg.
Miscellaneous	170,153	neg.	76,645	neg.	93,508	neg.
No religion	21,953,315	49.3	11,782,401	26.4	10,170,914	22.8
Unknown	2,571	neg.	1,523	neg.	1,048	neg.
Total population	44,553,710	100.00	22,357,352	–	22,196,358	–

Note: Due to the rounding of the raw statistical figures, the percentages do not necessarily add up to one hundred per cent. Figures too small for a significant statistical comparison are designated as being 'negligible', or *neg.*

249

First, because children under the age of fifteen are included in the gross statistics, the statistics as presented only give an indication of the size of the communities of adherents to a particular religion including all members of their families rather than an indication of all people who self-identify as members of a particular group or faith. Second, there is a large group of people identified as belonging to miscellaneous groups. Because there is an open-ended question in the questionnaire, it would have been useful if the persons preparing the report of the Census had included in the report statistics on those organisations which do not appear as an option in the questionnaire. For example, we know that there is a sizeable Korean Muslim community, and also that there is a small community of Orthodox Christians. It would have been interesting to know the size of the Muslims and Orthodox Christians as they would appear to be as large as some of the designated groups whose statistics are reported in the Census. In addition, there may be other groups which are not reported. Third, the category 'No Religion' is nearly as large as the religious population (approximately 49.3 per cent of the national population). This group is assuredly not just the numbers of atheists and agnostics in Korea. The author strongly suspects that in this category may be found a large number of people who, because they didn't fit any of the designated categories, or who did not feel that they belonged to any organised religion as such, put themselves down or were put down by the census recorder as having no religion. 'No Religion' in this case must mean no attachment to a designated religious organisation. I think that most of the people in this category are in fact practitioners of the cults of folk religion and other traditional practices. This point also raises an issue with regard to the Buddhist statistics. It is known that many of the followers of shamanistic practices will refer to their beliefs as being 'Buddhist', and consequently some people may have self-identified themselves as being Buddhist. Fourth, there are also issues regarding the Protestant statistics. In previous reports, the author has seen cases where statistics for Protestantism included figures for the Unification Church, the Mormon Church and the Jehovah's Witnesses which on strict theological grounds (Christology) are not mainline denominations but new religious movements. Are groups such as those included in the Protestant statistics in this Census, or are they (or some of them) included in the miscellaneous category?

Even taking into consideration these problems, the Census does reveal some interesting characteristics about the practice of religion in Korea at the end of the twentieth century. First, the identified religious population of Korea constitutes about 50.7 per cent of the total national population. Adjusting the statistics by eliminating all children under the age of fifteen, the proportion between the general population and the religious population remains similar at 49.5 per cent. Second, of those people who identified themselves as adhering to an organised form of religion, 51.8 per cent claimed to belong to a Christian denomination, six per cent more than the 45.7 per cent of the respondents who claimed adherence to a form of Buddhism. Third, there were usually more female adherents of a religious group than male adherents, although the difference was not great. The female/male differential in Buddhism was 52.8 per cent versus 47.2 per cent, in Protestantism 53.3 per cent versus 46.7 per cent, and in Catholicism, 54.6 per cent versus 45.4. This same gender distribution held true for the minor designated religions. The gender distribution amongst the designated religious traditions is striking because the female/male sex ratio in the general population is the reverse of this profile at 49.8 females to 50.2 males per hundred members of the population. The only case where the religious gender distribution was reversed is Confucianism where the female/male ratio is 46 per cent versus 54 per cent. What is interesting in this case is not that there are more male adherents, given the emphasis on the male in Confucianism, but the high proportion of females who self-identified as being Confucianists. Even allowing for the 'family' principle, this is a very high percentage. Interestingly enough, this same proportion of gender distribution held true for those listed as of 'No Religion' with a female/male ratio of 46.3 per cent versus 53.7. This category, however, is problematic as mentioned above because it contains information about the practitioners of traditional religion and those who are genuinely agnostics or atheists, as well as those who have made no conscious choice one way or the other.

The Census (Table 2) also reveals interesting characteristics regarding the age distribution of the different designated religious traditions. Christianity in its Protestant and Catholic forms is primarily a young religion in terms of its age composition. Taking together all adults and youth above the age of fifteen, 72.5 per cent of self-identified Protestants are between fifteen and forty-four years of ago. Catholic respondents produce a similar result at 69.2 per cent. This compares with an age profile of 60.2 per cent for self-identified Buddhists. Thus, the three major religious traditions have a generally young profile, but Christians tend to be even younger compared with Buddhists. Indeed, Protestant statistics indicate that the largest single group of adherents is found amongst the youngest

Table 2 Age Distribution of Different Religions (Adults and Youth 15 and Above)

Religious Group	Percentage of Age Group 15–24	25–34	35–44	45–54	55–64	65–
Buddhism	17.7	19.4	23.1	16.9	13.4	9.4
Protestantism	26.5	23.6	22.4	13.2	8.1	6.8
Catholicism	22.9	21.3	25	14.2	8.8	7.7
Confucianism	11	11.6	13.3	17.3	24.8	22.3
Wŏn Buddhism	18.5	17.8	20.1	16.1	14.1	13.5
Ch'ŏndo-gyo	18.3	19.9	18.8	13.8	14	15.2
Taejong-gyo	20.2	16.6	19.8	16.3	14.1	12.9
Taesun Chilli-gyo	20	27.4	23	13.4	9.7	6.6

group, persons aged between fifteen and twenty-four years. This group accounts for more than a quarter of all self-identified Protestants. Self-identified Confucianists, on the other hand, show a reverse age profile with 64.4 per cent of the respondents being 45 years of age or over. Taesun Chilli-gyo, a development of Chŭngsan-gyo, shows a different age profile from the other minor designated traditions which generally have a profile of around 50 per cent below the age of 45. However, respondents identifying themselves as members of Taesun Chilli-gyo, and who are between fifteen and forty-four years of age, account for 70.4 per cent of its self-identified membership, giving it an age profile which is similar to Protestantism. This confirms the general impression of a revival of interest in this group and its teaching. It would be useful to have an educational profile of this group as it is often thought that it has gained a large number of its recent converts from amongst university students.

In the table below (Table 3), the different designated religious traditions are compared as a proportion of the regional population. The Sŏul Metropolitan Region includes the self-governing cities of Sŏul and Inch'ŏn as well as the surrounding province of Kyŏnggi-do. The eastern region refers to the province of Kangwŏn-do on the east coast, the central region to the provinces of North Ch'ungch'ŏng-do and South Ch'ungch'ŏng-do and the self-governing city of Taejŏn, the southwest region to the provinces of North Chŏlla-do and South Chŏlla-do and the self-governing city of Kwangju, and the southeast region to the provinces of North Kyŏngsang-do and South Kyŏngsang-do and the self-governing cities of Taegu and Pusan.

This table shows that in those places where Buddhism is strong, Christianity tends to be weaker and vice versa. In the area of the nation's capital, Christianity

Table 3 Religions as a Proportion of Regional Populations

Type of religion	Sŏul Metropolitan Region	East	Central	Southwest	Southeast	Cheju-do
Buddhism	18	23.2	22	13.5	35.7	34.6
Christianity	33.6	21.2	24.2	28.9	15.5	14.3
Protestantism	25.2	16.2	18.5	22.9	10.9	8.3
Catholicism	8.4	5	5.7	6	4.6	6
Confucianism	0.003	0.005	0.005	1.1	0.004	0.004
Wŏn Buddhism	0.0001	neg.	neg.	0.007	0.001	0.004
Ch'ŏndo-gyo	neg.	neg.	neg.	neg.	neg.	neg.
Taejong-gyo	neg.	neg.	neg.	neg.	neg.	neg.
Taesun Chilli-gyo	neg.	neg.	neg.	neg.	0.001	neg.
Miscellaneous	0.004	0.003	0.003	0.003	0.005	0.004

represents a third of the population, or nearly twice the size of the Buddhist groups in the same area. In the southeast and on the island of Cheju-do, the situation is reversed. In the eastern and central region of the Republic of Korea, there is rough parity between Buddhism and Christianity. Generally, the proportion of Catholics to Protestants throughout the country tends to be on the order of one to three except in Cheju-do where the Catholic population is about three-quarters the size of the Protestant community. Confucianism generally represents three to five tenths of one per cent of any of the regional populations except for the southwest where the representation of Confucianism within the population is more than twice the national average. This is particularly interesting in contrast with the southeast region which has often been depicted as being a particularly Confucian and conservative sector of the nation. Interestingly enough, it is this same southwest region in which Buddhism is strongest and Christianity weakest. It is also in this region that Wŏn Buddhism and Taesun Chilli-gyo have a representation within the population which rises above statistical negligibility. Both of these movements arose in this area, and Wŏn Buddhism currently has its headquarters there and its associated university. Doing a separate calculation (not shown) for the self-governing municipalities apart from their regions indicates that the proportion within the populations for the various religious traditions remains the same except for the representation of Confucianism in the population of the city of Kwangju in the southwest. At 4.4 per cent, it is half the regional representation of Confucianism, but still twice the national average for self-governing municipalities, again pointing out the strength of Confucianism in the southwest area. Taking all of these observations together along with some of the points made in earlier paragraphs, they point to the general fact that Christianity is strongest proportionately in the capital region, the area of the country which is the most highly urbanised and undergoing the greatest social change, whereas Buddhism is strongest in the most traditional areas of the country. Moreover, Protestantism has the highest proportion of any religious tradition amongst the youngest group of adults and youth.

The final table (Table 4), which takes the regional self-identified member-ship of different groups as a proportion of the groups' national adherency, indicates that all groups have a strong presence in the nation's capital, and usually with a strength which is greater than in any other part of the country. The only exceptions to this observation are Buddhism and Wŏn Buddhism which find their greatest strength in either the southeastern or southwestern part of the nation. It is interesting to note that the traditional religions of the country are weaker in the capital than in comparison with new religious movements, either Christianity in its Protestant or Roman Catholic forms or movements such as Ch'ŏndo-gyo or Taesun Chilli-gyo. Furthermore, certain traditions such as Wŏn Buddhism and Ch'ŏndo-gyo remain strongest in those parts of the country in which they originated. Confucianism maintains its comparative strength in the southwest and the southeast with a proportion of its membership

Table 4 Regional Religious Adherence as a Proportion of National Adherence

Type of religion	Sŏul Metropolitan Region	East	Central	Southwest	Southeast	Cheju-do
Buddhism	35.2	3.3	9.4	6.8	44.2	1.6
Protestantism	58	2.7	9.3	13.6	15.8	0.004
Catholicism	57	2.6	8.6	10.8	20	1
Confucianism	30	4.1	11.1	27.6	26.1	1
Wŏn Buddhism	27.7	0.007	6	45.3	18.3	0.008
Ch'ŏndo-gyo	45.8	3.2	10.6	11.7	27.9	0.008
Taejong-gyo	48.3	4.3	11.1	11.3	24.6	0.003
Taesun Chilli-gyo	47.1	2.5	12.5	7.1	29.6	1.2
Miscellaneous	42.8	2.8	7.7	10.2	35.2	1.5

in both regions which is equivalent to its strength in the capital. This chart also shows that there are certain regions of the country, such as the eastern, central and Cheju Island areas, which remain peripheral or of less importance to all traditions.

SELECT BIBLIOGRAPHY

Because this book has been written as a general introduction to the subject of the history of religion in Korea, the following bibliography contains works mostly in English and in other Western languages. Works in the Korean language are principally general works on various subjects or important primary resources. The bibliography is also not comprehensive, but a selection of readily available materials. For further works, interested readers should consult generalist and specialist journals such as *Acta Koreana, Asian Folklore Studies, History of Religion, Journal of Asian Studies, Journal of Korean Studies, Korea Journal, Korean Studies, Religion, Transactions of the Korea Branch of the Royal Asiatic Society* and other sources.

1. Reference and General Works

Academy of Korean Studies, *Han'guk munhwa tae paekkwa sajŏn* [Encyclopaedia of Korean Culture], 27 vols. (Sŏngnam, Korea, Academy of Korean Studies, 1994).

Chindan hakhoe [Chindae Society], *Han'guk-sa* [History of Korea], 7 vols. (Sŏul, Ilchi munhwa-sa, 1959).

Ch'oe, Sŏgu, ed., *Han'guk kat'ollik tae sajŏn* [A Dictionary of Korean Catholicism], 2 vols. (Sŏul, Han'guk kyohoe yŏn'gu-so, 1985).

Courant, Maurice, *Bibliographie Coréenne* (Paris, E. Leroux, 1894–6).

Eliade, Mircea, et al, eds., *The Encyclopedia of Religion*, 16 vols. (London, Macmillian, 1987).

Hanayama, Shinsho, *Bibliography on Buddhism* (Tōkyō, Hokuseido, 1961).

Hasting, James, et al, eds., *Encyclopaedia of Religion and Ethics*, 13 vols. (Edinburgh, T & T Clark, 1908–26).

Kang, Man'gil, et al, eds., *Han'guk-sa* [History of Korea], 27 vols. (Sŏul, Korea Univ. Press, 1994).

Kim, Han-kyo, *Studies on Korea: A Scholar's Guide* (Honolulu, Univ. of Hawaii Press, 1980).

Kim, Tai-jin, *A Bibliographical Guide to Traditional Korean Sources* (Sŏul, Korea Univ. Press, 1976).

Kuksa p'yŏnch'an wiwŏn-hoe [National History Compilation Committee, South Korea], *Han'guk-sa* [History of Korea] 25 vols. (Sŏul, 1981).

Marcus, Richard, ed., *Korean Studies Guide* (Berkeley, Univ. of California Press, 1954).

Murphy, Sunny, and Yi Myung-hui, *Koreana Collection* (Sŏul, United States Eighth Army Yongsan Library, 1982).

Pratt, Keith and Richard Rutt, *Korea: A Historical and Cultural Dictionary* (London, Curzon, 1999).

Sahoe kwahak-wŏn, yŏksa yŏn'gu-so [Historical Research Centre, Academy of Social Science, North Korea], *Chosŏn chŏnsa* [A Complete History of Korea], 15 vols. (P'yŏngyang, 1979).

Shulman, Frank Joseph, *Japan and Korea: An Annotated Bibliography of Doctoral Dissertations in Western Languages, 1877–1970* (Chicago, American Library Association, 1970).

Song, Minako I., and Masato Matsui, *Japanese Sources on Korea in Hawaii* (Honolulu, Center for Korean Studies, 1980).

Wallace, Anthony F. C., *Religion: An Anthropological View* (New York, Random House, 1966).

—— 'Revitalization Movements', *American Anthropologist*, 58 (1956), 264–81.

Yi, Hongjik, *Kuksa tae sajŏn* [Encyclopedia of Korean History], 5 vols. Sŏul, Paengman-sa, 1973).

—— *Chungbo sae kuksa sajŏn* [A New Encyclopedia of Korean History, Enlarged] (Sŏul, Ch'ŏnga ch'ulp'an-sa, 1983).

Yi, Hŭisŭng, et al., ed., *Han'guk inmyŏng taesajŏn* [Korean Biographical Dictionary] (Sŏul, Sin'gu munhwa-sa, 1976).

Yi, Unhŏ, *Pulgyo sajŏn* [A Dictionary of Buddhism] (Sŏul, Hongbŏb-wŏn, 1971).

Yu, Hongnyŏl, *Han'guk-sa sajŏn* [A Dictionary of Korean History] (Sŏul, P'ungmun-sa, 1975).

Yugyo sajŏn p'yŏnch'an wiwŏn-hoe [Dictionary of Confucianism Compilation Committee], *Yugyo tae sajŏn* [Encyclopaedia of Confucianism], 2 vols. (Sŏul, Pagyŏng-sa 1990).

2. Korean History, General

Bishop, Isabella Bird, *Korea and Her Neighbours* (1898; repr. Sŏul, Yonsei Univ. Press, 1970).

Fischer, J. Earnest, *Pioneers of Modern Korea* (Sŏul, Christian Literature Society of Korea, 1977).

Gale, James Scarth, *Korean Sketches* (1898; repr. Sŏul, Royal Asiatic Society, Korea Branch, 1975).

Han, Woo-keun, *The History of Korea*, trans. Kyong-shik Lee (Sŏul, Ulyu Publishing, 1971).

Henthorn, William E., *A History of Korea* (New York, Free Press, 1971).

Hoare, James and Susan Pares, *Korea: An Introduction* (London, KPI, 1988).

Hulbert, Homer B., *The History of Korea*, 2 vols. (1905; repr., ed. Clarence N. Weems, New York, Hillary House, 1962).

Iryŏn, *Wŏnmun-kyŏm yŏkchu Samguk yusa* [The 'Samguk yusa', Incorporating the Original Text, a Modern Translation, and Annotations], ed. Yi Pyŏngdo (Sŏul, Kwangjo Publishing, 1975).

Joe, Wanne J., *Traditional Korea: A Cultural History* (Sŏul, Chung'ang Univ. Press, 1972).

Kim, Pusik, *Wanyŏk Samguk sagi* [A Complete Translation of the 'Samguk sagi'], trans. Kim Chunggwan (Sŏul, Kwangjo Publishing, 1974).

Ledyard, Gari, *The Dutch Come to Korea* (Sŏul, Royal Asiatic Society, Korea Branch, 1971).

Lee, Ki-baik, *A New History of Korea*, trans. Edward W. Wagner (Sŏul, Ilcho-gak, 1984).

3. Korean Religion, General

Banier, l'Abbé Antoine, *La Mythologie et les fables expliquées par l'histoire* (Paris, Briasson, 1738).

Clark, Charles Allen, *The Religions of Old Korea* (1932, repr. Sŏul, Christian Literature Society of Korea, 1961).

Courant, Maurice, 'Sommaire et historique des cultes coreéns', *T'oung Pao* (Leiden and Paris, 1900), pp. 295–326.

Grayson, James Huntley, 'Ideology, Religion and the Roots of Nationalism: Two Case Studies of Revitalization in Late Koryŏ and Late Chosŏn Times', *Religion*, 24 (1994).

Han'guk chonggyo sahoe yŏn'gu-so [Korean Religion and Society Research Institute], *Han'guk chonggyo yŏn'gam* [Yearbook of Korean Religion], (Sŏul, Korea Halimwon, various years).

Kendall, Laurel, and Griffin Dix, *Religion and Ritual in Korean Society* (Berkeley, Univ. of California, Center for Korean Studies, 1987).

Kim, Duk-Hwang, see Kim, Tŭkhwang.

Kim, T'aegon, et al., *Han'guk chonggyo* [Korean Religions] Han'guk chonggyo taegye, 1 [Korean Religions Series, 1] (Iri, Korea, Wŏn'gwang taehakkyo chonggyo munje yŏn'gu-so, 1973).

Kim, Tŭkhwang, *Han'guk chonggyo-sa* [A History of Religions in Korea] (1963; repr. Sŏul, Ep'el ch'ulp'an-sa, 1970).

——, *A History of Religions in Korea*, transl. of *Han'guk chonggyo-sa* (Sŏul, Daeji, 1988).

Korean National Statistical Office, *In'gu chut'aek ch'ongjosa pogosŏ* [Report on the (Korean) National Population Household Census], 15 vols. (Sŏul, T'onggye-ch'ŏng [National Statistical Office], 1997).

Lancaster, Lewis R., and Richard K. Payne, eds., *Religion and Society in Contemporary Korea*, Institute for East Asian Studies Korea Research Monograph 24 (Berkeley, Univ. of California, Institute of East Asian Studies, 1997).

Lee, Hyo-jae, et al., 'Religion and Social Values', *Transactions of the Korea Branch of the Royal Asiatic Society*, 46 (1971).

Lee, Peter H., *Sourcebook of Korean Civilization* 2 vols. (New York, Columbia Univ. Press, 1993/1996).

Linton, Stephen Winn, *Patterns in Korean Civil Religions*, Ph.D. thesis (New York, Columbia Univ., 1989).

Morse, Robert, ed., *Wild Asters: Explorations in Korean Thought, Culture and Society* (Lanham, Md., and London, Univ. Press of America, 1987).

Osgood, Cornelius, *The Koreans and Their Culture* (New York, Ronald Press, 1951).

Phillips, Earl H., and Eui-young Yu, eds., *Religions in Korea: Beliefs and Cultural Values*, Korean-American and Korean Studies Publication 1 (Los Angeles, Center for Korean-American and Korean Studies, California State Univ. at Los Angeles, 1982).

Sørensen, Henrik Hjort, ed., *Religions in Traditional Korea*, Seminar for Buddhist Studies Monograph 3 (Copenhagen, University of Copenhagen, Seminar for Buddhist Studies, 1995).

Vos, Frits, *Die Religionen Koreas* (Stuttgart, Verlag W. Kohlhammer, 1977).

Yi, Ŭnbong, *Han'guk kodae chonggyo sasang* [Religious Thought in Ancient Korea] (Sŏul, Chimmun-dang, 1984).

Yu, Chai-shin, ed., *Korean and Asian Religious Traditions*, (Toronto, Korean and Related Studies Press, 1977).

4. Buddhism

An, Kyehyŏn, *Han'guk pulgyo-sa yŏn'gu* [Research in the History of Korean Buddhism] (Sŏul, Tonghwa ch'ulp'an kongsa, 1982).

—— 'Silla Buddhism and the Spirit of the Protection of the Fatherland', *Korea Journal*, 17:4 (1977).

Buswell, Robert E., jun., *The Formation of Ch'an Ideology in China and Korea: The Vajrasamādhi Sūtra, A Buddhist Apocryphon* (Princeton, Princeton Univ. Press, 1989).

—— *The Korean Approach to Zen: The Collected Works of Chinul* (Honolulu, Univ. of Hawaii Press, 1983).

—— 'Monastery Lay Associations in Contemporary Korean Buddhism: A Study of the Puril Hoe' in Lewis R. Lancaster and Richard K. Payne, eds., *Religion and Society in Contemporary Korea*, Institute for East Asian Studies Korea Research Monograph 24 (Berkeley, Univ. of California, Institute of East Asian Studies, 1997).

—— *Tracing Back the Radiance: Chinul's Korean Way of Zen* (Honolulu, Univ. of Hawai'i Press, 1991).

—— *The Zen Monastic Experience: Buddhist Practice in Contemporary Korea* (Princeton, Princeton Univ. Press, 1992).

Buzo, Adrian, and Tony Prince, trans., *Kyunyŏ-jŏn: The Life, Times and Songs of a Tenth Century Korean Monk* (Broadway, N.S.W., Australia, Wild Peony, 1993).

Ch'egwan, *T'ien-t'ai Buddhism: An Outline of the Fourfold Teachings*, ed. David W. Chappell, compiled by Masao Ichishima (Honolulu, Univ. of Hawaii Press, 1984).

Chin, Hongsŏp, *Han'gug-ŭi pulsang* [Korean Buddhist Statuary] (Sŏul, Ilchi-sa, 1976).

Cho, Myŏnggi, 'Prominent Buddhist Leaders and Their Doctrines', *Korea Journal*, 4:5 (1964).

—— 'Venerable Pojo's Life, Thought, Achievement', *Korea Journal*, 4:6 (1964).

Chong, Key Ray, *Won Buddhism: A History and Theology of Korea's New Religion* (Lewiston, N.Y., Mellen, 1997).

Chung, Bong-kil, 'What Is Wŏn Buddhism?', *Korea Journal*, 24:5 (1984).

Chung, Byung-jo, 'The Buddhist Lay Movement in Korean Society' in Lewis R. Lancaster and Richard K. Payne, eds., *Religion and Society in Contemporary Korea*, Institute for East Asian Studies Korea Research Monograph 24 (Berkeley, Univ. of California, Institute of East Asian Studies, 1997).

Cleary, Jonathan Christopher, trans., *A Buddha from Korea: Zen Teachings of T'aego* (Boston, Mass., Shaftesbury/Shambala, 1988).

Cohn, William, 'Zur Koreanischen Kunst', *Ostasiatische Zeitschrift* (Berlin), 7:3/4 (1918–19).

Dumoulin, Heinrich, 'Contemporary Buddhism in Korea', in Heinrich Dumoulin, ed., *Buddhism in the Modern World* (New York, Macmillan, 1976).

Ennin, *Ennin's Diary*, trans. and ed. Edwin O. Reischauer (New York, Ronald Press, 1955).

Fuchs, Walter, 'Heui-ch'ao's Pilgerreise durch Nordwest Indien und Zentral-Asien um 726', *Sitzungsberichte der Preussicher Akademie der Wissenschaften* (Sitzung der Philosophisch-historischen Klasse, 30; 1938).

Forte, Antonino, *A Jewel in Indra's Net: The Letter Sent by Fazang in China to Ŭisang in Korea*, Italian School of East Asian Studies Occasional Papers 8 (Kyōto, 2000).

Gottsche, Bertha, 'Sok-kul-am, Das Steinhohlen-Kloster', *Ostasiatische Zeitschrift*, 7:3/4 (1918–19).

Grayson, James Huntley, *Early Buddhism and Christianity in Korea: A Study in the Emplantation of Religion* (Leiden, E. J. Brill, 1985).

—— 'The Role of Early Korean Buddhism in the History of East Asia', *Asiatische Studien* (Zurich), 34:2 (1980).

—— 'Religious Syncretism in the Shilla Period: The Relationship between Esoteric Buddhism and Korean Primeval Religion', *Asian Folklore Studies* (Nagoya), 43:2 (1984).

Hackmann, H., *Buddhism as a Religion: Its Historical Development and its Present Condition*, trans. by the author from German (London, Probsthain, 1910).

Han'guk pulgyo yŏn'gu-wŏn [Korean Buddhist Research Institute], *Han'gug-ŭi sach'al* [The Buddhist Temples of Korea], series in progress, 18 vols. (Sŏul, Ilchi-sa, 1974–).

Han, Kidu, *Han'guk sŏn sasang yŏn'gu* [Research into the Thought of Korean Sŏn Buddhism] (Sŏul, Ilchi-sa, 1992).

Han, Kidu, and Hong Yusik, *Han'guk pulgyo-sa* [A History of Korean Buddhism] (Iri, Korea, Wŏn'gwang Univ. Press, 1974).

Hwang, Suyŏng, ed., *Pulsang* [Buddhist Statues] (Sŏul, Chung'ang ilbo-sa, 1979).

International Cultural Foundation, *Buddhist Culture in Korea* (Sŏul, Si-sa-yŏng-ŏ-sa, 1982).

Jan, Yun-hwa, 'Hui Ch'ao and His Works: A Reassessment', *Indo-Asian Culture* (New Delhi), 12 (Jan 1964).

Jung, Hee-Soo, *Kyŏnghŭng's Commentary on the Larger Sukhāvatīvyūha sūtra and the Formation of Pure Land Buddhism in Silla*, Ph.D. thesis (Madison, Wisc., Univ. of Wisconsin, 1994).

Kang, Sŏksu, and Pak Kyŏnghun, *Pulgyo kŭnse paengnyŏn* [Buddhism's Recent Century] (Sŏul, Chung'ang sŏrim, 1979).

Kang, Wi-jo, 'The Secularization of Buddhism Under the Japanese Colonialism', *Korea Journal*, 19:7 (1980).

Keel, Hee Sung, *Chinul: The Founder of the Korean Sŏn Tradition* (Berkeley, Institute of Buddhist Studies, 1984).

Kim, Tonghwa, *Pulgyo-hak kaeron* [Introduction to Buddhist Studies] (Sŏul, Paegyŏng-sa, 1967).

—— 'The Buddhist Thought in the Paekche Period', *Journal of Asiatic Studies* (Sŏul), 5:1 (1962).

—— 'The Buddhist Thought in the Silla Period', *Journal of Asiatic Studies* (Sŏul), 5:2 (1962).

Kim, Yŏngt'ae, and U Chŏngsang, *Han'guk pulgyo-sa* [A History of Korean Buddhism] (2nd edn. Sŏul, Chinsu-dang, 1970).

Korean Buddhist Research Institute, *Buddhist Thought in Korea* (Sŏul, Dongguk Univ. Press, 1994).

—— *The History and Culture of Buddhism in Korea* (Sŏul, Dongguk Univ. Press, 1993).

Kusan, *The Way of Korean Zen*, Martine Fages, trans. (New York, Weatherhill, 1985).

Lancaster, Lewis R., and Chai-Shin Yu, *Assimilation of Buddhism in Korea: Religious Maturity and Innovation in the Silla Dynasty* (Berkeley, Asian Humanities Press, 1991).

—— *Introduction of Buddhism to Korea: New Cultural Patterns* (Berkeley, Asian Humanities Press, 1989).

Lancaster, Lewis R., et al, eds., *Buddhism in the Early Chosŏn: Suppression and Transformation*, Institute of East Asian Studies Korea Research Monograph 23 (Berkeley, Univ. of California, Institute of East Asian Studies, 1996).

—— *Buddhism in Koryŏ: A Royal Religion*, Institute of East Asian Studies Korea Research Monograph 22 (Berkeley, Univ. of California, Institute of East Asian Studies, 1996).

Lancaster, Lewis R. and Sung-bae Park, *The Korean Buddhist Canon: A Descriptive Catalogue* (Berkeley, Univ. of California Press, 1979).

Landis, E. B., 'Buddhist Chants and Processions', *Korean Repository*, 2 (1895).

Lee, Peter H., *Lives of Eminent Korean Monks: The Haedong Kosŭng Chŏn* (Cambridge, Mass., Harvard Univ. Press, 1969).

—— 'The Life of the Korean Poet-Priest Kyunyŏ', *Asiatische Studien*, 9 (1958).

Leverrier, Roger, 'Buddhism and Ancestral Religious Beliefs in Korea', *Korea Journal*, 12:5 (1972).

Mu Seong, *Thousand Peaks: Korean Zen – Traditions and Teachers* (Cumberland, Rhode Island, Primary Point, 1991).

Mun, Myŏngdae, *Chosŏn purhwa* [Buddhist Paintings of the Chosŏn Period] (Sŏul, Chung'ang ilbo-sa, 1984).

Ohlinger, F., 'Buddhism in Korean History and Language', *Korean Repository*, 1 (1892).

Pak, Sŏng-bae, 'The Life of the Ven. Chinul', *Korea Journal*, 11:2 (1971).

Park, Chong-hong, 'Buddhist Influence on Korean Thought', *Korea Journal*, 4:5 (1964).

Park, Kwangsoo, *The Wŏn Buddhism (Wŏnbulgyo) of Sot'aesan; A Twentieth-century Religious Movement in Korea* (San Francisco, International Scholars Publications, 1997).

Pratt, James Bissett, *The Pilgrimage of Buddhism and a Buddhist Pilgrimage* (New York, Macmillan, 1928).

Seo, Kyung Bo, 'A Study of Korean Zen Buddhism Approached through the Chodangjip', Ph.D. dissertation (Temple Univ., Philadelphia, 1969).

Sim, Chaeyŏl, *Wŏnhyo sasang: Nolli-gwan* [Wŏnhyo's Thought: His Logic] (Sŏul, Hongbŏb-wŏn, 1983).

Sok, Do-ryun, 'Buddhist Images of Popular Worship', *Korea Journal*, 10:7 (1970).

Sŏngjŏn p'yŏnch'an ŭiwŏn-hoe [Scriptural Compilation Committee], *Uri mal p'alman taejang-gyŏng* [The Tripitaka Koreanum in Modern Korean] (Sŏul, Kungmin sŏgwan, 1963).

Song Kwang Sa Monastery, *Nine Mountains: Dharma Lectures of the Korean Meditation Master Ku San* (Songju-gun, Korea, Songgwang-sa, 1976).

Sørensen, Henrik, 'A Bibliographical Survey of Buddhist Ritual Texts from Korea' in Ecole Française de l'Extrême-Orient, Section de Kyōto, *Cahiers d'Extrême-Asie, Numéro spécial sur le chamanisme coréen*, 6 (1991–92).

—— *The Contents of Chinul's Sŏn Seen in Relation to the 'Nine mountains schools'* (Sŏul, Pojo sasang yŏn'gu-wŏn, 1990?).

—— 'Ennin's Account of a Korean Buddhist Monastery, 839–840', *Acta Orientalia* (Copenhagen), 47 (1986).

—— *The Esoteric Buddhist Tradition*, Seminar for Buddhist Studies Monograph 2 (Copenhagen, Univ. of Copenhagen, Seminar for Buddhist Studies, 1994).

—— 'Problems with Using the *Samguk yusa* as a Source for the History of Korean Buddhism' in *Cahiers d'études coréennes 7* (Paris, Centre d'Études Coréennes, Collège de France, 2000).

Starr, Frederick, *Korean Buddhism* (Boston, Marshall Jones, 1918).

Sungsan Pak Kilchin paksa hwan'gap kinyŏm saŏp-hoe [60th Birthday Commemorative Committee for Dr. Pak Kilchin], *Han'guk pulgyo sasang-sa* [History of Korean Buddhist Thought] (Iri, Korea, Wŏn Pulgyo sasang yŏn'gu-wŏn, 1975).

Tongguk taehakkyo pulchŏn kanhaeng wiwŏn-hoe [Tongguk University Buddhist Scripture Publication Committee], *Han'guk pulgyo chŏnsŏ* [A Compendium of Korean Buddhism], 6 vols. (Sŏul, Tongguk University Press, 1984).

Tongguk taehakkyo sŏngnim tongmun-hoe [Tongguk Univ. Monastic Alumni Association], ed., *Han'guk pulgyo hyŏndae-sa* [Modern History of Korean Buddhism] (Sŏul, Sigong-sa, 1997).

Tongguk taehakkyo yŏkkyŏng-wŏn [Tongguk Univ. Scripture Translation Bureau], *Koryŏ taejang-gyŏng* [Tripitaka Koreanum], 48 vols. (Sŏul, Tongguk Univ. Press, 1957–76).

Trollope, Mark Napier, 'Introduction to the Study of Buddhism in Corea', *Transactions of the Korea Branch of the Royal Asiatic Society*, 8 (1917).

U, Chŏngsang, 'High Priest Hyujŏng: Unity of Zen and Doctrinal Buddhism', *Korea Journal*, 13:2 (1973).

Wŏn Pulgyo Chŏnghwa-sa [General Secretariat of Wŏn Pulgyo], *Wŏn pulgyo chŏnsŏ* [Complete Scriptures of Wŏn Pulgyo (Iri, Korea, Wŏn Pulgyo ch'ulp'an-sa, 1989).

Won, Yi Beom, *A History of Korean Buddhist Culture and Some Essays: The Buddhist Pure Land and the Christian Kingdom of Heaven* (Sŏul, Jipmoondang, 1992).

Yang, Han-sung, et al., transls., eds., *The Hye Ch'o Diary: Memoir of the Pilgrimage to the Five Regions of India* (Sŏul, Po Chin Chai, 1984).

Yi, Hyŏnt'aek, *Wŏn pulgyo ŭn sasang-ŭi yŏn'gu* [Research on the Concept of *ŭn* in Wŏn Pulgyo] (Iri, Korea, Wŏn'gwang Univ. Wŏn Pulgyo sasang yŏn'gu-wŏn, 1989).

Yi, Kibaek, 'Samguk sidae pulgyo chŏllae-wa kŭ sahoe-jŏk sŏnggyŏk' [The Transmission and Social Characteristics of Korean Buddhism in the Three Kingdoms Period], *Yŏksa hakpo*, 6 (1954).

—— 'Wŏn'gwang and His Thought', *Korea Journal*, 14:6 (1975).

Yi, Kiyŏng, *Wŏnhyo sasang: segye-gwan* [The Thought of Wŏnhyo: His World-view] (Sŏul, Hongbŏb-wŏn, 1967).

—— 'Wŏnhyo and His Thought', *Korea Journal*, 11:1 (1971).

Yi, Nŭnghwa, *Chosŏn pulgyo t'ongsa* [A Complete History of Korean Buddhism] (Sŏul, Sinmun-gwan 1918).

Yi, Tongju, ed, *Koryŏ purhwa* [Buddhist Paintings of the Koryŏ Period] (Sŏul, Chung'ang ilbo-sa, 1981).

Yu, Chaesin, *Pulgyo-wa kidokkyo pigyo yŏn'gu* [A Comparative Study of the Founder's Authority, the Community, and the Discipline in Early Buddhism and Early Christianity] (Sŏul, Christian Literature Society of Korea, 1980).

5. Christianity

An, Ŭngyŏl, *Han'guk sun'gyo pokcha-jŏn* [A Record of the Blessed Martyrs of Korea] (Sŏul, Kat'ollik ch'ulp'an-sa, 1974).

Baker, Donald, 'From Pottery to Politics: The Transformation of Korean Catholicism' in Lewis R. Lancaster and Richard K. Payne, eds., *Religion and Society in Contemporary Korea*, Institute for East Asian Studies Korea Research Monograph 24 (Berkeley, Univ. of California, Institute of East Asian Studies, 1997).

Biernatzki, William E., et al, *Korean Catholicism in the 1970s: A Christian Community Comes of Age* (Maryknoll, N.Y., Orbis Books, 1975).

Brown, Arthur Judson, *The Korea Conspiracy Case* (New York, Board of Foreign Missions of the Presbyterian Church, USA, 1912).

Ch'oi, Andreas, 'L'Érection du premier vicariate et les origines du Catholicisme en Corée, 1592–1837', *Nouvelle revue des sciences missionnaires* (Schöneck-Beckenried, Suisse, 1961).

Christian Conference of Asia, ed., *Minjung Theology: People as the Subjects of History* (Singapore, Christian Conference of Asia, Commission on Theological Concerns, 1981).

Chung, David, *Syncretism: The Religious Context of Religious Beginnings in Korea* (Albany, N.Y., State Univ. of New York Press, 2001).

Clark, Allen D., *A History of the Church in Korea* (1961; rev. Sŏul, Christian Literature Society of Korea, 1971).

Clark, Donald N., *Christianity in Modern Korea* (Lanham, Maryland and London, Univ. Press of America, 1986).

—— 'History and Religion in Modern Korea: The Case of Protestant Christianity' in Lewis R. Lancaster and Richard K. Payne, eds., *Religion and Society in Contemporary Korea*, Institute for East Asian Studies Korea Research Monograph 24 (Berkeley, Univ. of California, Institute of East Asian Studies, 1997).

—— ed., *Yanghwajin: Seoul Foreigners Cemetery, Korea, An Informal History, 1890–1984* (Sŏul, Yongsan Library, 1984).

Corfe, C. J., *The Anglican Church in Corea* (Sŏul, The Seoul Press, 1905).

Dallet, Charles, *Histoire de l'Église de Corée*, 2 vols. (1874; repr. Sŏul, Royal Asiatic Society, Korea Branch, 1975).

Davies, Daniel M., *The Life and Thought of Henry Gerhard Appenzeller (1858–1902), Missionary to Korea* (Lewiston, N.Y., Edwin Mellen, 1988).

Goh, Moo Song, *Western and Asian Portrayals of Robert Jermain Thomas (1839–1866), Pioneer Missionary to Korea: A Historical Study of an East-West Encounter through his Mission*, Ph.D. thesis (Univ. of Birmingham, UK, Department of Theology, 1995).

Grayson, James Huntley, 'Cultural Encounter: Korean Protestantism and Other Religious Traditions', *International Bulletin of Missionary Research*, 25:2 (2001).

—— 'Dynamic Complementarity: Korean Confucianism and Christianity' in Richard H. Roberts, ed., *Religion and the Transformations of Capitalism: Comparative Approaches* (London, Routledge, 1995).

—— *Early Buddhism and Christianity in Korea: A Study in the Emplantation of Religion* (Leiden, E. J. Brill, 1985).

—— (under Korean name, Kim Chŏnghyŏn), *Chon Rosŭ, Han'gug-ŭi ch'ŏt sŏn'gyo-sa* [John Ross, Korea's First Missionary] (Taegu, Korea, Kyemyŏng Univ. Press, 1982).

—— 'The Shintō Shrine Conflict and Protestant Martyrs in Korea, 1938–1945', *Missiology*, 29:3 (2001).

Griffis, W. E., *A Modern Pioneer in Korea: The Life of Henry G. Appenzeller* (New York, Fleming H. Revell, 1912).

Han, Gil Soo, *Social Sources of Church Growth: Korean Churches in the Homeland and Overseas* (Lanham, Md., Univ. Press of America, 1994).

Han'guk kidokkyo yŏksa yŏn'gu-so [Korean Church History Research Institute], *Puk Han kyohoe-sa* [North Korean Church History] (Sŏul, Han'guk kidokkyo yŏksa yŏn'gu-so, 1996).

Harrington, F. H., *God, Mammon, and the Japanese* (Madison, Univ. of Wisconsin Press, 1944).

Hunt, E. N., jun., *Protestant Pioneers in Korea* (Maryknoll, New York, Orbis Books, 1980).

Huntley, Martha, *Caring, Growing, Changing: A History of the Protestant Mission in Korea* (New York, Friendship Press, 1984).

Im, Luke Jinchang, Anselm Kyong Suk Kim, et al, *Catholic Socio-religious Survey of Korea*, 2 vols. (Sŏul, Social Research Institute, Sŏgang Univ., 1971).

Kang, Wi Jo, *Christ and Caesar in Modern Korea: A History of Christianity and Politics* (Albany, N.Y., State Univ. of New York Press, 1997).

Kim, Changseok Thaddeus, *Holy Places of the Korean Martyrs* (Sŏul, Lay Apostolate Council of Korea, 1986).

—— *Lives of 103 Martyr Saints of Korea* (Sŏul, Catholic Publishing House, 1984).

Kim, Sujin, *6.25 chŏnnan-ŭi sun'gyoja-dŭl* [Christian Martyrs of the Korean War] (Sŏul, Christian Literature Society of Korea, 1981).

Kŭrisŭdogyo-wa kyŏre munhwa yŏn'gu-hoe [Christianity and Indigenous Culture Research Society], *Han'gŭl sŏngsŏ-wa kyŏre munhwa* [The Korean Script Bible and Indigenous Culture] (Sŏul, Kidokkyo mun-sa, 1985).

Lee, Jong Hyeong, *Samuel Austin Moffett: His Life and Work in the Development of the Presbyterian Church of Korea, 1890–1936*, Ph.D. thesis (Richmond, Virginia, Union Theological Seminary in Virginia, 1983).

Lee, Jung-young (Yi Chungyŏng), ed., *Ancestor Worship and Christianity in Korea* (Lewiston, N.Y., Edwin Mellen, 1988).

Min, Kyŏngbae, *Han'guk kidok kyohoe-sa* [A History of the Korean Church] (1968; rev. Sŏul, Christian Literature Society of Korea, 1979).

Min, Pyŏngho, *R. J. T'omasŭ moksa yŏn'gu* [Research on the Revd Robert Jermain Thomas] (Sŏul, Hongik-chae, 1984).

Min, Yŏngjin, *Kugyŏk sŏngsŏ yŏn'gu* [Research into the Korean Translations of the Bible] (Sŏul, Sŏnggwang munhwa-sa, 1984).

Moffett, Samuel H., *The Christians of Korea* (New York, Friendship Press, 1962).

—— *Samuel A. Moffett: First Letters from Korea, 1890–1891* (Sŏul, Presbyterian Theological Seminary, Institute of Missions, 1975).

—— 'The Independence Movement and the Missionaries', *Transactions of the Korea Branch of the Royal Asiatic Society*, 54 (1979).

Moltmann, Jürgen, et al, eds., *Minjung: Theologie des Volkes Gottes in Südkorea* (Neukirchen-Vlyun, Neukirchener Verlag, 1984).

Monod, René, *The Korean Revival*, trans. Anthea Bell (London, Hodder and Stoughton, 1971).

Mullins, Mark R., and Richard Fox Young, eds., *Perspectives on Christianity in Korea and Japan: the Gospel and Culture in East Asia* (Lewiston, N.Y., Edwin Mellen, 1995).

Mutel, Gustave, *Documents relatifs aux martyrs de Corée de 1839 et 1846* (Hong Kong, Société des missions étrangères de Paris, 1924).

Paik, Lak-Geoon George, *The History of Protestant Missions in Korea, 1832–1910* (1927; repr. Sŏul, Yonsei Univ. Press, 1970).

Rhodes, Harry A., *History of the Korea Mission, Presbyterian Church USA:* vol. 1, *1884–1934*, (Sŏul, Chosen Mission of the Presbyterian Church USA, 1934).

—— *History of the Korea Mission, Presbyterian Church USA*, vol. 2, *1935–1950*, vol. 3, *1950–1954*, mimeograph (New York, United Presbyterian Library, 1954).

Ri, Jean Sangbae, *Confucius et Jésus Christ: la première théologie chrétieene en Corée d'après l'oeuvre de Yi Piek, lettré confucéen, 1754–1786* (Paris, Beauchesne, 1979).

Ro, Bong-Rin, and Marlin L. Nelson, eds., *Korean Church Growth Explosion*, (Sŏul, Word of Life Press, 1983).

Ruiz de Medina, Juan G., *Orígenes de la Iglesia Católica Coreana desde 1566 hasta 1784: según documentos inéditos de la época*, Bibliotheca Instituti Historici S.I., 45 (Roma, Institutum Historicum S.I., 1986).

—— *The Catholic Church in Korea: Its Origins 1566–1784*, John Bridges, trans., (Roma, Instituto Storico, 1991).

Sauer, Charles A., *Methodists in Korea* (Sŏul, Christian Literature Society of Korea, 1970).

Shearer, Roy E., *Wildfire, Church Growth in Korea* (Grand Rapids, Michigan, William B. Eerdmans, 1966).

Strawn, Sonia Reid, *Where There is no Path: Lee Tai-young, Her Story* (Sŏul, Korea Legal Aid Center for Family Relations, 1988).

Suh, David Kwang-sun, *The Korean Minjung in Christ* (Hong Kong, Christian Conference of Asia, Commission on Theological Concerns, 1991).

Underwood, Lillias, *Underwood of Korea* (1918; repr. Sŏul, Yonsei Univ. Press, 1983).

Wasson, Alfred W., *Church Growth in Korea* (New York, International Missionary Council, 1934).

Wells, Kenneth M., *New God, New Nation: Protestants and Self-reconstruction Nationalism in Korea, 1896–1937* (Honolulu, Univ. of Hawai'i Press, 1990).

Yi, Ch'anyŏng, *Han'guk kidok kyohoe-sa ch'ongnam* [Materials on Korean Church History] (Sŏul, Somang-sa, 1994).

Yi, Hwasŏn, *Minjung sinhak pip'an* [A Critical View of *Minjung* Theology] (Sŏul, Sŏnggwang munhwa-sa, 1989).

Yi, Manyŏl, *Ap'enchellŏ, Han'guk-e on ch'ŏt sŏn'gyo-sa* [Appenzeller, the First Missionary to Come to Korea] (Sŏul, Yonsei Univ. Press, 1985).

Yi, Manyŏl, et al, *Han'guk kidokkyo wa minjok undong* [The (Korean) People's Movement and Korean Christianity] (Sŏul, Posŏng, 1986).

Yi, Nŭnghwa, *Chosŏn kidokkyo-gŭp oegyo-sa* [A History of Korean Foreign Relations and Christianity] (Sŏul, Kidokkyo ch'angmun-sa, 1925).

Yu, Chai-Shin, ed., *The Founding of the Catholic Tradition in Korea* (Sŏul, Myung Hwa Publishing, 1996).

—— *Korea and Christianity* (Sŏul, Korean Scholar Press, 1996).

Yu, Hongnyŏl, *Han'guk ch'ŏnju kyohoe-sa* [The History of the Korean Catholic Church] (Sŏul, Kat'ollik ch'ulp'an-sa, 1964).

—— *Han'gug-ŭi ch'ŏnju-gyo* [Korean Catholicism] (Sŏul, Sejong taewang kinyŏm saŏp-hoe, 1976).

Yu, Tongsik, *Han'guk chonggyo-wa kidokkyo* [Christianity and Korean Religion] (Sŏul, Christian Literature Society of Korea, 1965).

6. Confucianism

Boot, Willem Jan, *The Adoption and Adaptation of Neo-Confucianism in Japan: The Role of Fujiwara Seika and Hayashi Razan* (University of Leiden Ph.D., 1983).

de Bary, Wm. Theodore and JaHyun Kim Haboush, *The Rise of Neo-Confucianism in Korea* (New York, Columbia Univ. Press, 1985).

Choung, Haechang, and Hyong-jo Han, eds., *Confucian Philosophy in Korea* (Sŏngnam, Academy of Korean Studies, 1996).

Chung, Chai-sik, *A Korean Confucian Encounter with the Modern World: Yi Hang-no and the West*, Institute of East Asian Studies Korea Research Monograph 20 (Berkeley, Univ. of California Institute of East Asian Studies, 1995).

Chung, Edward Y. J., *Korean Neo-Confucianism of Yi T'oegye and Yi Yulgok; A Reappraisal of the 'Four-Seven Thesis' and its Practical Implications for Self-cultivation* (Albany, N.Y., State Univ. of New York Press, 1995).

Deuchler, Martina, *The Confucian Transformation of Korea: A Study of Society and Ideology*, Harvard-Yenching Institute Monograph 36 (Cambridge, Mass., Council on East Asian Studies, Harvard Univ., 1992).

—— 'Neo-Confucianism: The Impulse for Social Action in Early Yi Korea', *Journal of Korean Studies*, 2 (1980).

—— 'Neo-Confucianism in Action: Agnation and Ancestor Worship in Early Yi Korea', in Laurel Kendall and Griffin Dix, *Religion and Ritual in Korean Society*, (Berkeley, Univ. of California, Center for Korean Studies, 1987).

Duncan, John, 'Confucian Social Values in Contemporary South Korea' in Lewis R. Lancaster and Richard K. Payne, eds., *Religion and Society in Contemporary Korea*, Institute for East Asian Studies Korea Research Monograph 24 (Berkeley, Univ. of California, Institute of East Asian Studies, 1997).

Fu, Charles Wei-hsun, 'T'oegye's Thesis on the Four Beginnings and Seven Feelings', *Korea Journal*, 25:7 (1985).

Government-General of Chōsen, *Chōsen saishi sōzoku hō ron josetsu* [Introduction to the Rules of Confucian Ceremonial in Korea] (Sŏul, 1939).

Henderson, Gregory, 'Chŏng Ta-san: A Study in Korea's Intellectual History', *Journal of Asian Studies*, 16:3 (1957).

—— and Key P. Yang, 'An Outline of Korean Confucianism: I and II', *Journal of Asian Studies*, 17:1–22 (1958).

Janelli, Roger L., and Dawnhee Yim Janelli, *Ancestor Worship and Korean Society* (Stanford, California, Stanford Univ. Press, 1982).

Kalton, Michael C., *To Become a Sage; The Ten Diagrams on Sage Learning by Yi T'oegye* (New York, Columbia Univ. Press, 1988).

Kalton, Michael C., et al, *The Four-Seven Debate: An Annotated Translation of the Most Famous Controversy in Korean Neo-Confucian Thought* (Albany, N.Y., State Univ. of New York Press, 1994).

Kim, Chong-guk, and Kim Chin-man, 'Some Notes on the Sŏnggyun'gwan', *Transactions of the Korea Branch of the Royal Asiatic Society*, 38 (1961).

Kim, Doo-hun, 'The Rise of Neo-Confucianism against Buddhism in Late Koryo', *Bulletin of the Korean Research Center*, 12 (May 1960).

Kim, Ha-tai, 'The Transmission of Neo-Confucianism to Japan by Kang Hang, a Prisoner of War', *Transactions of the Korea Branch of the Royal Asiatic Society*, 37 (Apr. 1961).

Korean National Commission for UNESCO, *Main Currents of Korean Thought* (Sŏul, Si-sa-yŏng-ŏ-sa, 1983).

Palmer, Spencer J., *Confucian Rituals in Korea* (Berkeley/Sŏul, Asian Humanities Press/ Po Chin Chai, 1984?).

Provine, Robert C., *Essays on Sino-Korean Musicology: Early Sources for Korean Ritual* (Sŏul, Il Ji Sa, 1988).

—— 'The Sacrifice to Confucius in Korea and its Music', *Transactions of the Korea Branch of the Royal Asiatic Society*, 50 (1975).

Ro, Young-chan, *The Korean Neo-Confucianism of Yi Yulgok* (Albany, N.Y., State Univ. of New York Press, 1989).

Seoh, Roy Munsang, 'The Ultimate Concern of Yi Korean Confucians: An Analysis of the *I-Ki* Debates', Joint Committee on Korean Studies of the American Council of Learned Societies and the Social Science Research Council, *Occasional Papers on Korea*, 5 (Mar. 1977).

—— 'Dynamics of Stability and Longevity of the Yi Dynasty: A Contribution of Korean Neo-Confucians', *Korea Journal*, 18:9 (1978).

Setton, Mark, *Chŏng Yagyong: Korea's Challenge to Orthodox Neo-Confucianism* (Albany, N.Y., State Univ. of New York Press, 1997).

Tu, Wei-ming, 'Yi Hwang's Perception of the Mind', *Korea Journal*, 18:9 (1979).

—— 'T'oegye's Anthropocosmic Vision: An Interpretation', *Korea Journal*, 25:7 (1985).

Yi, In-gi, 'Yi T'oegye and the Cultural Unity of East Asia', *Korea Journal*, 18:9 (1979).

Yi, Myonggyu, and William A. Douglas, 'Korean Confucianism Today', *Pacific Affairs*, 40 (1967).

Yi, Ŭrho, *Han'guk kaesin yuhak-sa siron* [An Essay on a New History of Korean Confucianism] (Sŏul, Pagyŏng-sa, 1980).

Yun, Sasoon, see Yun, Sa-sun.

Yun, Sa-sun, *Critical Issues in Neo-Confucian Thought: The Philosophy of Yi T'oegye*, trans. Michael C. Kalton (Sŏul, Korea Univ. Press, 1992).

—— 'T'oegye's View of Human Nature as Fundamentally Good', *Korea Journal*, 25:7 (1985).

7. Folk Religion and Shamanism

Akiba, Takashi, *Chōsen minzoku-shi* [Records of Korean Folk Customs] (Tōkyō, Rokusan Shoin, 1954).

Allen, H. N., 'Some Korean Customs, the Mootang', *Korean Repository*, 3 (1896).

Canda, Edward R., 'The Korean Mountain Spirit', *Korea Journal*, 20:9 (1980).

Chang, Sugŭn, *Han'gug-ŭi hyangt'o sinang* [The Indigenous Faith of Korea] (Sŏul, Ŭryu, 1975).

Chin, Song-gi, *Cheju-do musok non'go* [Essays on Cheju Shamanism] (Cheju, Korea, Cheju minsok yŏn'gu-so, 1993).

—— 'Tangsin: Cheju Shamanism', *Korea Journal*, 17:8 (1977).

Cho, Ch'ang-su, 'The Five Blessings and Korean Coin Charms: A Psychocultural Analysis', *Korea Journal*, 17:2 (1977).

Cho, Hung-youn (Cho Hŭngyun), 'Le chamanisme au début de la dynastie Chosŏn' in Ecole Française de l'Extrême-Orient, Section de Kyōto, *Cahiers d'Extrême-Asie, Numéro spécial sur le chamanisme coréen*, 6 (1991–92).

266

—— *Koreanischer Schamanismus: Eine Einführung* (Hamburg, Im Selbstvertrag Hamburgisches Museum für Völkerkunde, Wegweiser zur Völkerkunde, 27, 1982).

—— *Han'gug-ŭi mu* [The Shamans of Korea] (Sŏul, Chŏngŭm-sa, 1983).

—— 'Zum Problem der sogenannten Yŏltugŏri des Ch'ŏnsin'gut im Koreanischen Schamanismus', *Mitteilungen aus dem Museum für Völkerkunde Hamburg*, 10 (1980).

—— 'Die Initiationszeremonie im Koreanischen Schamanismus', *Mitteilungen aus dem Museum für Völkerkunde Hamburg*, 11 (1981).

—— 'Problems in the Study of Korean Shamanism', *Korea Journal*, 25:5 (1985).

Ch'oe, Kilsŏng, *Han'guk musog-ŭi yŏn'gu* [Research on Korean Shamanism] (Sŏul, Asea munhwa-sa, 1978).

—— *Han'gug-ŭi mudang* [The Shamans of Korea] (Sŏul, Yŏrhwa-dang, 1981).

—— *Han'guk musong-non* [The Concept of Korean Shamanism] (Taegu, Korea, Hyŏngsŏl ch'ulp'an-sa, 1981).

—— 'Community Ritual and Social Structure in Village Korea', *Asian Folklore Studies* (Nagoya), 41 (1982).

Choi, Chungmoo, 'Hegemony and Shamanism: The State, the Elite, and Shamans in Contemporary Korea' in Lewis R. Lancaster and Richard K. Payne, eds., *Religion and Society in Contemporary Korea*, Institute for East Asian Studies Korea Research Monograph 24 (Berkeley, Univ. of California Institute of East Asian Studies, 1997).

Deschamps, Christian, 'Min'gan sinang-ŭi hyŏngt'ae-wa t'ŭksŏng' [Formes et Caractéristiques de la Religion Populaire Coréenne] MA thesis (Seoul National. Univ. Graduate School, Dep. of History, 1972).

Ecole Française de l'Extrême-Orient, Section de Kyōto, *Cahiers d'Extrême-Asie, Numéro spécial sur le chamanisme coréen*, 6 (1991–92).

Gale, J. S., 'Korean Beliefs', *Folklore*, 11 (1900).

Government-General of Chōsen, *Chōsen-no semboku-to yogen* [Fortune-telling and Divination in Korea] (Sŏul, 1933).

—— *Chōsen-no kyōdo shinshi* [Folk Rituals of Korea] (Sŏul, 1937–8).

Grayson, James Huntley, 'Female Mountain Spirits in Korea: A Neglected Tradition', *Asian Folklore Studies*, 55: 1 (1996).

—— '*Sŏngha sindang*: The Tutelary Shrine of T'aeha Village, Ullŭng Island, Korea', *Asian Folklore Studies*, 57:2 (1998).

Guillemoz, Alexandre, *Les Algues, les anciens, les dieux* (Paris, Leopard d'Or, 1983).

—— 'La descente d'un chamane coréene' in *Cahiers d'études coréennes 7* (Paris, Centre d'Études Coréennes, Collège de France, 2000).

—— 'The Religious Spirit of the Korean People', *Korea Journal*, 13:5 (1973).

Guisso, Richard W., and Chai-Shin Yu, eds., *Shamanism: The Spirit World of Korea* (Berkeley, Asian Humanities Press, 1988).

Harvey, Youngsook Kim, *Six Korean Women: The Socialization of Shamans* (St Paul, Minnesota, West, 1979).

Hentze, H., 'Schamanenkronen zur Han-Zeit in Korea', *Ostasiatische Zeitschrift* (Berlin), NS 19:5 (1933).

Hogarth, Hyun-key Kim, *Korean Shamanism and Cultural Nationalism* (Sŏul, Jimoondang, 1999).

Howard, Keith, ed., *Korean Shamanism: Revivals, Survivals, and Change* (Sŏul, Royal Asiatic Society, Korea Branch, 1998).

—— 'Paper Symbols in Chindo *Ssikkim kut*: A Korean Shamanistic Ceremony' in Ecole Française de l'Extrême-Orient, Section de Kyōto, *Cahiers d'Extrême-Asie, Numéro spécial sur le chamanisme coréen*, 6 (1991–92).

Huhm, Halla Pai, *Kut, Korean Shamanist Rituals* (Sŏul, Hollym, 1980).

Hulbert, Homer B., *The Passing of Korea* (1906; repr. Sŏul, Yonsei Univ. Press, 1969).

—— 'The Geomancer', *Korean Repository*, 3 (1896).

—— 'The Korean Mudang and P'ansu', *Korea Review*, 3 (1903).

Hwang, Lusi, *P'alto kut* [Eight Provinces *Kut*] (Sŏul, Taewŏn-sa, 1989).

—— *Sŏul tang-gut* [Local Shrine *Kut* in Sŏul] (Sŏul, Taewŏn-sa, 1989).

Janelli, Roger L. and Dawnhee Yim Janelli, *Ancestor Worship and Korean Society* (Stanford, Calif., Stanford Univ. Press, 1982).

—— 'Ritual Change in a Korean Village', *Chōsen Gakuho*, no. 89 (Oct. 1978).

Jones, George Herber, 'The Spirit Worship of the Koreans', *Transactions of the Korea Branch of the Royal Asiatic Society*, 2 (1902).

Kendall, Laurel, *The Life and Hard Times of a Korean Shaman: of Tales and the Telling of Tales* (Honolulu, Univ. of Hawai'i Press, 1988).

—— 'Of Gods and Men: Performance, Possession, and Flirtation in Korean Shaman Ritual' in Ecole Française de l'Extrême-Orient, Section de Kyōto, *Cahiers d'Extrême-Asie, Numéro spécial sur le chamanisme coréen*, 6 (1991–92).

—— *Shamans, Housewives, and Other Restless Spirits* (Honolulu, Univ. of Hawaii Press, 1985).

—— 'Receiving the *Samsin* Grandmother: Conception Rituals in Korea', *Transactions of the Korea Branch of the Royal Asiatic Society*, 52 (1977).

Kim, Ch'ŏl-chun, 'Native Beliefs in Ancient Korea', *Korea Journal*, 3:5 (1963).

Kim, T'aegon, 'Components of Korean Shamanism', *Korea Journal*, 12:12 (1972).

—— *Han'guk musok torok* [A Pictorial Record of Korean Shamanism] (Sŏul, Chimmun-dang, 1982).

—— *Han'guk muga-jip* [A Collection of Korean Shaman's Songs], 4 vols., (Sŏul, Chimmun-dang, 1971).

—— *Korean Shamanism – Muism*, Chang Soo-kyung, ed., trans., (Sŏul, Jimoondang, 1998).

—— 'Shamanism in the Seoul Area', *Korea Journal*, 18:6 (1978).

—— 'A Study on the Rite of *Changsŭng*, Korea's Totem Pole', *Korea Journal*, 23:3 (1983).

—— *Tongsin-dang* [Village shrines] (Sŏul, Taewŏn-sa, 1992).

Kister, Daniel A., *Korean Shamanist Ritual: Symbols and Dramas of Transformation*, Bibliotheca Shamanistica 5 (Budapest, Akadémiai Kiadó, 1997).

Korean National Commission for UNESCO, *Korean Folklore* (Sŏul, Si-sa-yŏng-ŏ-sa, 1983).

Landis, E. B., 'Notes on the Exorcism of Spirits in Korea', *Journal of the Buddhist Text and Research Society*, 3:3 (1895).

—— 'Geomancy in Korea', *Korean Repository*, 5 (1898).

Lee, Jung-young (Yi Chungyŏng), *Korean Shamanistic Rituals* (The Hague, Mouton, 1981).

—— 'The Seasonal Rituals of Korean Shamanism', *History of Religions*, 12 (1972/3), 271–85.

—— 'Concerning the Origin and Formation of Korean Shamanism', *Numen*, 22:2 (1973/4).

—— 'Divination in Korean Shamanistic Thought', *Korea Journal*, 16:11 (1976).

Owens, Donald Dean, *Korean Shamanism: Its Components, Context and Functions*, Ph.D. thesis (Univ. of Oklahoma, 1975).

Republic of Korea, Ministry of Culture and Information, Bureau of Cultural Properties, *Han'guk minsin chonghap chosa pogosŏ* [Cumulative Report of Research on Korean Folk Belief] (Sŏul, 1969).

Starr, Frederick, 'Corean Coin Charms and Amulets; A Supplement', *Transactions of the Korea Branch of the Royal Asiatic Society*, 8 (1917).

Walraven, Boudewijn Christiaan Alexander, 'The Social Significance of Sorcery and Sorcery Accusations in Korea', *Asiatische Studien* (Zurich), 342 (1980).

—— *The Songs of the Shaman: The Ritual Chants of the Korean Mudang* (London, Kegan Paul International, 1994).

Yi, Nŭnghwa, *Chosŏn musok-ko* [Records of Korean Shamanism], ed. Yi Chaegon (1927; repr. Sŏul, Paengnok, 1976).

—— *Han'guk togyo-sa* [A History of Korean Taoism] (Sŏul, Tongguk Univ. Press, 1959).

Yi, Sangil (text), and Chu Myŏngdŏk (photographs), *Han'gug-ŭi changsŭng* [Village Tutelary Spirit Poles in Korea] (Sŏul, Yŏrhwa-dang, 1976).

Yŏrhwa-dang Publishers, *Han'gug-ŭi kut* [Korean Shamanistic Rituals], series in 20 vols.

Young, Barbara Elizabeth, *Spirits and Other Signs: The Practice of Divination in Seoul, Republic of Korea*, Ph.D. thesis (Seattle, University of Washington, 1980).

Yu, Tongsik, *Han'guk Mugyo-ŭi yŏksa-wa kujo* [The History and Structure of Korean Shamanism] (Sŏul, Yonsei Univ. Press, 1975).

—— *Minsok chonggyo-wa Han'guk munhwa* [Korean Culture and Folk Religion] (Sŏul, Hyŏndae sasang-sa, 1978).

—— 'The World of *Kut* and Korean Optimism', *Korea Journal*, 13:8 (1973).

Yun, Sunyŏng, 'Magic, Science, and Religion on Cheju Island', *Korea Journal*, 16:3 (1976).

8. Folklore

Ch'oe, Sangsu, *Han'gug-ŭi susukkekki* [Korean Riddles] (Sŏul, Sŏmun mun'go, 1973).

Deschamps, Christian, 'La Lutte a la corde en Corée', *Memoires du Centre d'études coréennes* (Paris, College de France), 6 (1985).

—— 'Deux fêtes de village en Corée', *Cahiers d'Extrême-Asie* (Kyōto), 2 (1986).

Gale, James S., trans., *Korean Folk Tales; Imps, Ghosts, and Fairies, trans. from the Korean of Im Bang and Yi Ryuk* (1913; repr. Tōkyō, Charles E. Tuttle, 1962).

Grayson, James Huntley, 'Foundation Myths, Sacred Sites and Ritual: The Case of the Myth of the Three Clan Ancestors of Cheju-do Island', *Korea Journal* 38:4 (1998).

—— 'The Myth of Tan'gun: A Dramatic Structural Analysis of a Korean Foundation Myth', *Korea Journal* 37:1 (1997).

—— *Myths and Legends from Korea: An Annotated Compendium of Ancient and Modern Materials* (London, Curzon Press, 2001).

—— 'Some Patterns of Korean Folk Narrative', *Korea Journal*, 16:6 (1976).

Ha, Tae Hung, *Maxims and Proverbs of Old Korea* (Sŏul, Yonsei Univ. Press, 1970).

Han'guk minsok hakhoe [Korean Folklore Society], *Han'guk soktam-jip* [A Collection of Korean Proverbs] (Sŏul, Sŏmun mun'go, 1972).

Hodges, Cecil H. N., 'A Plea for the Investigation of Korean Myths and Folklore', *Transactions of the Korea Branch of the Royal Asiatic Society*, 5 (1914).

Hulbert, Homer B., *Omjee the Wizard: Korean Folk Stories* (Springfield, Mass., Milton Bradley, 1925).

—— 'Korean Folk-tales', *Transactions of the Korea Branch of the Royal Asiatic Society*, 2 (1902).

Im, Tonggwŏn, *Han'gug-ŭi mindam* [Proverbs of Korea] (Sŏul, Sŏmun mun'go, 1972).

International Cultural Foundation, *Folk Culture in Korea* (Sŏul, Si-sa-yŏng-ŏ-sa, 1982).

Kim, So-un, *The Story Bag: A Collection of Korean Folktales*, trans. Setsu Higashi (Tōkyō, Charles E. Tuttle, 1955).

Kim, T'aegon, 'Korean Folklore Data Collected Prior to Liberation', *Korea Journal*, 12:4 (1972).

Kim, Yŏlgyu, *Han'gug-ŭi sinhwa* [Korean Myths] (Sŏul, Ilcho-gak, 1976).

—— *Han'gug-ŭi chŏnsŏl* [Korean Legends] (Sŏul, Chung'ang ilbo-sa, 1980).

—— 'Some Aspects of Korean Mythology', *Korea Journal*, 15:12 (1975).

Kungnip minsok pangmul-gwan [National Folklore Museum (of Korea)] untitled catalogue (Sŏul, T'ongch'ŏn munhwa-sa, 1980).

Moes, Robert, ed., *Auspicious Spirits: Korean Folk Paintings and Related Objects* (Washington DC, International Exhibitions Foundation, 1983).

Orange, Marc, 'De quelques aspects du renard coréen', *Études mongoles et siberiennes*, 15 (1984).

Pak, Taeyong, *A Korean Decameron* (Sŏul, Korea Literature Editing Committee, 1961).

Varat, Charles, 'Voyage en Corée, 1888–1889', *Le Tour de Monde*, no. 1635 (7 Mai 1892), 289–368.

Walraven, Boudewijn Christiaan Alexander, *De redder der armen: Koreaanse verhalen* [The Saviour of the Poor: Korean Tales] (Amsterdam, 1980).

Yi Minsu, *Kwan, Hon, Sang-je* [Funeral, Marriage, and Initiation Rites (in Korea)] (Sŏul, Ŭryu munhwa-sa, 1975).

Yi, Ŏnyŏng, *Han'gugin-ŭi sinhwa* [Myths of the Korean People] (Sŏul, Sŏmun mun'go, 1972).

Yi, Sinbok, *Han'gug-ŭi sŏrhwa* [Folk-tales of Korea] (Sŏul, Ŭryu munhwa-sa, 1974).

Zong, In-sob, *Folk Tales from Korea* (Sŏul, Hollym, 1970).

Zozayong (Cho Chayong), *Guardians of Happiness, Shamanistic Tradition in Korean Folk Painting* (Sŏul, Emileh Museum, 1982).

9. Syncretic Religions

An, Ho-sang; 'Taejong-gyo: Religion of God-Human Being', *Korea Journal*, 3:5 (1963).

Boyer, Jean-François, *L'empire Moon* (Paris, Editions La Découverte, 1986).

Choi, Dong-hi, 'Tonghak Movement and Chundogyo', *Korea Journal*, 3:5 (1963).

Choi, Jai-sok, 'A Socio-religious Study of Sindonae', *Transactions of the Korea Branch of the Royal Asiatic Society*, 43 (1967).

Choi, Joon Sik, *The Development of the 'Three-Religions-Are-One' Principle from China to Korea: A Study in Kang Chungsan's Religious Teachings as Exemplifying the Principle*, Ph.D. thesis (Philadelphia, Temple Univ., 1989).

Choi, Syn-duk (Ch'oe Sindŏk), 'Korea's Tong-il Movement', *Transactions of the Korea Branch of the Royal Asiatic Society*, 43 (1967).

Ch'ŏndo-gyo ch'anggŏn-sa (Sŏul, Taedong Press, 1933).

Chryssides, George D., *The Advent of Sun Myung Moon: The Origins, Beliefs, and Practices of the Unification Church* (Basingstoke, Macmillan, 1991).

Chun, Young-bok, 'The Korean Background of the Unification Church', *Japanese Religions*, 9:2 (1976).

Earhart, H. Byron, 'The New Religions of Korea: A Preliminary Interpretation', *Transactions of the Korea Branch of the Royal Asiatic Society*, 49 (1974).

Government-General of Chōsen, *Chōsen-no ruiji shūkyō* [The Pseudo-religions of Korea] (1935; repr. Sŏul, Sinhan sŏrim, 1971).

Hulbert, Homer B., 'The Religion of the Heavenly Way', *Korea Review*, 6 (1906).

Kang, Wi Jo, 'Belief and Political Behavior in Ch'ŏndogyo', *Review of Religious Research*, 19 (1968).

Kim, Yong Choon, *The Ch'ŏndogyo Concept of Man* (Sŏul, Pan Korea Book Corp., 1978).

Landis, E. B., 'The Tonghaks and their Doctrine', *Journal of the North China Branch of the Royal Asiatic Society*, 21 (1903).

Lee, Kang-o, 'Jingsan-gyo: Its History, Doctrines, and Ritual Practices', *Transactions of the Korea Branch of the Royal Asiatic Society*, 43 (1967).

Moos, Felix, 'Leadership and Organization in the Olive Tree Movement', *Transactions of the Korea Branch of the Royal Asiatic Society*, 43 (1967).

Mun, Sanghŭi, 'Fundamental Doctrines of the New Religions in Korea', *Korea Journal*, 11:12 (1971).

Pak, Kimin, *Han'guk sinhŭng chonggyo yŏn'gu* [The New Religions of Korea] (Kyŏngnam, Kosŏng County, Hyerim-sa, 1985).

Prunner, Gernot, 'New Religions – New Eras: A Preliminary Enquiry into the Nature of Chronological Systems Used by the New Religions of Korea', *Proceedings of the Second International Symposium on Asian Studies* (1980).

Ryu, Tong-shik, 'Religion and the Changing Society of Korea', *East Asian Cultural Studies*, 11:1–4 (1972).

Thelle, Notto R., 'The Unification Church: A New Religion', *Japanese Religions*, 9:2 (1976).

Weems, Benjamin B., *Reform, Rebellion and the Heavenly Way* (Tucson, Univ. of Arizona Press, 1964).

—— 'Ch'ŏndogyo Enters its Second Century', *Transactions of the Korea Branch of the Royal Asiatic Society*, 43 (1967).

Weldon, John, 'A Sampling of the New Religions', *International Review of Mission*, 67:268 (1978).

CONVERSION TABLE FROM WADE-GILES TO PINYIN

Note: Words and terms are in alphabetical order by syllable. Consonant sounds with an apostrophe, such as T' or Ch' are placed in a separate sequence from standard consonants, such as T or Ch.

Chan-ch'a Ching – Zhan-cha Jing
Chan-jan – Zhan-ran
Chang Tao-ling – Zhang Dao-ling
Chang Tsai – Zhang Cai
Chang-ching – Zhang-jing
Chên-yen – Zhen-yan
Chien-cha Wên – Jian-zha Wen
Chih-fou – Zhi-fou
Chih-hsiang – Zhi-xiang
Chih-i – Zhi-yi
Chih-yen -Zhi-yan
Chilin – Jilin
Chin – Jin
Chou Tun-i – Zhou Dun-yi
Chou Wên-mu – Zhou Wen-mu
Chu Hsi – Zhu Xi
Chu Hsi Chia-li – Zhu Xi Jia-li
chüan – juan
Chuang-tzu – Zhuang-zi
Chung-nan Shan – Zhong-nan Shan
Chung-yung – Zhong-yong

Ch'a-kou – Cha-gou
Ch'an – Chan
Ch'ang-an – Changan
Ch'ên – Chen
Ch'eng Hao – Cheng Hao
Ch'eng I – Cheng Yi

ch'i – qi
Ch'i-an – Qi-an
ch'ih – chi
Ch'ing – Qing
Ch'un-ch'iu – Chun-chui

Fa-hsiang – Fa-xiang
Fa-hsien – Fa-xian
Fa-tsang – Fa-zang
fêngshui – fengshui
Fo-t'u-teng – Fo-tu-deng
Fu-ch'ien – Fu-qian

Hai-tung shêng-kuo – Hai-dong sheng-guo
Han – Han
Hsi-ming – Xi-ming
Hsi-tang – Xi-dang
Hsiao-ching – Xiao-jing
Hsienpei – Xianbei
hsien-tao- xian-dao
Hsing-li hsüeh – Xing-li xue
Hsü Kuang-ch'i – Xu Guang-qi
Hsüan-chang – Xuan-zhang
Hsüan-hsüeh – Xuan-xue
Hsüan-tsang – Xuan-zang
Hsüan-t'u – Xuan-tu
hua-t'ou – hua-tou
Hua-yen – Hua-yan
Hua-yen Ching – Hua-yan Jing
Huai-hai – Huai-hai
Huang Tsan – Huang Zan
Hui-ssu / Hui-szu – Hui-si
Hung-chou – Hong-zhou

I-ching – Yi-jing
I-ching – Yi-ching

Jên-wang Ching – Ren-wang Jing

Kao-li Mên – Gao-li Men
Kao-tsung – Gao-zong
Kuanchung – Guan-zhong
Kuei-feng – Gui-feng

K'ai-yüan – Kai-yuan
K'uei-chi – Kuei-ji

li – li
Li Chin-ch'ung – Li Jin-chong
Li-ki – Li-ji
Liang – Liang
Liang Kao-sêng ch'uan – Liang Gao-seng chuan
Liao – Liao
Liaotung – Liao-dong
Lolang – Luo-lang
Lu-tsung – Lu-zong
Lun-yü – Lun-yu

Ma-ku – Ma-gu
Ma-tsu – Ma-zu
Mao Hêng – Mao Heng

Nan-ch'uan – Nan-juan
Nan-hai chi-kuei nei-fa ch'uan – Nan-hai ji-gui nei-fa juan
Nieh-p'an tsung – Nie-ban zong

Pê-chang Shan – Bei-zhang Shan
Peiching – Beijing
P'o-hai – Po-hai
P'u-yü Ching – Pu-yu Jing

San-lun – San-lun
Sêng-lang – Seng-lang
Shantung – Shandong
Shangti – Shangdi
Shensi – Shenxi
Shenyang – Shenyang
Shih-chi – Shi-ji
Shih-ching – Shi-jing
Shih Ch'uan – Shi Chuan
Shu Ching – Shu Jing
Shu-pên – Shu-ben
shu-yüan – shu-yuan
Shun-tsung – Shu-zong
Ssu-fen-lü – Si-fen-lu
Ssu-Ma Ch'ien – Si-ma Qian
Sui – Sui
Sung – Song

Sung Kao-sêng Ch'uan – Song Gao-seng Chuan

Ta-ch'êng Hsien-shih Ching – Da-cheng Xian-shi Jing
Ta-hsüeh – Da-xue
Ta-hui Tsung-kao – Da-hui Zong-gao
Ta T'ang hsi-yü ch'iu-fa kao-sêng ch'uan – Da-tang xi-yu qui-fa gao-seng chuan
Tao-hsin – Dao-xin
Tao-hsüan – Dao-xuan
Tao-sheng – Dao-sheng
Tao-tê Ching – Dao-de Jing
Tso Ch'uan – Cuo Chuan
Tso Ch'iu-ming – Cuo Qiu-ming
Tso-ch'iu Ming – Cuo-qui Ming
Tunhua – Dunhua
Tung-fang Ta P'u-sa – Dong-fang Da Pu-sa

T'ai-chi – Tai-ji
T'ai-chi-t'u shuo – Tai-ji-tu shuo
T'aiping – Taibing
T'an-shih – Tan-shi
T'ang – Tang
T'ien-chien – Tian-jian
T'ien-chu Shih-i – Tian-zhu Shi-yi
T'ien-li – Tian-li
T'ien-t'ai – Tian-tai
T'ung-shu – Tong-shu

Ts'ao-tung – Cao-dong

Wang Yang-ming – Wang Yang-ming
Wei – Wei
Wei-shih Lun – Wei-shi Lun
Wei-yen – Wei-yan
Wu-ti – Wu-di
Wu-tsung – Wu-zong
Wu-t'ai Shan – Wu-tai Shan

Yin-Yang – Yin-Yang
Yingk'ou – Ying-gou
Yu-chia Lun – Yu-jia Lun
Yüan – Yuan

INDEX AND CHINESE
CHARACTER GLOSSARY

Note: All entries are in alphabetical order, ignoring distinctions between letters with or without an apostrophe (such as t or t', ch or ch'), and also ignoring breaks between syllables, whether the entry items are hyphenated or not.